To Dream of Dreams

To Dream of Dreams

Religious Freedom and Constitutional Politics in Postwar Japan

DAVID M. O'BRIEN
with Yasuo Ohkoshi

UNIVERSITY OF HAWAI'I PRESS

Honolulu

Library of Congress Cataloging-in-Publication Data
O'Brien, David M.
　To dream of dreams : religious freedom and
constitutional politics in postwar Japan / David M.
O'Brien with Yasuo Ohkoshi.
　　　p.　cm.
　Includes bibliographical references and index.
　ISBN 0–8248–1757–5 (cloth : alk. paper). —
ISBN 0–8248–1166–6　(paper : alk. paper)
　1. Freedom of religion—Japan. 2. Church and
state—Japan. 3. Separation of powers—Japan.
4. Japan—Constitutional history.
I. Ōgoshi, Yasuo, 1946– . II. Title.
KNX2472.O27　1996
342.52'0852—dc20　　　　　　　　　95–45936
[345.202852]　　　　　　　　　　　CIP

University of Hawai'i Press books are printed on
acid-free paper and meet the guidelines for permanence
and durability of the Council on Library Resources

Designed by Paula Newcomb

Contents

Preface

RELIGIOUS FREEDOM is precious and precarious in any country, but especially in Japan. After World War II, in 1946–1947, the United States imposed on Japan a constitution with stricter provisions both for the separation of government from religion and for religious liberty than were enforced in the United States at the time. Moreover, it did so in a country with a very different religious scenery and history. Before the war, a new religion, State Shinto, centered on worship of the emperor *(tennō)** and Yasukuni Shrine's cult of war dead, was invented and established as a "nonreligion" in support of the government and militarism. Although other countries have adopted or adapted provisions from the U.S. Constitution, no other country has had a similarly modeled constitution imposed on it.

This book is about the controversies arising over religious freedom and militarism under Japan's postwar constitution. As such, it underscores that the governmental structure, social infrastructure, and legal culture matter far more than constitutional provisions for determining the scope of reli-

---

*The convention of translating *"tennō"* as "emperor" is followed here, even though there are several reasons for not doing so. Although commonly translated as "emperor," the Japanese *tennō,* German *kaiser,* Russian *tsar,* and the Holy Roman Emperor are not precisely equivalent. The *tennō* is a "kingly diety," a "manifest deity," a "living god" in an "unbroken line" of descendents from the ancestral Sun Goddess Amaterasu. As discussed later, the word *"tennō"* has special connotations, ambiguities, and associations with other important words and concepts relating to the Japanese mental structure. Lastly and most importantly, this book is about the legal and political battles over attempts to reestablish the institutions and symbolism of Yasukuni's cult of war dead and the emperor system. The emperor system was a new religion invented and established before World War II and disestablished during the Occupation afterward. For those on both sides of the postwar controversy over religious freedom and militarism, especially for those who lived through the war, the emperor *(tennō)* retains very special meaning and significance.

gious freedom and, more generally, civil rights and liberties. Japan is no exception in this regard.

Religious freedom litigation in postwar Japan is also vexing because it is intertwined with another, larger political controversy over the incremental buildup of the military, the Land, Air, and Maritime Self Defense Forces (SDF). There are actually three overlapping lines of litigation, or underlying themes:

First, litigation has been brought by pacificists, communists, and others opposed to what they deem renewed militarism. Article 9 of Japan's "peace constitution" not only renounces "war as a sovereign right of the nation" but in no uncertain terms stipulates that "land, sea, and air forces, as well as other war potential, will never be maintained." Yet spending for the SDF has grown steadily, to the point that Japan now ranks among the top five countries of the world in its military expenditures.

Second, and closely related, some survivors of World War II object fiercely to renewed governmental support for the symbolism and institutions of State Shinto, particularly Yasukuni Shrine's cult of the war dead. They, too, have turned to the courts for the enforcement of the Constitution's provisions for the disestablishment of state support for religion.

Third, religious minorities, Christians, and other supporters of human rights have sought the enforcement of constitutional provisions for the free exercise of religion.

Religious freedom litigation thus represents three separate yet interwoven undercurrents of social conflict—conflict over militarism, the revival of governmental support for Yasukuni and the emperor system, and demands for human rights.

In focusing on religious freedom litigation, several often self-perpetuated and imported myths about religion, law, and politics in Japan are dispelled. Although Japan has a history of religious syncretism and ambivalence, religious ambivalence harbors a darker side: an indifference, bordering on righteous intolerance, of minorities who hold strong beliefs or who demand religious freedom. As the conflicts over religious freedom here illustrate, Japan is far less harmonious and homogeneous than usually portrayed. Deep-seated disagreements cut along generational, geographical, gender, and political lines. In addition, although the Japanese are no less ambivalent about law, Japan is not, as so often claimed, a country of "reluctant litigants."

Organized around three case studies, new material is brought together in this volume with interdisciplinary work on religion, law, and politics in Japan. The first case study deals with a series of lawsuits involving the separation of the state from religion that were brought by survivors of World War II, Satoshi and Reiko Kamisaka and a few of their neighbors. Chapter 1 introduces their lawsuits and dispute with Minoo city officials over expenditures for a prewar *chūkonhi* war monument that enshrines the souls of 298 soldiers as "country-protecting deities."

Their story also provides a basis for exploring Japanese attitudes toward religion and law, which some Japanologists may find elementary but which will be helpful for nonspecialists and students of comparative law and society. The Kamisakas' suits pitted them against other survivors in the local and national Japan Association of War Bereaved Families (JAWBF), a powerful interest group and constituent of the conservative Liberal Democratic Party (LDP). The Kamisakas' suits thus represent generational and ideological conflict among survivors of World War II and, due to the postwar educational system, a conflict not well understood by younger generations. Their litigation also played into the larger political struggle over resurrecting governmental support for the Yasukuni Shrine's cult of war dead and glorification of militarism.

Why the Kamisakas sued the government and persisted in battling it out in the courts for two decades is explored in greater depth in Chapter 2, in terms of both the prewar history of the political dynamics that established State Shinto and the drafting of Japan's 1947 Constitution. Apart from the Kamisakas' experience, some of the discussion covers old ground for Shinto scholars and historians of Japan, but nonspecialists will find it useful for understanding the lawsuits in question as well as contemporary struggles for religious freedom. The development of State Shinto is briefly traced from the Meiji Restoration in 1868 to the eventual emergence of what became known as "the emperor system" of indoctrination into the militarism of Yasukuni's cult of war dead. By the 1930s, when the Kamisakas were growing up, State Shinto and the military held a vicelike grip on the people. That ended with Japan's surrender and occupation by the Allied forces, which the latter half of the chapter takes up when dealing with the drafting of the postwar constitution, and specifically the provisions for religious freedom.

Chapter 3 examines the Kamisakas' litigation within the context of the operation of the judiciary and the Supreme Court's first major ruling on governmental support for religion in the *Tsu City Ground-Purification Ceremony* case. Although the 1947 Constitution laid a basis for judicial independence and gave the courts the power of "American-style" judicial review, judicial independence has failed to take root. The Liberal Democratic Party's control over the government (and judicial appointments) for thirty-eight years, until the 1993 elections, along with the politics of the judicial bureaucracy, conspired in various ways to suppress judicial independence and the exercise of judicial review.

Although experts on Japanese courts may find some of the discussion of the judiciary's organization to be basic, there is new evidence here documenting the decline of judicial independence, and this provides a background for understanding the courts' rulings and for explaining their deference to the government. The watershed ruling in the *Tsu City Ground-Purification Ceremony* case is analyzed in the second half of the chapter. As a kind of case study in the Supreme Court's methods of constitutional interpretation, the discussion of the *Tsu City* ruling focuses on the Court's construction of the "social reality" of religion both in postwar Japan itself and in relation to rulings by the U.S. Supreme Court that the Japanese Supreme Court has drawn on but not followed entirely. The Court's *Tsu City* ruling, moreover, hung over the Kamisakas' and subsequent religious freedom litigation. Here and in the remaining chapters, previously untranslated material is presented that will interest those concerned not only with religious freedom but with comparative constitutional law and judicial politics as well.

Having laid a basis for understanding Japanese attitudes toward religion and law, the development of State Shinto, and the political dynamics of interest-group litigation and the judiciary, Chapter 4 provides a detailed analysis of the Kamisakas' lawsuits, the *Minoo War Memorial* cases. Their three suits against Minoo city are analyzed both in terms of their tortuous course up through the lower courts to the Supreme Court, and within the broader political context of interest-group conflicts over resurgent ultranationalism and militarism.

The related litigation over the free exercise of religion and the struggles of Christian minorities for religious liberty are examined in Chapters 5 and 6. These chapters are based on a third case study, that of a well-publicized suit in Japan known as the *Self Defense Forces Enshrinement* case. This lawsuit was brought by a Christian woman, Mrs. Yasuko Nakaya, who objected to the enshrinement of her dead husband's soul as a "country-protecting deity" in Yamaguchi prefecture's *gokoku* (country-protecting) shrine. Her suit became entangled with the major controversy in the 1970s and 1980s over pressures to reestablish governmental support for Yasukuni Shrine, which is dealt with at length in Chapter 5.

Unlike the Kamisakas' litigation, Mrs. Nakaya's case became a rallying point, a human rights cause commanding the support of major Christian and Buddhist organizations. This occurred because, in addition to actively opposing renewed governmental efforts to support Yasukuni, Mrs. Nakaya raised a novel and untested claim to constitutional protection for religious liberty. Chapter 6 discusses how and why the Supreme Court reached its in some ways surprising decision. The chapter closes by addressing the bearing of the Court's ruling on controversies over Emperor Hirohito's funeral in 1989 and Akihito's enthronement ceremonies in 1990, along with the continuing struggles over religious freedom on the eve of the fiftieth anniversary of Japan's postwar constitution and the government's quest for an expanded military role in international affairs.

Together, these studies offer revealing accounts of religion, law, and politics in contemporary Japan. In doing so, they tie together struggles over religious freedom and show the interrelationship of opposition to LDP ultranationalists' attempts to revive the symbols and institutions of the prewar emperor system at all three levels on which they previously operated: (1) at local *chūkonhi* war memorials, as in Minoo city; (2) at regional State Shinto shrines, such as Yamaguchi's *gokoku* shrine; and (3) at the national level, at Tokyo's Yasukuni Shrine. As such, they explain much about political conflict and conflict resolution in postwar Japan. They also dispel widely circulated myths and provide explanations for the role played by litigation, law, and the courts in the postwar politics of Japan's constitutional democracy.

Acknowledgments

I T   I S   F A I R   T O   S A Y   that this book would never have been undertaken without the encouragement and assistance of Professor Yasuo Ohkoshi of Tokyo International University. At the outset, he suggested narrowing the project to religious freedom litigation. Later, he provided translations of crucial materials and arranged some interviews. In addition, Professor Ohkoshi read and commented on drafts (and there were many). Beyond being a valued collaborator, Professor Ohkoshi remains a good friend and colleague.

The book also would not have been possible without a Fulbright research serial grant from the Japan–United States Educational Commission. That award enabled several trips to Japan in 1993–1994, as well as spending six months there. I am indebted to the anonymous reviewers on several Fulbright committees, both in the United States and Japan, for their favorable reviews and faith in the project application. A special debt is owed to the former director of the Japan–United States Educational Commission, Mrs. Caroline A. Matano Yang, and to program officer Ms. Teruyo Kuramoto for their interest and help.

I had as well the good fortune of having the advice and support of one of the United States' leading authorities on Japanese constitutional law and courts, Professor Lawrence W. Beer, F. M. Kirby Professor of Civil Rights at Lafayette College. He graciously provided introductions to some of Japan's leading constitutional-law scholars, journalists, and friends acquired over almost four decades. Professor Beer generously read the penultimate draft, for which I am especially indebted and grateful.

Both because so little has been written in either English or Japanese about religious freedom litigation in postwar Japan, and because the book is organized around three case studies of the *Minoo War Memorial* litigation, the *Tsu City Ground-Purification Ceremony* case, and the *Self Defense Forces*

Enshrinement case, opportunities to interview plaintiffs, attorneys, expert witnesses, and judges, along with constitutional scholars and commentators, proved invaluable.

Quite by chance, at the suggestion of Mrs. Yang, I met Katsuyuki Kumano, the lead attorney for the plaintiffs in the *Minoo War Memorial* litigation. An indefatigable crusader, he generously spent many days and nights discussing with me both that litigation and courts, law, and religion more generally. He also introduced Mrs. Reiko Kamisaka and her son Naoki, along with two other plaintiffs, Mrs. Yoshiko Furukawa and Mrs. Hiroko Hamuro. They, in turn, graciously spent time discussing the litigation. Besides arranging to hear the Osaka High Court's 1994 ruling, Mr. Kumano carefully read and commented on the first four chapters. Three of his friends—Dōshisha University professor Hiroyuki Ōta, his wife Lucinda Lohman Ōta, and Tatsuhiro Koyama—provided translations of some materials. In Osaka, former judge Shigeyuki Uehara, who participated in the first ruling of the Osaka District Court, kindly granted an interview. In Tokyo, a lengthy meeting with Supreme Court Justice Itsuo Sonobe was also enormously informative and helpful.

Mrs. Yasuko Nakaya cheerfully discussed her background and clarified crucial points concerning the *Self Defense Forces Enshrinement* case. In addition, she generously spent time showing her church, the Yamaguchi *gokoku* shrine, and the Yamaguchi District Court, as well as introducing some of her supporters. Two of her attorneys, both associated with the Japan Civil Liberties Union (JCLU), were also extraordinarily helpful. Takashi Kōno took several evenings from his busy schedule to discuss the case and appeal to the Supreme Court. Through the JCLU's international liaison officer, Emiko (Amy) Furuya, Tsuguo Imamura made some very useful materials available.

Others connected with the JCLU also kindly spent time discussing the courts, litigation, and religious liberty. Those deserving of special mention include Hideo Shimizu, former professor, prolific author, and head of the Motion Picture Ethics Committee (Eirin); Lawrence Repeta, who brought the *Note Takings* case, which resulted in the Supreme Court's ruling that Japanese courts may not bar spectators from taking notes during court proceedings; and attorney Hiroshi Miyake. Finally, Masami Itō, former Supreme Court justice and the solo dissenter in the *Self Defense Forces Enshrinement* case, kindly offered his reflections on the case and the Japanese judiciary.

A number of other scholars, lawyers, and commentators were no less helpful. Among them, I am particularly grateful to International Christian University professor Yasuhiro Okudaira; Gakushūin University constitutional-law professor Hidenori Tomatsu; Kokugakuin University professor of Shinto Studies Yoshiya Abe; retired journalist and editor Yukio Matsuyama; Kitakyūshū University professor Nobuhiko Takizawa; Kyoto University law-school professor Takao Tanase; Tokyo University professors Takashi Igarashi and Shōjirō Sakaguchi; and Keiō University law professor Setsu Kobayashi.

University of the Ryūkyū law professor Tetsumi Takara and his wonderful family were generous hosts on Okinawa. Ms. Claire Debenham of the National Christian Council in Japan also made some useful materials available. The project benefited as well from informal discussions with other scholars, lawyers, and journalists during the course of lecturing for the United States Information Agency. Although they remain nameless, I remain grateful to those in the College of Social Sciences at Tsukuba University in Tokyo; the University of Nagoya; Dōshisha University, Kyoto University Law School, and the American Cultural Center in Kyoto; as well as to the prefectural bar associations in Nagoya and Fukuoka.

The staffs at a number of institutions were invariably helpful. Tokyo International University kindly provided an office and other support. Others who deserve mention include the Clerk's Office of the Supreme Court of Japan for making unpublished opinions available; the Library of the Diet; the Japan Association of War Bereaved Families and the Kudan Kaikan in Tokyo; and the MacArthur Foundation and Library in Norfolk, Virginia.

Because drafts of the manuscript were written on a laptop computer while traveling, another debt was incurred to those who made conditions conducive to writing. Almost three months were spent, at different times, at the International House of Japan in Roppongi, Tokyo. The staff, especially of its library, was unfailingly helpful and efficient. Other places meriting mention are the Sanjo Karasuma Hotel in Kyoto; the Plaza Hotel Osaka; the Karatsu City Hotel in Karatsu, Kyushu; the Shangri-La Hotel in Bangkok, Thailand; the Bagan Inn in Yangon, Myanmar (Burma); the Prince Hotel in Penang, Malaysia; and the Hotel Le Passey in Juan-le-Pins, France.

At the University of Virginia, I have always enjoyed the strong support and friendship of certain colleagues. My senior colleague and friend Henry J. Abraham, the Miller Center's director Kenneth W. Thompson, and former department chair R. K. Ramazani wrote letters of recommendation, once again. The latter also had the wisdom to create the Rowland Egger Memorial Research Fund, which made available a grant to present a portion of the study at the 1994 Interim Meeting of the International Political Science Association's Committee on Comparative Judicial Studies in Florence, Italy. As departmental chair, Paula McClain approved a grant from the Rowland Egger Small Grants Program, which was appreciated. A summer grant from the Office of the Vice President for Research and a Sesquicentennial Award from the University's Center for Advanced Studies enabled completion of the project. Both are gratefully acknowledged.

History professor and Japanologist Gary Allinson kindly offered his encouragement. A number of graduate students were also helpful in ways directly and indirectly bearing on the project. Steven Brown deserves special mention for his proofreading and other skills. Others include Christopher Banks, Stephen Bragaw, Charles Kromkowski, James Staab, Laura Mirsky, and Stephen Tauber.

Besides the comments on drafts of the manuscript offered by Professors Ohkoshi and Beer, and Katsuyuki Kumano, I am grateful that several others took the time to read and comment on portions of the manuscript, including Professors Yasuhiro Okudaira, Hidenori Tomatsu, and Shōjirō Sakaguchi, along with Lawrence Repeta and the Reverend Thomas W. Grubbs. Several anonymous reviewers were no less helpful with their comments and favorable reviews. While their corrections and suggestions steered me away from some mistakes and otherwise greatly strengthened the book, they are absolved of all remaining mistaken omissions and commissions. Finally, I am indebted to Patricia Crosby and Cheri Dunn of the University of Hawai'i Press for their assistance.

Last but by no means least, I am grateful for the understanding and affection of my wife Claudine and our children Benjamin, Sara, and Talia. As always, they were supportive and not only tolerated my travels but took a keen interest in the project. Without their love and understanding, the book would never have been completed.

CHAPTER I

The Nail That Sticks Up

ORDINARY IN SO MANY WAYS and yet extraordinary, Satoshi Kamisaka and his wife, Reiko,[1] represented a certain segment of the generation that survived World War II. Disillusioned by the massive destruction that ended the war, they later benefited from the economic prosperity that followed in the 1970s and 1980s. They lived quietly in Minoo city. Once a village in the mountains, Minoo gradually became a city, part of the postwar suburban sprawl a 40-minute train ride from Osaka, Japan's third-largest city. Yet the Kamisakas were destined to become "nails that stick up." Drawn into a major controversy over religious freedom, they confronted the old Japanese proverb, "The nail that sticks up gets hammered down."

Satoshi and Reiko Kamisaka tested the courage of their convictions when they sued the mayor of Minoo city, Buhei Nakai, and the chairman of the board of education, Ryōsaku Kōno. They sued over the city's paying for the relocation and rededication of a *chūkonhi* war memorial on public school grounds. Their lawsuit—actually, a series of suits filed in the mid-1970s—went against the grain. In challenging the city, the Kamisakas raised the sensitive issue of the separation of the state from religion under Japan's 1947 Constitution. The litigation would drag on for nearly two decades, past Satoshi Kamisaka's death in 1986, at the age of fifty-five.

The Kamisakas' clash with Minoo city authorities stemmed from the decision in 1975 to build a swimming pool and a new classroom wing at an elementary school. To do so required removing a *chūkonhi* war memorial or cenotaph located on the school's playground. Originally constructed in 1916 by the Minoo chapter of the Sasayama Veterans' Association, the "Monument to the Fallen Soldier" commemorates the "loyal souls" (*chūkon*) of 298 soldiers who died in Japan's wars. Save for the litigation sparked by its relocation, the memorial is unexceptional.

Hundreds of *chūkonhi* war memorials were erected during and following the Meiji era (1868–1912), especially in the period leading up to World War II. With the Meiji Restoration in 1867–1868, Japan entered the age of modern nation-states. Still, the fighting among clans continued for another decade, until the conclusion in 1877 of the "West South War" against a rebellion by the Satsuma clan. During this period, the Meiji forces were plagued with insurrections and desertions. In order to establish its legitimacy and to build loyalty, the Meiji government promoted "the unity of Shinto and the state" *(saisei itchi)*. The emperor was venerated as the divine descendant of the great Sun Goddess, Amaterasu-Ōmikami. And soldiers who gave their lives for the emperor and the country were glorified and deified.

A major national spirit-invoking shrine was erected in 1869 in Tokyo, originally to honor and comfort the spirits of 7,751 soldiers who had died after 1853 and in the Meiji civil war. In 1875, however, there was a massive joint enshrinement there for loyalists who had died in the name of Meiji. Four years later, in 1879, after the defeat of the Satsuma rebellion, the "Tokyo Shinto Shrine Dedicated to the Souls of War Dead" *(Tokyo Shokon Sha)* was renamed the Yasukuni Shrine *(Yasukuni Jinja)*. It was designated a special government shrine, administered by the ministries of Home Affairs and War, and later by the army and navy ministries.[2]

By the beginning of World War II, 124,191 soldiers were enshrined at the Yasukuni Shrine. In 1939, 117 regional shrines for war dead became local branches of Yasukuni and were renamed *gokoku jinja* (country-protecting shrines, or shrines to defenders of the country). Over 2.4 million souls are now enshrined at Yasukuni, including the wartime prime minister, General Hideki Tojo, and thirteen other class-A convicted war criminals. The latter were enshrined there in 1979, amid controversy and protests from other Asian countries.

Minoo's *chūkonhi* war memorial and the Yasukuni and *gokoku* shrines are not quite what they appear to be. *"Yasukuni"* means "peaceful country," or "to pacify the state and country." Soldiers are enshrined there solely because they died fighting for the emperor and the country in holy wars. Yasukuni, *gokoku* shrines, and other *chūkonhi* war memorials are unlike monuments to unknown soldiers elsewhere in the world. The soldiers are known, glorified, and venerated as national *kami* (gods, or deities) and *gokoku* (country-protecting gods). The spirits of the enshrined soldiers alone are honored with worship by the emperor, himself a manifest *kami*. These national shrines and regional war memorials are places of cult worship. They commemorate Japan's divine origins and the legendary unity of Shinto and the state.

Hundreds of other war memorials were destroyed after World War II on the orders of the Allied Occupation Forces. Minoo's *chūkonhi* war memorial, however, was cut down, buried, and preserved by people in the village. In 1950, following the outbreak of the Korean War, the memorial was restored with private funds of the Minoo Association of War Bereaved Families of Fallen Soldiers.

The Minoo Association of War Bereaved Families is the local affiliate of the national Japan Association of War Bereaved Families (JAWBF). That organization was founded originally as the Japan War Bereaved Welfare League on November 17, 1947, at Kanda Temple in Tokyo. Its creation was due largely to the work of the secretary general of Yasukuni Shrine, Tōnosuke Ōtani. He traveled throughout Japan organizing war-bereaved families at the end of War World II. There were an estimated seven million war-bereaved families at that time. Following the end of the Occupation (1945–1952), the league was reorganized as a legal, nonprofit foundation on March 22, 1953, and renamed the Japan Association of War Bereaved Families on June 4, 1953. The association's resources and status then increased dramatically. For its headquarters, the government gave the JAWBF the Kudan Kaikan, the old Soldiers' Association Institute. During the Occupation, the U.S. Army had taken possession of the institute because of its central location, using it as an army hall. When the Kudan Kaikan was returned to the Japanese government, the latter turned it over to the Japan Association of War Bereaved Families.

Position, prestige, and money are often said to be the driving forces of interest-group politics, and this is especially so in the interest-group struggles animating Japanese politics. The JAWBF's acquisition of the Kudan Kaikan represented the postwar government's frequent support for conservative and ultranationalist groups, who continue to seek to revive the prewar symbolism of emperor worship and State Shinto. The Kudan Kaikan sits in the heart of Tokyo, not far from the hilltop occupied by Yasukuni Shrine. Directly across the northern part of the moat that surrounds the Imperial Palace, it occupies a place that is technically on the palace grounds. The Kudan Kaikan, in other words, sits in a privileged position and enhances the association's prestige and resources.

The Kudan Kaikan was transformed not only into the headquarters for the JAWBF, which are very modest and located in the basement, but into a huge hotel and annex as well, for visiting veterans' groups and regional affiliates of war bereaved families on their trips to Yasukuni and Tokyo. The building and annex now house a number of restaurants, a wedding palace, an auditorium, meeting rooms, and a rooftop beer garden, from which Yasukuni's massive metal *torii* (gateway) and surrounding greenery may be seen.

The reorganization of the Japan War Bereaved Welfare League into the Japan Association of War Bereaved Families and its relocation to the Kudan Kaikan further solidified its ties to Yasukuni. Those ties remain strong due to the two organizations' overlapping memberships on their boards of directors. The first chairman of the JAWBF's board of directors, Fujimaro Tsukuba, also served as the first chief president of Yasukuni. The reorganization also signaled a renewed dedication to reviving the symbolism and rituals of State Shinto, which hard-line conservatives continue to back. In a 1952 address to the executives of Japan's Safety Force, the forerunner of the Self Defense Forces, for instance, Prime Minister Shigeru Yoshida observed that, "If we intend to rearm Japan, we need to prepare for it in both ways, materially and emotionally. We have to restore a military pension, and the like."[3]

The shift in the focus and objectives of the JAWBF is reflected in the change in its statement of purpose. The league's founding charter had stated: "The League aims at mutual aid and consolation relief, promotes morality and cultivates character, strives for constructing peaceful Japan, and intends to contribute to the welfare of the whole human being, expecting prevention of war and establishment of permanent world peace." In contrast, the JAWBF's 1953 charter gives much greater emphasis to the glorification of the country's war dead. Article 2, for example, provides that "The Association aims at admiring the spirit of the war dead, promoting the welfare of the war bereaved, opening the way to consolation relief, and at the same time, trying for the improvement of morality and cultivation of character, and contributing to the establishment of peaceful Japan."

Article 3 further specifies that the association aims to achieve its goals by promoting activities related to the "admiration and consolation of the spirit of the war dead," the "improvement of treatment of war bereaved," "consultation about living for war bereaved," and "bringing up and guidance of their children."[4] In the following decades, the JAWBF promoted enshrinements and other ceremonies at local *chūkonhi* war memorials and *gokoku* shrines, lobbied for increased benefits for war-bereaved families, and organized trips for members of its regional affiliates to visit Yasukuni.

A quarter of a century after Minoo's *chūkonhi* war memorial was restored, when the decision was made in 1975 to remove it, the local association of war-bereaved families demanded that the city pay for its relocation. The mayor and board of education agreed to move the memorial to some land a kilometer away, in front of the West Minoo Elementary School. Minoo city not only paid for the memorial's relocation, at a cost of 80 million yen (approximately $250,000), but leased free of charge the land on which the memorial was relocated to the local association of war-bereaved families.

Minoo's relocation of its war memorial on public land close to an elementary school was by no means an isolated event. Thousands of other war memorials are located on public property elsewhere in Japan. In 1983, Minoo city officials reported finding 10,344 memorials, based on a national survey the city commissioned of 2,700 communities (83 percent of the total, though excluding Tokyo). Of these, the largest number (4,088) were *chūkonhi* war memorials, accounting for 39.5 percent of the total. In addition, the survey found that 35 percent of the *chūkonhi* war memorials were located on public property.[5] The *chūkonhi* were followed in much smaller numbers by *ireihi* (soul mourning monuments), numbering 927, and by 525 *kinenhi*, (remembering stones, or memorial stones). The survey also reported that Shinto, Buddhist, and nonreligious rites had been held at *chūkonhi* and *kinenhi* monuments, along with seven Christian services reportedly held at *kinenhi*.[6]

The Kamisakas and others would, nevertheless, argue that public financial support for *chūkonhi* war memorials constitutes an entanglement of government with religion. Since *chūkonhi* war memorials are linked to Yasukuni, which is a religious corporation under law, governmental support or financial assistance for them arguably violates Articles 20 and 89 of the Constitution, which expressly bar government support for religion.

Like other *chūkonhi* war memorials, Minoo's is an imposing stone structure, measuring over 21 feet high. On the front is inscribed *"Chū Kon Hi"* in large characters and, in much smaller characters, "written by General Yasumasa Fukushima." On the back is recorded the year of its construction, "the Fifth Year of Taishō Emperor" (1916), thus registering the imperial system of calculating years, which is based on the accession of the emperor and the assigning of a special name to each emperor's reign. Akihito's assumption of the throne in 1990 thus began his reign in the Heisei era, while the reign of his father Hirohito is known as the Showa (Enlightened Peace) era (1926–1989).

"Chūkonhi" literally means "memorial for loyal souls" or, more precisely, "village memorial for the loyal souls of those who died fighting for the emperor." The souls enshrined in the *chūkonhi* are enshrined both there and at the great Yasukuni Shrine through a funeral ceremony or ritual known as *shokonsai*. The solemn rites of *shokonsai* call back the souls of the departed, which are believed to be drifting in the air. They are called back to a sacred place (the *chūkonhi, gokoku* shrines, and Yasukuni) in order to exalt and to comfort them.

According to Shinto tradition, people who suffer abnormal, untimely, or unusual deaths are believed to become spirits roaming about causing trouble, mischief, and grief. Through deification and ceremonies memorializing them, they are consoled. They become part of the "beautiful spirit" (*goryō shinkō*) protecting the people and continuing to intervene in everyday life in ways that contribute to Japan's prosperity. In this regard, State Shinto built on the centuries-old Japanese tradition of worshipping the ancestors of the household and the locality or clan. It did so by building Yasukuni, regional *gokoku* shrines, and local *chūkonhi* war memorials. The war dead enshrined in these special government-built and -sponsored shrines and memorials are the only national *kami* worshipped by the emperor, and State Shinto taught that this was the highest form of honor for its subjects.

The names and dates of death of the 298 souls enshrined in Minoo's *chūkonhi* war memorial were recorded on an 8-inch cedar plate. The plate was buried in a hole and covered with cement at the base of the *chūkonhi,* above the boulders on which the *chūkonhi* rests. The monument itself is sur-rounded by carefully arranged pine trees, azaleas, and other bushes. Although located in a residential area, the trees and plants create the atmo-sphere of a beautiful mountain garden over which the *chūkonhi* soars. The entire area is enclosed by a 5-foot-high fence made of *tamagaki* (granite pillars) exactly like those enclosing Shinto shrines. This wall of separation signifies a sacred place within. The area immediately outside the fence is covered with half-inch-wide white pebbles. In the Shinto tradition white represents purity, and in the midday sun the white ground shines brightly, giving the effect of a serene aura around the greenery from which the *chūkonhi* arises.

The Minoo *chūkonhi* war memorial stands literally in a garden sur-rounded by a "wall of separation." The metaphor of a "wall of separation" would appear at first glance to be highly inappropriate in Japan, for in the Shinto tradition there is no sharp division between heaven and earth or between the sacred and the secular. To the contrary, those realms are united, intersecting and interacting. In addition, the metaphor is rooted in biblical myths and teachings about creation and original sin. According to the Old Testament, Adam and Eve lived in harmony in the Garden of Eden until Eve, against God's command, took a bite from a forbidden apple and intro-duced sin into the world. The metaphor of a "wall of separation" thus evokes the imagery of God's creation of a pure and sacred garden, represent-ing the holiness of the church. The wall separates the sacred garden from the corruption, contamination, and sin in the wilderness outside.[7]

The metaphor of a "wall of separation" has been especially rhetorically powerful and central to controversies over the separation of government from religion in the United States. The metaphor was invoked by the U.S. Supreme Court in its first major rulings[8] on the disestablishment clause of

The Minoo *chūkonhi* war memorial. (Author photo)

the First Amendment to the U.S. Constitution, which provides simply that "Congress shall make no law respecting an establishment of religion."[9] A continuing controversy has revolved around the metaphor, and why and how far the government should be separated from religion.[10]

The controversy over a "wall of separation" in part registers the potency of the metaphor's ambiguity. The controversy actually runs back centuries in the West and has divided even advocates of a strict separation of government from religion. At least three principal positions have been staked out by separationists under the rubric of a "wall of separation" of government from religion.

Some advocates of a "high wall of separation" maintain that the disestablishment of religion was necessary to safeguard religion from the corrosive influence of politics. When celebrating the purity of evangelical faith in 1644, for instance, colonist Roger Williams proclaimed that God had commanded that "the most Paganish, Jewish, Turkish, or Antichristian consciences and worships, be granted to all men in all Nations and Countries." And Roger Williams invoked the metaphor of a wall of separation in defense of the integrity of religion:

> First, the faithful labors of many witnesses of Jesus Christ, extant to the world, abundantly proving that the church of the Jews under the Old Testament in the antitype were both separate from the world; and that when they have opened a gap in the hedge or *wall of separation* between the garden of the church and the wilderness of the world, God hath ever broke down the wall itself, removed the candlestick, and made His garden a wilderness, as at this day. And that therefore if He will ever please to restore His garden and paradise again, it must of necessity be walled in peculiarly unto Himself from the world; and that all that shall be saved out of the world are to be transplanted out of the wilderness of the world, and added unto His church or garden.[11]

More than 150 years later, President Thomas Jefferson again relied on the metaphor in his famous letter to the Danbury Baptist Association in 1802, in which he observed:[12]

> Believing with you that religion is a matter which lies solely between man and his God, that he owes account to none other for his faith or his worship, that the legislative powers of government reach actions only, and not opinions, I contemplate with sovereign reverence that act of the whole American people which declared that their legislature should "make no law respecting an establishment of religion, or prohibiting the free exercise thereof," thus building a wall of separation between Church and State.

Unlike those who shared Roger William's view, Jefferson was more concerned about insulating government from the influences of religion and religious fervor.

In Jefferson's home state of Virginia, however, James Madison was inclined toward a third view of the "wall of separation" between government and religion. Madison agreed that a wall would help preserve the integrity of government, but he also thought that it might benefit religion as well. Governmental assistance to religious establishments, Madison maintained, tended to divide society into factions and to produce "pride and indolence in the clergy; ignorance and servility in the laity; in both, superstition, bigotry and persecution." Nor did Madison think government depended on the support of religion. "That is not a just government," he wrote in 1792, a year after the ratification of the First Amendment, in which "a man's religious rights are violated by penalties, or fettered by tests, or taxed by a hierarchy."[13]

In short, the metaphor of a "high wall of separation" has been employed by advocates of disestablishment because they have feared and warned either (1) that governmental interference would pollute and corrupt religion, (2) that the entanglement of the state with religion could corrupt government, or (3) that both religion and government might be compromised and corrupted by their fusion, or by the uniting of the two.

Although the teachings of Christianity have made few inroads in Japan and, according to the prevailing Shinto tradition, the secular and the sacred intersect and interact, the metaphor of a "high wall of separation" still has utility in understanding the Kamisakas' lawsuits and disestablishment litigation in postwar Japan. Consider, again, the character of Minoo's *chūkonhi* war memorial and the Kamisakas' objections to the city's financial support for it.

Minoo's *chūkonhi* war memorial stands within a garden separated from the outside by a stone fence. The *tamagaki* fence signifies a special, sacred place within that is to be revered and considered holy. The 298 souls or deities enshrined there are exalted, praised, and comforted. For the faithful and for those in the association of war-bereaved families, the 298 are thereby consoled and pacified. No longer vengeful over their deaths, they will remain within the walls of the *tamagaki*, not wandering outside and making trouble for the living. These spirits, furthermore, are honored in special Shinto and Buddhist ceremonies conducted at the *chūkonhi* and are praised as the highest *kami* and buddhas. Because they died for the emperor, they have the most noble legacy of contributing to Japan's prosperity.

The Kamisakas maintained that, in relocating and reconstructing the *chūkonhi*, the garden, and the fence around it, Minoo city became inexorably entangled with the symbolism and institutions of the prewar establishment of State Shinto and its ideology of militarism. In their eyes, the city thus violated the explicit provisions of Articles 20 and 89 of Japan's 1947 Constitution, which bar governmental support both for Shinto and for religion more generally. What the Kamisakas sought in the courts was simply the enforcement of those constitutional provisions which mandate the strict separation of government from religion. Although raising a claim still unusual in Japan at the time, the Kamisakas' lawsuits posed precisely the kind of legal controversy that has animated disestablishment litigation in the United States, at least since the U.S. Supreme Court in 1947 wrote the metaphor of a "high wall of separation" into constitutional law.[14]

Even before the *chūkonhi* war memorial was moved and reconstructed, the Kamisakas opposed the city's plans to relocate it. They had moved to western Minoo just six years earlier, in 1970. At that time there was no *chūkonhi* to remind them of the war. When the city proposed to relocate the memorial, their two children were attending the elementary school that the *chūkonhi* would overlook. Their son Naoki was in sixth grade and his sister in second grade. The Kamisakas were very disturbed, especially Reiko. They profoundly disagreed with the city's rebuilding the memorial in front of the school. They did not like the prospect of their children walking by it every day or playing in a schoolyard overshadowed by the *chūkonhi*.

At first, Reiko Kamisaka and a few neighbors hoped to mobilize the Parent Teacher Association (PTA) of the West Minoo Elementary School against the proposed relocation of the memorial. At a committee meeting of the PTA, Reiko Kamisaka voiced her objections to moving the *chūkonhi* war memorial next to the school. A few other housewives supported her. But because she had been in a sanitarium recovering from tuberculosis after the war and had, as a result, married and had children later than most women, Reiko Kamisaka was somewhat older than the majority of the mothers at the meeting, who did not fully appreciate the role the *chūkonhi* had played before the war. Most did not even understand why the city planned to move it next to the school, or why the Kamisakas so opposed the move.[15]

Moreover, the school's principal, Mr. Kida, who was in his fifties and, as a public official, was entitled to respect, told the women that the city council was unanimous in deciding to reconstruct the war memorial, and that there was nothing they could do to change that. Besides, while admitting that State Shinto had promoted the war, he said the *chūkonhi* had not played a similar role. The *chūkonhi* was not religious, claimed Kida, and was quite different from State Shinto. The Kamisakas knew otherwise.

The PTA meeting did not go Reiko Kamisaka's way. Undaunted, she and a few neighbors collected about a hundred signatures protesting the memorial's relocation. Mayor Buhei Nakai, however, refused to meet with them. They next went to the chairman of the school board, Ryōsaku Kōno, but he tried to persuade them that the memorial's significance had changed 180 degrees after the war. The *chūkonhi,* Chairman Kōno said, was now "a peace statue"—more duplicity aimed at circumventing their objections.

When the *chūkonhi* war memorial was finally reconstructed on land that had been part of a playground, and across a narrow street directly in front of the entrance to West Minoo Elementary School, every boulder, pine tree, and shrub was moved and carefully put into place. The reconstruction was meticulous. Afterward, the Minoo Association of War Bereaved Families held annual spring services honoring the 298 enshrined there. In 1976 a Shinto ceremony was held, and in 1977 a Buddhist one. The mayor and chairman of the board of education made offerings of sprigs of the sacred *sakaki* evergreen tree *(tamagushi)* at the Shinto ceremony and burnt incense at the Buddhist one. They also approved city employees' participation in the ceremonies as well as the use of other public resources for them.

The ceremonies included prayers exalting and comforting the spirits of the dead soldiers, who were eulogized for having "fought bravely and died to build the basis for Japanese prosperity after the war."[16] For those in attendance, the message was unmistakable: Three decades after World War II, the mayor and officials of Minoo were celebrating the war dead as country-protecting gods *(go-koku)* who, in dying in a holy war, had contributed and would continue to contribute to Japan's prosperity.

For Satoshi and Reiko Kamisaka, along with a few other neighbors, mostly housewives living close to the school and the *chūkonhi* war memorial, the ceremonies brought back painful memories. Satoshi and Reiko Kamisaka had been born in 1930 and 1931, respectively. They had grown up during Japan's wars in Manchuria, China, and the Pacific. Indoctrinated into emperor worship at school, Satoshi Kamisaka had been a devoted follower, a true believer in the emperor and in the unity of Shinto and the state. With the crushing defeat in 1945 came a deep sense of betrayal and disillusionment, however. The Kamisakas wanted never again to witness the state's promotion of emperor worship. As one of their attorneys, Katsuyuki Kumano, recalled, Satoshi Kamisaka "did not want to go down the same road twice."[17]

Some other survivors of the war and neighbors of the Kamisakas felt the same way. Mrs. Yoshiko Furukawa, for one, had been born in 1927 and had lost two brothers fighting off the coasts of China and Burma (Myanmar). She remembered how, after the war, her mother Kazuko hated the emperor and felt that he had "killed her sons" Keisuke and Hiroshi. Mrs. Furukawa grew up seeing her mother torture herself every day. The depth of Kazuko's despair was almost unimaginable. She wrote special poems demanding that the emperor return her sons, and would cry out their names in the night on a dry river bed. This went directly against her upbringing and the government's teaching that loyal subjects should never lament the death of relatives who had died for emperor and country. "But how could I live long without becoming insane?" Yoshiko Furukawa remembers her 78-year-old mother saying.[18] For that reason, and because her parents had not opposed or objected to the emperor system, Mrs. Furukawa vehemently opposed the reerection of the *chūkonhi* war memorial and all it represented.

Another neighbor, Mrs. Hiroko Hamuro, born in 1935, remembers attending elementary school during the war. Virtually every day she would go to the local shrine, a 30-minute walk away, before her school day began in order to pray for victory in the war. At school, it seemed that almost every day she wrote a letter that would be sent to cheer up a soldier. For such activities, she received extra points from her teacher. In these and other ways, Mrs. Hamuro remembers how support for militarism and the emperor system was inculcated, even in elementary school.[19]

The Kamisakas, joined by the Furukawas and the Hamuros, decided in 1975 to petition city authorities to reconsider the matter. Under the Local Autonomy Law, residents may file petitions for inspection in order to obtain an audit and a determination of whether a local government's expenditures have been proper. This petition, though, was dismissed out of hand as well.

The turn of events continued to upset Reiko Kamisaka. Their efforts to halt the city's relocation of the *chūkonhi* war memorial had failed. She and her husband decided to file a lawsuit against Minoo city officials. They were joined by the Furukawas, Hamuros, and three others in filing a residents' or class action suit. Some slight pressure against their course of action was brought to bear. Mr. Furukawa consulted his company's lawyer, who said that challenging the city was impractical, since its decision to move the *chūkonhi* had been unanimous. The cost of hiring attorneys would also be great, and the Furukawas wondered how they could afford to pay them. Mrs. Hamuro remembers her parents and other relatives trying to persuade her to stay out of the lawsuit. She came from a landowning family and was married to a businessman. Her parents had lost most of their land after the war. If she persisted, there might be repercussions for her husband's business. But Mrs. Hamuro was determined, although she admits that joining the suit was "like driving off a cliff."[20]

The initial briefs were written and filed by Satoshi Kamisaka, who was a tax accountant, not an attorney. In those briefs, the issue of the separation of government from religion under Articles 20 and 89 of the Constitution was notably absent. Both at the outset and throughout the years of litigation, the Kamisakas' opposition centered on what they perceived to be the revival of the symbolism, institutions, and instruments of the prewar militarism of State Shinto. That is what drove them on.

In his initial briefs, Satoshi Kamisaka focused on the Articles 98 and 99, pertaining to public officials' oaths and duty to uphold the Constitution. He made two main arguments. First, Japan's 1947 Constitution contains, in Article 9, a provision renouncing war. Satoshi Kamisaka argued that Minoo's relocation and reconstruction of the *chūkonhi* war memorial amounted to a revival of prewar militarism in violation of the text and ideals of Japan's "peace constitution," which public officials are obligated to uphold. Second, he stressed the Constitution's declaration of popular sovereignty and argued that Minoo's support for the *chūkonhi,* a remnant of the prewar emperor system that was based on the emperor's sovereignty, ran contrary to that principle.

It was not until his ninth brief, in 1978, after filing his second suit against Minoo, that Satoshi Kamisaka raised the issue of the disestablishment of religion under Articles 20 and 89. He did so because, upon further research, those provisions appeared to be the best constitutional basis on which to challenge city officials. Ironically, that line of legal argumentation had first been suggested by District Court Judge Yoshinaga Kosaki. Judge Kosaki had a reputation for being arrogant, but he took an interest in the case and, in the Kamisakas' view, became helpful, rather atypically for a judge in Japan.[21] Like the Kamisakas, Judge Kosaki was a survivor. He had served as a soldier during the war. He understood the Kamisakas' concerns and had a sense of history. Consequently, he went out of his way to suggest that the Kamisakas frame their complaint in terms of the Constitution's separation of the state from religion.

The Minoo city war-memorial litigation, therefore, did not begin as a lawsuit calculated to test the constitutional boundaries of the separation of the government from religion. Yet it resulted in one of the first major lawsuits focusing public attention on the issue of religious disestablishment in postwar Japan. The Kamisakas' suit was also linked to larger political struggles over conservatives' attempts to revive the symbolism of the emperor and to encourage the steady buildup of the Self Defense Forces. Their litigation, as Mrs. Furukawa emphasizes, was "the first case asking the emperor system to accept responsibility for the war, and attacking it at the base of the system,"[22] that is, at the local level, where conservatives after the war understood the need to revive support for the prewar system before carrying it forth on the national level.

The Minoo war-memorial litigation eventually evolved into three separate lawsuits. In each suit the Kamisakas argued that the principle of religious disestablishment had been violated, albeit in different ways, namely, by

(1) Minoo's relocation of the *chūkonhi* war memorial and its lease of land at public expense to the local association of war-bereaved families;
(2) the participation of the mayor, the school board chairman, and other city officials in the memorial services held at the monument; and
(3) the city's payment of subsidies to the local association of war-bereaved families, which helped pay for the memorial services.

Each of these governmental activities, the Kamisakas claimed, ran afoul of the Constitution. Each entangled the government with religion, fostering the revival of State Shinto. These three lawsuits became known as the *Minoo Memorial* case, the *Minoo Memorial Service* case, and the *Minoo Subsidy* case, respectively.

The Kamisakas' lawsuits commanded media coverage and attracted public attention. That, of course, was part of their strategy. Lawsuits against the government raising large issues of public policy remain relatively rare in Japan, though they increased in the last few decades. When such "public-interest" suits are brought, the plaintiffs often have little expectation of actually winning in the courts. Instead, the litigation is a kind of political tool that uses the courts as a public forum for presenting their views and gaining publicity for their causes. "The greatest power of the Japanese court may lie not in the traditional judicial function of rendering decisions," as Lawrence Repeta, among others, has observed. Repeta— an American attorney living in Tokyo who brought a widely known suit that led to the Supreme Court's holding, in 1989, that members of the public have the right to take notes in courtrooms during trials[23]—explains that the judiciary's power instead resides "in its position of focusing the attention of the community on issues raised by the litigants."[24]

Although interest-group politics is well established in Japan, interest-group litigation is still in its infancy. Only since the 1970s has public-interest litigation emerged over issues such as the environment, reapportionment, and employment discrimination.[25] Interest-group litigation in Japan remains by no means as well structured, well orchestrated, or as pervasive as in the United States.[26]

In the United States, groups such as the National Association for the Advancement of Colored People's (NAACP's) Legal Defense and Education Fund, the American Civil Liberties Union (ACLU), and, in the 1970s and

1980s, conservative legal-defense funds, have been founded for the purpose of litigating the interests of their constituents.[27] Organized litigation affords opportunities to select test cases and to develop an organization's litigation expertise and strategies. It also has the potential for moving a body of law in one direction or another.

In addition, studies in the United States have found that, besides the primary goal of achieving legal victories, interest-group litigation may serve secondary functions such as gaining publicity for the interest group's cause, maintaining and expanding a litigating organization's constituency, fund-raising, and bringing other pressures to bear on the government so as to influence the political process through the judicial process.[28] For some groups, these secondary functions may at times become as important as actually winning in the courts. Success in the courts, or at least the promise thereof, nonetheless remains the primary goal, and the basis for maintaining a group's constituency and funding.

In Japan, the primary and secondary functions of public-interest litigation as they are understood in the United States are often inverted. In litigating major issues of public policy, there is less expectation of achieving court victories. Instead, the publicity and media attention given to the litigation are deemed extremely important, for therein lies the opportunity for mobilizing supporters and influencing public opinion. Well-established groups and organizations that already command public attention rarely initiate litigation, although, in the 1960s and 1970s, the Communist Party did initiate some suits to gain publicity for its opposition to the Liberal Democratic Party (LDP) government's policies. Rather, well-established groups concentrate on lobbying and waging campaigns in the media to build public support. They infrequently turn to the courts. Even an organization like the Japan Civil Liberties Union (JCLU) does not have an overall litigation strategy or participate in litigation itself. Instead, its individual members and directors join in suits that they deem important to advancing the cause of civil rights and liberties.[29]

In other words, in Japan small groups of citizens, instead of well-established special-interest groups or organizations, tend to bring public-interest litigation in order to gain publicity for their causes. They aim to thereby influence public opinion, which may in turn eventually influence the courts and the government.

The Kamisakas were not part of a large special-interest group or organization when filing their suits. No other groups or organizations offered financial assistance. All their support came from individual citizens, mostly pensioners. In this regard, the Kamisakas' litigation differed from the so-called *Self Defense Forces Enshrinement* case.[30] In that case, major Christian and Buddhist organizations rallied around Mrs. Yasuko Nakaya in her fight over the Self Defense Forces' enshrinement of her husband's soul as a country-protecting *kami*. Christian and Buddhist priests, along with their followers, also brought other cases in the 1970s and 1980s, as discussed further in Chapter 4.

However, the Kamisakas' litigation did generate publicity for a cause shared by others, and it was also among the first cases to elevate the issue of disestablishment to the level of national debate. "Without our fight," as Reiko Kamisaka puts it, "we could not have submitted the problem to the people, to get them to think about the emperor system, and it's very important for them to think over the emperor system."[31]

Had the Kamisakas directly raised the controversial issue of militarism and Japan's peace constitution, it would have been much easier for people to understand. But that was too abstract a basis on which to legally challenge Minoo's support for the *chūkonhi* war memorial. They therefore posed the issue indirectly, in terms of Minoo city's violating constitutional guarantees for the separation of government from religion. Such subtlety made their litigation more difficult for the public to appreciate, however. Moreover, the central issue was transformed into one that most Japanese and courts would rather avoid—namely, the disestablishment of religion. With the exception of the relatively few Christians, some Buddhists, and others opposed to militarism, most Japanese probably think that the issue of the disestablishment of governmental support for religion is not worth the bother.

Religious (In)Tolerance

Religious freedom litigation in Japan is perplexing. It remains so in part because religious toleration is generally taken for granted, being assumed in the expression, "Born Shinto, die Buddhist." The Japanese tend either to deny that Shinto customs are "religious" or to dismiss religion as unimportant anyway.

Shinto (literally, *"kami* way," or "way of the gods") is the ancient, indigenous religion of Japan.[32] Centered on neither a founder nor a doctrine, it has no organized theology or monotheistic creed. Instead, Shinto rites and rituals revolve around the special character of the Japanese and their relationship to the *kami* according to centuries-old myths and legends. Japan's religion has repeatedly been said to be a "religion of Japaneseness."[33] Devotion to "things Japanese" is undeniable, and Shinto is the heartbeat of "things Japanese" in a country for centuries populated basically by one race, under one government. At least symbolically, the emperor and the imperial family have reigned for 1,600 years (2,600 mythologically). Moreover, for more than two centuries (1638–1853) Japan remained virtually isolated from foreign contact, and it was not invaded until the end of World War II.

The expression "religion of Japaneseness" became popular in the 1970s. Although Japanese and other scholars enthusiastically embraced it in their theories of "Japanese uniqueness" *(Nihonjin-ron),*[34] the idea itself is centuries old. The expression was popularized in the 1970s by several best-selling books, in particular *The Japanese and the Jews,* by Isaiah Ben-Dasan, a pseudonym allegedly used by a Hebrew University historian, Ben-Ami Shillony. That work drew some illuminating analogies between the Jews and the Japanese in terms of both groups identifying with divine origins, being a chosen people, and living in a promised holy land. "Both the Jews and the Japanese regard themselves," Ben-Dasan wrote, "as categorically different from any other peoples. The feeling of 'us' and 'them' is, of course, common to all ethnic groups, but few peoples have drawn that line so sharply and clearly and maintained it for so long as have the Jews and the Japanese."

Other cultural characteristics are ostensibly shared as well. Both reject celibacy and the Christian view of sex as a weakness of the flesh. Both focus as well on well-being in this world. But no similarity is stronger than their religious-cultural identification with separateness as a divine and chosen people. There are, of course, profound religious-cultural differences between the Jews and the Japanese, especially in each group's treatment of other religions. Those differences stem fundamentally from the monotheism of Judaism, Christianity, and Islam versus the animistic polytheism of Shinto. Central to those differences, Ben-Dasan observed, is the fact that "Judaism places God at the center of the universe and regards nature as his creation. Nature worships God, but the beauty of nature has rarely occupied an important place in Judaism. . . . Shinto is a religion that worships the gods manifested in the exquisite beauty or the frightening awe of nature. . . . Unlike Judaism, which is ethically oriented, Shinto is aesthetically oriented."[35]

Although in some ways illuminating Shinto and Japanese culture, *The Japanese and the Jews* was deceptive and self-serving, because it aimed to legitimize the idea of Japanese uniqueness by cleverly expropriating stereotypes of Jewish cultural identity. The book largely succeeded in that regard and sold more than a million copies in Japan before it was translated into English. Yet the book's author was not in fact Jewish. There was no Ben-Dasan or Professor Shillony. That was a hoax. Years later, the supposed translator and publisher of the book, Shichihei Yamamoto, a well-known novelist and Christian, finally admitted to having written the book.[36]

As a collective noun, "Shinto" actually embraces a wide range of cults and animistic folkways related to the worship of a pantheon of *kami.* Everything above the individual, both in space and hierarchical order, is called *kami,* and the word itself may mean "above," "one's superior," or "hair." Heads of clans and political rulers were once referred to as *"okami." Kami* abound everywhere, in beautiful streams, trees, and mountains.

Shinto shrines are also dedicated to great leaders and warriors, as well as to special crafts and skills. Today, major corporations typically have shrines built on their headquarters' rooftops. The Asahi beer company has an Asahi shrine. Many others, like the Yokohama Rubber Company, have *inari* (fox) shrines. The fox, believed to be a messenger for the gods and to possess spiritual powers, traditionally represents the *kami* of cultivation and has come to stand for corporate productivity and success.

Shinto consists in the rituals for honoring ancestors, sacred places, special skills, and the spiritual forces of nature, as well as rites for personal purification and for the community's or country's prosperity. The word "Shinto" was not even coined until the early eighth century, and then largely to distinguish traditional indigenous rituals from Buddhism and other religions imported from China and Korea. Ancestor worship in Japan differs, for example, from that in China, where offerings and prayers at shrines for other people's ancestral spirits are considered insulting to a person's own ancestral spirits. No such sharp distinction is made in Japan, in part because ancestors are honored at home and in part because of the traditional belief that unless the departed are properly enshrined and honored their vengeful, unpacified spirits will wander about making trouble. By honoring the deceased, their spirits are comforted and, over time, pacified. The rough edges of their individual personalities are, as it were, worn down, and they become part of the divine collective spirit of the country.

Shinto is thoroughly ritualistic, polytheistic, and highly superstitious. Babies are customarily taken to local Shinto shrines for blessings and the protection of the *kami.* Other rites of passage are observed as well, such as when children come of age and when people marry or die. Throughout each year at local shrines people purify themselves and enjoy small festivals. Large Shinto festivals are held at major shrines in Tokyo, Kyoto, and elsewhere. They mark changes in the cycle of seasons, times for paying respect to ancestors, and occasions to pray for prosperity and to buy charms, as well as to ask for personal favors and good fortune. Through purification rituals, according to Shinto tradition, the body and soul are cleansed and connections with the *kami* are magically restored in an aesthetic sense, not in a moral or metaphysical one.[37]

To be sure, Shinto shrines and Buddhist temples now serve for the most part simply as places for people to stop during the day. They ring the bell in front, clap their hands, awake the *kami*, make a wish, and then go on their way. There is no concern with other-worldly salvation, guilt or sin, or religious truth. What matters are this-worldly benefits and well-being, such as passing an examination or making a business deal. For that reason, though, the Japanese find no contradiction in praying for the fulfillment of their wishes at a Shinto shrine and later at a Buddhist temple, or even at a Christian church, for that matter.

As a legacy of Buddhism's influence, most Japanese are cremated after death according to Buddhist funeral rites. Buddhism was introduced in the sixth century A.D. from China through Korea, yet had a tumultuous history afterward in Japan. During the Nara period (710–794), Buddhism was first embraced by the government and grew in power. Nara, not far from Kyoto in western Honshu, became the first "permanent" capital. Prior to that, the capital had changed with each successive emperor in order to escape, according to Shinto beliefs, the pollutions arising from the death of the preceding one.

The ties between Buddhism and the government were severed in the Heian period (794–1185), and the capital was moved to Kyoto to distance the government from the influence wielded by Buddhist priests. Buddhism regained governmental support under the military shoguns who governed during the Kamakura era (1192–1333). In this period, the emperor remained isolated in Kyoto but was still the nominal ruler. Buddhism's influence gradually waned over the course of the next two hundred years. In the Muromachi (1336–1573) and Momoyama (1576–1600) periods, warring clans, rival aristocratic courts and priesthoods clashed in long-running struggles for power. Finally, in the feudal Tokugawa period (1603–1867), initiated after a decisive battle by Ieyasu Tokugawa, the governing shogunates seized control of major cities and ports. The shoguns imposed a kind of unity and national seclusion. They also reembraced and consolidated Buddhism as a state institution. Buddhism was thus reestablished, and until the Meiji revolution, in 1868, every citizen was required to register births, deaths, and other matters at a Buddhist temple.

Over the centuries, many schools of Buddhism—Rinzai and Sōtō Zen, for instance, and later Jōdo ("Pure Land") and Nichiren Buddhism—developed along individual lines. However, Buddhism in Japan, as in China and Korea, remained rooted in the Mahayana ("Greater Vehicle") tradition, while what is termed Hinayana ("Lesser Vehicle") predominated in southern India, Burma (Myanmar), Thailand, Vietnam, Cambodia, and Laos. The basic yet crucial difference between the two is that Mahayana is concerned with the collective, whereas Hinayana teaches individual enlightenment and salvation. Significantly, Buddhism as imported into and refined in Japan stresses the communal and the collective, not the individual.[38]

As imported into Japan, Buddhism both reinforced traditional Shinto customs governing the worship of ancestral deities and was transformed by Shinto's preoccupation with this-worldliness. In other words, Buddhism was converted in accord with the indigenous tribalism of Shinto, and was thus simplified. Shinto deities were considered manifestations of buddhas, and vice versa.

Because of concerns with purification and avoidance of pollutions, Shinto priests had traditionally declined to perform funeral rites, which thus came to be conducted by Buddhist priests, the remains being placed in a family plot in a Buddhist cemetery. The departed might then be remembered according to either Shinto or Buddhist traditions, or both. They may become either buddhas or wandering, vengeful spirits, depending on whether their death is considered normal or abnormal. Through ritual and remembrance by surviving family members, their spirits are comforted and purified of the unhappiness associated with their death. Depending on the region, 33 or 49 days after memorial services have been held, the ancestral souls become *kami,* and hence a part of the collective and protective spirit of the survivors' household.[39]

The pragmatic overlay and interweaving of Shinto and Buddhism, along with elements of Confucianism, Taoism, and shamanism, created a background of religious ambivalence against which the Kamisakas' lawsuits were difficult to appreciate. Surveys conducted in the early 1980s revealed that about 60 percent of the households in Japan had a Shinto *kamidana* (*kami*-shelf) honoring ancestors of the household as deities. Another 61 percent had Buddhist altars (*butsudan*) memorializing family ancestors, and 45 percent had both; only 24 percent neither.[40] (According to tradition, daily rites are performed before the *kamidana,* on which are placed cenotaphs recording the names of ancestors, their ages and dates of death; memorial tablets or "representatives of their souls," which are placed in small boxes on the shelves; and offerings of rice, *sake,* and fish.)

The surveys also found that 60 percent "turn to the gods in time of distress." However, only 35.9 percent said they believed that *kami* "certainly" or "perhaps" exist, while 42.8 believed in buddhas and 54 percent professed belief in the existence of the soul after death. Strikingly, more members of younger generations claimed to believe in the existence of *kami* and buddhas than did their grandparents. Yet they were far less likely to pray at home Shinto and Buddhist altars or to visit ancestral tombs.

Although the percentage of households with *kami*-shelves has almost certainly declined due to continuing urbanization and changing life-styles, religious ambivalence and syncretism still hold. Reports on religious membership by the Japanese Agency for Cultural Affairs in the 1970s and 1980s invariably found multiple religious affiliations. Religious affiliations, moreover, amounted to twice Japan's entire population. Approximately 76 percent claim Buddhist affiliation, while almost 95 percent identify with Shinto. Another 12 percent claim to belong to one or another of the "new religions,"[41] and less than 1 percent identify with Christianity.[42] The number of religious adherents, although increasing throughout much of the last quarter of a century, dropped sharply in the late 1980s and early 1990s. Indeed, a 1994 poll found that only one in four Japanese claim to follow any particular religion, and that over 70 percent do not believe in any religion, though only 23 percent call themselves atheists.[43]

Religious ambivalence, nevertheless, harbors a darker side: an indifference, bordering on righteous intolerance, toward those who hold strong religious beliefs. Christians and other religious minorities invariably confront a lack of sympathy, particularly when claiming the free exercise of religion as an exception to governmental regulations. Strong religious beliefs, sharply defined creeds, and concerns about other-worldly salvation appear not merely unneccessary disturbances but foreign and abnormal. Christians and others who abide by their religious convictions stand out and apart when, for example, they refuse to contribute to neighborhood associations for the performance of annual Shinto festivals. Their refusal to do so appears strange and oddly uncivil.

Table 1   Religious Affiliations of the Japanese

YEAR	SHINTO	BUDDHIST	CHRISTIAN	OTHER
1965	76,973	70,003	740	8,190
1970	83,329	84,960	804	9.878
1975	89,063	86,607	886	11,655
1980	95,848	87,745	1,019	15,783
1985	115,602	92,065	1,688	14,444
1990	109,000	96,255	1,464	10,511

Source: Japan Statistical Yearbook—1992 (Tokyo: Statistics Bureau, Management and Coordination Agency, 1992), p. 695.

Note: Amounts are in thousands.

A young Jehovah's Witnesses student at Kobe Technical College, for instance, refused on religious grounds to participate in a required gym class's kendo exercises. Kendo, a martial arts somewhat similar to karate, involves exchanges of blows with long wooden sticks. When dismissed from the college for declining to participate in the kendo exercises, he sued, claiming a denial of religious freedom as guaranteed in Article 20 of Japan's Constitution. But in its 1993 ruling in the *Kobe Technical College* case, the district court rejected the student's claim out of hand. The court held that it would be too burdensome and disruptive to make an exception for him, and eventually for other religious minorities.[44] The college's regimen had to be respected. The student was simply relieved of attending the college. Such claims by religious minorities remain somewhat novel and are generally deemed of little interest, or viewed as strange assertions of individual differences, "much ado about nothing."

With over 140,000 Jehovah's Witnesses and their numbers slightly increasing in Japan, litigation like that in the *Kobe Technical College* case is certain to continue. Jehovah's Witnesses, like religious fundamentalists who are in the minority elsewhere, inevitably face uphill battles over their beliefs. The Witnesses, in particular, are well known for putting their sharply held faith on the line and challenging governmental authorities. Founded in the 1870s in Pittsburgh, Pennsylvania, by Charles Russell, the Jehovah's Witnesses believe that the Bible is literally and historically accurate. And it prophesies the coming of Armageddon. Their reading of the Bible leads them to refuse to pledge allegiance to any national flag or to serve in the military. Because the Apostles were missionaries, Jehovah's Witnesses believe that they must engage in door-to-door proselytizing as well.

As a result of their strongly held beliefs, and with only about four million members worldwide, the Jehovah's Witnesses frequently clash with authorities over their claims of exemption from generally applicable laws. In the United States, claims of religious freedom first brought by Jehovah's Witnesses led to a series of Supreme Court rulings in the 1940s that greatly expanded the scope of the First Amendment's guarantees for the free exercise of religion and for the freedoms of speech and press.[45] Although Japan's constitutional guarantees for religious freedom and disestablishment were modeled on those contained in the First Amendment, a similar development in Japan appears unlikely, at least in the near term, because of the very different underlying orientation toward religion and the role of courts and law more generally. The ruling in the *Kobe Technical College* case reflects that communitarian orientation.

Although the Jehovah's Witnesses' claim in the *Kobe Technical College* case was unusual, the district court's ruling was by no means isolated or atypical. On the contrary, it reflected the judiciary's propensity for deferring to the government and reinforcing traditional cultural values and norms. In 1986, for instance, the Tokyo District Court rejected the religious claims of a United Church of Christ minister's two daughters who had not attended scheduled classes on a Sunday but instead had gone to church. When their absences were recorded on their report cards, they filed suit to expunge the records, on the grounds that the school was penalizing their freedom of religious exercise.[46] Noting that holy days fall on other days of the week as well, however, the district court held that to exempt them would violate the religious neutrality of the school. To carve out an exemption for them would also result in children attending school for unequal numbers of days. Moreover, the school held classes on Sundays only a couple of times of the year. And for most fathers, Saturdays and Sundays were the only days they could visit their children's classes. Finally, the court noted that religious freedom, like other freedoms, may be restricted by law when necessary to serve the interests of the government and the public.

Subsequently, in 1989, the Sapporo District Court granted a divorce on the grounds of religious incompatibility. In that case, a husband sued to dissolve his sixteen-year marriage because his wife had become a Jehovah's Witness. She had refused to continue participating in Shinto and Buddhist family rituals.[47] The Kobe, Tokyo, and Sapporo district courts' reinforcement of the government's position and underlying communal-folkways-orientation also reflects the Japanese Supreme Court's interpretation of constitutional guarantees for religious freedom and disestablishment.

Periodic surveys by the Ministry of Education underscore the distinctive disaffection in Japan for sharply held individual religious beliefs. They consistently show that, despite claims of multiple religious affiliations, more than 65 percent of Japanese profess no religious beliefs, and only slightly more than 30 percent claim any.[48] Indeed, this religious ambivalence led no less an authority than Edwin O. Reischauer, former U.S. ambassador to Japan, to conclude that "religion in contemporary Japan is not central to society and culture."[49] Most Japanese would probably agree. Yet this assessment is due in part to the fact that Shinto does not accord with Western theories of religion, which are based on monotheism and on concern for personal, other-worldly salvation. A leading Japanese scholar of religion, Keiichi Yanagawa, puts the point as follows:

> In Japan, the unit of religion is human relationships and religion is indistinguishably mixed with customs. Since the European Reformation, the idea that religion is a personal affair has been predominant. But I do not think

that it is right, using this as a criterion, to criticize the religion of the Japanese as being in some way not genuine, since religion based on human relationships does in fact exist.[50]

Part of the explanation for the apparent religious ambivalence and lack of religious belief among Japanese may be semantic. Questionnaires continue to employ the word *shūkyō* for "religion," although the term did not gain currency until nineteenth-century encounters with Christian missionaries. "*Shūkyō*" is a compound of *shū* (sect or denomination) and *kyō* (teaching or doctrine). As Japanologist Ian Reader points out, *shūkyō* "implies a separation of that which is religious from other aspects of society and culture, . . . [and] conjure[s] up notions of narrow commitment to a particular teaching to the implicit exclusion and denial of others—something which goes against the general complementary nature of the Japanese religious tradition."[51] In other words, the only available Japanese word for "religion" conjures up notions of non-Japaneseness.

Claims of religious freedom by Christians and other religious minorities remain little appreciated precisely because of Shinto's pervasive presence. In the words of one Shinto scholar, Kokugakuin University professor Sokyo Ono,

> Shinto is more than a religious faith. It is an amalgam of attitudes, ideas, and ways of doing things that through two millenniums and more have become an integral part of the *way* of the Japanese people. Thus, Shinto is both a personal faith in the *kami* and a communal way of life according to the mind of the *kami,* which emerged in the course of the centuries as various ethnic and cultural influences, both indigenous and foreign, were fused, and the country attained unity under the Imperial Family.[52]

For that and other reasons, many Japanese, including members of the Supreme Court of Japan and other governmental officials, are inclined to deny that Shinto is a "religion," at least according to Western standards. They thereby play down the postwar controversy over its status. In the words of Supreme Court Justice Itsuo Sonobe, "we almost don't have any religion in the true meaning."[53] Shinto rituals are explained away as a unique folkway, rather than as religious observances per se. The matter is further compounded by the fact that the idea of "the unity of Shinto and the state" *(saisei itchi)* is deeply rooted in Japanese history and culture. Even an archaic word for "government" *(matsuri-goto)* also meant "affairs of worship."

Major public-opinion polls conducted by leading newspapers support the view of Shinto as a folkway, a custom, a kind of national nonreligious-religious faith. Barely 51 percent of those questioned professed a belief "in God or Buddha." Yet over 82 percent claimed to "have an amulet of a shrine or a temple in [their] house," and 71 percent said that at least sometimes, if not every year, they go to a shrine or temple on New Year's Day to pray. When asked why they do so, 31 percent said it was "custom," 25 percent said they did so to "feel purified," and 15 percent claimed they wanted their requests and wishes granted.[54]

In suing the officials of Minoo city, the Kamisakas appeared to turn against bonds rooted in ancient Shinto myths and traditions, as well as popular theories of "Japanese uniqueness." Those formidable bonds of "things Japanese" are manifest in everyday life in a myriad of ways: in the traditions of tea ceremony rituals, in the standardized mat flooring of houses, and in the ubiquitous uniforms of high school boys, in middle-school girls' "sailor outfits," and in the bright, same-colored skirts of office ladies. Indeed, Japanese intellectuals frequently contrast the idealism of the harmonious communal ties of Japanese uniqueness with that of the rugged individualism of liberalism and American exceptionalism.[55]

Yet the Kamisakas' aim was both more limited than a broadside attack on traditional tribal bonds and far more incisive and penetrating. They aimed to drive a wedge through Japanese ambivalence about religion and state support for Shinto war memorials. They remained primarily concerned about governmental attempts to revive militarism and the symbolism of the emperor system that had supported it. That one thread—the emperor system and State Shinto—which had been woven into the traditional fabric of Japanese society during the prewar era, and unwoven during the Occupation, is what the Kamisakas' suits sought to prevent the Japan Association of War Bereaved Families, veteran groups, and the government from stitching back together again.

Law and Ordinary Litigation

The Kamisakas' lawsuits also ran counter to another traditional ambivalence or, more exactly, antipathy: antipathy about law. In a nation of so-called reluctant litigants,[56] recourse to courts is generally said to be anathema. The myths of homogeneity that prevail, along with the undeniable social density of Japan, do register a social order without the kind of dependence on courts and law found in the United States. Social rather than legal sanctions still tend to predominate.

In the old village communities *(mura),* social sanctions, hierarchical and parental-filial group relationships, and the spirit of communal accommodation were especially strong. They continue to carry weight even after the exodus from rural farming communities into the sprawling urban centers and metropolitan areas of postwar Japan. Admittedly, the social sanctions or "reciprocal dependency"[57] of the *mura* have largely been replaced by those of companies and the workplace. Still, the ties of family, household, neighborhood, and the group or community, although transformed after the war and continuing to change, more or less hold.[58]

A poll taken at the time the Kamisakas filed their suit underscores the self-claimed aversion to litigation of the Japanese. When asked, "When you feel your right is violated, are you going to bring a case before the court?" over 60 percent of the respondents said "No," followed by 23.7 percent who said "Yes, sometimes." Only 11.1 percent responded, "Yes, I am going to do so at once." Asked whether they preferred a lawsuit or arbitration, only 8.1 percent favored a suit, whereas 42.7 percent preferred to "arbitrate or negotiate publicly in the court," and another 41.3 percent claimed they "should make efforts to resolve conflicts by talking to each other privately."[59]

But this by no means suggests that the Japanese are not conflictual or that they are entirely adverse to litigation. On the contrary, they are very emotional, contentious, and keen disputants. Indeed, it seems fair to say that the Japanese are hardly the "reluctant litigants" they are portrayed to be, and that it is a myth that they are significantly less litigious than other peoples.[60] As further discussed in Chapter 3, for instance, in the 1990s, the Japanese Supreme Court and the U.S. Supreme Court had dockets and disposed of approximately the same number of cases. Filings and pending cases on both dockets reached over seven thousand, and each disposed annually of about five thousand cases. In terms of the large number of filings and crowded dockets in the lower courts, the Japanese also appear to be far from reluctant litigants (see Appendix A).

In other words, the Japanese are ambivalent about law but hardly reluctant litigants. The role of lawyers, judges, and law does remain circumscribed. The legal profession, which did not emerge until the Meiji era (1868–1912), remains small in spite of its modest growth after World War II. In fact, the ratio of judges to the population has dropped by two-thirds since 1890.[61] Citizens typically do not go to attorneys even for matters such as advice on drawing up wills and real-estate transactions.[62]

Satoshi Kamisaka, as noted earlier, initially filed the Minoo city war-memorial cases without the assistance of an attorney. Moreover, as is common when governmental actions and laws are challenged, the Kamisakas were joined by some neighbors in filing their lawsuits. Unlike Americans who may strike out on their own when asserting claims to individual rights, the Japanese tend to assert legal claims as part of a group, or in the company and with the support of a group.

Because there exists no strong sense of the individual outside the context of the group, community, and country, libertarian ideas about civil rights and liberties have largely failed to take hold in postwar Japan. Social relations take precedence over the individual—a legacy of centuries-old clan-consciousness and tribalism. "Generally speaking," in the words of law-school professor Yasuhiro Okudaira, "Japanese are equality-minded rather than liberty-minded, and the Japanese concern for equality is socio-economic and substantive in nature."[63] The Japanese have little or no interest in abstract theories of legal equality or liberty.

The kind of equality, or mutual concern and respect, that prevails remains confined largely to the clannishness of a particular group's, company's, or community's concerns. Communal equality within a group or among the Japanese, however, lasts only as long as shifting coalitions and consensus-building are not ruptured by deep-seated conflict from within, and perhaps by a faction's turning to the courts. Outsiders are simply excluded and widely discriminated against. The Burakumin, Japanese descendants of a caste of laborers, were declared "new citizens" in 1872, but despite recent progress toward social acceptance and equality, they remain looked down upon by some as outcasts, untouchables.[64] Korean citizens and other resident foreigners are also considered outsiders. They are dealt with differently.

The professed reluctance of Japanese to litigate disputes has been attributed to a number of other factors as well, including the high costs of litigation, crowded dockets, lengthy court delays, notoriously slow judicial proceedings, and the overarching influence of legal and political elites.[65] There are also pressures and procedures in the lower courts, especially in family courts, that promote conciliation and discourage adjudication of ordinary disputes. In addition, the influence of a civil law tradition may contribute to the role courts play and to the judiciary's deference to the Diet and other governmental bodies.[66] The "rights talk" and adversarial culture found in the United States remain foreign.[67]

No less important in explaining the Japanese ambivalence about law may be how language structures social interaction and conflict resolution. Whereas English speakers generally regard their spoken and written language as two alternative ways of expression, the Japanese are more apt to regard their spoken and written language as two different kinds of communication. Spoken Japanese is more direct and personal, of course. But it is also highly complex and inflected, with multiple verb endings and adjectives. The inflections or sounds change the meaning of spoken words, and often cannot be written or captured entirely in *kanji* (characters).

Written Japanese is one of the most complex languages in the world, combining three different scripts (or four, if the increasingly popular Roman script, *rōmaji*, is included). The *kanji* were inherited from the Chinese and are more like painting. Furthermore, the characters may be pronounced in a number of ways and, individually or in combination, stand for many different things. In addition, there are two separate alphabets or syllabaries, *hiragana* and *katakana*. The former is used primarily for native Japanese words, the latter for words and ideas borrowed from abroad (*feminisuto*, for example, represents "feminist").

Throughout Japan's history, new characters were introduced as needed. The term "Shinto," as noted earlier, was introduced to distinguish the native worship of *kami* from Buddhism and other foreign religions. Consequently, written Japanese is extremely rich and complex, especially in highly technical areas like law. Indeed, many Japanese cannot master the written word at all, especially highly technical legal terminology. To put the matter into perspective, high school students, according to the Ministry of Education, are expected to know about 1,850 characters. A well-educated person can write some 5,000 and recognize thousands more, while encyclopedias use about 50,000 different characters.[68]

Ambivalence about law may thus stem partially from the very introduction of *hō* (law) into the language. The word was introduced to represent the Western concept of law and individual legal rights. "Such a conception of law," however, as Professor Yoshiyuki Noda explains, "is not something that arose naturally out of the traditional character of the ordinary Japanese. Therefore, when a Japanese views the law from his tradition-tinted perspective, he tends to see it in a different light."[69]

Virtually everything in Japan is considered in terms of opposing yet mutually self-defining concepts, from the dualistic perspective of having two sides (the *yin* and *yang* in Chinese). Take, for instance, *tatemae-honne* (conventions, principles, or institutions versus what is the underlying practice, what is true and natural) and *omote-ura* (that which is public or offical versus that which is not and remains hidden). *Tatemae* and *honne* are always potentially in tension and holding out the possibility of coming together to produce harmony. *Tatemae* and *omote* conceal *honne* and *ura,* that which is more natural and basic.[70]

This dualistic perspective rooted in language and culture may also explain why the Japanese are not especially surprised by scandals. The individual *(honne)* exists within a group's or community's consensus *(tatemae).*

The individual is submerged, sheltered by, and subservient to the community or group. At the same time, he or she may try to manipulate the *tatemae* from within and behind, as it were, in subtle and often unspoken ways. In any event, life is never solitary. People are always contextualized as part of, in relation to, or together with others—whether the family, company, community, or country.

No less crucially, neither *tatemae* nor *honne* is identified with either moral goodness or evil. Western conceptions of moral praiseworthiness, guilt, and blameworthiness simply have no place. For that reason, some scholars, including anthropologist Ruth Benedict, in her popular postwar work *The Chrysanthemum and the Sword,* have characterized Japan's culture as a "shame culture" based on external social sanctions, in contrast to Western "guilt cultures," which inculcate an internalization of personal sin and guilt.[71] Yet traditional Japanese concerns with purification and related rites are unencumbered by notions of sin. Instead, they revolve around removing physical or mental defilements and pollutions, thus cleansing impurities that separate one from others and from the *kami.* Neither are there external, objective, or universal standards, or a sharp division between earth and heaven. Rather, everything depends on context and the politics of situational ethics. Context dictates obligations and duties, and remains backed by strong social sanctions. Context, although powerfully controlling, always remains open to the possiblity of subtle manipulation.

Imported into the language to convey Western concepts of law and legal rights, *hō* (law) is a governing institution. But courts and law stand in opposition to that which is most natural and determinative. Thus law as *tatemae* is a facade. Law is a governing pretense. It is somewhat indistinct, less pressing than other concerns, and amenable to evasion and manipulation. That is why, for most Japanese, in the words of Professor Noda, "the ideal life is one in which they have no truck whatsoever with either the court or the law. . . . The Japanese feel they are better off when not bothered by law. If they can do without law, so much the better."[72]

Language may contribute to less weight being placed on law in another way, namely, due to the multiple meanings of Japanese characters. Because spoken words change meaning depending on context, and written characters may represent different things, the Japanese expect less precision.[73] As former Tokyo University law-school professor Takeyoshi Kawashima points out,

> In Japan the traditional notion or expectation concerning language is that every word has some meaning which represents only the core of its many possible meanings. Around this core there lies rather an area of ambiguous

meaning which fades away into zero through the process of interpretation. The meaning of a word is not expected to be definite, limited and fixed. It is intended to undergo change according to its use and application in a wide variety of possible situations.[74]

Accordingly, indirection, vagueness, and ambiguity are regarded as polite and respectful. Differences and potential disagreements are thereby blurred and diffused. The Japanese are thus tolerant of ambiguity, elasticity, and discretionary applications of legal documents. As a result, Takeyoshi Kawashima contrasts what he terms "the naive realism" of Japanese culture with the "logical realism" of American legal culture. "Here," Kawashima says, "the people would not be surprised to discover that the meaning of law sometimes is changed, shaped and sometimes distorted by policemen, prosecutors, lawyers and by judges during the legal process. . . . In Japan it is understood from the beginning of a legal enactment that the meaning of law is changeable and not definite."[75]

Finally, despite constitutional provisions for individual civil rights and liberties, such as freedom of speech and religion, they have largely failed to take hold in postwar Japan. Individual civil rights and liberties are simply far less important than in the West. The libertarian tradition of civil rights and liberties in the West has always rested on a fundamental distinction between the public and the private. Indeed, the public-private distinction is not only pivotal for the separation of the state and religion but central to libertarianism and all of Western liberalism. Simply put, in the separation of the two—the public from the private, and the state from religion—lies liberty and freedom.

The point of the public-private distinction was well expressed by James Otis in a famous colonial case, *The Paxton's Case,* in 1761. In that case, Otis contended that general warrants for searches and seizures ran contrary to the *Magna Carta* of 1215 (the first great English charter expressing the ideas of the supremacy of law and fundamental individual rights that the state may not deny). "A man's house is his castle," argued Otis, "and while he is quiet, he is well guarded as a prince in castle."[76] That position, central as it is to Western liberalism, was echoed even more eloquently by William Pitt the Elder, who exclaimed that "The Poorest man may in his cottage bid defiance to all the force of the Crown. It may be frail—its roof may shake—the wind may blow through it—the storm may enter—the rain may enter—but the King of England cannot enter—all his force dares not cross the threshold of the ruined tenement."[77]

In Japan, not only has the crucial Western distinction between the public and the private failed to take root, but the connotations and implications of the words for "public" (ōyake) and "private" (watakushi) are radically different: they are turned upside down, as it were. Ōyake is highly ambiguous, and stands also for that which is official and traditionally associated with the emperor. The Japanese character for ōyake or kō, moreover, is the last character of the prewar slogan, "Self-annihilation for the sake of the country" (messhi hōkō). In short, the public (ōyake) and the private (watakushi) have historically suggested a hierarchical relationship between ruler and subordinate, of superiority and inferiority in position and in importance.

Conflict amid Conformity

Given the ambivalence about religion and law, as well as the general apathy about claims to individual rights, the Kamisakas' challenge to Minoo city was remarkable in many ways. Their claim that city officials had violated constitutional provisions for the separation of the state from religion—and their insistence on the enforcement of a strict separation between the two—cut across deeply ingrained predispositions. At the same time, the Kamisakas' lawsuits represented an undercurrent of diversity within Japan.

Far less homogeneous and much more conflictual than usually portrayed, deep-seated differences and disagreements in Japan cut along generational, geographical, gender, and political lines. In addition, while the Japanese are ambivalent about law, they are far from reluctant litigants. Moreover, in postwar Japan an embryonic movement has emerged toward litigating issues of public policy. Rather than an institution for conflict resolution per se, however, the judiciary generally functions more as a public forum for raising issues and criticizing the government. Such interest-group litigation commands publicity. It is used to mobilize support and to attempt to sway public opinion on major issues of social policy.

In bringing the Minoo War Memorial litigation, the Kamisakas registered political dissent and the incipient turn toward interest-group or public-interest litigation in postwar Japan. They also became part of the larger, ongoing political struggle between liberal and conservative forces within the country. That continuing controversy is between those who dream of religious freedom and a strict separation of the state from religion, on the one hand, and those who dream of reinvigorating the myths and symbols of emperor worship and the prewar status of State Shinto, on the other.

CHAPTER 2

Paradoxes of (Dis)Establishment

SHINTO'S STATUS and separation from the state remain problematic because of its complex history and role in supporting militarism during and after the Meiji Restoration. That is also why the Kamisakas and their neighbors were so determined to push for an official acknowledgment of the Constitution's mandate for the strict separation of the state from religion. They recalled being indoctrinated into the emperor system in the 1930s and 1940s: how the great national myths of the divine origins and superiority of the emperor and Japan were rigorously inculcated in school; how students recited daily prayers to the emperor and were required to pay homage at state shrines and *chūkonhi* war memorials.

What the Kamisakas remembered of their youth was an accumulation of state-sponsored Shinto that began in 1868, with the Meiji Restoration, and culminated in World War II. This is not to say that state sponsorship of Shinto emerged full blown and remained static throughout the period. On the contrary, the history of the state's sponsorship of Shinto was turbulent, complex, and at times mired in contradiction. It is a history of competing factions, warring bureaucracies, and Shinto priests rising to and falling in and out of positions of political power; it is also a history of the military's finally gaining a vicelike grip on the government and the people.

The Establishment of State Shinto

The state's relationship with Shinto evolved through at least four distinct periods.[1] First, in the decade or so following the Meiji civil war (from 1868 to 1880), Shinto was separated from Buddhism. Its sacred myths and rituals were embraced as a national religious creed that aimed at both uniting the people and legitimizing the newly formed Meiji regime. Second, during roughly the last quarter of the nineteenth century (1880 to 1905), the government's financial support for Shinto declined and Shinto priests faced an identity crisis. During this period, however, Shinto became more sharply defined through a classification system, while State Shinto was redefined as "nonreligious" and set apart from popular and traditional religious Shinto sects. Third, in the period between 1905 and 1930, financial support for State Shinto was renewed and its influence grew, while "new religions" also emerged and Christians, Buddhists, and others generally enjoyed religious freedom. Finally, for a brief and very oppressive period (from 1930 to 1945), State Shinto became so pervasive that it became known as the "emperor system." Emperor worship and State Shinto were rigorously taught in schools, perpetuated in propaganda films, and glorified in public ceremonies for the cult of the war dead at Yasukuni, regional *gokoku* shrines, and local *chūkonhi* war memorials.

The Meiji Restoration was actually a revolution. The feudal government of kingdoms overseen by the Tokugawa shogunates was overthrown, and the basis was laid for a more centralized, modern nation-state under the governing authority of the emperor.[2] During the previous period (1603–1868), Tokugawa shoguns had also governed in the name of the emperor, but the emperor had remained isolated and removed from power in the western capital of Kyoto. The shoguns embraced Buddhism, and Buddhist temples served as the smallest unit of feudal control. Buddhist festivals were affairs of state, and Buddhist priests were in charge of keeping records on all births, marriages, deaths, travel, and other matters. Although Shinto was Japan's indigenous religious folkway, it remained undifferentiated, disorganized, and subordinated. To put it differently, although, technically speaking, it was the emperor who reigned, Buddhism was the established religion while traditional Shinto cults were basically assimilated: priests prayed to Shinto *kami* under Buddhist names, and Buddhist rites were conducted at Shinto shrines.

In the late Tokugawa period, there emerged a movement to restore pure Shinto—a kind of Japanese renaissance. To call this movement a revival or restoration is in some ways misleading, however. For centuries Buddhist and Shinto rituals and institutions had been amalgamated and thoroughly integrated. In the sixth century, when Buddhism had first been introduced in Japan, there had been a power struggle. But with the support of Prince Shōtoku (593–633), Buddhism had gained the upper hand. Shinto rituals and customs were assimilated with those of Buddhism. The spirits of the forces of nature and the *kami* of ancestors, heads of clans and warriors were worshipped as buddhas at both Buddhist temples and Shinto shrines, without differentiation. In short, the movement to revive Shinto actually aimed self-consciously to identify Shinto qua Shinto.

Led by Atsutane Hirata (1776–1843), who was from the "national learning" school of thought *(kokugaku),* the movement sought to purify Shinto. It aimed to separate Shinto from Buddhism and to celebrate the distinctiveness of traditional Shinto rituals and rites. While building on traditional local rituals and shrines, this nativist movement also emphasized the worship of national deities in state rites. In contrast to the prevailing practice of only worshipping local cults, this movement sought to unify the people through identification with the deities of ancient myths and legends of Japan's divine origins and race. More attention was paid to Japanese classics and to the elimination of all pollutions of foreign influence. In other words, a new tradition was in the process of being forged, albeit in the name of restoring something that may or may not have existed eleven hundred years before.

As the movement to differentiate Shinto gradually increased in popularity, Tokugawa warlords censured Hirata's books and teachings in the 1840s. That proved counterproductive, however. Over the next twenty years, the movement for establishing Shinto grew alongside forces of rebellion. Samurai-intellectuals, merchant-landlord-industrialists opposed to the system of feudal lords, Shinto priests, artisans, lower-class warriors, and rich farmers finally turned against the Tokugawa military government. In the end, they succeeded in establishing the imperial rule of the emperor according to ancient myths and legends.[3]

During the Meiji civil war, the emperor performed unprecedented Shinto rites. He worshipped the heavenly and earthly *kami* of war and prayed for the Meiji forces. Amid the continuing civil war, in the fall of 1868, the first year of the Meiji era, the 15-year-old emperor traveled from the capital of Kyoto, in western Honshu, to Edo to take up residence at the palace of the deposed Tokugawa shoguns. Edo was renamed Tokyo, the eastern capital, and in 1871 became the capital of the new government and the country. Moving the capital to Tokyo was more than just symbolic of the Meiji forces' victory over the Tokugawa shogunates. It aimed to distance (and eventually eliminate) the influence of the old imperial bureaucracy in Kyoto. A new central government with a different cast of players, who would also rule in the name of the emperor, was gradually established.

Emperor Meiji also made a historic pilgrimage to Ise, the most venerated Shinto shrine. The Ise Shrine complex dates back to the third century A.D. and, according to Shinto tradition, is rebuilt every twenty years (most recently in 1993, at a cost of 5 billion yen, or approximately $50 million). Representing, again, the renewal, restoration, and purification of all Japan, the Ise shrines are built anew, exactly like the old ones, out of wood and without using nails, on a purified site next to the old shrines. Ise is the most sacred shrine because it is dedicated to the ancestral sun goddess, the guardian of the imperial family and the nation. The inner shrine at Ise preserves one of the three sacred treasures of the emperor: a mirror which, along with a sacred sword and jewel, symbolize the emperor's divine right to rule. According to legend, these sacred regalia were given by the Sun Goddess Amaterasu-Ōmikami to her grandson Niniginomikoto when he left the heavens for the earth to rule with her divine descendants.

As the divine descendant of an "unbroken line" that reaches back to the great sun goddess herself, the emperor embodies the unity of Shinto and the state. He is the highest Shinto priest, performing the most sacred Shinto rites for the fertility and harvest of the country's rice. Ise's outer shrine enshrines the goddess of agriculture, Toyouke-Ōmikami. Throughout the centuries, because of its religious symbolism for Shinto and Japanese folkways, Ise has been a magnet for pilgrims. Indeed, in the 1990s about six million people a year visit Ise, even though its inner shrines remain closed to the public.

On April 6, 1868, Emperor Meiji proclaimed the Charter Oath of Five Articles, the "national polity or policy" *(kokutai)* of imperial sovereignty. A new era was thus inaugurated. Reforms followed that established compulsory education and military service, as well as a system of taxation. Notably, though, "the national polity or policy" stood ambiguously for the legal recognition of the emperor's sovereignty and/or the national belief in—or moral sentiments promulgated by the Meiji reforms toward—the emperor.

Central to the Meiji reforms was the separation of the *kami* and buddhas *(shinbutsu-bunri)*. The unity of Shinto and the state was embodied in and symbolized by the emperor. Shinto was separated from and elevated above Buddhism by the Separation Edict of 1868. Prior to that, as earlier noted, there was no rigid separation between Shinto shrines and Buddhist temples. In fact, until the Meiji policy of separating the *kami* from buddhas, the great shrine at Ise was surrounded by hundreds of Buddhist temples, monuments, and statues. Imperial funerals had been conducted according to Buddhist rites. Prayers for the longevity and health of the emperor were said at Buddhist temples, and imperial tombs were located in them. But the Buddhist temples and statues at Ise were now purged and plundered. Many Buddhist priests gave up celibacy and married or took concubines, as well as started eating fish and meat in violation of their vows.

Shinto priests took over from Buddhist priests responsibilities for registering births, marriages, deaths, and other administrative matters. A Department of Divinity was created as the highest agency within the new government. It assumed the mission of promulgating the teachings of the Meiji regime. Shinto priests, however, were divided over how to exercise their newly acquired power. The quarreling soon resulted in the dissolution of the department and the creation of both the Bureau of Shinto and Ministry of Education in its place. The overriding objective nonetheless remained that of propagating the national teaching (*kokkyō,* or "state religion") of reverence for the emperor and the unity of Shinto and the state.

Along with the initial appearance of bureaucratic structures dominated by Shinto priests came the continued persecution of Christians and the pillage of Buddhist temples, which accompanied the "anti-Buddhist storm"[4] that swept the land, especially in the provinces of the leaders of the Meiji government. When, in 1868, it was discovered that the village of Urakami had for two hundred years secretly practiced Christianity, the entire village was purged. Urakami is on the rural, western island of Kyushu and has now become absorbed into Nagasaki, where Christianity was first introduced by Saint Francis Xavier in 1549. Nagasaki's governor had the leaders of the Urakami Christians tortured and 3,384 villagers relocated and reeducated by Shinto priests. Many died in the process.

The Meiji state's embrace of Shinto was further advanced in 1872 with

Yasukuni Shrine, Tokyo. (Author photo)

the promulgation of "Three Articles of Teaching Principles,"[5] which were announced for the purpose of disseminating the teachings of the Meiji regime. Students were taught (1) the principle of veneration of *kami* and love of country, (2) the importance of the law of heaven and the way of humanity, and (3) that the emperor and imperial instructions must be reverently defended and obeyed.

Shinto priests and the emerging governmental bureaucracies nonetheless remained entangled in long-running disputes over the relationship between Shinto and the state. Indeed, that relationship, along with the structure of the Shinto bureaucracy itself, underwent several transformations for a number of reasons. Recall that before the Meiji era the word "Shinto" had not been widely used, and Shinto and Buddhism were basically amalgamated. Nor was there an understanding of Western conceptions of religion, either as a matter of private individual belief or along the lines of established state religion in Europe. Such Western conceptions were (and remain) foreign. Indigenous rites and rituals were undifferentiated aspects of everyday communal life. Shrines were disorganized, their priests generally preoccupied with local concerns and indifferent to sharing in common what State Shinto would come to represent and superimpose on them.

Following the Meiji revolution, government support for Buddhism came to an end. And although Shinto had always been the indigenous, traditional folk religion of Japan, it for the first time came into bold relief. Shinto alone now received state support. A bureaucracy headed by Shinto priests was created to legitimize the newly formed government through a "great promulgation campaign."[6] Yet this experiment, aimed at unifying the people in support of the Meiji government, lasted for little more than a decade (1868–1880): the campaign encountered resistence; quarrelling among local priests doomed the newly created Shinto bureaucracy; and Shinto itself remained largely disorganized. Shinto shrines and rites remained closely tied to their villages and to historical preoccupations with matters such as fertility, diseases, and the glorification of local *kami*. As a result, there were demotions, reorganizations, and, eventually, a decline in government support for Shinto priests.

For the next quarter of a century, from roughly 1880 to 1905, the Shinto priesthood faced a kind of identity crisis. In the words of Japanologist Helen Hardacre, the priesthood "saw itself as an embattled minority, misunderstood by government,"[7] yet identified with the Meiji government. The priesthood was also bitter and dispirited over its loss of previous (though short-lived) prestige, positions of power, and financial assistance. Without funding from the government, Shinto priests had to depend on local supporters' offerings. This in turn meant performing certain rites and rituals, including funerals, which ran against what some Shinto priests conceived of as their higher calling—namely, promulgating the teachings of the Meiji government and the unity of Shinto and the state.

During this period, some important State Shinto shrines were nevertheless built. A system of classifying shrines and temples was put into place, which finally organized Shinto into a rigid hierarchical structure. No less importantly, in 1898, the National Association of Shinto Priests was founded: it took more than thirty years, but the Shinto priesthood finally became more or less unified in order to fight against competing interests. Notably, in 1899 the government enacted a law forbidding religious leaders—whether Shinto, Buddhist, or Christian—from participating in political parties or holding elective office. That same year, however, the government also granted a request from the priests of the Grand Ise Shrine to abandon their status as a religious body. Ise became a secular juridical corporation. It did so on the grounds that its priests were preserving the country's historical heritage and most sacred teaching of veneration for ancestor worship and the emperor.

The Meiji government's recognition of the Grand Ise Shrine as a secular institution underscores one of the major and enduring disputes over State Shinto. From the outset of the Meiji era, there was disagreement over no less a matter than whether Shinto was indeed a religion. State Shinto incorporated traditional local Shinto rites, nationalized certain rituals and holidays, and built on them to promote worship of the emperor and Yasukuni's cult of war dead. Still, disagreement raged over whether Shinto was comparable to the established religions of Europe, a grand civil religion, or patriotism and civic responsibility. Some Shinto priests maintained that State Shinto was above and beyond all religion. Veneration of the emperor and the country's ancestors and war dead, they argued, was at the heart of civic responsibility and patriotism. Others saw their mission in more religious terms. For them, what was at stake was nothing less than a national purification. They aimed to dismantle the bureaucratic structure and influence of Buddhism that had held sway during the preceding Tokugawa era.

The debate over whether state-sponsored Shinto constituted an established religion was complicated by international pressures on the Meiji government in the late nineteenth century. As the Meiji government sought recognition and favorable treaty terms, it confronted opposition due to Japan's treatment of Christians and other religious minorities. Outraged by incidents like the purge of the Urakami Christians, Catholic and Protestant leaders in Europe pushed Western governments to demand guarantees of religious freedom and the rights of the accused in exchange for more favorable treaty agreements. At the same time, the Meiji government resented treaties that had been negotiated prior to the revolution. Some of these included extraterritorial clauses that permitted foreign powers to station military forces on Japanese soil and that exempted foreign nationals from Japan's courts. Along with adopting new legal codes in the process of renegotiating its treaties, the Meiji government reassessed its position on State Shinto. As a result—and despite the fact that the Meiji revolution had been fought as a holy war to restore the unity of Shinto and the state—the government came to the rather paradoxical conclusion that State Shinto was fundamentally nonreligious.

The Meiji government thus not only distanced Shinto from Buddhism but also pursued a policy of distancing State Shinto from all religion. For the first time in Japan's long history, a distinction was made between the state and politics versus religion. From the pre-Nara age through the Tokugawa period and up to the Meiji Restoration, the political and the religious had been intertwined within the fabric of Japanese society. Ironically, the Meiji government embraced the Western dichotomy of the state versus religion in order to advance its creation of State Shinto as a kind of super-religious, national nonreligion.

The Meiji government implemented its seemingly counterintuitive policy by organizing all Shinto cults and shrines and dividing them into classes. Each shrine was ranked on the basis of its proximity to the emperor. The sacred rites of the emperor performed at the imperial palace (*kōshitsu* Shinto) were set apart and continue to be closed to the public. Next in importance were state shrines, or shrine Shinto (*jinja* Shinto).[8] Although the Grand Ise Shrine ranked at the top, these state shrines were classified as nonreligious. By contrast, popular Shinto cults and shrines were officially recognized as religious or sect Shinto (*kyōha* Shinto). In 1900, the old Bureau of Shrines and Temples was abolished, and in its place a Bureau of Shrines and a Bureau of Religion were created.

Thirteen Shinto sects were eventually classified as religious. With a few exceptions, each had been founded by a charismatic person, but their followers also worshipped the most revered national *kami* of State Shinto. In addition, the broader amalgam of cults and magical rites observed by families, neighborhoods, villages, and regional or corporate groups was dubbed "folk Shinto" (*minkan* Shinto). While embracing the worship of national *kami* and observance of the principal traditional Shinto festivals, folk Shinto included local customs and rituals that had been deemed non-religious and linked to State Shinto.[9]

The classification system developed during the Meiji era (which remains in place) organized Shinto for the first time in its long history. It also provided a basis for rationalizing both the government's establishment of State Shinto and its claim that religious freedom was guaranteed. Yet even as the classification system brought Shinto into bold relief, it masked the overlapping and coalescing rituals of traditional Shinto and state-sponsored Shinto, particularly in Yasukuni's cult of the war dead.

The Meiji classification system also reinforced the further development of a burgeoning Shinto bureaucracy. Under the system, it was on the basis of rank that shrines received more or less state support, or none at all. State-supported shrines received public funding according to their ranking as an imperial or national shrine. Within each of those divisions there were major, middle-grade, and minor shrines. All state shrines were considered nonreligious, and their priests served as teachers of civic responsibility and the national policy announced in imperial rescripts. In contrast, religious shrines—those of sectarian and folk Shinto—received no governmental support but were nevertheless registered as prefectual, district, town, village, or unranked shrines. Each town or village was required to have at least one shrine, and after 1939 to have one *chūkonhi* memorial to war dead in a schoolyard or other prominent public place.

In short, by (1) building important state shrines, such as Yasukuni and those to Emperor Meiji and other major figures who had been devoted to the emperor; (2) organizing and classifying other Shinto shrines that had roots in the traditional customs of the people; and (3) proclaiming the nonreligious character of State Shinto, the Meiji government achieved a pretense of religious freedom. That pretense was perpetuated in the Meiji Constitution in Article 28 of Chapter 2, headed "Rights and Duties of Subjects," which was finally promulgated in 1889, after twenty years of study and debate.[10]

Article 28 of the Meiji Constitution specifically guaranteed that "Japanese subjects shall, within the limits of law, not prejudicial to peace and order, and not antagonistic to their duties as subjects, enjoy freedom of religious belief." Yet religious freedom was guaranteed only to the extent that it did not interfere with civic duties or responsibilities and "except as provided by law." No less crucially, the right of religious freedom, among other freedoms, existed merely as one of the "rights of *the subjects*" extended by the "will of the emperor." The very idea that individual rights trump political power remained (and to a large extent remains) alien and foreign. The obligations and duties of citizens were more familiar and overriding. Christians and other religious minorities would thus eventually be forced to publicly honor the emperor, Yasukuni's war dead, and other rituals of State Shinto, even though for them that amounted to blasphemy or a denial of religious freedom.

Other provisions of the Meiji Constitution were also in apparent contradiction to the guarantee of religious freedom in Article 28. The first article of the Constitution recognized the emperor as a divine, "manifest *kami* who possesses sovereign religious authority over Shinto rituals and ceremonies." It also proclaimed that "The Empire of Japan shall be reigned over and governed by a line of emperors unbroken for ages eternal." The third article declared the emperor "sacred and inviolable."

These constitutional provisions misleadingly suggest that the emperor was indeed an all-powerful sovereign. To the contrary, and paradoxically, the emperor exercised little or no independent decisionmaking power. He had no veto power and could wield the power of subtle persuasion at most. Even the Emperor Meiji remained a virtual recluse during his reign, served by nobles and advisors in the imperial palace. Historically, the emperor played the role of a sacred sovereign authority without wielding actual political power. The Meiji Constitution merely gave constitutional effect to that long-standing tradition. Elite clans claiming divine origins, and even the shoguns in the Tokugawa period, had governed in the name of the emperor.

As the highest Shinto priest and titular head of the government under the Meiji Constitution, the emperor reigned as a legitimizing symbol. He was a centripetal force standing against the centrifugal forces of rival clans and foreign influences. Until 1885, the actual decisionmaking power resided behind the imperial throne, with ministers in the Grand Council of State *(Daijōkan)* thereafter, it resided with the heads of governmental ministeries and leaders in the Diet.

Despite being a "manifest *kami* who possesses sovereign religious authority over Shinto rituals and ceremonies," the emperor functioned politically somewhat like a constitutionally limited monarch within the imperial court and the government. The emperor gave legitimacy and public expression to the consensus or ultimate decision of the ruling elites. That the emperor was constitutionally limited under the Meiji Constitution is evident from any number of provisions. Article 55, for instance, specifically limited the emperor's administrative powers by specifying that "The respective Ministers of State shall give their advice to the Emperor and be responsible for it." The article also provided that "All Laws, Imperial Ordinances, and Imperial Rescripts of whatever kind, that relate to the affairs of the State, require the countersignature of a Minister of State." The emperor's authority was constitutionally limited in other ways as well. Article 5 stipulated that "The Emperor exercises the legislative power with the consent of the Diet." Article 8 further specified that, when the Diet was not in session, "Imperial Ordinances are to be laid before the Imperial Diet at its next session, and when the Diet does not approve said Ordinances, the Government shall declare them to be invalid for the future."[11]

Under the Meiji Constitution, and according to centuries-old tradition, the emperor was thus a reigning, though not a de facto ruling, monarch. The Emperor Meiji (1868–1912) actively questioned his ministers and the government leaders in his court, and thereby influenced decisionmaking. But he made few decisions himself, and then only when ministerial advisors were divided. The mere existence of the emperor was sufficient. The emperor provided "sacred legitimacy" for the government's policies.[12] During the brief reign of Meiji's son, Emperor Taishō (1912–1926), constant poor health caused the emperor to be even more removed from political decisionmaking. By contrast, Hirohito, like his grandfather, actively questioned ministers during his long reign (1926–1989). Yet he, too, rarely directly intervened or asserted independent judgment, except at the very end of World War II.

An extraordinary creation of the illusion of authority with power, what over time developed into the emperor system rested on a profound paradox: While the government cultivated State Shinto—and the people thus came to venerate the emperor as "the son of the heavens," an all-powerful sovereign embodying the unity of Shinto and the state—the emperor was in fact constitutionally constrained. In 1873, Toshimichi Ōkubo (a samurai-intellectual and one of the leaders who orchestrated the coup d'etat that became the Meiji revolution) put it this way, when proposing a draft constitution:

> The more the outward appearance of the power of the Emperor is strengthened, the less his actual power will be. . . . The basic law which will determine the powers of the Emperor and limit the powers of the people must be based on a profound love of the nation. It must maintain the Emperor's position for all ages to come and make the people keep their natural order.[13]

In practice, then, the emperor wielded little political power. By incorporating, organizing, and finally superimposing State Shinto and Yasukuni's cult of the war dead on traditional yet diverse local rituals and shrines, the government nevertheless endeavored to create a national, civil religion centered on worship of the emperor. State Shinto at once legitimized the government and perpetuated the grand illusion of unity and harmony. All the while, State Shinto masked the internal power struggles of those elite factions and warring bureaucracies that governed in the name of the emperor.

The depth of the devotion to "restoring" pure Shinto and to establishing the unity of Shinto and the state was dramatized on the very day the Meiji Constitution was promulgated. A group of Shinto priests from Ise Shrine assassinated the minister of education. He had been a leader in the movement for Westernization and allegedly had poked a cane at a curtain to try to see a secret ritual performed at Ise. Two years later, Kanzo Uchimura, a great evangelist and the founder of the "Non-Church" Christianity Movement, was censured for refusing to pay homage to the Imperial Rescript on Education.[14] Issued on October 30, 1890, the document itself was deified, and students were required to memorize it, along with the names of each emperor. The rescript merits quoting at length:[15]

Know ye, Our Subjects:

Our Imperial Ancestors have founded our Empire on a basis broad and everlasting, and have deeply and firmly implanted virtue; Our subjects, ever united in loyalty and filial piety, have from generation to generation illustrated the beauty thereof. This is the glory of the fundamental character of Our Empire, and herein also lies the source of our education. Ye, Our subjects, be filial to your parents, affectionate to your brothers and sisters; as husbands and wives be harmonious, as friends true; bear yourselves in modesty and moderation; extend your benevolence to all; pursue learning and cultivate arts, and thereby cultivate intellectual faculties and perfect moral powers; furthermore advance public good and promote common interests; always respect the Constitution and observe the laws; should emergency arise, offer yourselves courageously to the State; and thus guard and maintain the prosperity of Our Imperial Throne coeval with heaven and earth. So shall ye be not only Our good and faithful subjects but render illustrious the best tradition of your forefathers.

The Way here set forth is indeed the teaching bequeathed by Our Imperial Ancestors, to be observed by Their Descendants and the subjects, infallible in all ages and true in all places. It is Our wish to lay it to heart in all reverence, in common with you, Our subjects, that we may attain to the same virtue.

Although state financial support for Shinto ebbed during the last quarter of the nineteenth century, State Shinto became further entrenched. State Shinto then expanded after the turn of the century, at a steadily increasing cost to religious freedom. Following the Russo-Japanese war (1904–1905), appropriations for State Shinto and Yasukuni's cult of war dead gradually increased until 1930. State Shinto slowly became more pervasive, due not only to greater funding and renewed government support for the training of Shinto priests, but also to the fact that several generations had been conscripted into the military. The military's policy was to keep soldiers from the same region together in troop units. In addition, military codes prohibited commanders and soldiers from surrendering or becoming prisoners of war, admonishing them not to be taken alive.[16] In these ways, the military built on soldiers' local affiliations and allegiances while instilling devotion to the emperor and Yasukuni's cult of the war dead.

Beginning with the Sino-Japanese war (1894–1895), then the Russo-Japanese war (1904–1905), the annexation of Korea in 1910, and the subsequent colonization of China, the number of enshrinements grew incrementally at Yasukuni. In addition, construction began on the great Meiji Shrine in Tokyo in 1915 and was completed in 1926. The Meiji Shrine stands as an impressive national monument to emperor worship, enshrining both the emperor Meiji and the empress as *kami*. In 1928, the Peace Preservation Law was amended in order to suppress new religious movements by providing harsh penalties, including death, for those who opposed the national policy and teachings of State Shinto. Antiwar publications and books on socialism and pacifism were censored, along with other means of mass communications.[17]

During the world economic depression of the 1930s, the military gained even greater influence within the imperial household. Military officials worked closely with the Bureau of Shrines in promoting militarism in the name of the emperor.[18] After the Manchurian Incident in 1931, and the escalation of Japan's war campaign thereafter, there was a rising toll of war dead who were glorified in public rituals at Yasukuni, regional *gokoku* shrines, and *chūkonhi* war memorials.

With so many soldiers dying in the decades following the turn of the century, the symbols and rituals of State Shinto took hold. State Shinto captured the people's imagination, or was, at least, vigorously imposed throughout the country. In 1932, the Ministry of Education required all schoolchildren above the sixth grade to give their salutations to the dead who were enshrined at local *chūkonhi* war memorials and *gokoku* shrines. Schoolchildren also had to participate in class field trips to Yasukuni. Three years later, college students were ordered to worship at the *chūkonhi* war memorials.[19]

Due to the escalation of the war with China in 1937, the number of war dead continued to rise. Services at war memorials and *gokoku* shrines became almost daily rituals for schoolchildren to attend. The services sought to provide "role models" and to inspire unconditional allegiance from the children. From their classrooms, fireworks could be heard. Like exciting bombs, they exploded in mid-morning of the days on which services were to be held. In the afternoon the children were taken outside to *chūkonhi* war memorials, where Shinto priests conducted ceremonies for the dead. Food and *sake* were offered to the *kami*. The mayor or other government officials would deliver funeral orations. More Shinto rituals would follow. The orations were delivered against a quiet, somber background, broken only by the crying of relatives of those who were being enshrined. Sprigs of the sacred *sakaki* evergreen tree would be offered. Finally, the food and *sake* would be taken away.

Back in their classrooms, the students were instructed that dying for their country and the emperor would bring deification, the highest honor. With the exception of four soldiers who had died in the Russo-Japanese war, 294 of the 298 souls enshrined at Minoo city's war memorial were from the generations that grew up immediately preceding and during World War II. Thus virtually all those enshrined in the Minoo *chūkonhi* had been forced to worship there as children.

The highwater mark of State Shinto had arrived. The government's experiment with "the invention of a new religion," to borrow Basil Hall Chamberlain's phrase, had succeeded.[20] Although State Shinto lasted only fifteen years (1930–1945), it took a heavy toll. In 1940, the twenty-six-hundredth anniversary of the mythical founding of Japan, the government enacted the notorious Religious Organizations Law. This law tightened control over religion even more, by regulating religious organizations like other corporations. Under the law, religious organizations had to apply for and be granted government recognition to operate legally. Moreover, recognition depended on the religious body's agreeing to teachings and rites supportive of the emperor's divinity. For Christian organizations to operate legally, they had to compromise their creeds and doctrines. Religious bodies not recognized by the government were thus illegal, becoming subject to persecution and prosecution. At the same time, the Bureau of Shrines became the Board of Shrine Rites, and its power and prestige were greatly expanded. In 1941, the Peace Preservation Law was again revised to authorize police to go after religious groups that denied or opposed the national policy of emperor worship.

During World War II, Christians and other religious minorities were ruthlessly persecuted both at home and abroad, in Korea and elsewhere. In Yokohama, several Catholic priests were shot to death. Outspoken Christians, such as Yanaihara of the Non-Church Christianity Movement, were driven from their posts at Tokyo University and elsewhere. In June 1942, more than a hundred ministers of the United Church of Christ of Japan were arrested and charged with disturbing the peace. During their trials, their faith was tested as well. They confronted the horns of a calculated dilemma when asked, "Who do you think is greater, the Emperor or Christ?" To safely affirm the former constituted the sin of blasphemy, while maintaining allegiance to the latter meant imprisonment.

Many ministers died in prison, while others submitted or left the country. Still, a majority of Christians acquiesced and participated in the rituals of State Shinto. They defended their actions as participation in accepted social practices, thus yielding to the government's tortured logic that worship of the emperor and Yasukuni's war dead was not religious worship. Some Christian pastors even went so far as to incorporate the Imperial Rescript on Education into their sermons.

Christians were not alone in opposition to or suppression by State Shinto. Some Buddhist sects also spoke out in defiance. They likewise faced surveillance and other reprisals. Just how oppressive State Shinto had become was made clear by Prime Minister Kiichirō Hiranuma. When presenting the Religious Organizations Law to the Diet, Hiranuma claimed that, "In our country the way of the *kami* is the absolute way," and added, "Teachings which differ from this and confict with it are not allowed to exist."[21]

In sum, the Meiji Constitution rejected an established religion. Religious freedom was ostensibly guaranteed. And the government was thereby left free to promote State Shinto as patriotism and civic responsibility, as well as to glorify militarism in the name of the emperor and Yasukuni's cult of war dead. Yet this by no means suggests that, as Sheldon Garon puts it, there was "a straight line between the Meiji regime's attempt to establish an absolute national religion in the early 1870s and the wartime creation of the Board of Rites in 1940."[22] The history of Shinto and the state was richer and more complex than that. The path was far more circuitous and cumbersome. Still, the Meiji revolution and identification with the unity of Shinto and the state had laid the basis for the emergence of State Shinto.

By the 1930s, when Satoshi and Reiko Kamisaka were growing up, the government had fully absorbed regional and local rituals and shrines into a vast bureaucratic system centered on the worship of the emperor and Yasukuni's cult of war dead. As was customary, babies continued to be taken to local shrines. But, in addition to receiving the blessings of the local *kami,* their lives were dedicated to the emperor. Families were required to purchase a talisman from the Grand Shrine at Ise for their altars at home. Along with the traditional *kami*-shelf honoring household ancestors, each home was expected to have another plain wooden *kami*-shelf for the "great offering" to Ise and the nation's imperial and divine ancestors. In these and other ways, State Shinto was integrated into and superimposed on traditional Shinto customs and practices.[23]

In schools, along with the trips to *chūkonhi* war memorials and *gokoku* shrines, books prescribed by the Ministry of Education introduced and reinforced national myths and learning policies that blurred the lines between secular and religious Shinto. In *The Basic Meaning of the National Policy (Kokutai no Hongi)*, State Shinto was treated basically as religious, and students were instructed that "To give up one's life for the sake of the Emperor cannot be called self-sacrifice. It is rather discarding one's lesser self to live in the great Imperial Virtue, and exalting one's true life as a national subject."[24] Such were the daily recitals of schoolchildren—children who were taken to pray at state shrines, who played in schoolyards overshadowed by *chūkonhi* war memorials, and who would be conscripted to fight in the country's wars.

"Every facet of the curriculum was permeated with emperor worship and militarism. Young children were indoctrined to believe that the Greater East Asian War was a holy war,"[25] recalls Saburo Ienaga. He was a high school teacher during the war. "The government monopolized the writing of history textbooks and they taught children only things that were in line with their policies." "During the war," Ienaga adds, "there was the ever-present danger that some of the students might be informants and might report us to the police if we said something wrong in class."[26] Another scholar, Joseph Kitagawa, recalls his schooling in the prewar days as follows:

> Every individual who was educated in Japan before World War II was sub-jected to, and personally witnessed the intensification of, the emperor cult and the exaggerated propaganda of patriotism. If my memory is correct, schools in Japan in those days—especially primary and middle schools—devoted less and less energy to education and more and more time to military training and ritual obeisance to Shinto shrines and/or imperial portraits.[27]

Indoctrination comes in many forms. Before the war, the emperor system was rigorously and rigidly imposed. That ended with the Occupation. Afterward, however, the bureaucracy set about perpetuating a kind of historical amnesia in younger generations. Postwar education changed and yet remained the same, only different. Textbooks were screened, and selective recollection and revisionism were notorious. The emperor, militarism, and State Shinto were played down. Japan's aggressions were whitewashed. Japan's invasion of China, annexation of Korea, and attack on Pearl Harbor were dealt with offhandedly. They were described as simply an "advance" or an "incident" that had just happened. Instead of *shinryaku* (aggression), the word *"shinshutsu"* (advance, or entry into) was used in textbooks to describe Japan's invasion of Korea and China. *Tenshin* (changing course) rather than *tettai* (fleeing from the front line) was used to describe Japanese troops' retreats from the battlefield.

Time for teaching history remains limited. Classes generally begin with premodern periods and often do not get to the twentieth century by the end of the school year. As a result, not a few of those in the postwar generations have only vague, ambiguous ideas about World War II. Not until 1994, five years after the death of Emperor Hirohito (Shōwa), were textbooks finally beginning to deal with his role in the war and his reluctance to end it.

Ironically, Ienaga, who became a prolific historian at Tokyo University of Education, had his own textbooks censored by the Ministry of Education after the war. He had pointed out Japan's aggressions, the procurement of "comfort women" for soldiers, and other atrocities during the war. In the mid-1960s, Ienaga filed a series of suits challenging the government. Like the Kamisakas' litigation, his lawsuits dragged on until the Supreme Court finally handed down its ruling in 1993, upholding the Ministry of Education's policy of screening books and rejecting Ienaga's claim for damages.[28]

Consequently, the generations of Japanese schooled in the 1960s, 1970s, and 1980s have little understanding of State Shinto. They have even less interest in litigation like that brought by the Kamisakas, or in controversies over the separation of the state from religion and over claims to religious liberty.

Such is, nevertheless, what Satoshi and Reiko Kamisaka remembered, and more. "Japan, the land of the *kami*" was the government's slogan. Pilots leaving for battle became *kamikaze* (the divine wind), swearing, "We will meet in Yasukuni."[29] The depth of commitment inculcated by State Shinto remains preserved not only at Yasukuni but at the Japanese Underground Navy Headquarters on Okinawa. There, in the closing days of the battle over Okinawa, more than four thousand soldiers committed suicide rather than submit to the Allied forces.

Disestablishment and Japan's 1947 Constitution

World War II ended, for Japan, with all the devastation of a huge earthquake, or as though an unimaginably large tidal wave had swept the land, as it did centuries earlier when the temple that housed the enormous Kamakura buddha was swept away. Virtually every major city was leveled and incinerated. On August 6, 1945, Hiroshima exploded, burning under the dropping of a uranium atomic bomb. Two days later, the former Soviet Union formally declared war against Japan. The next day, August 9, a plutonium bomb flattened most of Nagasaki, though missing its industrial port. For the first time in its long history, Japan stood invaded and defeated.

For most Japanese, the war was an enormous national natural disaster, nothing less and nothing more. In the words of Yosiyuki Noda,

> As the Japanese view it, the Pacific War just happened to break out. None of the former government leaders who was tried at the International Military Tribunal for the Far East as first-class war criminals identified himself as someone responsible for having started the war. This is in sharp contrast with the Nazi leaders who positively identified themselves as the ones who had deliberately started the war in Europe. This episode clearly reveals an idiosyncracy unique to the Japanese people. In Japan, even her declaration of war against the Allied Powers is regarded as an incident that happened "in some way or another" without any premeditated design.[30]

Precisely because the war is generally considered little more than a huge natural disaster, without any sense of culpability, and because the emperor was (and remains) answerable to no one, apologizing or admitting responsibility for it remains highly controversial. Even a half-century later, it arouses the fierce passions of right-wing ultranationalists. The government still uses the word *"shūsen"* (the end of the war) instead of *haisen* (defeat in the war). The U.S. and Allied forces in Japan also continue to be referred to as "stationed forces" *(shinchūgun)* rather than "occupation forces" *(senryōgun).*[31]

The controversy over the war was stirred further when the conservative Liberal Democratic Party finally fell out of office in 1993. For the first time since the war, newly elected Prime Minister Morihiro Hosokawa called World War II a "war of aggression and a wrong war." He also apologized publicly for Japan's wartime conduct, specifically its forcing thousands of Asian women to become sex slaves or "comfort women." That drew angry responses from conservatives and the far right. At a small protest rally in Tokyo, Dokkyō University professor Akira Nakamura, among others, demanded that Hosokawa retract his statement. "It was Japan's fate to stand up to the white man," said Nakamura, "and save Asia."[32]

Less than a year later, in May 1994, after a scandal over his financial dealings drove him from office, Hosokawa was shot at by a right-wing extremist (in a country that bans guns) who was angry over the former prime minister's remarks about the war. Just weeks before, Hosokawa's successor, Tsutomu Hata, had been forced by a related incident to fire his coalition government's justice minister, Shigeto Nagano. Nagano, a veteran of the imperial army and a retired chief of staff of the Self Defense Forces, had dismissed as a "fabrication" the so-called Massacre of Nanjing, Japan's invasion of China in 1937, during which China claims that more than three hundred thousand of its citizens died. His comment outraged liberals and the Chinese but played to conservatives and right-wing supporters. These were not isolated events. They are expressions of the undercurrent of ultranationalism in Japan on the approach of the fiftieth anniversary of its 1947 Constitution.[33]

When in the summer of 1995, the Diet finally passed a resolution on the fiftieth anniversary of the end of World War II, which many still refer to as the "Greater East Asian War," an apology still remained too controversial. Instead, the resolution expressed "remorse" *(hansei)* over Japan's having "inflicted suffering on people of other nations, particularly Asian nations." Even that watered-down resolution required Prime Minister Tomiichi Murayama to threaten to resign (and to dissolve his coalition government) if it was not passed. That secured the resolution's passage, but did not deter two-thirds of the Liberal Democratic Party's members in the lower house of the Diet from boycotting the vote. Moreover, neither side considered apologizing for the raid on Pearl Harbor or Japan's aggression against the United States or its Western allies. Conservative LDP members and veterans groups maintain that Japan's wartime aggressions aimed honorably at liberating other Asian countries from Western colonialism, while liberals counter that their country waged war solely to benefit Japan, not other Asians.

The massive destruction that brought an end to World War II nevertheless dictated submission, as Hirohito acknowledged in an extraordinary radio broadcast on August 15, 1945. The broadcast was the first time the Japanese people had heard his voice. Prior to the end of the war they were not even permitted to look in the direction of the emperor when he made an infrequent "public" appearance. How else, Hirohito explained, "are we to save millions of our subjects, or to atone ourselves before the hallowed spirits of our imperial ancestors?" Yet, recalling ancient legends, Hirohito held out hope:

> Let the entire nation [*kokka,* or "national family"] continue as one family from generation to generation, ever firm in its faith of the imperishableness of its divine land, and mindful of its heavy burden of responsibilities, and the long road before it. Unite your total strength to be devoted to the construction for the future. Cultivate the ways of rectitude, nobility of spirit, and

work with resolution so that you may enhance the innate glory of the imperial state and keep pace with the progress of the world.[34]

Japan's rendezvous with destiny had arrived. The terms of surrender
were signed on September 2, 1945, and on January 1, 1946, Hirohito publicly disavowed being a *kami* in human guise. In an imperial rescript that
began by reaffirming the "national policy" announced by the Emperor
Meiji in 1868, Hirohito reached the conclusion that

> The ties between Us and Our people have always stood upon mutual trust
> and affection. They do not depend upon mere legends and myths. They are
> not predicated on the false conception that the Emperor is divine, and that
> the Japanese people are superior to other races and fated to rule the world.[35]

In other words, the fundamental character and uniqueness of the nation
remained, only the form of government would change. No longer sovereign, the emperor conceded popular sovereignty.

From the beginning of the Allied Occupation (September 2, 1945 to
April 28, 1952), dismantling State Shinto was a primary objective. A
complete separation of Shinto from the state was considered imperative.
Without fully understanding Shinto, the staff of the General Headquarters (GHQ) of the Supreme Commander for Allied Powers (SCAP), General Douglas MacArthur, was convinced that Shinto underlay Japanese
militarism. It was considered to be the main obstacle to establishing popular sovereignty, democracy, and religious freedom.[36] For this reason, the
GHQ created a Religions Division (later the Religions and Cultural
Resources Division) to oversee the disestablishment of State Shinto, along
with several other divisions that censored publications, movies, and other
means of mass communications, as well as waging a propaganda war of
their own.[37]

MacArthur and the GHQ were at the same time committed to using
Emperor Hirohoto to legitimate the postwar government. They were also
initially inclined to let the government take the lead in forging reforms.[38]
The latter assumption proved remarkably naive. The Cabinet and the Constitutional Problem Investigation Committee, chaired by Dr. Jōji Matsumoto, were more concerned with preserving the emperor's status under the
old constitution. And the people had no experience with religious freedom
or democracy.[39]

The emperor's role during the Occupation deserves some brief attention, both because Hirohito has been sharply criticized and wrongly portrayed as a tragic figure unable to control the military before the war,[40] and

because of the role he played after it. Few topics are as sensitive or subject to as much revisionism. Yet there is ample evidence that Hirohito was neither the sole instigator of the war nor always manipulated by his military advisors.[41] Like his grandfather Meiji, whom he greatly admired, he actively questioned his advisors and stayed thoroughly abreast of military strategy and maneuvers. Still, the tradition of supreme political authority without independent power was deeply rooted in the imperial institution and basically written into the Meiji Constitution. Under that constitution, as political scientist David Titus underscores, "the political centrality of the imperial institution was created *for,* not *by,* the emperor and imperial family, and the emperor's role from 1889 to 1947 was managed *for* him, not *by* him."[42]

Hirohito has been said to have been neither constitutionally nor politically positioned to override his military advisors or the Cabinet. But many survivors doubt that he was so personally or politically unsuited as to have been unable to intervene in the escalation of the conflict in the Pacific. In February 1945, Hirohito was advised to curtail the war effort but refused. He remained reluctant to come to the decision to end the fighting. As the war took increasingly grueling turns in the spring of 1945, top ministers remained split over whether or not to surrender. They were still divided when they met a few days after the bombing of Hiroshima.

Only after another meeting did Hirohito finally move to break the deadlock over Japan's surrender. Had Hirohito taken a different course in February, the ugly battle over Okinawa and the devastating bombings of Nagasaki and Hiroshima might have been avoided. Hundreds of thousands of lives might have been saved. Not until after the war did Hirohito appear to arise to the occasion. He then urged cooperation with the Occupation forces, eased the transition to a constitutional democracy, and encouraged the development of a postwar industrial economy.[43]

The GHQ's first step toward separating the state from Shinto was the issuance, on October 4, 1945, of a Civil Liberties Directive on the "Removal of Restrictions on Political, Civil, and Religious Liberties."[44] This ordered the government to suspend and abrogate "all provisions of all laws, decrees, orders, ordinances and regulations which establish or maintain restrictions on freedom . . . of religion . . . [or] operate unequally in favor of/or against any person by reasons of . . . creed." Accordingly, the Religious Organizations Law and the Peace Preservation Law were suspended, and those imprisoned for their religious beliefs were released.

The directive was followed, on December 15, 1945, by another, more sweeping one. The so-called Shinto Directive *(Shinto Shirei)* aimed at disestablishing State Shinto. Its objective and breadth were crystal clear:

The purpose of this directive is to separate religion from the state, to prevent misuse of religion for political ends, and to put all religions, faiths, and creeds upon exactly the same legal basis, entitled to precisely the same opportunities and protection. It forbids affiliation with the government and the propagation and dissemination of militaristic and ultra-nationalistic ideology not only to Shinto but to the followers of all religions, faiths, sects, creeds or philosophies.[45]

In four detailed pages, the directive proscribed all financial support for Shinto shrines from public funds. The Shrine Board was abolished, and public schools were barred from providing instruction on Shinto and sponsoring any Shinto rites or practices. *Kami*-shelves were removed from all public buildings, and all public officials were forbidden to visit any shrine in an official capacity or otherwise participate in Shinto rites, ceremonies, and practices.

Drafted by the SCAP's staff, the Shinto Directive was interpreted broadly to ban not only the government's funding and teaching of religion in the schools, but also traditional customs such as the participation of public officials in Shinto ceremonies, including state funerals and memorial services for the war dead. As such, the directive mandated a stricter and more extensive separation of the state from Shinto than that then (and now) required between church and state under the First Amendment to the U.S. Constitution.

With no real choice in the matter, the Japanese government, religious groups, and the public accepted the Shinto Directive with little resistance. Reactions were nonetheless mixed. For Christians and liberals, the directive was a welcome move in the direction of securing religious freedom. In contrast, Prime Minister Yoshida and State Shinto leaders resented it as a blow to "folk faith *(minzoku shinkō)*, the fountainhead of the spiritual strength of the Japanese."[46] At the same time, the directive was not as severe as Shinto leaders had feared. Yasukuni and the Grand Ise Shrine were left untouched. Yasukuni lost its status and its financial support as a special governmental shrine, but otherwise remained intact. And under the Shinto Directive and the 1951 Religious Corporation Law, Yasukuni and other religious organizations were permitted to register as private religious corporations. As a result, they gained tax-exempt status and protection from state interference.

The Shinto Directive, which expired with the signing of the 1952 Peace Treaty, remains a source of debate. That debate continues to carry over into rival interpretations of the provisions for religious freedom eventually incorporated into Japan's new constitution.[47] Moreover, the GHQ's own vacillations exacerbated confusion over the extent to which the Shinto Directive mandated separation of the state from religion. Policies were modified, even reversed, depending on circumstances and as the Occupation wound down. Initially, thousands of war memorials were destroyed, and early in 1946 the head of the GHQ's Religious Division, William Bunce, issued orders forbidding both the government and private groups from constructing monuments for war dead. But within weeks war memorials were allowed to stand "unless they carried ultra-nationalistic or militaristic sentiments."[48] As 1946 drew to a close, the policy changed to allow associations of war-bereaved families to erect new war memorials.

Despite the Shinto Directive, memorial rites for the war dead continued, often with public officials in attendance. Indeed, in November 1945, the GHQ gave approval for a massive joint enshrinement at Yasukuni of the souls of all who had died in the days before September 2, 1945. The GHQ did so with the understanding and agreement of Shinto priests that no more enshrinements would take place during the Occupation and that the emperor would no longer attend public ceremonies at Yasukuni. Still, on November 20, Emperor Hirohito and high-ranking Japanese and American officers, including some in military uniform, attended the enshrinement ceremony at Yasukuni.[49] Given that well-publicized event, it is not surprising that enshrinements and other ceremonies continued during the Occupation at regional shrines, frequently with the sponsorship or participation of local officals.

Amid the confusion, conflicting orders, and forces working at cross-purposes, General MacArthur tried to impress on Cabinet members the need for constitutional reform. The SCAP's initial policy was to have the government initiate necessary reforms, but the Cabinet and the Constitutional Problem Investigation Committee, chaired by Dr. Matsumoto, remained conservative in their approach to constitutional revision. At the same time, there were fears that the Far Eastern Commission (composed of representatives of the Allied nations) might press for even more radical changes than the GHQ. Specifically, the fear was that Hirohito might be put on trial for war crimes.[50]

After months of the GHQ's persistent but ineffective pressure on the Cabinet and committee, quite by chance, on February 1, 1946, the *Mainichi Shinbun* published what it (mistakenly) claimed was the final draft of constitutional revisions proposed by Matsumoto's committee. The draft proposed minimal revisions that in fact had been rejected in favor of an even more conservative version. Among the proposed provisions for the "Rights and Duties of Subjects" was a limited guarantee for religious freedom. Article 28 of the draft provided that "Every Japanese subject shall have freedom of religious belief and the restrictions necessary to maintain public peace shall be under the provision of the law. The special privileges that every shrine has ever had shall be abolished."[51]

The publication of the Matsumoto committee's draft persuaded MacArthur that the GHQ staff should press ahead with a new constitution. Three days after the *Mainichi Shinbun* article, a meeting of the government section of GHQ was called by Brigadier General Courtney Whitney for that purpose. Whitney laid out MacArthur's three "musts" for reform: (1) the emperor would remain head of the state, but "His duties and powers will be exercised in accordance with the Constitution and responsive to the basic will of the people"; (2) the Constitution would renounce Japan's "sovereign right" to engage in war; and (3) the feudal system would be abolished.[52] He also created a steering committee to oversee the work of several committees set up to draft particular provisions.

A Committee on Civil Rights was assigned to work on a guarantee for religious freedom and related provisions. It initially proposed the following:

> Freedom of religion is guaranteed to all. No religious organization shall receive privileges from the State, or its national or local authorities, nor may ecclesiastical functionaries abuse their spiritual authority for political purposes. No person shall be compelled or pressed to take part in any religious sects, celebrations, rites or practices. No religious body will be recognized as such if under the disguise of religion, it should stir up and practice antagonism to others or should weaken instead of strengthen public order and morality. The State and its organs shall refrain from religious education or any other religious activity.[53]

At a meeting of the steering committee on February 8, however, questions arose about the draft's practicality and whether its prohibition on ecclesiastical involvement in politics amounted to a denial of freedom of speech and the press as well.

Defenders of the draft insisted on making it clear that religious organizations were not to exercise any political authority. Alfred R. Hussey, an attorney on the steering committee, agreed that people might be persuaded to undertake political activities because of their religious beliefs, but pointed out that that was a matter of individual conscience unlikely to be prevented by any constitutional prohibition. Furthermore, the provision that "no religious body will be recognized as such if under the disguise of religion, it should stir up and practice antagonism to others or should weaken instead of strengthen public order and morality" appeared too broad. As under the Meiji Constitution, such a provision might be used to justify suppression of new religions that were viewed as disruptive. In short, the proposed draft appeared to forbid religious organizations from any involvement in politics, while leaving the government free to meddle with religion. As a result, the steering committee agreed to have the article redrafted.

The Committee on Civil Rights subsequently submitted the following, much shorter provision for religious freedom and the separation of religion from the state:

> Freedom of religion is guaranteed to all. No religious organization shall receive special privileges from the State, nor exercise political authority. No person shall be compelled to take part in any religious acts, celebrations, rites or practices. The State and its organs shall refrain from religious education or any other religious activity.[54]

And the Committee on Public Finance submitted another, specifically barring state financial support for religion:

> No public money or property shall be appropriated for use, benefit or support of any system of religion, or religious institution or association, or for any charitable, educational or benevolent purposes not under the control of the State.[55]

More concise and explicit than the initial draft, both these draft provisions were accepted by the steering committee. They are also virtually identical to those eventually incorporated as Articles 20 and 89 of Japan's Constitution. Their basic objective was clear. In the words of Frank Rizzo, one of the officers responsible for drafting the latter provision, "We simply wanted to separate religion from the state. That was all there was to it. We were not concerned about any theories regarding church-state relations."[56]

Within eight days of receiving the assignment, Whitney's steering committee submitted its draft to General MacArthur. At a pivotal meeting on February 13, Whitney presented the draft to Matsumoto, Foreign Minister Yoshida, and two others. They were stunned. Matsumoto later claimed they were coerced into accepting "MacArthur's Constitution."[57] They were understandably alarmed, both by some of the provisions and by Whitney's telling them that unless they accepted the draft "the person of the Emperor could not be guaranteed." "As you may or may not know," Whitney explained firmly,

The Supreme Commander has been unyielding in his defense of your Emperor against increasing pressure from the outside to render him subject to war criminal investigation. He has thus defended the Emperor because he considered that that was the cause of right and justice, and will continue along that course to the extent of his ability. But, gentlemen, the Supreme Commander is not omnipotent. He feels, however, that acceptance of the provisions of this new Constitution would render the Emperor practically unassailable.[58]

Whitney appeared to cross the line between forceful persuasion and coercion when, without authorization, he added that MacArthur was prepared "to leave the sponsorship of the document to your government with his firm approval, but failing in that, if necessary, he is prepared to lay it before the people himself."[59]

Matsumoto and others hoped to put off what they deemed far too radical revisions, but the GHQ quickly countered their diversions and demanded a response from the Cabinet by February 20 (later extended for two more days). On February 21, MacArthur personally pressed Prime Minister Shidehara to accept the draft, and the next day the Cabinet agreed to its "fundamental principles." In the meantime, Shidehara secured the approval of Hirohito. For three more weeks, GHQ staff and members of the Japanese government conferred on the language of the proposed constitution. They worked through a number of changes and adopted new amendments before publishing a final version on March 6. The Diet spent several more months debating further amendments. The Constitution was finally promulgated on November 3, 1946, going into effect on May 3, 1947.

Forged of compromise and still resented by conservatives as an imposition, the new constitution remains in many respects revolutionary.[60] Yet it also contains provisions conserving as much as possible of the Meiji Constitution. There is little doubt that the Occupation forces aimed to separate the state from Shinto, while the Japanese government sought to preserve the emperor's status and the fundamentals of the old order.

Disagreement immediately arose over, and continues to revolve around, whether the Constitution incorporates the far-reaching disestablishment principles of the Shinto Directive and whether the strict separation imposed by the Occupation should remain permanently in place. However, as William Woodard stresses, the Occupation's General Headquarters

did not think it should or could formulate a permanent policy for the Japanese people. . . . Throughout the Occupation, it was a fundamental assumption that ... it was the function of the Japanese people themselves ... to implement and interpret the basic principles of religious freedom and separation of "church" and state in a manner suitable to themselves alone.[61]

Almost as soon as the Occupation ended in 1952, controversy emerged over revising the Constitution, on which the conservative Liberal Democratic Party has, throughout the postwar period, tried to capitalize.[62] Conservative opposition to the 1947 Constitution and occasional calls for revision have focused on two fundamental matters: (1) formal reestablishment of the status accorded the emperor under the Meiji Constitution, or at least regaining recognition of the continuity in the emperor's status and "the national polity" under the Meiji and World War II constitutions,[63] and (2) revision of the controversial pacifist provision in Article 9, along with securing an expanded role for the Self Defense Forces. Article 9 declares in part that "the Japanese people forever renounce war as a sovereign right of the nation and the threat or use of force as a means of settling international disputes."[64]

A commission on constitutional revision studied the matter for six years in the late 1950s and early 1960s, only to issue a noncommittal report.[65] In the 1970s, the Liberal Democratic Party repeatedly, though unsuccessfully, sought passage of a bill to renew state control over Yasukuni.[66] State support for Yasukuni was subsequently addressed in a major and controversial report on government officials' worship at Yasukuni the mid-1980s.[67] Controversy again erupted with the enshrinement ceremonies held for Hirohito in 1989, and with the enthronement rituals for his successor, Akihito, in 1990.[68]

The postwar constitutional controversy over Shinto and the state stems in part from the very first article of the Constitution. While the preamble "proclaim[s] that sovereign power resides with the people," Article 1 retains a constitutional basis for the emperor system in declaring that "The Emperor shall be the symbol of the State and of the unity of the people, deriving his position from the will of the people with whom resides sovereign power." That provision, conservatives argue, reaffirms the tradition of the emperor system, as well as provides a basis for reviving state support for Yasukuni and Shinto ceremonies.[69]

Revisionism by postwar conservatives and ultranationalists is far from unprecedented. Actually, their arguments are in many ways little more than a replay of prior constitutional constructions. They further reflect how little weight law, even constitutional law, may carry in postwar Japan. For example, during World War II, on January 1, 1944, in *Direct Imperial Rule (Tennō Seiji),* a book published in English, French, German, and Japanese, a Waseda and Nippon University law professor, Shin'chi Fujii, defended the emperor system on ancient grounds both deeper than and superior to the provisions of the Meiji Constitution.

Recall that Article 1 of the Meiji Constitution stated that "The Empire of Japan shall be reigned over and governed by a line of Emperors unbroken for ages eternal." Professor Fujii nonetheless maintained that that constitutional provision was merely "a confirmation in writing of the historical fact" that the ancestral sun goddess had declared that "*Mizuho-no-Kuni* (The Country of Goodly Grain) with the promise of one thousand and five hundred mellow autumns to come is the land over which Our descendants shall become Sovereigns. . . . The prosperity of the Imperial Throne shall be coeval with heaven and earth." The divine proclamation, not Article 1 of the Meiji Constitution, insisted Fujii, established the emperor's sovereignty, "the essence of our national polity."[70]

Fujii had looked into the abyss of war and seen the future in the past, and continuity amid great change. After the war—and almost half a century after the enactment of Japan's 1947 Constitution—some conservatives advance virtually identical arguments about its Article 1. In their view, the Constitution remains, after all, an imposition. At the same time, the Constitution is only a parchment document, *tatemae* (a pretense, a facade), not the *honne* (the actuality or truth) of the matter. Japan's ultraconservatives still cling to the dream spun by Fujii and countless others before him.

Conservatives and ultranationalists are not the only ones to dismiss or explain away the constitutional change ostensibly forged by Japan's 1947 Constitution. The bestselling author and psychologist Takeo Doi, among others, argues that, in Article 1, "far from denying Japan's ancient traditions and institutions, this constitution actually upholds a position that respects them above all else—not only for Japan's own people but also for the rest of the world to see." "In short," concludes Doi, "this constitution adopted democracy as something that would reinforce Japan's most ancient tradition."[71]

Even some liberal professors concede that the theoretical change in the constitutional status of the emperor may not be widely understood or embraced. In the words of Nobuhiko Takizawa,

> It, however, is doubtful whether the basic change in the Emperor's position has changed [the] consciousness of the Japanese people from that of the subjects "reigned over and governed by" the Emperor, to that of the people "with whom resides sovereign power." . . . For, unfortunately, the Emperor as "the symbol of the State and of the unity of the people" under the New Constitution has been the same person who, as Manifest Deity, was under the Meiji Constitution, which called him "the head of the Empire, combining in Himself the rights of sovereignty."[72]

Conservative law professors and politicans also hasten to emphasize that the emperor's status was preserved in Article 7 of the 1947 Constitution. That article recognizes that the emperor shall perform ceremonial functions "on behalf of the people." In other words, Article 7 is an exception to the separation of the state from religion set forth in Articles 20 and 89. On that basis, Setsu Kobayashi, a Keiō University law-school professor and advisor to the LDP, argues that the government may finance and officials may attend ceremonies at Yasukuni.[73]

Admittedly, Article 20 is not entirely unambiguous. It combines a guarantee of religious freedom with the separation of the state from religion (*saisei bunri*). In three brief clauses, the article provides:[74]

Freedom of religion is guaranteed to all. No religious organization shall receive any privileges from the State nor exercise any political authority.

No person shall be compelled to take part in any religious acts, celebration, rite or practice.

The State and its organs shall refrain from religious education or any other religious activity.

The principle of separation, though, is reinforced by the stipulation in Article 89 that "No public money or other property shall be expended or appropriated for the use, benefit or maintenance of any religious institution or association, or for any charitable, educational or benevolent enterprises not under the control of public authority."

Although modeled after the guarantees in the First Amendment to the U.S. Constitution, the provisions for disestablishment in Japan's Constitution go far beyond the scope of the First Amendment's disestablishment clause. Indeed, the U.S. Supreme Court had infrequently enforced the First Amendment's guarantee before 1947. Not until its ruling in *Everson v. Board of Education of Ewing Township, New Jersey*,[75] which was handed down just three months before Japan's Constitution went into effect, did the U.S. Supreme Court enforce the First Amendment's disestablishment clause as a limitation on state and local governments, no less than the federal government.

Writing for a bare majority in *Everson*, Justice Hugo Black elevated into constitutional law the metaphor of a "high wall of separation" between religion and the state. But, notably, Justice Black backed away from strictly enforcing that principle in *Everson*. His opinion, joined by Chief Justice Fred Vinson and Justices William O. Douglas, Frank Murphy, and Stanley Reed, upheld the government's reimbursing parents for the cost of busing their children to private parochial schools as a "subsidy to parents, not churches." In their view, a strict separation need not preclude the state's "benevolent neutrality" toward religion. Dissenting Justices Felix Frankfurter, Harold Burton, Robert Jackson, and Wiley Rutledge thought otherwise. They argued that the principle of a "high wall of separation" requires "strict neutrality," an absolute separation. *Everson's* ruling proved highly controversial, and thereafter the Court became embroiled in a long-running controversy over defining the boundaries of disestablishment of religion and the state.[76]

A Basis for Dialogue amid Disagreement

Articles 20 and 89 of Japan's 1947 Constitution, like those of other written constitutions, are not self-interpreting. They invite rival constructions, particularly when superimposed on a country in which Shinto and the state, religion and politics, had been interwoven in the social fabric of life for centuries. Conservative politicans in the LDP, right-wing organizations, the SDF leadership, associations of war-bereaved families, and the Association of Shinto Shrines have persistently sought to reclaim the prewar symbolism of the emperor system, along with the glorification of those enshrined at Yasukuni, through state support for Yasukuni and official visits to its shrine.[77]

In addition, among the many "new religions" gaining popularity after the war, some preach the explicit fusion of politics and religion, such as the Sōka Gakkai and its political arm, the Kōmeitō (Clean Government Party).[78] By contrast, Christians, communists, socialists, and liberal law professors maintain that Articles 20 and 89 mandate a strict separation of the state from religion, and that this remains a crucial barrier against the revival of militarism.[79]

Moreover, even liberals differ on the scope of Articles 20 and 89, just as the disestablishment clause of the First Amendment to the U.S. Constitution has been subject to competing interpretations.[80] How strict a separation of the state from religion is required? As in the United States, there are those who press for a "high wall of separation," whereas others complain that Article 20 should not be construed so rigorously as to result in state hostility toward religion, especially in Japan, where Shinto remains undeniably pervasive. Peter Herzog, an author and former Jesuit from Germany who for over fifty years has lived in Japan, takes the latter view. "The intent of Article 20 of the constitution is often summarised by the expression 'separation of state and religion' *(saisei bunri).* This is a tendentious and biased interpretation," in Hertzog's view. "The state (and its organs) must be neutral in the sense that it cannot perform religious activities, order or direct religious actions, but it does not say that the state must be irreligious."[81]

The continuing constitutional controversy over Shinto and the state is further clouded by the old debate over whether Shinto is a religion, a non-religious folkway, or a traditional civil religion.[82] The idea of Shinto as a civil religion has had considerable attraction in postwar Japan for some conservatives. This is in part due to the concept's potential utility in their efforts to find ways around constitutional restrictions on state support for religion. In this regard, the writings of American sociologist Robert Bellah have been highly influential. Bellah, who in the 1950s wrote a dissertation and later a book entitled *Tokugawa Religion,*[83] championed the idea of civil religion with respect to both Japan and the United States.[84]

The concept of civil religion, however, remains controversial and, in some ways, less than helpful. It is neither unambiguous about whether "civil religion" refers to a folk religion, religious patriotism, democratic faith, civil piety, or socio-religious solidarity,[85] nor is it unproblematic in describing the constitutional culture of either country.[86] Bellah and his followers nevertheless argue, for instance, that U.S. presidents have, in speeches, appealed to God, and that the U.S. Congress opens its sessions with a prayer, as does the U.S. Supreme Court, with its clerk crying "God save this honorable Court." The Pledge of Allegiance refers to "one nation, under God," and coins and currency bear the national motto, "In God We Trust."[87]

Still, critics counter that the increasing religious diversity, ethnic pluralism, and secularism of the United States render the concept of civil religion misleading and, at best, obsolete.[88] Other critics charge that appeals to an American civil religion are dangerous. Such appeals have historically been made at times of war and within a militaristic context.[89] Moreover, even some Shinto scholars, like Yoshiya Abe, stress that "the concept of civil religion does not fit well with the animistic ways of Shinto."[90] In Japan, appeals to civil religion invite potentially dangerous confusion as well, because the concept of civil religion blurs the institutionalization of State Shinto and militarism of the emperor system before and during World War II with the rich history of centuries-old indigenous Shinto cults and customs.

In sum, Japan's 1947 Constitution did not lay to rest the controversy over Shinto and the state. Instead, the basis was laid for legal battles and ongoing political struggles between defenders of the Constitution's disestablishment of religion and those who would reinvigorate government support for Shinto and Yasukuni's cult of war dead.

CHAPTER 3

Manipulating Law's Social Reality

THE KAMISAKAS SUED Minoo city officials in 1976, amid resurging nationalism and a movement to revive state support for Yasukuni and the symbolism of the emperor system. Led by conservative politicans in the Liberal Democractic Party (LDP), the Japan Association of War Bereaved Families (JAWBF), and other veterans' groups, the movement for greater accommodation of Shinto by the state had built up gradually over the course of two decades. In the 1950s, Shinto leaders and conservative politicians looked for a Shinto revival, but economic recovery took priority. There were a few signs of continuity amid great change, such as Crown Prince Akihito's installation according to Shinto rites and the rebuilding of the Grand Ise Shrine in 1952. In 1959, the government treated as a state affair the crown prince's wedding, at which the traditional Shinto rites were performed. By the 1960s, economic expansion was in full swing. Japan's gross national product (GNP) was growing faster than that of any other country.[1] Except for a downturn in the early 1970s, this economic prosperity continued throughout most of the 1980s.[2]

For thirty-eight years, until the 1993 elections, the LDP remained in power. During this period, the far right wing of the LDP incrementally pushed for renewed state support for Shinto. In 1963, the government sponsored memorial rites for war dead on August 15, the anniversary of Japan's surrender in World War II. In 1967, the prewar Empire Day *(Kigensetsu),* celebrated on February 11, was restored as National Foundation Day *(Kenkoku Kinenbi).* The mythical legends of Japan's uniqueness were thereby reintroduced into popular culture. A year later, the government sponsored the Meiji centennial celebration. That celebration symbolically restored the linkages between the Constitution's proclamation of popular sovereignty and the age-old tradition of imperial sovereignty.

In symbolic yet important ways, the lines between Shinto and the

From right: Satoshi and Reiko Kamisaka, their children, and Mrs. Kamisaka's father in 1976. (Courtesy of Mrs. Reiko Kamisaka)

state continued to be blurred. After the rebuilding of the Grand Ise Shrine in 1973, for example, Hirohito's third daughter served briefly as the chief priestess there. The following year, Hirohito made a pilgrimage to Ise and revived a ritual *(kenji doza),* abolished after the war, in which two of the three sacred regalia (the sword and jewel) were taken to Ise. But in addition to such symbolic reassertions of Shinto traditions, conservative LDP leaders and right-wing groups pressed for more in their assault on the Constitution's separation of religion and the state. In 1969, and several times thereafter (as discussed in Chapter 5), the LDP presented to the Diet a bill to reestablish Yasukuni Shrine as a nonreligious foundation under the government's control, thereby directly challenging the disestablishment of religion.

The Liberal Democratic Party was not alone in turning somersaults with history. In November 1976, on the fiftieth anniversary of Hirohito's rule, ceremonies were staged on a grander scale than for the 1968 centennial of the Meiji Restoration. Incredibly, the next year Hirohito publicly denied that on January 1, 1946 he had renounced being a manifest *kami* and had proclaimed his human character.[3] Also in 1977, over protests from a number of citizen groups, the Ministry of Education reestablished the *Kimigayo,* which contains verses praising the emperor, as the national anthem. And two years after that, the Diet enacted a law reinstituting the practice of counting years from the first year of the reign of each emperor.[4] In short, in small but calculated ways, the postwar LDP government sought to revive, step by step, the prewar symbolism of State Shinto.

By the time the Kamisakas filed their lawsuits, a major political and constitutional controversy was brewing. That controversy (discussed further in Chapter 5) intensified when the LDP unveiled its Memorial Respect Proposal, offering rationalizations for its earlier proposals that government officials be allowed to worship at Yasukuni. The LDP attempted to justify officials' visits to Yasukuni on the ground that they were not religious per se. Rather, public officials' visits to Yasukuni would simply pay respect to those who had died for Japan and thereby laid the foundation for its current prosperity. The logic of the LDP was little more than a return to the prewar rationalization that observance of State Shinto was a nonreligious patriotic duty. Despite strong opposition from liberals, Christians, Buddhists, and some others, on August 15, 1985, for the first time since the war, a prime minister paid an "official" visit to Yasukuni Shrine.

The Kamisakas' challenge to Minoo city officials played into the larger political controversy over the LDP's push for both explicit governmental support for Yasukuni and greater accommodation of the prewar institutions of State Shinto. Their constitutional claims also remained novel and untested in the highest court in the land. Remarkably, in light of the growing national controversy and a few other suits against local officials' sponsorship of Shinto ceremonies, the Supreme Court had yet to rule on the separation of religion from the state.

In 1977, a year after the Kamisakas had filed their first suit—and thirty years after the Constitution had taken effect—the Supreme Court finally handed down its first major ruling on the separation of the government from religion in the *Tsu City Ground-Purification Ceremony* case.[5]

Stifling Judicial Independence

The wheels of justice grind slowly in Japanese courts, in part because, following the civil law tradition, trials are scheduled one day at a time at monthly intervals. Hence a case heard on October 1 is not heard again until November 1. As a result, the average trial takes two or more years to complete.[6] Still, there is much more to lengthy court proceedings than that. The lower courts are understaffed by judges who are closely monitored and whose careers are carefully manipulated. The Supreme Court and the judiciary as a whole are bureaucratically driven. There are hierarchies within hierarchies in the judiciary. Judicial independence on the bench is touted, but falls far short of that enjoyed by federal judges in the United States.

The Japanese judicial system is unitary, unlike the system of judicial federalism in the United States, which has both a national judicial system and separate judiciaries in each of the fifty states.[7] At its apex is the Supreme Court of Japan, which is composed of fifteen justices who generally sit and decide cases as petty benches composed of five justices each. Each of the three petty benches has its own courtroom and sits twice a week. The First Petty Bench sits on Mondays and Thursdays, the Second on Mondays and Fridays, and the Third on Tuesdays and Fridays. Major cases and administrative matters are referred for decision to the entire Court, which sits *en banc* as the Grand Bench to hear cases, and as the Judicial Conference to dispose of administrative matters. These meetings of the entire Court are held on Wednesdays throughout the year, except during holidays and vacation time in August.

The Supreme Court's docket of cases is unbelievably crowded, as are those of the lower courts. The size of the docket runs contrary to the self-perpetuated myth of harmony in a country of "reluctant litigants." More than seven thousand cases have been filed or pending annually in the 1990s, with the Court disposing of approximately five thousand each year. This docket is as large as that of the U.S. Supreme Court, but in a country with less than half the population of the United States.[8]

Unlike the U.S. Supreme Court, the Japanese Supreme Court has no discretionary jurisdiction. Technically, it must decide all appeals. Appeals are basically of two sorts. The first are *kōso* appeals to high courts and *jōkoku* appeals to the Supreme Court, which are limited to review for errors in legal interpretation, alleged conflicts with precedents, and misapplications of the Code of Criminal Procedure, although they also allow for *de novo* review and a determination of whether there are other grounds for appeal. Second are *kōkoku* appeals, which must raise an alleged constitutional violation or conflict with precedent.[9] In practice, both kinds of appeals are treated basically alike. Well over 95 percent are summarily dismissed, leaving the lower court rulings intact.

Of the 5,000-odd cases disposed of each year, only about a hundred are granted oral arguments and decided by full written opinion. Each justice ostensibly reads all filings, but they are first screened by the Court's law clerks or research officials *(chōsakan)* and then divided among the justices on the three petty benches. Unlike law clerks at the U.S. Supreme Court, who are recent law school graduates, serve only a year, and work for a single justice,[10] the law clerks in Japan are experienced judges assigned to the Court for three to five years. Notably, they work for the Court as a whole, not individual justices. They screen and research cases, as well as draft most of the opinions of the petty and grand benches.[11] There are currently 29 law clerks. Among them, a chief supervises the work of 17 who are assigned to a division handling civil and administrative cases, while the remaining 11 are assigned to the criminal law division.

On the three petty benches, each case is in turn assigned to an individual justice, who further studies it and recommends whether it should be granted at the twice-weekly conference of each petty bench. Each justice reports on about 100 to 150 cases a month, for about 800 cases per petty bench each month. Yet, according to Justice Sonobe, only a dozen or so of these "are seriously deliberated."

The most important cases—those that raise unresolved constitutional issues, or in which precedents will be established or changed—are transferred to the Grand Bench. These select few are further researched by the law clerks, and some are eventually granted oral arguments. Oral argumentation carries little weight, however. As Justice Itsuo Sonobe candidly concedes, "Oral argument is admitted in cases in which the lower court decision is [to be] reversed, and such oral argument is pretty formal and not substantial."[12] Justices rarely ask questions from the bench. In the words of one Tokyo University law professor, they "sit like Buddha until the lawyer finishes."[13]

In addition—and again unlike the U.S. Supreme Court, which publishes all its opinions and decisions—the Japanese Supreme Court publishes only a few of its most important rulings each year. Two justices from each of the petty benches, along with two law clerks, form a publication committee that decides which ones should appear in the reporter of abridged Supreme Court decisions, the *Saikō Saibansho Hanreishū*. The cases and opinions in that reporter are thus deemed important enough to have precedential value and to prove useful for practitioners. A more complete collection, containing many more but not all opinions, is available in a so-called unabridged reporter, the *Saikō Saibansho Saibanshū*, for criminal (*keiji*) and civil (*minji*) cases. This reporter of decisions neither includes all opinions nor is it widely available, even in libraries.

In short, the decisionmaking process and operation of the Supreme Court, which is basically mirrored in the lower courts, push away from individualism and reinforce collective judgments. In the words of political scientist Hiroshi Itoh,

> The stress for harmony has led to groupism in which collective interests supersede individual interests. Decisions are always group products, and a [formal] vote is seldom taken either in the cabinet or in the Supreme Court.

The Supreme Court is the only tribunal in which dissents are published, but only the majority is made [generally] known in lower courts.[14]

Below the Supreme Court are eight high courts, located in the major cities of Tokyo, Osaka, Nagoya, Hiroshima, Fukuoka, Sendai, Sapporo, and Takamatsu, as well as six branches in other cities (see Map). These courts have territorial jurisdiction over their designated regions. They also have both appellate and original jurisdiction over civil and criminal cases. Each is supervised by a chief judge (or president) and typically functions in three-judge panels, with a senior judge presiding, although cases involving insurrection are heard by five-judge courts. There are approximately 285 high court judges. Appointed by the Cabinet on the recommendation of the Supreme Court, they remain subject to periodic reappointment and to mandatory retirement at age 65.

The number of judges sitting on a high court depends on its caseload and regional population. Assignments are made basically on the basis of seniority, along with the ranking of individual judges and courts. In 1991, there were 30,690 appeals filed and another 15,824 cases pending, for a total of 46,514 cases. Of these, decisions were rendered in 30,706 cases. Notably, there were roughly the same number of cases (a total of 44,465) in U.S. federal appellate courts.[15]

Appeals to high courts come from district courts and family courts, along with some cases directly from summary courts. District courts are the principal trial courts of the system. There are 50 of them, located in all major cities, and another 201 branches in other towns. District courts generally function as single-judge courts without juries. Three-judge district courts, however, decide appeals from summary courts and cases deemed especially important because of the constitutional issues raised. There are 910 district court judges and 460 assistant judges. They face heavy caseloads as well. In 1991, for instance, the district courts had 822,590 filings, another 405,458 cases pending, and reached decisions in 813,634 cases. By contrast, U.S. district courts in 1991 faced filings of only 217,656 civil cases and 45,215 criminal cases, though state courts confronted far larger numbers.

The 50 family courts and their 201 branches are located alongside the district courts. Unlike district courts, they have specialized jurisdiction over family affairs and domestic matters, such as divorce and estates, as well as juvenile delinquency. These courts utilize conciliation procedures to discourage adjudication of disputes. They are staffed by approximately 200 judges and 150 assistant judges, along with 1,500 probation officers. Below the district and family courts are 452 summary courts with about

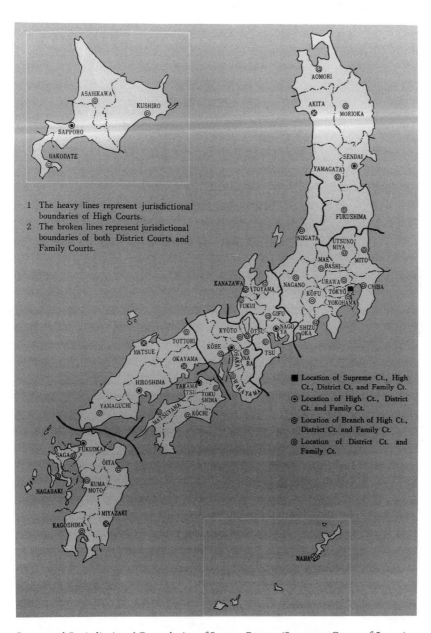

Japan and Jurisdictional Boundaries of Lower Courts (Supreme Court of Japan)

810 judges. These single-judge courts have original jurisdiction over civil cases involving claims of less than 900,000 yen ($9,000) and minor criminal cases for which fines may not exceed 200,000 yen ($2,000).[16] The filings and pending cases in 1991 totaled 2,741,230, with decisions handed down in 2,637,938 cases.

The creation of Japan's postwar judicial system aimed to forge revolutionary change in the role of courts. Under the prewar Meiji Constitution, the courts and the Diet exercised their powers in the name of the emperor. That constitution specifically stipulated that the "Judicature shall be exercised by the Courts of Law according to Law, in the name of the Emperor." Although judicial independence was proclaimed and judges had lifetime appointments, subject to good behavior and disciplinary action, they functioned like bureaucrats under the supervision of the Ministry of Justice. Courts had no power of judicial review over either legislation or administrative actions. They could not even adjudicate disputes between citizens and the government; disputes with the government were handled by separate administrative courts.[17]

Against this background of the prewar judiciary, the reorganization of the courts in 1947 was revolutionary, or potentially revolutionary, in three respects. First, the 1947 Constitution established a parliamentary system but, unlike the system of parliamentary sovereignty in Great Britain, it also separated the courts from the rest of the government for the first time in Japan's long history. Second, American-style judicial review was provided for, and courts were given the power to strike down laws that violate the Constitution. Third, the basis for judicial independence was laid, at least on paper.

In practice, the reorganization of the judicial system resulted in far less revolutionary change. Article 76 vests the "whole judicial power" in the courts, and Article 77 shifts responsibility for judicial administration from the prewar Ministry of Justice to the Supreme Court. The latter acquired extensive rule-making powers and authority over the training, nomination, assignment, and oversight of lower court judges and other judicial personnel. The courts were also empowered for the first time to exercise judicial review over legislation and administrative actions. Yet despite these parchment guarantees, courts infrequently assert their power or challenge the government.[18] This is due in large measure to the fact that judicial independence has failed to develop within the ranks of the postwar judiciary. Institutional independence and autonomy were secured but have, ironically, worked to thwart the assertion of judicial independence on the bench, at least along the lines of the tradition of judicial independence found in U.S. federal courts.[19]

Judicial independence was ostensibly guaranteed by the reorganization of the postwar judiciary and by provisions providing for the removal of judges from the bench primarily through impeachment proceedings.[20] Yet it has amounted to little more than the institutional separation of the courts from the rest of the government. There are a number of reasons for the failure of judicial independence to take root, as it has in some other countries. The legacies of the prewar judicial tradition, the infrastructure, and legal culture all boded ill for judges' assertion of independence. In addition, although the forces of the Occupation "purged" many high government officials, prewar judges were not among them,[21] being deemed not important enough to purge. Prewar judges thus continued to exercise influence, and arguably wielded greater power due to the reorganization of the courts.[22] They were positioned to conserve as much as possible of the past and to rebuff efforts to enforce new constitutional guarantees for civil rights and liberties.

Moreover, after 1947–1948, the conservative Liberal Democratic Party remained in power for almost four decades, and therefore retained control over judicial appointments. No less importantly, the Supreme Court—and, in particular, the chief justice and General Secretariat—oversee the training, nomination, reappointment, assignments, and salaries of lower court judges. The General Secretariat, it bears emphasizing, consists of one secretary general, seven bureau chiefs, and about eight hundred judges and other officials. As a result, Japanese judges and courts are tightly controlled, in contrast to the decentralized, relatively nonbureaucratic,[23] and far more independent federal courts in the United States.

The configuration of judicial politics changed in the postwar era, but in ways that perpetuated bureaucratic methods for punishing assertions of judicial independence. No longer part of the prewar Ministry of Justice, the judiciary became a large bureaucracy in its own right. The judicial system now employs more than twenty-one thousand judges, clerks, secretaries, marshals, and other personnel.[24] There are bureaus for civil, criminal, administrative, personnel, and financial affairs. The Legal Training and Research Institute turns out virtually all the country's attorneys, prosecutors, and judges. There is also a research and training institute for court clerks, and another for probation officers. The entire system is supervised by the Supreme Court, with the primary responsibility under the direction of the chief justice and the General Secretariat.

Central to the operation of contemporary Japanese courts is their system of producing and promoting an elite cadre of professional judges. With the exception of Supreme Court justices,[25] the lower courts are staffed by career judges who must survive a series of professional and personal hurdles, beginning with their admission to a university. Unlike legal education in the United States, but like that in Great Britain, Germany, and France, students study law as undergraduates. After graduation, most students now take bar-exam cram courses in preparation for the National Law Examination. The test, which may be taken numerous times, is rigorous. Out of the more than twenty thousand students a year who take the test, only about seven hundred pass. (Prior to 1993, when the government increased the number, only about five hundred a year were successful.) Graduates of the leading law schools at the universities of Tokyo, Waseda, Chūō, Kyoto, and Keiō tend to be favored.

Only after passing the examination, submitting a thesis, and passing an interview is a student admitted to the Legal Training and Research Institute. There, at government expense, he or she pursues a two-year course of study. During their time at the institute, students have four four-month internships—in an attorney's office, a prosecutor's office, a criminal court, and a civil court. After graduating they may apply to become assistant judges, although there are only as many positions as there are vacancies, which amount to about a hundred per year. Some students are thus discouraged by faculty at the institute from applying for judgeships. Still others may be deemed unsuited for judicial service and denied an appointment.[26]

Judicial careers begin with a ten-year appointment as an assistant judge, an apprenticeship. In actuality, assistant judges function like full judges after five years. They may become associate judges on a three-judge court or preside over a single-judge court. After a decade, they become full judges, subject to reappointment every ten years. During the course of their careers, they are reassigned many times and to several courts, or to other positions within the judiciary.

A judge may move from a district court to being an acting high court judge, sitting as a so-called left-hand associate. After five more years, the judge may then become a regular high court judge, sitting on the right side of a more senior presiding judge. Eventually, a judge may be elevated to the position of presiding judge on a three-judge court. A very few are then given an opportunity to become chief judges (presidents) on the country's most prestigious high courts, those located in Tokyo, Osaka, and Nagoya. Later, from that select group, a few who have reached their midsixties will be rewarded with an appointment to the Supreme Court, or to the most coveted position of chief justice. The chief justice ranks in status with the prime minister, the only other government official ceremoniously appointed by the emperor. The chief justice recommends to the Judicial Conference and to the Cabinet all lower court appointees and reassignments, consults on appointments to the Supreme Court, and otherwise oversees the operation of the judiciary.[27]

Already selective, the judicial system becomes increasingly competitive the higher up a judge moves within the hierarchy of courts. Over the years and along the way, many are encouraged to abandon their judicial careers and go into private legal practice. Reassignment to less desirable courts, salary rankings, and the remote but real possibility of being denied reappointment are powerful incentives for achieving conformity. In addition, some judges are put on fast tracks, while many others reach dead-ends sooner or later. Those serving on the Tokyo District and High Courts fall into the former category. Within legal circles, the elite among the judicial elite are referred to as "triple crown winners." They have worked on the staff of the General Secretariat, served as law clerks at the Supreme Court, and later become teachers at the Legal Training and Research Institute. In contrast, those known as "triple handicaps" are kept in the lowest (fourth) pay grade, assigned to local branch courts, and never become presiding judges.[28]

The career of Supreme Court Justice Itsuo Sonobe, appointed to the Court in 1989 at age sixty, illustrates the fast track of a select few. After teaching administrative law for more than a decade at Kyoto University, he began a fifteen-year judicial career destined to culminate in a Supreme Court appointment. After two years as a district court judge, he moved to a high court for three years, and then became a chief judge on a district court for three years. Afterward, he served for five years as the head law clerk in charge of civil and administrative cases at the Supreme Court, followed by two more years as the chief judge of the Tokyo District Court. Sonobe then returned to academia, teaching in Tokyo for two years at Tsukuba University and another two at Seikei University, whereupon he was appointed to the Court as a professor despite his extensive experience within the judiciary.[29] His career was distinguished and exceptional. Rarely are legal scholars elevated to the highest bench. "In Japan," as Justice Sonobe explains, "the academic world is completely separated from the practicing world. Scholars are like an octopus (tako) living in a small trap (tsubo). They don't know the outside world. So the academic world is called tako-tsubo (octopus-trap) society."[30]

The experience of the majority of career judges is vastly different, and the pressures for conformity enormous. As further discussed in subsequent chapters, some lower court judges have asserted their independence and ruled liberally on claims to civil rights and liberties. Their rulings tend to be reversed on appeal by higher courts.[31] Moreover, a range of personal and professional sanctions may be brought to bear on them. Even former Chief

Justice Takaaki Hattori acknowledged that "There is a potential conflict here between the judges' independence to decide cases and the Supreme Court's power of administrative supervision" over lower court judges.[32] Many lawyers and former judges contend that the conflict is blatant, with assignments and salary adjustments manipulated so as to reprimand certain judges.[33]

Judges who are too independent or too liberal may be offered reassignment to less prestigious courts or to courts in less desirable locations, necessitating their moving their families. In this way they are encouraged to leave the judiciary instead. That is what happened to the young assistant judge who participated in the Osaka District Court's ruling in favor of the Kamisakas on the first of the Minoo city war-memorial cases. When former judge Shigeyuki Uehara's time for reassignment came up, he was offered a position that required moving his family away from Osaka. For Judge Uehara that was personally unacceptable, and he resigned.[34] Judge Uehara was far from alone in being encouraged by superiors to leave the bench.[35]

Other former judges and lawyers report that the General Secretariat regularly discriminates in salary rankings against those who, after ten or twenty years, have proven to be too independent or less than absolutely loyal.[36] After twenty years, career judges who are favored are promoted to the third grade of the salary scale, receiving 18.4 million yen (about $184,000). If they serve on a prestigious court in a major city like Tokyo or Osaka, they receive an additional 2.2 million yen ($22,000), for a total of 20.60 million yen ($206,000).

By contrast, some of their peers, those who began their careers at the same time but who have fallen out of favor, remain stuck in the fourth salary grade. Because these judges are typically assigned to branch courts located in small towns, they receive no salary supplement and earn 15.42 million yen ($154,200). The prospect is not bright for these judges. The favored judges will continue to be promoted, while they will be kept in the lowest salary grade.

The disparity in salaries continues to grow throughout their careers. Favored judges will reach the first grade, earning 24.81 million yen ($248,100) a year, while the disfavored who remain on the bench earn 9.39 million yen ($93,900) less. The burden on these judges grows greater as their children reach college age and they face the expenses of sending them to live in Tokyo, Kyoto, or Osaka, where the major universities are located. Yet such discrimination is defended as necessary to maintaining a judicial meritocracy, promoting the best and the brightest.

More direct assaults have been made on judicial independence in the lower courts. On occasion, a senior judge or the chief justice has tried to influence lower courts' rulings on sensitive issues. One well-known instance occurred when the *Naganuma* case[37] was pending before the Sapporo District Court. That case, which is further discussed in Chapter 5,[38] involved a major controversy over the construction of a missile base. The plaintiffs also challenged the constitutionality of the Self Defense Forces under Article 9's stipulation that "land, sea, and air forces, as well as other war potential, will never be maintained" in postwar Japan. Chief Judge Kenta Hiraga sent to two of the three judges deciding the case a letter that became known as the "Hiraga Memorandum." In the letter, he offered Presiding Judge Shigeo Fukushima and Assistant Judge Hiroshi Hirata some "friendly advice from a senior colleague."[39] And he proceeded to counsel them to be circumspect in their ruling.

After handing down the court's decision, Judge Fukushima brought Hiraga's letter to the attention of the Sapporo District Court's judicial conference, which leaked the matter to the press. Chief Judge Hiraga defended his action on the ground that Judge Fukushima was a member of the Young Jurists Association, a group of lawyers, judges, and professors founded in 1954 to counter the influence and fierce anti-communist stance of Chief Justice Kōtarō Tanaka, who headed the judiciary from 1950 to 1960. Amid protests on all sides, Chief Judge Hiraga was subsequently "reprimanded" by being transferred to the more prestigious Tokyo High Court! The Supreme Court also admonished Judge Fukushima that "judges should not fall into the error of self-importance but should always be humble enough to try to build up character and competence by exchanging experience and knowledge among themselves."[40]

Judges belonging to the Young Jurists Association were specifically singled out for recrimination. The association was far too liberal in the view of the Supreme Court and the General Secretariat. Attorneys in the association were in the vanguard of defending victims of environmental pollution, and some of the judges ruling in their favor and against the government were also members.[41] As a result, they faced retaliation from the Supreme Court under both Chief Justice Tanaka and his successors in the 1970s. In particular, ultraconservative Chief Justice Kazuto Ishida (1963–1973) sought to purge the bench of members of the association. (Chief Justice Ishida later helped found the Association for Honoring the Glorious War Dead, which has campaigned for renewed governmental support for Yasukuni and is further discussed in Chapter 5.)

In addition, the National Conference of High, District, and Family

Courts passed a resolution calling for judges to resign from the Young Jurists Association. A number of lawyers in the General Secretariat resigned. Others belonging to the association were denied assistant judgeships. And some of the association's judges were given undesirable transfer assignments.[42] In these ways, judicial independence in the lower courts was directly assaulted and undermined.

Unlike lower court judges, not all members of the Supreme Court are career judges. Still, judicial independence is discouraged in a variety of ways, ranging from the selection process to the operation of the Court itself. The appointment process and tenure are different for Supreme Court justices than for lower court judges.[43] The drafters of the Constitution and the hastily written Court Organization Law of 1947 modeled the appointment process for justices along the lines of the so-called Missouri Plan.[44] The Missouri Plan was first adopted by that state in 1940; subsequently, almost half the other states enacted some version of it.[45] The plan embodies a merit selection system that the American Bar Association and the American Judicature Society championed as an alternative to partisan judicial elections, and also as a means to improve the quality of judges sitting on state benches in the United States. The basic elements of the plan are as follows: (1) a nonpartisan commission nominates three candidates for every vacancy, (2) from those three, the governor appoints one, and (3) the judge must then be approved by the voters at the next general election; if approved, he or she receives a twelve-year appointment.

Although modeled after the Missouri Plan, the constitutional and statutory provisions for the selection, appointment, and tenure of Japanese Supreme Court justices have been modified or circumvented in practice. The use of a nominating commission was short-lived, for instance. In April 1947, an eleven-member Advisory Committee for Appointing Justices was appointed, and it nominated thirty candidates for justiceships and three for the chief justiceship. Later that year, however, the Japan Socialist Party (JSP) won the general election and temporarily controlled the government for one year.

Again, the selection process changed. A new fifteen-member nominating committee was created. This committee recommended thirty candidates, from which the Cabinet named the first fifteen justices to the postwar Supreme Court. A year later, in 1948, the JSP was driven from office. Nominating committees for selecting justices were never used again. Instead, when a vacancy occurs, Cabinet officials consult with the chief justice and the General Secretariat, who exercise extraordinary influence over the appointments, especially if a career judge is elevated.

As with the selection and promotion of lower court judges, the chief justice largely determines the appointment of members of the Supreme Court, including his own successor. Appointments are made by the prime minister and the Cabinet, but only on the recommendation of the chief justice. There is no "advice and consent" process, as with the U.S. Senate's confirmation of the president's judicial nominees. As a result, little media attention is paid to judicial appointments, and the appointment of Supreme Court justices frequently becomes known only after the fact. Moreover, during the 1980s and 1990s, all chief justices—specifically, Chief Justices Jirō Terada (1980–1985), Kōichi Yaguchi (1985–1990), and Ryōhachi Kusaba (1991–)—have risen through the ranks of the General Secretariat. Each had served previously as a chief of one or more of its bureaus before their elevation to the Court.

The selection of justices is also conditioned by stipulations in Article 31(1) of the Court Organization Law that they "shall be among persons of broad vision and extensive knowledge of law, who are not less than 40 years of age." That article further specifies that

> At least 10 of them shall be persons who have held one of the positions mentioned in item (1) or (2) for not less than 10 years, or one or more of the positions mentioned in the following items for the total period of 20 years or more: (1) President of the High Court; (2) Judges; (3) Judges of the Summary Court; (4) Public Prosecutors; (5) Lawyers; (6) Professors or assistant professors in legal science in universities which shall be determined elsewhere by law.

In practice, only those who have reached the pinnacles of their careers are considered. And an appointment to the Court is considered the crowning glory for those favored few.

A convention was established, in the words of former Chief Justice Takaaki Hattori, that "Supreme Court justices are appointed in roughly equal numbers from among three broad groups: (1) inferior court judges; (2) practicing lawyers; and (3) public prosecutors, law professors, or other persons of broad knowledge and experience."[46] However, that ratio in representation has changed over the years. The rule instead has become six career judges, four lawyers, two former bureaucrats, two prosecutors, and one law professor. The prior positions of the 116 justices who have served on the Court between 1947 and 1994 are shown in Table 2.

Notably, as the ratio of career judges, lawyers, bureaucrats, and law professors changed, the balance tipped farther toward reinforcing the influence of the chief justice and the General Secretariat over the composition and, arguably, the direction of the Court. With one exception, all

Table 2   Prior Positions of Japanese Supreme Court Justices,
           1947–1994

IMMEDIATE PRIOR POSITION	NUMBER	PERCENT
Judge	44	37.9
Attorney	38	32.7
Prosecutor	12	10.4
Professor	10	8.6
Administrator	7	6.0
Diplomat	5	4.3
Total	116	99.9%

appointees have been male. In 1994, Prime Minister Morihiro Hosokawa named the first female, a 66-year-old former conservative Labor Ministry official, Hisako Takahashi.[47]

Somewhat like the Missouri Plan, the Constitution of Japan provides for a system of popular review. After their appointment, according to Article 79(2), justices "shall be reviewed by the people at the first general election of the members of the House of Representatives following their appointment." Thereafter, justices face election after each ten years of service. This provision is ostensibly a reflection of the postwar Constitution's rejection of the emperor's sovereignty and recognition of popular sovereignty. Under the system, voters place an "X" in a box next to the name of a justice they think should be dismissed. Otherwise, their ballot is counted as a vote for retaining the justice.

Popular review nevertheless has been rendered virtually meaningless. Criticism has been leveled on several scores: Voters are more concerned with the election of representatives and pay little attention to justices on the ballot. They generally know little about the justices' qualifications or voting records. And the ten-year interval is too long.[48] In addition, Justice Sonobe points out, the "mass media doesn't take it seriously." Votes are cast "against some of the justices half in fun," because they were once bureaucrats. Votes for dismissal usually amount to only "10 percent or 15 percent at most." Justice Sonobe, among others, thus doubts whether "this system is effective and that the cost of carrying it out in every election of the House of Representatives has enough benefit."[49]

Whatever the merits of popular review, an end-run around the system has been made by the practice of appointing older and older justices. Justices are simply not on the bench long enough to stand for election after ten years. Article 50 of the Court Organization Law mandates retirement at age 70, and because justices are appointed in their sixties, few face elections. Furthermore, the average age of appointees has incrementally inched up. In the 1950s, the average age of justices at the time of their appointments was 61.2 years. In the 1960s, the average rose to 62.9 years, then reached 63.7 years in the 1970s, and 64 years for appointees in the 1980s. The average age of the 11 justices appointed between 1990 and 1993 was 65. As indicated in Table 3, the average length of service is a little over 6 years.[50] And as the average age of appointees has risen, their corresponding average tenure has declined. The average length of service for those justices appointed in the 1940s and 1950s was over 8 years, compared to little more than 5 years for those named in the 1990s.

Age discrimination appears in the recruitment of justices from different career paths as well. The largest number of justices are either elevated from within the lower courts or named from private legal practice. The latter are deemed potentially more independent because they have not toiled within the judicial bureaucracy. Considering all justices recruited from 1947 through 1993, 43 were former judges and 36 practicing attorneys. The average length of service for the former was 6.79 years, while the latter averaged 5.22 years. The average service for others was as follows: the 5 former administrators averaged 8.8 years, followed by 10 law professors with 8.1 years, 11 prosecutors with 8 years, and 5 diplomats with an average of 7.4 years. Thus while the latter have longer tenures than former lower court judges or lawyers, their numbers are severely limited.

Justices appointed from outside the ranks of career judges may have some experience in the courts or the government, as the earlier discussion of Justice Sonobe's career illustrates. Still, law professors, lawyers, and others appointed from outside the judiciary or the government are considered by the General Secretariat to be potentially far too independent on the bench. By design, their numbers and length of service are thus limited. When the average tenure of the 54 justices elevated from lower court judgeships or prosecutorial positions is compared to that of the remaining 56, those in the former category served on average a full year more (i.e., 7 rather than 6 years). The disparity between "outsiders" and "insiders" is even more striking when the average tenure of law professors and lawyers is compared to that of those promoted from within the judiciary and the government. The average tenure of the 46 former law professors and private attorneys was only 5.6 years, whereas that of the 64 justices who were elevated from positions as judges, prosecutors, administrators, and diplomats was 7.2 years.

Appointing older justices to the Court results in higher levels of turnover. The General Secretariat and the government thus have more opportunities to reward a greater number of those who have reached the

Table 3   Average Length of Service of Supreme Court Justices,
           1947–1993

PRIME MINISTER	DATE OF APPOINTMENTS	NUMBER OF APPOINTEES	AVERAGE NUMBER OF YEARS OF SERVICE
Katayama	1947	15	8.93
Yoshida	1948–1954	7	8.28
Hatoyama	1955–1956	4	8.75
Ishibashi	1956	1	4
Kishi	1958–1960	2	6
Ikeda	1960–1964	13	6.61
Satō	1964–1972	13	7
Tanaka	1972–1974	6	7
Miki	1974–1976	4	5.75
Fukuda	1976–1978	5	5.2
Ōhira	1978–1980	7	6.57
Suzuki	1980–1982	5	5.6
Nakasone	1982–1987	13	5.3
Takeshita	1987–1989	2	6
Kaifu	1989–1991	9	5.55
Miyazawa	1992–1993	4	5.25
Total		110	6.72

peak of their careers and proven loyal. Limited tenures, though, may also work to discourage judicial independence.[51] Moreover, there was no tradition of individual concurring or dissenting opinions prior to the postwar Court. The Great Court of Cassation, under the Meiji Constitution, announced decisions in *per curiam* (unsigned) opinions. All decisions were unanimous. No dissenting or concurring opinions were filed, as remains the contemporary practice in Japanese lower courts.

The Court Organization Law of 1947, though, mandates that "The opinion of every judge shall be expressed in written decisions."[52] A basis was thus laid for introducing the practice of individual dissenting and concurring opinions, as is well established in the U.S. Supreme Court.[53] The practice of the postwar Japanese Supreme Court has largely proven otherwise, however. All the justices sign opinions for the Court, and occasionally some attach supplemental opinions that are neither concurring nor dissenting per se and that may only invite confusion over the Court's ruling.[54] Still, it seems fair to say that judicial independence, as registered in concurring or dissenting opinions and non-unanimous decisions, remains far from the norm.

Because not all opinions are published, serious issues of the justices' accountablilty are apparent and major methodological problems arise in measuring judicial independence.[55] Most studies of the Supreme Court's decisionmaking are based on decisions reported in *Saikō Saibansho Hanreishū*. Yet, as noted earlier, many more (but still not all) opinions are published in the less accessible reporter *Saikō Saibansho Saibanshū*. An examination of all published and unpublished decisions and opinions, kept for civil and administrative cases in the Clerk's Office of the Supreme Court, underscores how few individual opinions are actually produced.[56] In 1989, the three petty benches and the Grand Bench rendered decisions in 2,243 cases, issued 474 orders, and ruled on another 464 miscellaneous matters. The Court took a total of 3,181 actions on pending civil and administrative filings. In addition, the Court disposed of 1,509 filings in criminal cases with 76 written decisions, issued 1,101 orders, and took action on another 332 miscellaneous filings.

Of the civil and administrative cases, only 30 decided by the three petty benches were not unanimous decisions. Justices filed only 16 dissenting opinions, 7 concurring opinions, and 5 separate opinions. The Grand Bench handed down only one non-unanimous ruling with a single separate opinion filed. By that measure, the norm remains collective, not individualized, decisionmaking. Moreover, the *Saikō Saibansho Saibanshū* published only the 1 non-unanimous Grand Bench decision and 16 of the 30 non-unanimous petty bench rulings in civil cases, plus 65 unanimous decisions in civil cases, along with the decisions in 70 criminal cases, for a total of 152 reported decisions.

Even fewer were published in the *Saikō Saibansho Hanreishū*. It reported just the Grand Bench's 1 non-unanimous decision, 8 other non-unanimous civil decisions, and 3 non-unanimous criminal cases, with another 44 unanimous rulings (in 26 civil and 18 criminal cases), for a total of 56 reported decisions out of the 4,690 decisions and orders handed down by the Court in its 1989 term.

A major study of the postwar Court's decisionmaking, based on published opinions in *Saikō Saibansho Saibanshū*, suggested a basis for optimism about the development of judicial independence. Of the cases decided from 1947 through 1962, political scientist Takeyoshi Kawashima found 589 criminal cases and 161 civil cases in which non-unanimous decisions were rendered.[57] In total, there were 750 non-unanimous votes out of the 5,716 votes taken in 4,729 criminal cases and 987 civil cases. Further analyzing those data, Kawashima found that the number of concurring and dissenting opinions gradually increased, and did so in relation to justices' length of service. Those who were elevated to the Court from outside the ranks of lower-court career judges filed almost three times the number of concurring and dissenting opinions in the initial period from 1947 to 1950. But Kawashima concluded that by the late 1950s and early 1960s, each group tended to concur and to dissent about as often as the other.

However, whatever movement there initially appeared to be toward individualism in decisionmaking on the postwar Court soon abated. Indeed, judicial independence, as recorded in non-unanimous decisions, concurrences, and dissents, has declined significantly over the last decade. A review of the published opinions in *Saikō Saibansho Saibanshū* over the twelve years from 1981 to 1993 reveals only 331 dissenting, concurring, and separate opinions (see Appendix B).[58] Notably, the number of individual opinions dropped to less than half the number filed during the Court's first fifteen years: 331 separate opinions were filed between 1981 and 1993, as compared with 750 between 1947 and 1962. As Table 3 indicates, justices sitting during the Court's first decades had longer tenures (an average of seven years) than those serving in the 1980s and early 1990s (who averaged a little over five years). Moreover, Kawashima found that the initial conventional ratio of five former judges, five lawyers, and five administrators or professors held true: among those serving in the period from 1947 to 1962, former judges constituted 34 percent, lawyers 34 percent, and administrators or professors 31 percent.[59] By contrast, of the justices serving between 1981 and 1993, 40 percent were former lower-court judges, 32 percent were attorneys, 10 percent were prosecutors, and the percentage of administrators, diplomats, and professors had dropped to 18 percent.

What remains no less striking about individual opinion writing in the contemporary Japanese Supreme Court is how a very small number of justices authored a majority of all separate opinions. In other words, many justices authored few or no separate opinions. Thirty percent of the justices between 1981 and 1993 never filed a single individual opinion, whether separate, concurring, or dissenting. Moreover, little more than a handful of the justices wrote more than 50 percent of all separate opinions, or 171 of the 331 individual opinions issued. The six justices listed in Table 4 were the only ones to file more than 15 separate opinions during their tenures on the bench.

The sole former career judge to file a large number of individual opinions was Justice Masataka Taniguchi. Among the career judges appointed to the Court, he was truly exceptional in this regard. His productivity, however, was exceeded by former University of Tokyo law-school professor Masami Itō. The remaining "frequent filers" of dissenting, concurring, and separate opinions also had professional careers in areas other than the judiciary. If Justice Taniguchi's opinions are excluded,

Table 4   Separate Opinion Writing in the Japanese Supreme Court, 1981–1993

Justice	Prior Position	Years on Court	Concurring	Dissenting	Other	Total
Itō	professor	9	34	12	2	48
Taniguchi	judge	7	16	13	15	44
Dandō	professor	9	9	11	4	24
Shimatani	lawyer	6	4	13	2	19
Fujisaki	diplomat	7		14	3	17
Yokoi	prosecutor	6	2	11	6	19
Total			65	74	33	171

then three law professors accounted for 27.2 percent of all individual opinions; ten attorneys contributed 23.4 percent; and nine former administrators, prosecutors, and diplomats wrote 23.2 percent. The number of individual opinions filed by twelve former lower-court judges amounted to 20.7 percent (if Taniguchi's opinion writing is included, this rises to 31.7 percent). Notably, law professors are the most prolific independent-opinion writers, yet their representation on the Court is the most severely limited as well. By contrast, former lower court judges are generally the least independent but comprise the largest percentage of the occupational groups represented on the Court.

One more factor may contribute to the decline in the number of dissenting and concurring opinions. Besides the shift toward naming older appointees and more career judges to the Supreme Court, the justices' opinion-writing process itself discourages individualism. As Justice Sonobe emphasizes, opinions for the Court are drafted by law clerks, not the justices themselves.[60] A justice filing a dissent or concurrence thus must draft the opinion alone. This not only entails a lot of work but pits the justice against his colleagues, the law clerks, the Court's norms, and the legal culture.

In sum, judicial independence in the Supreme Court and the lower courts is discouraged by various means: the prewar tradition weighs against individual expression; separate opinions remain prohibited in the lower courts; the LDP's long reign ensured its ultimate control over judicial appointments throughout most of the postwar era; the judicial bureaucracy promotes judges in calculated ways to reward conformity; and the Supreme Court's composition and operation discourages individualism on the bench. In these ways, constitutional conflicts are minimalized, marginalized, and suppressed. Dialogue and debate over constitutional politics remains constrained in the Supreme Court, the lower courts, and the country. The politics of the judicial bureaucracy, elections, and the governmental and social infrastructure matter far more than the Constitution's parchment guarantees for determining the scope of civil rights and liberties.

Secularizing Religion

The *Tsu City Ground-Purification Ceremony* case, which the Supreme Court finally handed down on July 13, 1977, had originated a decade earlier with a challenge to the Tsu municipal government. Tsu is in the Mie prefecture of Honshu, where the Grand Ise Shrine is located. In 1965, the city had sponsored a Shinto-style ground-purification ceremony *(jichinsai)* for the construction of a gymnasium. Four Shinto priests were paid an honorarium of 4,000 yen (about $20) to perform a ceremony for the purification of the ground, the pacification of earth *kami,* and for the construction to proceed without accidents. Another 3,663 yen was paid as an offering, for a total of 7,663 yen ($39).

Seiichi Sekiguchi, a city counselor who attended the ceremony along with more than a hundred other local officials and dignitaries, subsequently filed a suit against the city's mayor, Kiyoshi Kakunaga. Like the Kamisakas, Sekiguchi was a survivor of the war, born in 1915. Unlike them, he was also a member of the Communist Party, which adamantly opposed governmental support for religion and the LDP's efforts to expand military spending under Japan's "peace constitution." Sekiguchi demanded that the city be reimbursed for its expenditures because the mayor and other officials had violated Articles 20 and 89 of the Constitution. In addition, he sought 50,000 yen ($250) as compensation for the personal injury he had suffered by having been forced as a local official to attend a religious ceremony that ran against his beliefs.

Two years after the suit was filed, the Tsu District Court held that, although the Shinto-style ground-purification ceremony was religious, the city was not thereby propagating Shinto.[61] On the bench handing down the ruling were three relatively young judges. Presiding was 42-year-old Judge Takeshi Matsumoto, who had started his judicial career fifteen years earlier, after graduating from the prestigious Tokyo University. He was joined by two 36-year-olds: Judge Tadao Sugiyama, also a graduate of Tokyo University, and Judge Kōichi Aoyama, a graduate of Chūō University. Judges Matsumoto and Sugiyama would later be elevated to the Nagoya High Court.

District Court Judge Matsumoto reasoned that the ground-purification ceremony had a secular purpose and was merely a folkway. The city's payments to the Shinto priests were not unconstitutional under Article 89 because the priests were merely paid for their services. As for Sekiguchi's claim that he had been coerced and denied his religious freedom under Article 20, the court ruled that his attending the ceremony was not an official duty. Sekiguchi, said Judge Matsumoto—disregarding the pressures of local politics—could have simply declined to participate. Furthermore, if Sekiguchi had suffered mental anguish, that was his own doing, not the city's. Undeterred by that decision, Sekiguchi appealed to the Nagoya High Court.

Four years passed before the Nagoya High Court rendered a decision in 1971, reversing the Tsu District Court's ruling in part.[62] The high court's bench was composed of more senior judges than those who had decided the case in the district court. Presiding was 61-year-old Judge Junkichi Itō, a graduate of Tokyo University. With him were two graduates of Chūō University, 50-year-old Judge Kiyoshi Miyamoto and 43-year-old Judge Isamu Tsuchida. Thus Judges Itō and Miyamoto were old enough to have experienced the prewar period.

The Nagoya High Court's ruling was actually a mixed victory for Sekiguchi. On the one hand, the court found that the mayor and city had violated the disestablishment of state support for religion and ordered repayment of the 7,663 yen ($39). On the other hand, Sekiguchi's request for compensation for his personal injury was again rejected.

In arriving at the conclusion that Tsu city had violated the principle of separation of religion and the state, the Nagoya High Court took an expansive view of religious freedom under the Constitution. Freedom of religion, the court said, embraces beliefs and rituals of private and group religions, and newly advocated religions. The court also stressed the importance of considering Shinto's history before and after the war. Under the Meiji Constitution, state-sponsored Shrine Shinto enjoyed the status of an established "ultrareligion." It provided the basis for national policy. Although administratively separated from religion before the war, state-supported Shinto incorporated many traditional Shinto folkways. For those reasons, the Nagoya High Court stressed that the separation of the state and religion had to be taken seriously and strictly enforced.

Turning to Tsu city's argument that it had not violated the Constitution because the ceremony was a traditional folkway, the Nagoya High Court advanced a very sophisticated analysis of Shinto and the state. First, observed the court, folkways are norms or fixed customs passed down over at least three generations. Moreover, although they might once have had religious significance, they have over time become accepted as secular practices. The high court noted, for example, in rather curiously contorted logic, that the religious symbolism of Christmas trees and New Year's pine decorations had been largely diluted, becoming secular customs or seasonal events.[63] In any case, the Nagoya High Court underscored, traditional folkways are not regulated or financially supported by the state. Instead, folkways are voluntarily observed as customary practices.

On the basis of that analysis, the Nagoya High Court proposed three criteria for deciding whether Tsu city's ground-purification ceremony was an accepted folkway or a state-supported religious activity:

(1) Did religious officials preside over the ceremony?
(2) Did the ceremony follow that of a religious sect?
(3) Would ordinary people consider the ceremony to be a traditional folkway?

In Tsu city, Shinto priests in full traditional dress had conducted rituals in the manner prescribed by State Shinto and instituted by the Ministry of the Interior in 1907. Yet, because the ceremony had been performed for only a few decades in the prewar period and had been abandoned after the war, it would probably not, according to the Nagoya High Court's reasoning, be considered a folkway "without hesitation" by the people.

In addition, the high court pointed out that the postwar boom in building construction across the country had brought about an increase in the performance of many different kinds of ground-purification ceremonies. Subcontractors invariably expect the ground of a building site to have been purified. Not just Shinto but Buddhist and other kinds of ground-purification ceremonies are regularly performed. The Nagoya High Court, therefore, could not say firmly that the Shinto-style ground-purification ceremony was a national folkway. Tsu city thus had violated the Constitution by sponsoring a particular religion's ceremony.

The Nagoya High Court might have stopped at that, but its opinion continued. Since the war, people had become indifferent to religion. They lacked a clear distinction between the sacred and secular. Unlike Western countries in which there had been centuries-old struggles between the state and churches, there was little consciousness in Japan about the importance of separating the state from religion. After the war, the Shinto Directive had prescribed a strict separation of religion and the state. Moreover, the high court observed that, given the combination of religious pluralism and indifference in Japan, religious freedom could not be guaranteed without maintaining a thoroughgoing separation of the two.

The Nagoya High Court concluded with a statement aimed at educating as much as at explaining:

Freedom of religion cannot be completely guaranteed without separation of religion and the state. Separation of religion and the state is the actual method for realizing freedom of religion more concretely, and the principle of the constitutional guarantee for freedom of religion. The principle of separation of religion and the state aims at being protected against a crisis of destroying the state and of corrupting religion, caused by combining the state with religion. If the state combines with a particular religion, people believing in other religions would hate, disbelieve, and dislike the state. That invites the crisis of destroying the basis for the state. Besides, the state's political and financial support for a particular religion will cause the loss of the people's respect for, and bring about corruption of, that religion.[64]

Unpersuaded by the Nagoya High Court's bold ruling, Tsu city's mayor, Kiyoshi Kakunaga, appealed to the Supreme Court.[65] Under Article 10 of the Court Organization Law of 1947, which specifies the kinds of cases that the grand and petty benches may hear, a petty bench may not decide cases challenging the constitutionality of a law or regulation unless the case raises a challenge that has already been heard and decided by the Grand Bench. Neither may a petty bench declare a law or ordinance unconstitutional unless the Grand Bench has previously reached that conclusion, nor may it hand down a ruling contrary to an earlier ruling and interpretation rendered by the Grand Bench. Cases first go to a petty bench, which may refer them for decision to the Grand Bench. In important constitutional controversies, all fifteen justices thus sit as a Grand Bench and render a decision, typically after a considerable period of time.

Six more years passed after the Nagoya High Court's decision before the Supreme Court handed down its ruling in the *Tsu City Ground-Purification Ceremony* case on July 13, 1977. In overturning the Nagoya High Court's ruling, the justices were divided ten to five. According to the majority, the city's sponsorship of the Shinto-style ground-purification ceremony had been constitutional because, although it had religious aspects, the ceremony aimed neither at propogating Shintoism nor at interfering with other religions. In contrast to the Nagoya High Court, the majority construed the ground-purification ceremony to have become, after the war, basically a secular *(sezokuteki)* activity. Despite its religious origins, the Court's majority held that the ceremony had a secular purpose in conformity with traditional folkways.

In the majority's view, the Constitution mandated a separation of religion and the state. But the Constitution did not require the kind of rigid or complete separation proposed by the Nagoya High Court.

After briefly noting the close connection between Shinto and the state under the Meiji Constitution, and the new constitution's guarantees for religious freedom and the disestablishment of religion, the majority emphasized the impossibility of a completely strict separation in light of Japan's unique history and culture:

> In Japan, unlike Christian or Islamic countries, various kinds of religion had evolved and existed pluralistically, overlapping, and coexisted. In such a situation, it was not enough to only guarantee freedom of religion unconditionally. . . . It was necessary to prescribe a separation of religion and the state . . . [and that separation] should be interpreted to aim for complete separation and to ensure secularity or religious neutrality of the state.

The majority also pointed out that the state's regulations and support for education, welfare, and culture touch on religious activities and folkways. "Therefore, it is almost impossible to completely separate the state from religion in practice." A complete separation of the state from religion appeared unreasonable. Complete separation, said the majority, would mean that the state could not assist private schools that had some religious connection, for example, or subsidize religious groups for preserving architecture, shrines, or temples as cultural assets. Thus, concluded the Court's majority, "the principle of separation of religion and the state demands religious neutrality from the state, but does not completely prohibit all involvement of the state with religion."

Article 20, according to the Court's majority, bars only state sponsorship of "religious activities" that (1) "transcend the proper limit" in view of (2) whether the aim or "purpose" of the state-sponsored activities was to preach or propagate religion, and (3) whether they had the "effect" of assisting, encouraging, or promoting Shinto or any other particular religion. In short, the Court adopted a "purpose and effect" test requiring that the government not "endorse, facilitate, or advance religion in general." In arriving at that test for determining the application of section 3 of Article 20, the Supreme Court of Japan cited in support of its analysis the U.S. Supreme Court's 1971 ruling in *Lemon v. Kurtzman*.[66]

In *Lemon v. Kurtzman,* the Burger Court (1969–1986) had set forth a new test for applying the First Amendment's disestablishment clause. Writing for the Court, Chief Justice Warren E. Burger held that government policies and regulations must (1) have a secular purpose, (2) neither advance nor inhibit religion, and (3) not foster "an excessive government entanglement with religion." Although, in applying this three-pronged test in *Lemon,* Chief Justice Burger struck down direct financial assistance from states to parochial schools, including the use of public funds to pay parochial teachers' salaries, the ruling signaled a significant shift away from the Court's earlier defense of a "high wall of separation" between religion and the state. As such, *Lemon* represented retrenchment and Chief Justice Burger's concern with accommodating some governmental support for religion, while drawing a line at state support for any particular religion.

A year earlier, in *Walz v. Tax Commission of the City of New York,*[67] Chief Justice Burger had signaled the move away from enforcing a strict separation of the state and religion. Writing for the Court also in *Walz,* he rejected a challenge to New York's tax exemption for "real or personal property used exclusively for religious, educational or charitable purposes." In doing so, he took the occasion to return to *Everson's* theory of benevolent government neutrality toward religion, and thereupon to advance his own accommodationist interpretation of the First Amendment's religion clauses.

"There is room for play in the joints productive of a benevolent neutrality which will permit religious exercise to exist without sponsorship and without interference," claimed Chief Justice Burger, when explaining that

> The course of constitutional neutrality in this area cannot be an absolutely straight line; rigidity could well defeat the basic purpose of these provisions, which is to insure that no religion be sponsored or favored, none commanded, and none inhibited. The general principle deducible from the First Amendment and all that has been said by the Court is this: that we will not tolerate either governmentally established religion or governmental interference with religion.

Chief Justice Burger, however, went a step further. He held that government support of religion was permissible so long as there was "no excessive governmental entanglement with religion."

In *Walz,* Chief Justice Burger introduced the idea of "excessive government entanglement with religion," and the following year wrote it into *Lemon's* three-pronged test. But in *Walz* he rather conveniently failed to mention the two-pronged test laid down by the Warren Court (1953–1969) in *Abington School District v. Schempp.*[68] In that case, the Warren Court had enforced a "high wall of separation" between religion and the state by ruling that public schools could not require students to begin each school day with the recital of the Lord's Prayer and other verses from the Bible.

Schempp had laid down a two-pronged test for determining when the government ran afoul of the First Amendment's disestablishment clause:

whether laws and regulations have "a secular legislative purpose and a primary effect that neither advances nor inhibits religion." In *Lemon*, Chief Justice Burger merely turned *Schempp's* two-pronged test into a three-pronged one by adding that legislation must not "foster 'an excessive government entanglement with religion.' " While this might appear to buttress a "high wall" of strict separation, Chief Justice Burger had precisely the opposite goal in mind, namely, laying the basis for some accommodation of the state and religion. That twist in legal logic and tests also proved useful to the Supreme Court of Japan.

The *Lemon* test, in other words, represented a conservative reaction within the Burger Court to earlier rulings of the Warren Court that had basically entrenched a "high wall of separation" of the state and religion into constitutional law. During the Warren Court years, the First Amendment's disestablishment clause was held to bar public schools from requiring students to recite at the start of each school day either a nondenominational prayer[69] or the Lord's Prayer,[70] and to overturn state laws forbidding the teaching of evolution.[71] The Warren Court also upheld "Sunday closing laws" over the objections of Orthodox Jews, for whom Saturday is the Sabbath and who were thus forced to close their businesses two days a week.[72] As a result, the Warren Court's embrace of a strict separation of the state and religion was widely criticized for promoting governmental hostility toward religion, and, with changes in the Court's composition, this inspired a move in the opposite direction.

Even in the hands of the Burger Court, however, the *Lemon* test proved to be no talisman. Instead, it led to rather fine, often confusing line-drawing. The *Lemon* test failed to dictate any particular outcome or result other than that which a bare majority of the justices agreed on in each particular case. On the one hand, the Burger Court and the Rehnquist Court (1986–) upheld some forms of governmental aid to religion over First Amendment objections. Federal aid for the construction of academic buildings on private sectarian college campuses survived the *Lemon* test.[73] The loan of secular textbooks to parochial schools;[74] general-purpose grants for nonsectarian purposes to colleges with religious affiliations;[75] the provision of diagnostic and therapeutic testing services to primary and secondary schools associated with particular religions; reimbursement for the costs of recordkeeping and testing incurred by religious schools;[76] tax deductions for parents sending their children to religious schools[77]—all these have been upheld. In addition, in *Marsh v. Chambers*,[78] the Court upheld the practice of having chaplains open sessions of legislatures with prayers.

On the other hand, the Burger and Rehnquist Courts continued to draw the line at tax rebates for children attending religious schools;[79] prayers in schools;[80] governmental requirements that public schoolchildren begin their days with "a moment of silence, or prayer";[81] the posting of the Ten Commandments in public school classrooms;[82] as well as various forms of direct financial assistance to religion.[83] Because the *Lemon* test has been so problematically applied, and sometimes simply overlooked by the Court when reaching its result,[84] several of the justices have indicated that the Court should completely abandon the test.[85]

When adopting a *Lemon*-like test in the *Tsu City Ground-Purification Ceremony* case, the Supreme Court of Japan sought legitimacy for its ruling. In doing so, however, the Supreme Court's majority was even more deferential to the government's accommodation of and support for religion than the Burger Court had been when creating the *Lemon* test. The Court's majority very narrowly construed the ban on the government's engaging in "religious activities" in clause 3 of Article 20. Basically, according to the majority, Article 20 proscribes only "action the purpose of which is religious and that the effect of which is the assistance, promotion, and advancement of religion, or the oppression of or the interference in it." Drawing on clause 2 of Article 20, which forbids any person from being "compelled to take part in any religious acts, celebration, rite or practice," the Court narrowly interpreted the third clause's proscribing governmental support for "religious activities" to include solely those "religious ceremonies, rites, and practices the purpose and effect of which are stated above."

In addition, the Court's majority focused on how the general public viewed such ceremonies. "The generally accepted social idea" and "general public's judgment" of those ceremonies, rather than the fact that Shinto priests had performed them, was deemed controlling. Besides, the Court noted, the Shinto priests were not outwardly preaching or proselytizing. They were simply conducting traditional Shinto folkway rites.

Even more importantly, the majority supported its conclusion that Shinto ground-purification ceremonies would not, in "the general public's judgment," be considered a "religious activity" by emphasizing consideration of two societal factors: (1) the fact that there was a "pluralistic religious consciousness" but otherwise religious indifference in Japan, and (2) the idea that "Shrine Shinto itself is primarily concerned with ritual and ceremony, and not engaged in outward activities like preaching and missionary propagation." Unlike Christians and followers of Islam, Shinto priests and believers do not try to make converts. Although the Shinto-style ground-purification ceremony was a religious folkway, these two factors were held to lessen the effect of Tsu city's sponsorship of a religious activity, instead of contruing that sponsorship as promoting or advancing religion.

In short, the Court ruled that Tsu's sponsorship of the ground-purifi-cation ceremony, although religious, was probably not understood by the general public as a religious activity and was therefore constitutionally permissible. The Court thus very narrowly construed constitutional provi-sions for the separation of the state from Shinto, thereby arriving at its preordained conclusion that the religious significance of the Shinto cere-mony had basically become diluted in contemporary Japan. The municipal government's sponsorship of the ceremony had a secular purpose. The city neither advanced nor inhibited religion, let alone fostered an excessive entanglement—or, in the words of the Supreme Court of Japan, "tran-scend[ed] the proper limit"—of the state and Shinto.

The Court's analysis and ruling in the *Tsu City Ground-Purification Ceremony* case signaled the lower courts that Shinto ceremonies and monu-ments could once again be redefined as secular folkways. Governmental support for Shinto might be renewed. That construction of the Constitu-tion—and social reality—nevertheless appeared paradoxical and, some would say, disingenuous. However tortured, the Japanese Supreme Court's logic would reappear in lower courts' rulings, as well as mirror the reason-ing of the U.S. Supreme Court in its ruling in *Lynch v. Donnelly*.[86]

Lynch v. Donnelly bears emphasizing because there a bare majority of the Burger Court upheld the financial assistance and cooperation of the city of Pawtucket, Rhode Island, in the annual construction of a Christmas display that included a creche—a representation of the stable in which Jesus Christ was born—complete with the figures of Jesus, Mary and Joseph, and the three Magi (priests). Writing for a majority that included Justices Sandra Day O'Connor, William H. Rehnquist, Lewis F. Powell, and Byron White, Chief Justice Burger held that, even though the creche was a significant religious symbol for Christians, within the context of the times and of holiday displays at Christmas, the creche had taken on an overriding secular meaning.

Writing for the Court in *Lynch v. Donnelly,* Chief Justice Burger observed that,

> In this case, the focus of our inquiry must be on the creche in the context of the Christmas season. . . . The display is sponsored by the city to celebrate the Holiday and to depict the origins of that Holiday. These are legitimate secular purposes. . . . The display engenders a friendly community spirit of goodwill in keeping with the season. The creche may well have special mean-ing to those whose faith includes the celebration of religious Masses, but none

who sense the origins of the Christmas celebration would fail to be aware of its religious implications. That the display brings people into the central city, and serves commercial interests and benefits merchants and their employees, does not, as the dissent points out, determine the character of the display. That a prayer invoking Divine guidance in Congress is preceded and followed by debate and partisan conflict over taxes, budgets, national defense, and myriad mundane subjects, for example, has never been thought to demean or taint the sacredness of the invocation.[87]

"Of course the creche is identified with one religious faith," admitted Chief Justice Burger, but added that

> It would be ironic . . . if the inclusion of a single symbol of a particular historic religious event, as part of a celebration acknowledged in the Western World for 20 centuries, and in this country by the people, by the Executive Branch, by the Congress, and the courts for 2 centuries, would so "taint" the city's exhibit as to render it violative of the Establishment Clause. To forbid the use of this one passive symbol—the creche—at the very time people are taking note of the season with Christmas hymns and carols in public schools and in other public places, and while the Congress and legislatures open sessions with prayers by paid chaplains, would be a stilted overreaction contrary to our history and to our holdings. If the presence of the creche in this display violates the Establishment Clause, a host of other forms of taking official note of Christmas, and of our religious heritage, are equally offensive to the Constitution.

On the basis of that analysis, Chief Justice Burger held that Pawtucket's assistance and financial support in purchasing the creche for $1,365 were permissible under the First Amendment and *Lemon's* three-pronged test.

The four dissenting justices in *Lynch v. Donnelly* took strong exception to Chief Justice Burger's reasoning. Joined by Justices Harry Blackmun, Thurgood Marshall, and John Paul Stevens, Justice William J. Brennan, a Catholic, reminded the majority that,

> Unlike such secular figures as Santa Claus, reindeer, and carolers, a nativity scene represents far more than a mere "traditional" symbol of Christmas. The essence of the creche's symbolic purpose and effect is to prompt the observer to experience a sense of simple awe and wonder appropriate to the contemplation of one of the central elements of Christian dogma—that God sent His Son into the world to be a Messiah. Contrary to the Court's suggestion, the creche is far from a mere representation of a "particular historic religious

event." It is, instead, best understood as a mystical re-creation of an event that lies at the heart of Christian faith. To suggest, as the Court does, that such a symbol is merely "traditional" and therefore no different from Santa's house or reindeer is not only offensive to those for whom the creche has profound significance, but insulting to those who insist for religious or personal reasons that the story of Christ is in no sense a part of "history" nor an unavoidable element of our national "heritage."[88]

Chief Justice Burger's reasoning for the majority in *Lynch* and application of the *Lemon* test there represented a very hollow victory for true believers. The ruling was a nightmare for those who dreamed of a complete separation of the state from religion.

The Japanese Supreme Court majority's construction of Article 20 and of social reality in the *Tsu City Ground-Purification Ceremony* case drew a no less bitter dissent from Chief Justice Ekizō Fujibayashi. His dissenting opinion was joined by four others: Justices Yutaka Yoshido, Shigemitsu Dandō, Takaaki Hattori, and Shōichi Tamaki. The chief justice countered that the *Lemon*-like test was far too vague. "It is not enough to guarantee freedom of religion unconditionally," he insisted for the dissenters. "It is indispensable to eliminate, first of all, any entanglement of state in religion, in order to complete its guarantee."

Chief Justice Fujibayashi furthermore pointed out that

It is not clear what is the entanglement of state in religion referred to by the majority opinion, and it is vague as to when the entanglement exceeds the proper limit. We cannot help but fear that binding of the state with religion is easily permitted and that the guarantee of freedom of religion is violated, in the majority opinion's interpretation of the principle of separation of religion and the state.

The majority's ruling failed to make clear whether "excessive entanglement," or "the proper limits" of the separation of the state and Shinto, was an independent factor to be considered along with the "purpose" and "effect" of a state-sponsored activity associated with religion. Besides disagreeing with the majority's use of any test such as the *Lemon*-like "purpose and effect" test, the dissenters took exception to the majority's appeal to the "consciousness of the general public."

The bottom line for the dissenters was that the Shinto-style ground-purification ceremony was inevitably tainted with religious symbolism. Even if the ceremony's religious character had become so diluted over time that it was now accepted as a secular custom or folkway, the Shinto-style ground-purification ceremony inexorably remained religious. Shinto ground-purification ceremonies, however viewed, amounted to "religious activities," which clause 3 of Article 20 prohibits the state from supporting.

Chief Justice Fujibayashi, a 69-year-old follower of the Non-Church Christianity Movement, went further still. He filed an extraordinary, separate, solo dissenting opinion. "True religion," said Chief Justice Fujibayashi, "should stand without the help of the state or other secular power. And religion should be respected for its independence." In Japan, he agreed, people accept worshipping at shrines as not out of line with the constitutional guarantee of religious freedom. This was due to the "simplicity of Shrine Shinto" rituals, and to the fact that the "Japanese religious consciousness fostered by Shrine Shinto and Buddhism" had not instilled a "sufficient sensitivity to freedom of religion." Instead, explained Fujibayashi, the people's acceptance of State Shinto had made it easier for them to overlook the entanglement of the state and Shinto. For these reasons, an "absolute separation" of the state from religion was indispensable to guaranteeing freedom of religion.

Accordingly, Chief Justice Fujibayashi thought that the state should be required both to be neutral to all religions and not to interfere with any person's religion. Concluding, he underscored that,

> Since the ceremony in this case was held by those who wish for a power transcending that of humans for ensuring the safety of the construction, the ceremony is a religious event. For Shrine Shinto, a service or ceremony is the most important religious activity. When state power, prestige, and financial support of state and municipal government are put behind a particular religion, their pressure is exerted to force religious minorities to obey the state-sanctioned religion. Even if that is the opinion or feelings of a fastidious minority, the minority's freedom of religion or conscience should not be violated by majority rule. State or municipal government should avoid causing social conflicts over religion, and that is the true meaning of separation of religion and the state.

Law's Reflection of "Social Reality"

The Supreme Court's ruling in the *Tsu City Ground-Purification Ceremony* case provoked sharp criticism from liberal constitutional law scholars. If the Supreme Court was going to adopt a *Lemon*-like three-pronged test for determining the scope of the Constitution's disestablishment clause, then, argued constitutional law scholar Nobuyoshi Ashibe, it should stick to the

Lemon test and apply it exactly. Other scholars criticized the Court's majority for substituting its own prong of whether the government had "transcended the proper limit" of disestablishment for the *Lemon* test's third prong of fostering "an excessive government entanglement with religion." Still others countered that a *Lemon*-like test was inappropriate in the first place, because the Constitution expressly and strictly bars governmental support for religion.

Even some supporters of governmental support for Shinto remain critical of the majority's analysis in the *Tsu City Ground-Purification Ceremony* case. Just as the dissenters in *Lynch v. Donnelly* lamented Chief Justice Burger's treatment of the creche as having become a secular symbol, Kokugakuin University professor of Shinto studies and comparative religion Yoshiya Abe says, frankly, that the majority in the *Tsu City* case "trivialized the rituals" and "the animistic phenomenon of Shinto."[89] The ceremony at issue was, after all, a purification rite. It is deeply rooted in Shinto traditions and "fear of the revengence [*sic*] of unpacified spirits." The Court's announcement of its so-called *Lemon*-like test in the *Tsu City* case, Abe emphasizes, "doesn't really apply to a country with such a different religious scenery." As he goes on to explain,

> The Court took the position that folkway prevails over religious elements. But that is technique rather than criticial observation. In reality those animistic or revengeful ideas, you might say, are not religion in a similar way that prewar State Shinto was not religion. Or, you might say they were old ideas but, again, only when we define "religion" as "having a certain dogma" can something without dogma be said not to be religion. This hypothesis is necessary to say that [the ground-purification ceremonies] are not religious. This kind of analysis is not really taking religion very seriously.

Religion, Abe adds, "is sharing a worldview and otherworld view." Still, he agrees with the Court's bottom line. The government may financially support such ceremonies. These "animistic folkways," as he puts it, "are they really 'religion' in the sense that the Constitution prohibits religion?"[90] That is precisely the question which the Supreme Court's majority begged in construing social reality so as to fit its preconceived notion of the constitutional limitations on the establishment of religion.

The Supreme Court's ruling in the *Tsu City Ground-Purification Ceremony* case encouraged the Liberal Democratic Party and its supporters in the Japan Association of War Bereaved Families to keep pushing for renewed government control over and patronage of Yasukuni. Not surprisingly, the Association of Shinto Shrines praised the decision as sanctioning official, not merely private, visits by the prime minister and other government officials to Ise and Yasukuni shrines, as well as the state's sponsorship of other Shinto rites.[91] In contrast, the Roman Catholic Church criticized the ruling for blurring the line dividing the state and Shinto,[92] while the United Church of Christ warned that the ruling signaled "a dangerous trend."[93]

In treating the Shinto-style ground-purification ceremony as a secular, nonreligious folkway, the Court signaled that other Shinto ceremonies and monuments might be deemed nonreligious activities and folkways as well. Paradoxically, as some commentators pointed out, the *Tsu City Ground-Purification Ceremony* case strengthened the "ties between religious and political structures with a common orientation to the 'traditional unity' form of the *saisei itchi* ["the unity of Shinto and the state"] tradition. To change the metaphor, secularization here implies not the marginalization but the centralization of Shrine Shinto."[94]

And yet, it seems fair to say, the Court's ruling reflected and reinforced the postwar generations' ambivalence about and self-denial of religiosity. The Court basically construed social reality in such a way as to set aside the Constitution's principle of strict separation of the state from religion, thereby implicitly relegitimating the tradition of "the unity of Shinto and the state." In this regard, the Court's ruling accorded with the position of the majority of Shinto and Buddhist organizations.[95] Only Christian bodies and a few Buddhist sects reject that prewar principle but, of course, they are minorities in Japan.

The *Tsu City Ground-Purification Ceremony* case bore directly on the Kamisakas' challenge to Minoo city, which the Osaka District Court was considering at the time of the Supreme Court's ruling. Minoo's attorneys, moreover, were defending the city's relocation and reconstruction of the war memorial on the grounds that it was a secular monument, a *kinenhi* (remembering or memorializing stone). They also claimed that Mayor Nakai's and other local and national governmental officials' participation in the war memorial ceremonies was an unobjectionable secular folkway, a patriotic and customary practice.

CHAPTER 4

Past Remembering

FOR SATOSHI and Reiko Kamisaka, the political was personal. Their lawsuits were a continuation of life's struggles. Their dispute pitted them and a few supporters against others of their generation in the Japan Association of War Bereaved Families, against local Liberal Democratic Party loyalists, and against younger conservatives. Some of their friends tried to persuade them not to sue because the JAWBF generally enjoyed the support of the people. In addition, the association was headed by former high-ranking officers or their family members and received subsidies from the local and national government.

Reiko Kamisaka, though, recalls her husband frequently saying, "To change the opposite side, our side should change first."[1] Satoshi Kamisaka would stress that even so-called progressive local governments in the 1970s were subsidizing local associations of war-bereaved families to arrange ceremonies at *chūkonhi* war memorials. What was needed, he said, was a change in what was called "progressive local government." Like his wife, Satoshi Kamisaka was committed to fighting what they both perceived as the reemergence of state support for the emperor system and militarism. They were resolved to using the courts to air their grievance, to capture media attention, and to mobilize support for their cause. Still, most of those younger than the Kamisakas' generation probably did not fully appreciate what the couple felt was at stake, or their claim that the city of Minoo had violated constitutional provisions for the separation of government from religion. They had not suffered in the way of the survivors. They had grown up during the long postwar economic expansion.[2]

The Kamisakas' intense opposition to the government's revival of the symbolism of prewar militarism was rooted in the experience of those who had lived through World War II. After the war, Satoshi and Reiko Kamisaka found themselves hospitalized in the Okayama National Sanitarium.[3]

Like many others, they had contracted tuberculosis. At the time, tuberculosis was thought to be incurable, a virtual death sentence. They also remembered how the disabled had been abandoned during the war. Satoshi and Reiko met in the sanitarium, at a meeting of an antinuclear group. They married in 1960, after they were eventually released, in 1957 and 1959, respectively.

Much of Satoshi Kamisaka's childhood and youth were taken away by the war and by his bout with tuberculosis afterward. He had entered the sanitarium in 1949, at the age of nineteen, and was not released until he was twenty-seven years old. He lost one lung in surgery and never quite recovered his health. In the Okayama National Sanitarium, Satoshi Kamisaka also befriended another, older patient, Shigeru Asahi. Kamisaka and Asahi came to share the common cause of fighting the government over the expenses of their medical treatment in the sanitarium. Proud and far from a reluctant litigant, Asahi became well known for waging a battle in the courts against the bureaucracy and for taking his case all the way to the Supreme Court.

As a tuberculosis patient in the 1950s and early 1960s, Asahi received from the government a monthy allowance of 600 yen (about $1.75), along with free meals and medical treatment in the Okayama Sanitarium. When his brother began sending him 1,500 yen ($4.38) a month, the Social Welfare Office stopped the stipend and ordered him to pay 900 yen per month for his medical costs. That left Asahi with 600 yen from what his brother sent. Outraged, Asahi sued and won in the Tokyo District Court, which agreed that the government's allowance was inadequate. It fell below the minimum standards of health and living guaranteed by law and under Article 25 of the Constitution, which provides that "All persons shall have the right to maintain the minimum standards of wholesome and cultured living." The government was ordered to restore Asahi's monthly allowance. But the district court's decision was later reversed by the Tokyo High Court, so Asahi appealed to the Supreme Court.

Asahi died on February 14, 1964. Three years later, the Supreme Court finally rendered its decision, dismissing the suit: Asahi's death was held to have ended the controversy. Constitutional decisions are usually avoided by the Supreme Court, which ostensibly abides by a "rule of strict necessity." That is to say, "constitutional decision making is limited to the unavoidable."[4] In spite of its constitutional authority, the Supreme Court has ruled that many constitutional questions are either "matters of legislative discretion" or "political questions" reserved for the Diet and other governmental agencies, not for the courts, to decide.[5]

Only six times in the entire postwar period has a regulation or law been declared unconstitutional by the Supreme Court.[6] Moreover, none of these rulings brought about major social change. The Diet refused, for instance, to correct the malapportionment in the election of representatives which the Court deemed in 1976, and again in 1985, to be constitutionally impermissible.[7] "In short," as Professor Noriho Urabe puts it, "the Supreme Court of Japan has never said nay to the Government in a serious manner."[8]

When dismissing Asahi's suit, however, the Supreme Court went out of its way to broadly affirm the bureaucracy's discretionary powers. Here, said the Court in an unusually lengthy opinion, "the determination of what 'minimum standards of wholesome and cultured living' actually means [under particular circumstances] is within the discretion of the Minister of Health and Welfare."[9]

The Supreme Court's ruling in *Asahi v. Minister of Health and Welfare* registers the judiciary's deference to the bureaucracy and the primacy of the administrative process for conflict resolution in Japan.[10] The Court's rulings also tend to reverse lower court decisions that have gone against the government. The Court tends, in the words of Osaka University professor Yoshiharu Matsuura, "to legitimize the bureaucracy and to prepare a comfortable context for bureaucratic informalism."[11] In other words, the Court's decisions typically "function as triggers for the bureaucratic process; and the solution of most problems is committed to the bureaucracy."[12]

In 1962, five years before the Supreme Court's ruling on Shigeru Asahi's appeal, the government sued Satoshi Kamisaka for the cost of the medical supplies he had received while in the sanitarium. Despite the fact that the Kamisakas were not wealthy, the government demanded payment of 46,000 yen (approximately $134), which the couple resented. In 1966 a lower court found in favor of Satoshi Kamisaka, but the government remained adamant and appealed. An appellate court finally ruled in 1970 that the government had waited too long to bring its suit and awarded Satoshi Kamisaka 40,000 yen (about $116) in damages.

Inspired by that ruling, and despite the judiciary's well-known deference to the governmental bureaucracy, the Kamisakas persisted in suing Minoo city. "The war," Reiko Kamisaka explained, almost a half-century later, "made us ill, sick, and we have to fight to keep the peace."[13] The *chūkonhi* war memorial, she and her husband claimed, "worshipped as heroic souls men who had looked up to the emperor as a god and died in loyal devotion to the militaristic state. From every point of view, it is in conflict with the peace Constitution."[14]

On Recollection

In 1982, six years after the Kamisakas filed the first of their suits, the Osaka District Court handed down what became known in legal circles as the *Minoo Memorial* case.[15] The presiding judge in this suit remained Yoshinaga Kosaki. Judge Kosaki was a graduate of Tokyo University and the one who had intially suggested to the Kamisakas that they frame their objections to Minoo's expenditures for the *chūkonhi* in terms of the Constitution's separation of the state from religion. With him in finally deciding the case was Judge Takenori Haramiishi, a 43-year-old graduate of Chūō University, and Judge Shigeyuki Uehara, a 33-year-old graduate of Kyoto University, one of Tokyo's principal rivals in university rankings.

Litigation—all litigation—is about remembering, reconstructing the past. But, of course, attorneys and judges are not historians. In court, lawyers argue both about the interpretation and application of legal principles, as well as about disputed facts. Rival constructions of legal principles compete with individual and collective realities. Attorneys aim to persuade by debunking each other's arguments and by contradicting witnesses' testimony and evidence. Adjudication, in short, is neither a scientific process nor a process that would pass muster with historians. At its best, adjudication aims at fairness, not the truth. Inexorably, in the process courts perpetuate and legitimate scripted and selective recollections of the past.

Attorneys for Minoo city had defended the reconstruction of the *chūkonhi* war memorial on the ground that it was simply a secular monument, a remembering stone *(kinenhi)*. They also relied on the Supreme Court's 1977 ruling in the *Tsu City Ground-Purification Ceremony* case when defending the city against the claim that its expenditures for the *chūkonhi* impermissibly promoted religion. In contrast, Satoshi Kamisaka argued that Minoo's war memorial was more than just a *kinenhi*. It was also an object of religious veneration because of the history of the *chūkonhi* and the very inscription *"Chū Kon Hi"* on the memorial. The Kamisakas' attorneys would later concede that *chū-kon* (loyal souls) was a reference that had become less frequently used since the war, because during the Occupation worship of the emperor and other forms of government support for State Shinto had been prohibited. Still, the inscription *Chū Kon Hi* designated the special religious character of the Minoo war memorial. The city's financial support for it thus violated constitutional proscriptions on government assistance for religion.

It is worth noting that the Osaka District Court's ruling came down after the Supreme Court's landmark ruling in the *Tsu City Ground-Purifi-*

cation Ceremony case. Nevertheless, the Kamisakas were victorious. The Osaka District Court held that the war memorial was an object of religious worship. The loyal souls of the 298 war dead memorialized there were venerated and exalted as national deities. The memorial therefore stood as a facility for religious activities. In paying for its reconstruction, Minoo had violated the Constitution by becoming too entangled with religion.

Although Judge Kosaki presided over the district court and announced its ruling in the *Minoo Memorial* case, he was not in fact the drafter of the court's opinion. Instead, more than a year earlier, he had assigned a young assistant judge, Shigeyuki Uehara, who joined the bench in 1979, to draft it. District courts typically work in such a fashion, with the senior presiding judge supervising the business of the court and assigning responsibility for preparing draft opinions to one of the two other judges. As a practical matter, assuming the judges are in agreement, opinion assignments generally rotate back and forth between the two. Judge Kosaki also had Judge Uehara meet with Satoshi Kamisaka privately to discuss the case and the constitutional issues raised. Former judge Uehara recalls numerous meetings with Kamisaka more than half of a year prior to the court's ruling.[16] Because Satoshi Kamisaka was not an attorney and the disestablishment issues presented were complex and sensitive, Judge Uehara explained them to him and clarified legal arguments.

Judges Kosaki, Haramiishi, and Uehara were unanimous in reaching the decision to rule in favor of the Kamisakas. They also did not deem themselves constrained either by the Supreme Court's ruling in the *Tsu City* case or by its "purpose and effect" test. From the outset of their deliberations, they took a broad historical perspective. Presiding Judge Kosaki had personal experience with the role of Yasukuni and *chūkonhi* before and during the war. Although he brought that experience to bear on the case, Uehara remembers that the testimony and briefs filed by expert witnesses proved more influential. Among the four expert witnesses heard was prominent Shinto scholar Yoshiya Abe, who testified for Minoo city and argued that the *chūkonhi* was no longer a religious institution and that the city had not violated the Constitution. In opposition, Shigeyoshi Murakami, another outspoken authority on religion in Japan and the author of *Japanese Religion in the Modern Century,* testified. His view that Minoo had run afoul of the postwar constitution was reinforced by testimony of the highly regarded Gakushūin University constitutional-law professor Nobuyoshi Ashibe.

In reaching its decision, the Osaka District Court granted that there was much that was unprincipled about religion in Japan. Japan was, observed the court, "a peculiar nation which could not distinguish the divine from a human being." In support and as an illustration, the Osaka District Court cited Hirohito's 1946 imperial rescript denying his own divinity. "In order to make the principle of separation of religion from the state take root," the Osaka District Court continued, "we must interpret the principle strictly and carry it through." In addition, under the Local Autonomy Law, the Osaka District Court invalidated the city's rent-free lease of the land. Mayor Nakai was directed to refund 863,840 yen ($4,320), and he and School Board Chairman Kōno were ordered to repay 4,962,600 yen ($24,813) to Minoo city.

Virtually certain to provoke further controversy, the Osaka District Court's ruling was immediately denounced. Outcries of opposition came from Mayor Nakai, the Japan Association of War Bereaved Families, and the leadership of the Liberal Democratic Party. The latter criticized the ruling for striking at the heart of traditional folkways and denied any constitutional violation on the part of Minoo city officials. As the LDP explained in a public statement responding to the decision: "To remember our compatriots who gave their lives for society and the state represents a natural and universal human feeling. The District Court's judgement, which totally negates this natural sentiment of the Japanese people, challenges our traditional spiritual culture."[17]

Without the assistance of an attorney, the Kamisakas had won. Moreover, Reiko Kamisaka recalls that, after the Osaka District Court's ruling, groups and local associations of war-bereaved families in rural parts of Kyushu and Honshu that had been holding ceremonies at local *chūkonhi* war memorials and *gokoku* shrines stopped doing so. Some local governments became less involved with such activities as well. After the district court's decision, the fence around Minoo's *chūkonhi* war memorial was also defaced with spray paint. But leaders of the local association of war-bereaved families left it that way. Physically defiled, its atmosphere was now contaminated, its sacredness marred by controversy. In this way members of the local association for war-bereaved families sought to put the controversy over the *chūkonhi* behind them.

The Osaka District Court's decision in favor of the Kamisakas threw into question the constitutionality of local governments' support for such monuments. The controversy, as it were, escalated. Minoo city and other local government officials were more cautious. They sought ways to avoid becoming further embroiled in the controversy over the *chūkonhi* and the revival of State Shinto.

The Kamisakas' victory would be short-lived, nevertheless. The Kamisakas faced more years of litigation, the judicial bureaucracy, and

A Shinto ceremony conducted at the Minoo *chūkonhi,* April 4, 1978. (Courtesy of Mrs. Reiko Kamisaka)

powerful political forces. Mayor Nakai and his supporters remained defiant and appealed the district court's decision to the Osaka High Court.[18] Out of spite, the round cedar plate with the names of the 298 enshrined souls in Minoo's *chūkonhi* was dug out of the base of the monument. The Kamisakas' attorneys argued that the plate was further evidence of the religious nature of the *chūkonhi.* Now the name plate was gone and, according to the reasoning of local leaders of the association of war-bereaved families, everyone should admit that the monument was not religious.[19]

By the time the Osaka District Court issued its ruling in the *Minoo Memorial* case, Satoshi Kamisaka's health was not good. He doubted that he had the strength to complete the second and third suits filed against Minoo city. After winning the first round, he also thought that the nature of their litigation had changed and could no longer be dismissed as simply a private dispute. They had clearly raised a matter of public-interest litigation and needed the help of experts. The Kamisakas had to hire attorneys.

Over the course of the next decade, ten attorneys eventually worked together in carrying on the Kamisakas' challenge to Minoo city. The Kamisakas could not afford to pay all of their legal expenses. Satoshi Kamisaka had been a public accountant with only a modest income. His wife, Reiko, was a housewife. The attorneys were partially compensated from private contributions of pensioners and a few other supporters, which is not uncommon in interest-group litigation like that of the Kamisakas. Such lawsuits (as discussed in Chapter 1) are used to generate publicity and mobilize support for the plaintiffs' cause. Money was raised from all over Japan to pay for the Kamisakas' legal expenses. Still, the money raised did not cover all the attorneys' expenses. Each of the Kamisakas' lawyers received only about $2,000 a year for his work, about a tenth of what attorneys for Minoo city were paid.[20]

With no little irony, the Kamisakas' lead attorney, Katsuyuki Kumano, points out that, after lawyers were hired, there came a string of defeats in the courts. Like most attorneys in Japan, Kumano is a solo practitioner. He works out of a one-room office shared with a secretary. His office is above a rice store on the second floor of a building in downtown Osaka, not far from the district and high courts. Energetic and devoted to the Kamisakas' cause, Kumano is a Christian, unlike his clients. But like the Kamisakas, Kumano was born during Japan's wars, in 1939. When his mother was battling tuberculosis in 1951, he and his younger brother were baptized. After going to an Anglican Church for a year he stopped, however. He disliked the bickering and "ugly personal quarrels among church members."[21]

Not until the early 1960s, when studying law at Tokyo University, was Kumano truly converted to Christianity. At the time, a massive student-protest movement was on the upsurge. Demonstrations protesting the government's military buildup and the U.S.–Japan Mutual Security Treaty (Anpo) occasionally turned violent. During one such confrontation with police and right-wing supporters in 1960, a female student, Michiko Kanba, was killed, accidentally trampled by student protesters.[22] Kumano remembers later being deeply moved by a speech made by the president of Tokyo University, Tadao Yanaihara. Yanaihara had been purged from the university in 1937 for his antimilitary views, but never stopped criticizing the government's militarism. He was a disciple of

Kanzō Uchimura and the Non-Church Christianity Movement. He returned to the university after the war and eventually became its second president. Kumano recalls Yanaihara's saying, "However dangerous, a man or woman cannot be killed if God wants him or her to work his will in the world. But, if God thinks that he or she is better off going to heaven, he or she will die, however hard."[23] Kumano accepted faith, and it later made him determined to take up the Kamisakas' fight.

A year after the ruling in the *Minoo Memorial* case, the Osaka District Court ruled on the second of the Kamisakas' lawsuits, which had been filed in 1977. As in the first suit, Judge Kosaki presided and sat along with Judge Haramiishi, who had also participated in the earlier ruling. They were now joined by Judge Ryōichi Yagi, a 31-year-old born in Osaka after the war. This time, the outcome of the district court's decision was far less favorable toward the Kamisakas.

The Kamisakas' second suit, the *Minoo Memorial Service* case,[24] challenged the participation of Mayor Nakai and other city officials in memorial services as a violation of Articles 20 and 89 of the Constitution. The Kamisakas also contended that the violations had injured the city itself, and sought damages accordingly. From Mayor Nakai, the Kamisakas asked for 15,041 yen ($75) as a repayment of city officials' salaries for the time they had spent at the services and for the use of some city property. They also sought 3,833 yen ($19) from members of the Board of Education for the use of its property, and another 3,833 yen ($19) for a portion of the salary paid to its chairman, Ryōsaku Kōno, for the two hours he had participated in the memorial services. In total, they sought the repayment of 22,707 yen ($113).

This time, the Osaka District Court rejected on procedural grounds all of the Kamisakas' claims, except one: School Board Chairman Kōno was ordered to pay back 3,833 yen ($19), which was calculated to have been his earnings while participating in the services. The Kamisakas had argued that the services were unquestionably religious. Kōno's and other officials' participation in them thus violated the principle of separation of state and religion. In contrast, the city's lawyers countered that the memorial services were not a religious function per se. Like the Shinto-style ground-purification ceremony that was challenged in the *Tsu City Ground-Purification Ceremony* case, they were a custom that admittedly was accompanied by religious rituals. The services, argued Minoo city's lawyers, nevertheless were a traditional folkway. As for Kōno's and others' participation in the services, the city's attorneys contended, they were merely passive participants who were there as a matter of social courtesy. The city officials had received invitations from the local association of war-bereaved families, and it would have been discourteous for them not to have attended the ceremonies.

As in the *Minoo Memorial* case, the Osaka District Court granted that the Shinto and Buddhist services were religious activities. They were unlike the Shinto-style ground-purification ceremony that the Supreme Court had characterized as having a secular "purpose and effect" in the *Tsu City* case. However, this time the Osaka District Court did not dwell on the issue of the separation of government from religion. Nor did the district court even deal directly with what standard or test should determine whether the disestablishment principle was violated under the Constitution. Instead, the court turned the case virtually upside down.

Focusing on the local association of war-bereaved families, the Osaka District Court observed that such private associations were free to hold religious services. Indeed, the first clause of Article 20 constitutionally guarantees a right of "freedom of religion." That guarantee, held the court, safeguards the right of the association of war-bereaved families and others to hold religious services at the *chūkonhi* war memorial. In other words, the court turned the lawsuit from one over the disestablishment of state religion into one over the free exercise of religion.

Besides turning the controversy around, the Osaka District Court's opinion was narrowly crafted to focus exclusively on School Board Chairman Kōno's participation in the ceremonies—namely, his offerings of incense at the Buddhist ceremony and sprigs of a sacred *sakaki* evergreen tree in the Shinto ceremony. The Osaka District Court thereby managed to cleverly evade the arguments marshalled by the Kamisakas' attorneys.

Kamisaka and his attorneys had basically advanced a twofold argument. On the one hand, Kōno's participation could not be considered a private act, because of his status as chairman of the school board. On the other hand, if his participation were deemed an official act, then he would have violated the provision in clause 2 of Article 20, which stipulates that "No person shall be compelled to take part in any religious acts, celebration, rite or practice." In any event, his participation exceeded permissible conduct under a Local Education Administration Law and clause 3 of Article 20, which specifies in no uncertain terms that, "The State and its organs shall refrain from religious education or any other religious activity." And the city was not obliged to pay his salary while attending the ceremony.

Minoo city's attorneys countered that if Kōno's actions indeed had some relation to religion, they were still permissible because the local association of war-bereaved families was not a religious organization, so that his participation in its services at the *chūkonhi* had not been unconstitutional. In addition, they claimed that the *chūkonhi* was not a religious facility and that the city's support for the association was proper, well within constitutional bounds. Finally, assuming that Kōno's participation in the services were deemed unconstitutional, lawyers for Minoo city argued, his allegedly illegal act had been unintentional and he should not therefore be held liable for it.[25]

The Osaka District Court, however, managed to steer away from what appeared to be the central question: Did School Board Chairman Kōno's participation in the services violate the principle of separation of the state from religion? In the first place, the court observed, it was impossible to characterize Kōno's or other public officials' participation in religious services as official duties. This was an impossiblity because such a construction would violate clause 2 of Article 20, forbidding any person from being "compelled to take part in any religious acts, celebrations, rite or practice." Public officials could never be obligated to participate in a religious ceremony. In the district court's words, "such could never be the case, in view of the right to freedom of worship of the official in question." The Osaka District Court concluded that, "no matter for what purpose or out of what necessity a particular religious service is held, a public official's participation in that service can only be construed as the act of a private individual according to the Constitution."[26]

On the district court's keen reasoning, the principle of religious freedom in clause 2 of Article 20 could be considered to have been violated only if School Board Chairman Kōno's participation were deemed an official act. But that was impossible, according to the Osaka District Court, because it would violate the constitutional guarantee of freedom of religion spelled out in clause 2 of Article 20—a freedom enjoyed by public officials no less than private citizens. Thus the issue of the separation of the state from religion raised by Satoshi Kamisaka fell by the wayside, and Kōno's participation in the services could only be considered that of a private citizen.

The Osaka District Court effectively turned the Kamisakas' suit over the disestablishment of state-sponsored religion into one over the exercise of religious freedom. School Board Chairman Kōno's participation had to be deemed a private act under the Constitution. Still, since he had been paid by the city for the time he spent at the services in his capacity as a private citizen, the Osaka District Court reasoned that he had received an "unjust gain." Kōno had to repay 3,833 yen ($19), that portion of his salary paid by the government for the two hours he had spent as a private citizen participating in a religious service.

Kumano and the Kamisakas' other lawyers viewed the ruling as a defeat. Yet it remained a small victory. In the years ahead, their cause would be dealt far more serious blows. In 1986, Satoshi Kamisaka suddenly collapsed into unconsciousness and passed away. Not until the following year did the Osaka High Court finally hand down its ruling on Mayor Nakai's and Chairman Kōno's appeals of the district court's decisions. When it did, on July 16, 1987, the Osaka High Court wiped away all of the Kamisakas' earlier successes.[27]

Judge Shigeru Imatomi presided on the Osaka High Court. He sat with Judges Ikuo Hata and Kenji Endō, who were 56 and 44 years old, respectively. When vacating the district court's rulings and orders in the *Minoo Memorial* and the *Minoo Memorial Service* cases, 62-year-old Judge Imatomi dismissed the Kamisakas' claims out of hand, in an opinion that turned somersaults with history. First, Minoo was held not to have violated the Constitution in paying for the *chūkonhi* war memorial's relocation. Judge Imatomi held for the Osaka High Court that, contrary to the district court, the memorial was not an object of religious worship. Second, he ruled that the memorial services were not necessarily religious activities but social customs or folkways. Finally, Mayor Nakai's, School Board Chairman Kōno's, and other public officials' participation in the memorial services were deemed not to violate the Constitution.

In reviewing the history and role of war memorials, the Osaka High Court emphasized their part during the Meiji era in fostering civic responsibility and patriotism. Their connection with State Shinto was also acknowledged, though only briefly. Then, without mentioning the Occupation's destruction of hundreds of similar *chūkonhi* war memorials or the people's burial of Minoo's war memorial in order to escape that fate, the Osaka High Court claimed that, after World War II, such memorials were not generally understood as religious or used for the purpose of propagandizing militarism.

Regardless of the epitaph *"Chū Kon Hi"* inscribed on the stone memorial and its close connection with Yasukuni Shrine, the high court ruled that the memorial was not an object of religious worship. In so doing, the Osaka High Court conveniently neglected to address the Kamisakas' arguments that the epitaph *"Chū Kon Hi"*—and the fact that the memorial embodied the souls of 298 faithful war dead who were also enshrined in Yasukuni—clearly established Minoo city's war memorial as an object of religious veneration.

Turning next to the memorial services sponsored by the local association of war-bereaved families, the Osaka High Court stressed that the latter was a private association, not a religious organization aimed at promoting religion. The high court simply avoided mentioning, or even noting, the well-established historical ties between the Japan Association of War Bereaved Families and Yasukuni.

The Osaka High Court then turned to the purpose and effect of the memorial services. Its analysis of the memorial services and the city officials' participation in them was far from clear, however. Specifically, it remained unclear whether the high court was following the Supreme Court's reasoning in the *Tsu City Ground-Purification Ceremony* case.[28] The *Tsu City* case had been criticized by Tokyo University professor Shinichi Takayanagi, among others. He had challenged the Court's application of the so-called purpose and effect test and had criticized it for failing to distinguish between (a) instances where the government assists religion, and (b) instances when the government itself conducts religious activities, which arguably violate the U.S. Constitution's prohibition on the establishment of religion.

The Osaka High Court responded that such a distinction and the U.S. Supreme Court's rulings on disestablishment were not directly applicable in Japan. Still, the high court proceeded to stress that even the U.S. Supreme Court applies different tests or standards in cases involving challenges to governmental assistance for religion. Within that context, the Osaka High Court cited approvingly, but without further elaboration, rulings of the U.S. Supreme Court on the First Amendment's disestablishment of religion that are often cited by the Supreme Court of Japan.

Among those rulings cited by the high court were: *School District of Abington Township, Pennsylvania v. Schempp* (1963), striking down the mandatory reading of the Lord's Prayer in public schools at the start of each school day;[29] *McGowan v. State of Maryland* (1961), upholding "Sunday closing" laws over the objections of Orthodox Jews, for whom Saturday is the Sabbath;[30] *Stone v. Graham* (1980), striking down a state law requiring the posting of the Ten Commandments in public school classrooms;[31] and *Widmar v. Vincent* (1981), striking down a state law prohibiting state university buildings from being used for the "purpose of religious worship."[32]

The citation of these particular rulings suggests that the Osaka High Court deemed it unconstitutional for the government to directly endorse or advance religion, following *Schempp* and *Stone*. At the same time, the high court appeared to endorse the position that the general public's or community's interests overrode the interests of religious minorities, as in *McGowan*. Moreover, the court appeared to indicate that the government should not be hostile to religion or to the general public's or community's religious values, as in *Widmar*. The high court thereby implicitly drew a very fine thin line between the government and religion.

In any event, the purpose of the Shinto and Buddhist services, according to the Osaka High Court, was not primarily religious. Although the origins of the services were religious, the court held that their purpose was now merely to honor and console the souls of the 298 war dead. The primary effect of the services was to pay a social courtesy, to advance social welfare and harmony, not to endorse any particular religion. In short, the memorial services were a social custom, a folkway. Therefore, they certainly could not be construed to be unconstitutional.

Last but not least, the Osaka High Court ruled on the issue of public officials' participation in the memorial services. Not unexpectedly, given its earlier reasoning, the high court held that Mayor Nakai and School Board Chairman Kōno were merely paying a social courtesy by attending the ceremonies. They had done so, noted the court, at the invitation of the local association of war-bereaved families. Kōno, said Presiding Judge Imatomi, had a "social obligation" to attend the ceremonies. The Osaka High Court once again failed to mention that Minoo city officials had subsidized the association and that part of the city's subsidy had paid the costs of organizing the services in the first place. That, of course, made it easier for the high court to hold that the mayor's and other officials' participation in the services was a matter of social etiquette, a "social obligation." Mayor Nakai, School Board Chairman Kōno, and other public officials had thus neither done anything illegal nor "gained unjustly." They therefore did not have to reimburse Minoo city for the portions of their salaries they were paid while participating in the services.

The message of the Osaka High Court's ruling was unmistakable and hit home in the local district court. The following year, eleven years after the Kamisakas had filed the third of their suits, the *Minoo Subsidy* case,[33] the Osaka District Court finally handed down its decision. This time, 54-year-old Judge Norio Yamamoto presided. He was joined by 40-year-old Judge Norio Oikawa and Judge Yumiko Tokuoka, who at age 26 had just begun her judicial career the previous year. Neither the accumulation of earlier rulings, the operation of the judiciary, nor the district court's composition boded well for the Kamisakas' third suit against Minoo city.

In this suit, the Kamisakas and their neighbors challenged the city's payment of subsidies to the local association of war-bereaved families. The association received an annual subsidy as a member of the city's Social Welfare Council, along with other organized interest groups that had membership on the council. Part of that subsidy paid for the expenses of sponsoring the memorial services held at the *chūkonhi* war memorial. In addition, the city provided the association with services and the use of public property when organizing and holding the memorial services. The city provided the use of a conference room for meetings, for example, stationery for sending out invitations to the services, and the use of city cars and a microbus for transporting participants.

Minoo city's annual subsidy to the association of war-bereaved families was a benefit of membership on the local Social Welfare Council. In a country permeated by group consciousness and with interest-group politics so well entrenched, governmental subsidies are expected. Elected officials dole out financial assistance in exchange for support at the ballot box. Groups organize for the purpose of both advancing their interests and receiving governmental subsidies. The Minoo Association of War Bereaved Families was no exception in this regard. The Social Welfare Council included representatives of the Seniors' Group, the Childrens' Group, the Disabled Veterans' Group, the Boy Scouts, the Red Cross, and the Survivors of Atomic Bomb Group, among others.

The local association of war-bereaved families received the largest share of the subsidies given out by Minoo's Social Welfare Council. In 1975, when the controversy over relocating the *chūkonhi* war memorial began, the association received an allocation of 445,000 yen ($2,225), which was close to half of its total budget that year of 1,096,240 yen ($5,481). The largest expenditure, 330,900 yen ($1,654), of the association that year was for the expenses of members to travel to Yasukuni. Four years later, in 1979, that amount had increased to 617,000 yen ($3,085). In part because of the size of its membership, the association was allotted over 15 percent of the council's total budget, more than any other group. The Parents' Association received 10.7 percent of the council's budget, the Mother and Child Welfare Fund received 10.1 percent, the Seniors' Group got 9.96 percent, and the Red Cross was given 8.6 percent. All other groups on the council received subsidies of less than 10 percent of the budget. Several groups received a share that amounted to only 1 or 2 percent of the council's total budget for the year.[34]

The basis for the Kamisakas' challenge to Minoo city's financial support for the association of war-bereaved families was, perhaps, the most difficult of the three suits for some of their neighbors to appreciate. In the first place, the suit struck at the heart of the politics of money. It attacked the reciprocal dependency of elected officials and voters at the local level of government. Second, the association of war-bereaved families was singled out from all the other groups receiving financial assistance from the government.

The Minoo chapter of the Japan Association of War Bereaved Families (JAWBF), furthermore, had the largest local membership and was, of course, affiliated with a well-connected national organization. About half of all war-bereaved families in the country are estimated to belong to the

Japan Association of War Bereaved Families.[35] Not only do regional and local associations of war-bereaved families typically receive some financial support, virtually every household of a survivor of the prewar generations receives a pension paid by the national government upon the retirement or death of the head of the household.

The JAWBF had also been at the forefront of a drive for pension reform. It initially waged a campaign after the war and finally succeeded, in 1952, in persuading the Diet to pass legislation creating a pension system for servicemen's households. In 1955, the JAWBF successfully lobbied for an increase in the pensions and has relentlessly pressed for further increases ever since. The JAWBF's campaigns for pension reform were based on the rank of the servicemen and, not surprisingly, were advanced with arguments dear to the hearts of hard-line conservatives in the LDP and the government.[36] In a 1982 position statement calling for improved treatment and more governmental financial assistance, for instance, the JAWBF bluntly and controversially stated its bottom line: "Enriching the state compensation to war-deads' and war-bereaved families is the very foundation of advancement of [the] people's defense consciousness."[37]

The JAWBF's campaigns for pension reform proposed to increase the size of the pensions for those in the highest ranks. That would have honored and greatly compensated those who had held high positions of authority during the war; it would also have provided an incentive for younger servicemen to stay in the service and strive to rise in rank. In 1952, for example, when the JAWBF successfully lobbied for a pension system, under the pension system created, the highest-ranking officer received over six times the amount of the lowest. Subsequently, and in the face of its lack of success in getting further major pension reform, the association moderated its pension reform proposals. In 1978, for instance, the JAWBF sought an increase in support that was only three times as great for the highest-ranking officers as for the lowest-ranking servicemen.[38]

The JAWBF's move toward advocating pension reforms in the 1970s and 1980s that would have narrowed the gap between the highest and lowest pensions paid was prudent and tactical. By the late 1980s, there were fewer surviving high-ranking officials of the generation that had served during World War II. The numbers of younger generations of servicemen's sons, daughters, and families that the association needed to attract and retain as constituents were inexorably growing. The government, however, maintained its policy on pensions based on a combination of rank and parity considerations. In 1993, the highest-ranking officials were still eligible for pensions that remained more than six times larger than those given to the lowest-ranking servicemen. A general thus was eligible for up to 23 percent of the highest salary paid in that rank (7 million yen, or $67,307), whereas the lowest-ranking private would receive 46 percent of his salary (1.186 million yen, or $11,403).[39]

The Kamisakas' challenge to the financial support given by Minoo city to the association of war-bereaved families was thus difficult for some neighbors to appreciate. The local association, like other groups on the Social Welfare Council, was entitled to an annual subsidy, which was generally considered to be small. In addition, before the war, local governments had paid for such memorial services. That had ended during the Occupation. But after Minoo's *chūkonhi* war memorial was reconstructed in 1950, the city had resumed its subsidies, which continued for a quarter of a century without controversy, until the Kamisakas' lawsuit.

For some of their generation, and for those born after the Occupation, the Kamisakas' constitutional attack on the long-standing practice and policy of subsidizing the local association of war-bereaved families appeared to be unnecessary troublemaking. Many of those younger than the Kamisakas did not fully appreciate the significance of *chūkonhi* war memorials or the services held there. But members of the Kamisakas' generation who disagreed with them, and conservatives in the LDP, knew the significance of the *chūkonhi* and the memorial services held there. For them, such services represented continuity with the past and with prewar days.

The Kamisakas deemed their third suit to be just as critical as the first two. Although all three were equally important, Reiko Kamisaka points out that the third suit, challenging as it did the constitutionality of Minoo's subsidizing its local association of war-bereaved families, had in a certain respect the potential for the greatest impact. This was because, throughout the country, affiliates of the Japan Association of War Bereaved Families received subsidies from local governments—subsidies that were generally used in part to pay the expenses of their members traveling to Tokyo to visit Yasukuni.

Travel from rural areas and other parts of Japan to Yasukuni and Tokyo is expensive. For instance, to go from Minoo and Osaka to Tokyo by *shinkansen* (literally, "new trunk line" or, more commonly, "bullet train") takes three hours, and the round-trip costs well over $250. Tokyo hotels are expensive, even with special discounts at the Kudan Kaikan for members of the Japan Association of War Bereaved Families. Because the JAWBF is so closely linked to Yasukuni, a religious organization, Mrs. Kamisaka emphasizes, there is "no public interest served by giving money to the association." "To prohibit the subsidy" given by Minoo and other local governments, she adamantly maintains, "the Court should say the association is a kind of religious group."[40]

At the trial of the Kamisakas' third suit against Minoo city over its subsidies to the association of war-bereaved families, expert witnesses testified for both sides. The leading witness for the Kamisakas was Ken Arai, Tokyo's University of Komazawa (a Buddhist university) professor of literature and the sociology of religion. Professor Arai offered testimony about the nature of religion and its function as a "system of symbols." He also discussed Japanese religious consciousness and criticized the Supreme Court's reasoning in the *Tsu City Ground-Purification Ceremony* ruling.

Most poignantly, Arai testified that Yasukuni's cult of war dead was a manifestation of "a particular religion," and that Minoo's *chūkonhi* was the local representation of Yasukuni Shrine. Contrary to the city's attorneys and witnesses, he maintained that the association of war-bereaved families was basically a religious organization intimately engaged in promoting religious activities related to Yasukuni. Minoo's subsidies to the association, in Arai's opinion, violated the Constitution.[41]

The main expert witness for Minoo was Yoshiya Abe, a Kokugakuin University professor of Shinto studies. Kokugakuin University is one of two Shinto universities, has a department for training students who will become Shinto priests, and was once the Institute for the Study of Imperial Classics. Abe earned a Ph.D. at Claremont Graduate School in Claremont, California, and has the manner of the stereotypical Oxford don. Affable, charming, witty, and argumentative, he is also shrewdly serious. Abe, of course, testified in a written statement that Minoo's *chūkonhi* was not religious. "It has a tower-like stone," according to him, "and the rituals conducted in front of the *chūkonhi* are not religion." Drawing on the *Tsu City Ground-Purification Ceremony* case, Abe stressed that the Supreme Court had held that "other similar ceremonies are not religious."

As for the association of war-bereaved families, Abe claimed it was a "welfare organization" concerned with "the material and spiritual welfare of war-bereaved families. They are special people." Their activities and participation in rites at the *chūkonhi*, according to Abe, are no different from those conducted at the memorial for war dead in Hiroshima or the Tomb of the Unknown Soldier in Tokyo. "The Kamisakas saw them as religious," he says, "but I doubt that the believers would say so." So, too, Minoo's subsidies were not unconstitutional because, as Abe would have it, "public money is spent for the *chūkonhi* and therefore it's public, not religious." Precisely because of the disestablishment principle, he cleverly reasons, the constitutional separation of the state from religion means that "religion is only private under the Constitution."[42]

Outside the courtroom, much later, Abe agreed that "as a religious scientist I would not take that position. I was confining myself to this particular case and confining myself to how I can win." To say that the *chūkonhi* is not religious, he confessed, "requires a great deal of tricks and techniques. If you want to make the *chūkonhi* a Shinto shrine," he admitted, "you can." His strategy and tactic had been "to make the issue arguable, so no conclusion can be drawn." The controversy over religion was basically a smoke screen anyway. "The Kamisakas' attorneys," in Abe's words, "were really arguing about democracy versus militarism."[43]

In light of the Osaka High Court's earlier ruling reversing the lower court's decisions in the Kamisakas' first two cases, the Osaka District Court had, perhaps, little choice but to hold that the local association of war-bereaved families was not a religious organization engaged in religious activities. Indeed, the Osaka District Court ruled that the association had a secular purpose in honoring the souls of the 298 war dead. Although the court conceded the association's close connection to Yasukuni, it held that the association's purpose in honoring the souls of the war dead was not religious but secular, that is, aimed merely at comforting war-bereaved families.

Almost predictably, but still unbelievably, in the *Minoo Subsidy* case the Osaka District Court ruled that the association of war-bereaved families had a broad range of social activities. To be sure, the court admitted that the association had been "closely linked to Yasukuni Shrine from the beginning" and that, "The business of admiring the loyal war dead by the Association is essentially inclined to have an affinity with and link to the religious service and religious ideology of Yasukuni Shrine." But the Osaka District Court now stressed that, after World War II, "Yasukuni Shrine lost the character of a facility of religious service managed by the state, and State Shinto ceased to exist." The court thus reached the rather disingenuous conclusion that "the linkage of the war bereaved families and Yasukuni Shrine was not so strong as before."

While conceding that the JAWBF's "main purpose was the business of admiring the loyal war dead" and that "members support actively or at least implicitly the policy of the Association relating to raising the status of Yasukuni Shrine by reinstituting state support of the Shrine," the Osaka District Court emphasized that the association had been founded to promote the "welfare of bereaved families in poverty." Hence the district court concluded that "It can not be said that religious activities related to Yasukuni Shrine occupy an absolutely high percentage of all the business of the Association." Nor, said the court, contrary to the Kamisakas' claims, could the association be clearly characterized as having the religious activity of promoting the "teachings and belief of Yasukuni Shrine."

Minoo's *chūkonhi* war memorial, the Osaka District Court also conceded, had a "common religious and ideological basis with Yasukuni Shrine and Gokoku Shrine." Yet the court nevertheless characterized the *chūkonhi* as having "an essential character of the memorial stone for the war dead," not that of a "facility for religious service." Again the court made the points that "the system of State Shinto was destroyed" and that no governmental policy forced public officials to worship at the *chūkonhi*. The court did so to buttress its conclusion that it could not "help looking upon the *chūkonhi* as a monument for chiefly mourning and admiring the war dead." In sum, in the court's view, there was "no objective factor indicating that the *chūkonhi* itself continues to stand as a religious facility."

The financial assistance given by Minoo city to the local association of war-bereaved families was not unconstitutional. The city did not have to be repaid for its subsidies. Besides characterizing the association's activities as not primarily religious and dismissing the Kamisakas' contention that the *chūkonhi* remained a "religious facility" after the war, the court described the city's subsidy as having only a secular purpose and effect. In the words of the district court,

> The subsidy in question is secular in assisting the Association on a standpoint of welfare promotion for the bereaved families, and its effect only results in assisting indirectly its activity relating to religion by assisting it. Its activity relating to religion is only a link in the chain of activities for psychological consolation of the war bereaved families, like memorial service included naturally in its business, since it is the body of the war bereaved families. It does not aim at religious activity itself for spreading belief for a particular religion.

Finally, the Osaka District Court supported its dubious analysis by pointing out that Minoo city's subsidy for the association constituted "less than half of its annual revenue in 1976." The court thus claimed it could not be said either that the local association of war-bereaved families was "managed chiefly on the subsidy" or "that the subsidy was improper in its amount."

The issue of governmental subsidies raised in the *Minoo Subsidy* case had been submerged in the courts all along. Yet in certain respects it was pivotal to all the litigation: Minoo city subsidized the association of war-bereaved families, and its subsidies covered the costs of the memorial services in the first place. This remains the virtually hidden yet crucial aspect of the postwar government's assistance for religious activities. It was the root both of the government's entanglement with religion and of conservatives' endeavors to revive State Shinto.

Except for the controversy the Kamisakas had raised over the matter, Minoo's payments to the association were hardly unique. The Japan Association of War Bereaved Families, often with the support of the Self Defense Forces, had for over two decades been organizing regional and local affiliates, especially on the rural island of Kyushu. Money was funneled to these regional and local affiliates for conducting Shinto ceremonies, enshrining dead soldiers, and so that members could travel to Tokyo to visit the Yasukuni Shrine. Local government officials also catered to regional and local associations of war-bereaved families, disbursing small amounts of financial assistance to ensure their support at election time. Such practices, especially among conservative LDP politicans, were in accord with long-established patron-client social networks and the traditional understanding of reciprocal dependency in social and political relations.[44]

Such governmental support was precisely what the Kamisakas had found most objectionable and deemed the opening wedge for a possible return of State Shinto and renewed militarism. Their lawsuit sought to impress on people and the government the need to take seriously the constitutional provisions for the separation of government from religion.

After hearing of the Osaka District Court's decision, Mayor Nakai told reporters he was pleased and held the court in high esteem. The years of litigation and controversy, though, had made him more cautious and circumspect. Mayor Nakai now said that he would adhere to his policy of not attending memorial services at the *chūkonhi*. Nevertheless, Mrs. Kamisaka was further disappointed. She complained that the court had refused to see the "true nature" of *chūkonhi* and the JAWBF and that its decision cleared the way for renewed militarism and war.[45]

At a protest rally held outside of the Osaka District Court at the time of its ruling, Reiko Kamisaka's son, Naoki, carried a large banner reading, "The People Lost: 'The Way to Yasukuni' Is Coming." This was a particularly poignant expression of dissent, especially for World War II survivors. During the war, the expression "The Way to Yasukuni Shrine" was well known. It referred to the gruesome fact that soldiers fighting in the jungles of Asia would occasionally retreat from the battlefield on the orders of military commanders. Many then died in the jungle. Those who were wounded or too weak to keep up were ordered to kill themselves. They could then be reported by their commanders as "killed in action," rather than as missing or having surrendered.

Soldiers who were missing in action or who surrendered, which was illegal, could never be enshrined in Yasukuni, which was a precondition for their families to receive compensation and pensions from the government. Committing suicide was thus the only thing that wounded soldiers

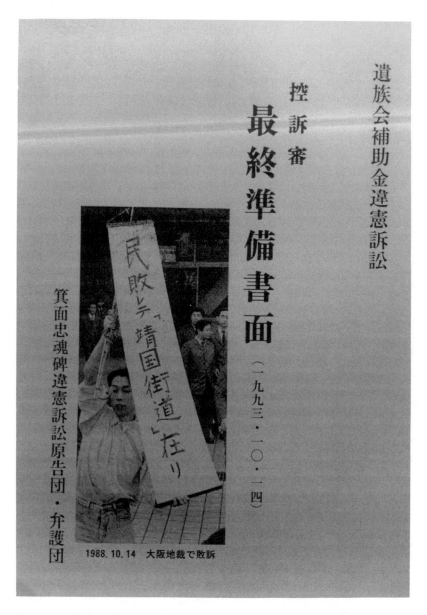

遺族会補助金違憲訴訟

控訴審

最終準備書面 （一九九三・一〇・一四）

箕面忠魂碑違憲訴訟原告団・弁護団

民敗レテ「靖国街道」在リ

1988.10.14　大阪地裁で敗訴

The cover of a brief filed by the Kamisakas' attorneys, with a picture of Naoki
Kamisaka carrying a protest banner at a rally in front of the Osaka District Court.
The banner reads, "The People Lost: The 'Way to Yasukuni' Is Coming."
(Courtesy of Mr. Katsuyuki Kumano)

could do to provide for their families. The soldiers' flesh would then be eaten away by insects, tropical flies, and maggots. A trail of white skeletons was left behind, and "the way of white skeletons" marked "the Way to Yasukuni." Such an emotional reminder of the past could not have sat well with Yasukuni's supporters either inside or outside of the government. It may also have proven costly for Naoki Kamisaka later on, in ways that he could not have foreseen at the time.

Reiko Kamisaka, who carried on after her husband's death as a plaintiff in the litigation, continued to lament the rulings of the Osaka District and High Courts. Mrs. Kamisaka, Mrs. Furukawa, and Mrs. Hamuro vowed to appeal to the Supreme Court of Japan. Their attorneys would appeal the Osaka High Court's ruling on grounds for appeals set forth in the Code of Civil Procedure. The high court's holding that the *chūkonhi* was not a religious monument had failed to fully address the Kamisakas' argument that the memorial had a dual character, that it was both secular and sacred. Their attorneys would contend that the Osaka High Court had violated Article 191 of the Code of Civil Procedure, which provides that a court's opinion must deal with the facts and issues presented, as well as set forth the reasons for its conclusions.

Articles 394 and 395 of the Code of Civil Procedure also provided bases for appeal. Article 394 authorizes appeals when a court's reasoning contradicts the "law of inference"; Article 395 stipulates that appeals for reconsideration of a ruling may be made when a court's judgment is inconsistent with the law and evidence at issue. Contrary to the district court, and without explanation, the high court had ruled that the *chūkonhi* was not religious. Wittingly or unwittingly, the high court's ruling gave the Kamisakas' attorneys a basis for appealing to the Supreme Court of Japan.

The issues represented in the *Minoo War Memorial* litigation would not go away. They remained linked to national and local governments' funding of Shinto ceremonies and public officials' participation in them, as well as their visits to Yasukuni. These would remain matters of litigation and political controversy. Still, given the appointment process and operation of the judiciary in Japan, the prospects for more favorable rulings on the Kamisakas' appeals appeared to be remote.

Transforming the Past

The Kamisakas and their attorneys were by no means alone in challenging what they considered to be a conspiracy to revive State Shinto. As the economic prosperity of the 1970s and 1980s grew, the Liberal Democratic

Party, the Self Defense Forces, and the Japan Association of War Bereaved Families gradually became more outspoken about renewing governmental support for Yasukuni, regional *gokoku* shrines, and *chūkonhi* war memorials.

In places besides Minoo, there were controversies over local governments' financial assistance for *chūkonhi* war memorials and Shinto ceremonies glorifying the souls of war dead. Almost invariably, the litigation arising from these controversies was brought by Christians, Buddhists, socialists, and liberals, who insisted on a "high wall of separation" between the state and religion. Their lawsuits tended to follow the same basic pattern of the *Minoo War Memorial* litigation: namely, lengthy delays, prolonged judicial decisionmaking, and district courts occasionally ruling against local governments, only to be overturned on appeal by regional high courts.

With the exception of two high court rulings on local officials' and the prime minister's official participation in Yasukuni Shrine services,[46] the district and appellate court rulings advancing a strict separation of the state and religion that came down in the 1970s and early 1980s were later reversed (see Table 5).

At least in the area of religious freedom litigation, and some other areas of public-interest litigation, lower courts tended to be somewhat more receptive to the claims of the plaintiffs, although higher courts remained less so.[47] In Japan, which is basically a civil law, not a common law country, the principle of *stare decisis* (precedent) has never been formally adopted, and lower court rulings occasionally run contrary to those of the Supreme Court.[48] Moreover, in the prewar era, Supreme Court decisions were not considered legally binding or controlling in other cases.[49] As Japan's postwar Court Organization Law stipulates, "a conclusion in a decision of a superior court shall bind courts below in respect of the case concerned," but not in respect to other, related cases.[50]

Consistency and avoidance of controversy are highly regarded, however. Hence lower courts appear generally to follow precedents laid down by higher courts, for a combination of reasons. First, in Japan's hierarchical judicial system, in which judges periodically come up for reappointment and may be reassigned to less desirable positions under the supervision of the chief justice and the General Secretariat of the Supreme Court, lower court judges may be disinclined to go against higher courts' rulings.

Second, jurisdictional and appellate procedures also contribute to lower courts' conformity with the Supreme Court's decisions: an appeal of a district court's decision to a high court, for instance, may concern both the facts and the law at stake, whereas an appeal from a high court to the Supreme Court may only raise questions of law, such as the constitutionality of a regulation or a lower court's failure to provide sound reasoning or analysis for its decision. As a result, the Supreme Court is technically bound by the lower courts' findings of facts and focuses only on questions of legal interpretation.[51]

Third, although the Supreme Court has occasionally expressly reversed itself, the justices' reliance on the Court's law clerks, plus its annual docket of more than five thousand cases that carries with it heavy workload, promotes reliance on precedent.

In the 1989 *Ehime Shrine Donation* case, for example, the Matsuyama District Court held that the governor of Ehime prefecture, Haruki Shiraishi, and six other government officials had violated Article 20 by using public funds to pay for offerings of flowers and sacred *sakaki* ever-green trees at the regional *gokoku* (country-protecting) shrine and at Yasukuni. The suit was brought by twenty-four local residents, led by the chief priest of the Buddhist Senneji Temple, Kenji Anzai. On twenty-two occasions between 1981 and 1987, the Ehime government had made small donations, ranging from 5,000 to 10,000 yen each, for a total of 166,000 yen (approximately $813) given to the shrines.

District Court Judge Kazuaki Yamashita ordered Governor Shiraishi to repay the money to the city because the donations constituted "a special bond" between the government and the Shinto shrines in direct violation of Article 20. While Chief Priest Anzai and his supporters applauded Judge Yamashita's decision as "brave," at a press conference afterward

Table 5   Major Rulings on Religious Disestablishment and Freedom

CASE	DISTRICT COURT	HIGH COURT	SUPREME COURT
Tsu Ground-Purification Ceremony	*	o	*
Minoo Memorial	o	*	*
Minoo Memorial Service	o	*	*
Minoo Subsidy	*	*	
Self Defense Force Enshrinement	o	o	*
Iwate Yasukuni Visitation	*	o	
Ehime Shrine Donation	o	*	
Osaka Yasukuni Visitation	*	o	
Fukuoka Yasukuni Visitation	*	*	
Kobe Yasukuni Visitation	*	*	
Nagasaki Monument Subsidy	o	*	
Kagoshima Imperial Rites Aid	*		

* = Rulings supporting the government.
o = Rulings against the government.

Governor Shiraishi denounced the ruling as "unreasonable" and swore to appeal. Confident that he would prevail, Governor Shiraishi claimed that "it is only natural" for the government to pay its respects to the war dead on behalf of local residents. The donations were, in his view, nothing more than "social protocol."[52]

The following year, the Nagasaki District Court likewise signaled a move, however slight, in the direction of a strict construction of the constitutional guarantees for the separation of the state from religion. In reaching its decision in the *Nagasaki Monument Subsidy* case, however, the district court carefully crafted an exceedingly narrow ruling. Ironically, this suit had been brought by Masaharu Oda, the pastor of the Nagasaki Evangelical Lutheran Church, and several of his followers against Hitoshi Motoshima, the city's outspoken and controversial mayor, who was a Catholic. Beginning in 1978, Mayor Motoshima had annually earmarked a maintenance subsidy of 40,000 yen for each of Nagasaki's fourteen monuments and memorial centopahs dedicated to war dead. Pastor Oka sued for the return of the maintenance subsidy set aside in 1981, which amounted to 560,000 yen (about $2,500 at the time).

Mayor Motoshima had once been a senior leader of the local chapter of the Liberal Democratic Party (LDP). He therefore had to cater to its conservative supporters in the Nagasaki Association of War Bereaved Families. Nagasaki, rebuilt after the war, lies on the coast of the beautiful rural island of Kyushu, the home of large rice producers and small farmers. Politically very conservative, Kyushu is also known for having sent large numbers of its youth into World War II, and for having the Self Defense Forces continue after the war to recruit disproportionately from the island. Associations of war-bereaved families remain especially active on Kyushu. In the 1970s, moreover, they began paying for new enshrinements of deceased soldiers and officers, typically with the assistance of regional SDF offices and local governments.

Mayor Motoshima let down his guard and was ousted from the local chapter of the LDP, however, because he refused to retract some highly inflammatory remarks made at a municipal assembly meeting. When, on December 7, 1988, a Communist Party member asked him to comment on the city's registry for imperial well-wishers and on the emperor's guilt for World War II, Mayor Motoshima—seemingly modestly but, as it turned out, extremely controversially—observed that,

> Forty-three years have passed since the end of the war, and I think we have been able to reflect sufficiently on the nature of that war. From reading various materials from abroad as well as the writings of Japanese historians, and

from my actual experiences in military service, where I was especially involved in educating the troops ... I think that the Emperor does bear responsibility for the war. However, by the will of the great majority of the Japanese people as well as of the Allied powers, he was released from having to take responsibility and became the symbol of the new Constitution. My interpretation is that we must adhere to that position.[53]

Later, in response to questions from reporters, the three-time mayor added fuel to what would erupt into a fireball of controversy by further stating that

It is clear from historical records that if the Emperor, in response to the reports of his senior statesmen, had resolved to end the war earlier, there would have been no Battle of Okinawa, no nuclear attacks on Hiroshima and Nagasaki. I myself belonged to the education unit in the western division of the army, and I instructed the troops to die for the Emperor. I have friends who died shouting "banzai" to the Emperor. I am a Christian, and I had difficult moments as a child when I was pressed to answer the question, "Who do you think is greater, the Emperor or Christ?"[54]

For those remarks, and for refusing to cave in to pressures from hard-line conservatives and ultranationalists, Mayor Motoshima confronted more than just bitter criticism. He was denounced as un-Japanese, thrown out of the local LDP chapter, and received numerous death threats. In fact, the 69-year-old mayor was in the hospital recovering from a serious gun-shot wound when the Nagasaki District Court announced its decision on February 20, 1990. A month earlier he had been shot in the back by an ultranationalist conservative in front of the Nagasaki City Hall.

When handing down the Nagasaki District Court's ruling, presiding Judge Shigetoshi Matsushima held that the subsidies for all but one of the fourteen memorials were constitutional under Article 20. The remaining one, the Sakoumegasaki *chūkonhi* war memorial, had been erected as a local affiliate of Yasukuni before the war. It remained a site for memorial services conducted by Shinto priests from the regional *gokoku* (country-protecting) shrine. That was too close an association or entanglement of the government with religion, Judge Matsushima concluded.

Judge Matsushima's opinion nonetheless stretched reason and history. He bent over backward to concede a great deal to the city and the local association of war-bereaved families. Before and during World War II, such war memorials had been considered sacred or divine, Judge Matsushima admitted. But after the war the late Emperor Hirohito, Shōwa, had renounced his divinity, and the Shinto Directive had mandated a complete separation of Shinto and the state. Under the 1947 Constitution, the emperor became only a symbol of the unity of the state and the people. Accordingly, state-supported Shinto was no longer permitted.

Nor, Judge Matsushima added, rather surprisingly, was the prewar militaristic ideology of apotheosis, of deifying those loyal souls who died for the sake of the emperor, supported any longer. Yet he conveniently failed to mention that enshrinements were still supported both by local associations of war-bereaved families and by some high-ranking officials in the LDP and the Self Defense Forces. The logic of this part of Judge Matsushima's opinion was tortured. It conspicuously and conveniently neglected aspects of social reality that were contrary to what the court said and held.

Drawing on the Supreme Court's ruling in the *Tsu City Ground-Purification Ceremony* case, Judge Matsushima ruled that ceremonies held at war memorials had become secular or social folkway ceremonies. As such, they were not unconstitutional, especially in light of the fact, Judge Matsushima emphasized, that Shinto, Buddhist, or Christian rites might be held there. Still, the judge drew the line at Mayor Motoshima's subsidy for the one *chūkonhi* war memorial. Its close identification with the regional *gokoku* shrine and Yasukuni rendered it, alone among the subsidized memorials, religious in nature. Hence Judge Matsushima ordered Mayor Motoshima to repay the 40,000 yen ($320) subsidy for that *chūkonhi* war memorial.

From his hospital bed, Mayor Motoshima told reporters that he was generally pleased with the ruling, although he regretted that the Sakou-megasaki *chūkonhi* war memorial had been deemed to be religious and would decide later whether to appeal that part of the court's decision. For his part, Pastor Oka said simply, "The ruling meant a 99.9 percent defeat for me, because the court rejected most of my argument."[55]

Two years later, in 1992, Pastor Oka's constitutional challenge was totally rejected when Mayor Motoshima's appeal resulted in the Fukuoka High Court's overruling the Nagasaki District Court's very narrow ruling. In announcing the appellate court's decision, Presiding Judge Morio Okudaira admitted that "some of the monuments were built in prewar days and retained their religious nature." Yet, he reasoned, "Now that the state administration over Shintoism and customs in worshiping war heroes are things of the past, their religious influences are slight. The city's subsidies, therefore, can be termed as constitutional."

Relying on the *Tsu City Ground-Purification Ceremony* case and its incorporation of the *Lemon*-like test for determining whether the government had violated disestablishment principles, Judge Okudaira observed that "The aim and effects [of the city's subsidies for the war memorials] were to provide psychological support for bereaved families of war dead, and the degree of their religious connotation and effects on the public are quite slight."[56] That left Pastor Oka with nothing but the hope of appealing, even though the outcome of an appeal to the Supreme Court appeared very unpromising. The Fukuoka High Court's ruling, Oka complained, "recognizes the revival of the state-administered Shintoism and only indicates the court's ignorance of religion."[57] A little over two years later, on July 27, 1994, Pastor Oka suddenly passed away at age seventy-five and further appeal of his suit was deemed moot.

In May 1992, the Takamatsu High Court also proved Governor Shiraishi correct about the *Ehime Shrine Donation* case. The Takamatsu High Court sided with the government, overturning the district court's decision holding unconstitutional the local government's donations for the performance of Shinto ceremonies. Contrary to the lower court, Presiding Judge Kazuo Takagi held that the Ehime prefectural government had not run afoul of Article 20's bar on governmental support for religion. "Spending such as donations to shrines remains in the realm of social protocol," Judge Takagi explained. The city's donations, therefore, had a secular purpose. The donations, Judge Takagi ruled, did not advance nor inhibit any particular religion, since they "were not considered activities that supported and promoted religion."

Hammering Down the Nail

A full decade after the Osaka District Court's initial decisions in the early 1980s on the Kamisakas' challenge to Minoo city officials, and almost six years after the appellate court's ruling on them, the Supreme Court finally handed down its decision on the appeal of the Osaka High Court's decision in the *Minoo Memorial* and *Minoo Memorial Service* cases.[58]

In appealing the Osaka High Court's ruling, the Kamisakas raised thirty-four specific objections, including that the high court had violated Articles 394 and 395 of the Code of Civil Procedure. These articles provide that appeals may be made when the reasoning of a high court contradicts "the law of inference" or is inconsistent with applicable law and evidence, as well as when its "judgment has not been furnished with reasons or there are discrepencies in the reasons." The Osaka High Court's decision, insisted the Kamisakas' lawyers, also misinterpreted the principles for religious freedom in Articles 20 and 89 of the Constitution.

The high court had wrongly concluded that the *chūkonhi* war memorial was secular in character, contrary to the district court's finding that it was "religious in nature." In reaching that result, the Kamisakas' attorneys argued, the Osaka High Court had neglected the abundant evidence they had presented demonstrating the *chūkonhi's* religious character. This conflict or contradiction provided the basis for their appeal and would, they hoped, afford the Supreme Court the opportunity to clarify both the status of the *chūkonhi* war memorial and the application of constitutional guarantees mandating the disestablishment of state support for religion.

On February 16, 1993, the Supreme Court's decision was announced by the Third Petty Bench, with Justice Katsumi Teika presiding. He was joined by Justices Hisao Sakaue, Itsuo Sonobe, Shōichirō Satō, and Tsuneo Kabe. It was a rather distinguished bench that included three former lower-court judges—one of whom, Justice Sonobe, had also been a prominent law-school professor—and two justices who had been private attorneys before their appointments to the Supreme Court.

In handing down the decision for the Court's Third Petty Bench, Justice Teika basically affirmed the ruling and reasoning of the Osaka High Court. Minoo city's *chūkonhi* war memorial, Justice Teika held, was not an object of religious worship per se. The *chūkonhi* had been built by people in the village to comfort the souls of war dead, and as such had the character of a cenotaph or monument. Justice Teika emphasized that the memorial services held there were alternately Shinto and Buddhist. Accordingly, he reasoned that the *chūkonhi's* relationship to specific religions after the war had become weak, no longer close *(kihaku)*. In other words, the *chūkonhi's* entanglement or association with Shinto—and with religion more generally—had become greatly diluted since World War II.

Nor, according to the Court, should the monument be considered an offshoot of Yasukuni, despite the fact that virtually all other parties in the controversy deemed the two to be intimately interrelated. As Justice Teika put it, "The cenotaph should be regarded as a monument to the war dead and not as an alter ego of Yasukuni Shrine."[59] Yet that very expression was ambiguous and self-serving. Indeed, the Court's opinion as a whole failed to come to terms with the fact that religion in Japan is syncretic, so that the war dead are comforted as supernatural beings and held in awe as both *kami* and buddhas.

Next, Justice Teika ruled that the Japan Association of War Bereaved Families was a private organization whose main purpose was not to engage in religious activities. Instead, the association's "essential purpose" was said to be that of supporting bereaved families and assisting them in remembering the glorified spirits of the war dead. The association, according to Justice Teika, had been founded for the purposes of promoting the welfare of war-bereaved families and "honoring the glorified spirits." Since the JAWBF was deemed to be neither a primarily religious organization nor engaged in principally religious activities, Minoo city was not precluded from offering its financial support under Articles 20 and 89 of the Constitution. Although Justice Teika conceded that the Minoo Association of War Bereaved Families does engage in activities with religious connotations, such as visiting Yasukuni and sponsoring Shinto ceremonies, he held that here "the purpose was of a secular nature, and it did not support or promote a particular religion."

Justice Teika conveniently omitted quoting the language of Article 3 of the JAWBF's charter, which states that "*comforting* the glorified spirits" is one of its two main goals, and which makes clear the association's involvement in religious activities from the beginning. He also failed to explain how he could justify focusing solely on the JAWBF's objective of promoting the welfare of war-bereaved families to the exclusion of its other objective, "comforting the glorified spirits." Even if the association's main purpose was deemed to be promoting the welfare of war-bereaved families, its charter makes it clear that glorifying the spirits of Yasukuni's war dead is at least a secondary purpose.

After almost half a century, the JAWBF's first objective of supporting war-bereaved families was, arguably, less important than it once had been, and hence had less priority. Hence Justice Teika's conclusion that the association's original or main purpose was not that of engaging in religious activities struck the Kamisakas' attorneys as both implausible and disingenuous. Furthermore, the Court once again declined either to define religion or to address the plaintiffs' arguments that Yasukuni's cult of war dead was a particular national religion.

The city's paying for the relocation of the monument and other financial assistance was therefore not unconstitutional. Justice Teika further reasoned that,

> The action of Minoo City is mainly secular and its effect is not recognized as assisting, encouraging, and promoting a particular religion, or as oppressing and interfering with other religions. Therefore, it is not recognized in view of social and cultural conditions as an entanglement with religion that goes beyond the proper limit in relation to the basic purpose of the guarantee for freedom of religion.

He also reaffirmed that Mayor Nakai, School Board Chairman Kōno, and other public officials attending the memorial services had not violated the constitutional separation of state and religion. As the Osaka High Court had ruled, the Supreme Court's Third Petty Bench held that, as local public figures and officials, Mayor Nakai and Chairman Kōno had attended the services as a matter of social protocol and courtesy.

In anticipation, perhaps, of the reactions of Reiko Kamisaka, Katsuyuki Kumano, and others opposed to the government's support for what they deemed objects of religious worship, Justice Sonobe filed a brief concurring opinion. He did allow that, generally speaking, facilities for mourning or comforting spirits—whether *chūkonhi* war memorials, *kinenhi* (remembering stones), or other monuments—could be considered not merely monuments, but as having a religious character as well. Ceremonies conducted at the *chūkonhi,* he conceded, might indeed stir the religious feelings of those in attendance. But Justice Sonobe rather cunningly added that "it is difficult to judge the character of such facilities as having only one nature based on the feelings of those in attendance. And," he claimed, "it cannot be said that to do it is an indispensable requisite for deciding whether the principle of separation of religion and the state is violated."

Turning to the case at hand, Justice Sonobe observed that, regardless of the actual character of Minoo's *chūkonhi,* it was therefore enough to judge the constitutionality of the city's financial support for the *chūkonhi* on the basis of the test laid down by the Grand Bench in the *Tsu City Ground-Purification Ceremony* case. From that perspective, he concluded, most people would probably neither associate the *chūkonhi* with a specific religion nor identify the ceremonies conducted there with a specific religion. In other words, the majority's or general public's view of war memorials and Shinto services as folkways or customs prevails, regardless of the religious significance they actually hold, both for those participating in them and for those criticizing the government's sponsorship of them.

Justice Sonobe's concurring opinion was hardly comforting for the Kamisakas' attorneys. In their view, his opinion should have been based solely on the arguments and evidence presented; instead, it proved no less troubling than the opinion of the Court. First of all, there had been no evidence presented about the "feelings" of either the participants in the ceremonies conducted at the *chūkonhi* or the general public. Second, how could Justice Sonobe decide whether the city had supported a religious activity without first determining the *chūkonhi's* character and whether or not it was religious? Third, why hadn't Justice Sonobe deemed Yasukuni's cult of war dead and State Shinto to be a particular religion? He had excluded from discussion all the "new religions," including State Shinto; yet Yasukuni's cult of war dead remained a creation of the Meiji regime, and thus a "new religion."

The Supreme Court's ruling was indeed open to criticism on several grounds. It invited sharp attacks from the Kamisakas' attorneys and from liberal constitutional-law professors. For one thing, the lawyers for Minoo city had argued all along that the war memorial and the ceremonies conducted there did not have religious symbolism. The monument was basically a *kinenhi* (a remembering stone), a secular memorial. The Kamisakas' attorneys had repeatedly countered that the Supreme Court should initially define "religion." And however the Court defined religion, they maintained, it should then relate its analysis to the *chūkonhi* and to the ceremonies conducted there.

Without a definition of religion, Kumano and other attorneys for the Kamisakas argued, the courts could say whatever they wanted and get away with arbitrary rulings. They could thereby deceive people about what constitutes those "religious activities" that the government is barred from engaging in under Articles 20 and 89 of the Constitution. A definition of religion was pivotal to any interpretation of those guarantees. It was a prerequisite, Kumano maintained—the minimal basis for rational reasoning—and ought to provide a standard that would prevent arbitrary decisions by the lower courts.

Still without defining religion, the Supreme Court appeared to disregard the Osaka High Court's findings when asserting that the Minoo *chūkonhi* originally had, and continues to have, something of the character of a cenotaph or religious monument. Moreover, without determining that the *chūkonhi* has religious symbolism, there was no reason for drawing on the "purpose and effect" test advanced in the *Tsu City Ground-Purification Ceremony* case. Nonetheless, the Court proceeded to stress that after the war the relationship between the *chūkonhi* war memorial and Yasukuni had become very subtle, so that it could not be said that the *chūkonhi* and Yasukuni were directly linked. This hardly responded to the arguments advanced by Kamisakas' attorneys. Nor did it honestly accord with the connections drawn between the *chūkonhi* and Yasukuni by the JAWBF, some conservatives, and members of the LDP or the Self Defense Forces.

The Kamisakas' attorneys had argued that the war memorial could be considered both as a religious symbol and as a secular remembering stone. But for them, the history of such memorials and the fact that *"Chū Kon Hi"* was inscribed on the monument were controlling and determinative. The Supreme Court not only avoided this argument but shrewdly went out of its way to avoid saying that the *chūkonhi* was *not* religious. The Court thereby left that issue to decide later and avoided criticism that had been leveled at the lower court for having taken that position.

In the course of its opinion, the Supreme Court also failed completely to address (or even to bother to explain why it refused to confront) the historical evidence amassed by the Kamisakas' attorneys in their lengthy briefs. In those briefs, they reviewed the history of State Shinto and high-lighted in considerable detail its disestablishment after the war. Included as supporting evidence were copies of documents sent by the U.S. State Department to the Allied Occupation Forces—documents which unequivocally stated that "National Shinto . . . is to be done away with."[60] In addition, more than 120 pages were reproduced from a publication of Yasukuni Shrine that surveyed individual *chūkonhi* war memorials and established beyond any doubt their linkages to Yasukuni and the prewar history of State Shinto.

In his brief, Katsuyuki Kumano argued that Minoo city's war memorial and Yasukuni were intimately and historically part of the government's sponsorship of what he called a "glorified spirit cycle." The glorified spirit cycle, he ingeniously argued, was analogous to the four-stroke cycle of a combustion engine: suction, compression, combustion, and exhaustion. Complete with diagrams to illustrate the analogy, Kumano stressed the interconnection among the four stages of the cycle: (1) the educational system indoctrinated loyalty and thereby supported (2) conscription into the military, which in turn (3) provided the bodies for "peacekeeping" and fighting, and inexorably resulted in soldiers' deaths, which (4) were then mitigated and celebrated by their enshrinement as national *kami* at Yasukuni and *chūkonhi* war memorials. The latter was in turn further celebrated and capitalized on by the educational system.

The fourth stage of the cycle, Kumano insisted, was pivotal to the whole system. He likened it to an engine's exhaust or "waste disposal" stage, for it disposed of the grief and anger toward the government of the families of the dead soldiers, raised the military's morale, and encouraged younger generations to go down the same path.

The glorified spirit cycle of the prewar emperor system, according to Kumano, was a vicious one. It had driven Japan into World War II and could conceivably come into play once again if the Supreme Court sanctioned governmental sponsorship of the symbolism, rituals, and institutions represented by Minoo's *chūkonhi* and associated with Yasukuni.

The Supreme Court neither paid attention to nor attempted to rebut that compelling historical evidence. This omission in the Court's opinion did not, however, go unnoticed. An editorial in the *Asahi Evening News,* for example, complained that the Court's opinion appeared to "lack a historical viewpoint."

No less seriously, in its ruling on the *Minoo Memorial* and *Minoo Memorial Service* cases, and in some other decisions on religious freedom,[61]

Mr. Katsuyuki Kumano in his office in downtown Osaka. (Author photo)

the Supreme Court conveniently avoided or manipulated the facts in dispute, apparently in order to reach its preordained outcome. The Osaka District Court had defined religion as including rites and ceremonies, but found that religion basically consists of firm beliefs in the supernatural and in other-worldliness. It concluded that Minoo city's war memorial *was* religious. The municipal government therefore should not have paid for its relocation, and School Board Chairman Kōno should not have received that portion of his salary paid while he was attending the ceremonies performed at the monument. It did not matter, according to the district court, that Shinto ceremonies were held one year and Buddhist ones the next. Yet the Osaka High Court reversed this and concluded that the *chūkonhi* was not religious.

The Supreme Court's Third Petty Bench then ruled, rather ambiguously, that the *chūkonhi* had originally been something in the nature of a memorial or remembering stone, implying but not specifically stating that it had no religious symbolism. Yet in manipulating the social reality of the *chūkonhi,* the petty bench simply ignored, and hence altered, the factual findings of the lower courts. Such a blatant manipulation of the facts, according to Kumano and some leading law-school professors, ran afoul of Article 403 of the Code of Civil Procedure, which specifically stipulates that "facts lawfully found by the original judgment are binding on the court of the second appeal."[62]

In ruling on the Kamisakas' appeals of the *Minoo Memorial* and *Minoo Memorial Service* cases, the Supreme Court's petty bench also relied on the "purpose and effect" test for determining the application of constitutional provisions for the separation of government from religion. That test had been endorsed in the *Tsu City Ground-Purification Ceremony* case and borrowed roughly from the U.S. Supreme Court's decision in *Lemon v. Kurtzman.*[63] Yet the Third Petty Bench twisted logic and facts when employing the test, so as to conclude that Minoo's *chūkonhi* war memorial was essentially a secular "memorial in character."

The purpose and effect test, however, is designed to gauge whether legislation or other governmental action has a purpose and effect of advancing religion. The test was not designed and remains inappropriate for making factual findings as to whether, for example, war memorials are or are not religious. Hence the Court should have analyzed whether or not Minoo's paying for the war memorial's relocation and reconstruction had the purpose and effect of advancing religion only *after* determining (contrary to its ruling implicitly denying) that the *chūkonhi* does indeed have religious symbolism.

In other words, the petty bench's opinion rationalized its decision in ways that confused matters and begged the important question of the religious character of Minoo's *chūkonhi* war memorial. By using the purpose and effect test as it did, the Third Petty Bench ignored the argument made by attorneys for the Kamisakas that the Osaka High Court's finding that the memorial had no religious character was inconsistent and unsubstantiated. In this respect, the petty bench arguably violated Article 395, section 1, clause 6 of the Code of Civil Procedures, which provides that a lower court's judgment should be reconsidered "if the judgment is not accompanied by reasons or the reasons are inconsistent."

After having decided that the war memorial was basically a secular "memorial in character" and cautiously avoiding saying explicitly that it was not religious, the Third Petty Bench further confused and obscured matters by continuing to invoke the purpose and effect test. On the one hand, since the war memorial had been held to be secular, the Court did not then need to apply the purpose and effect test to the city's use of public funds to relocate and reconstruct the monument. Again, the purpose and effect test was designed to gauge whether, with respect to some *admittedly* religious symbol or institution, governmental action has the result of entangling the government and religion in violation of the Constitution's prescriptions for the disestablishment of state support for religion.

But the Supreme Court had undercut the very basis for that analysis, and hence for applying the purpose and effect test. The Court had already eliminated the central premise for invoking that test by writing out of the case the crucial fact at dispute—namely, the religious character of the war memorial—and thus the presupposition for applying the test in the first place. In short, the petty bench's use of the purpose and effect test was both unnecessary and inappropriate.

On the other hand, had the Third Petty Bench clearly held that the Minoo city war memorial had been drained of its religious significance, so that it was now mainly a secular "memorial in character," it would at least have followed more closely and faithfully the reasoning in the landmark *Tsu City Ground-Purification Ceremony* case. There, the Supreme Court had held that the historical religious significance of the Shinto ground-purification ceremony at issue had indeed been diluted by changes in the times after the war. On that basis, the Court then applied the purpose and effect test.

If the Third Petty Bench in the *Minoo* case had adopted a similar sort of analysis, the purpose and effect test might have had some utility. The petty bench could have employed the test to determine whether Minoo city had become too entangled with religion or, as the Supreme Court in the *Tsu City Ground-Purification Ceremony* case put it, had "transcend[ed] the proper limit" of the state's relationship toward religion. Such an analysis would not have proven entirely unproblematic, however, in that it would have brought the petty bench into direct conflict with the Osaka High Court's bold finding that the Minoo city war memorial was definitely not a religious facility. Had the petty bench adopted this kind of analysis, it would have invited the criticism that it had manipulated the high court's factual findings, in violation of Article 403.

In addition, as Katsuyuki Kumano underscores, the petty bench concluded that the effect of the city's relocation and reconstruction of the war memorial was not to "endorse, facilitate, or advance any *particular religion.*"

That standard, arguably, is different from, and hence a departure from, the Supreme Court's earlier ruling in the *Tsu City Ground-Purification Ceremony* case. In that case, the Court had ruled that the constitutionality of the government's action depends on whether its effect is to "endorse, facilitate, or advance *religion in general.*" Under Article 10, clause 3 of the Judiciary Act, however, prior decisions of the Supreme Court may be revised only upon reconsideration by the Grand Bench, not a petty bench. Accordingly, Kumano charges that, since in the Minoo ruling the petty bench departed from, and thereby, arguably, revised, the standard set forth by the full Court in the *Tsu City* decision, it also ran afoul of Article 10, clause 3 of the Judiciary Act.

Finally, in dealing with the issue of whether or not the Minoo association of war-bereaved families was a religious organization, the Court's Third Petty Bench appeared to introduce a new qualification to the purpose and effect test by constantly referring to the association's "essential" purpose or activity. It could be argued that the Court thereby made new law and modified the test announced in the *Tsu City Ground-Purification Ceremony* case—and that it did so, according to critics of the ruling, simply in order to hold that the association is primarily a nonreligious organization.

Even more devastating, in the view of Katsuyuki Kumano and others, the *Minoo Memorial* ruling reveals once again the Supreme Court's failure to assert its judicial independence. The Court appeared willing to disregard procedures laid down in the Judiciary Act, the Code of Civil Procedure, and the Constitution. The Supreme Court and the lower courts almost invariably reinforce the government's position out of seemingly purblind deference. As a result, Kumano says frankly, the courts have "ceased to function as an independent judiciary, and merely follow the dictates of the administrative judgment."

What makes this all the more disturbing is that, as Kumano puts it, "the spirit of *messhi-hōkō*"—that is, sacrificing one's own life for the public good, as personified by the emperor—"which was inculcated in the Japanese minds by state Shintoism over the course of fifty years, is still alive in the minds of the people who hold the reins of national power."[64] Thus Kumano concludes that the challenge of achieving the Constitution's promise of the disestablishment of state sponsorship of religion depends on first securing judicial independence. The separation of the power of the courts from that of the government more generally appears to be a precondition or prerequisite for enforcing the Constitution's mandate for the separation of government from religion.

At a press conference called immediately after the Supreme Court announced its ruling, Reiko and Naoki Kamisaka, Kumano and other attorneys, and some of their supporters said that they felt "more than dis-appointment, just despair."[65] Reiko Kamisaka had been forty-five years old when the litigation over the Minoo city's war memorial began; she was now sixty-one. "I understand that there is a limit to what the court can do," she observed. "But since the court worked on the case for five and a half years," Mrs. Kamisaka said candidly, "I wish it had more clearly shed light on the relations between the war and Yasukuni Shrine and the relations between the shrine and the cenotaph, which is the city's Yasukuni Shrine, so to speak." Regretfully, she lamented, the Court had managed to avoid entirely the issue of war memorials and state-supported Shinto ceremonies being used once again to glorify militarism. The Supreme Court, in her view, had failed completely to appreciate the reli-gious nature of *chūkonhi* war memorials and of the ceremonies conducted at them.

Reiko Kamisaka, her son Naoki Kamisaka, and their attorneys remained determined to continue their appeals and battle in the courts. A little over a year later, though, they faced further setbacks. During the course of the litigation, Naoki Kamisaka had grown up and pursued a legal education. While attending the Legal Training and Research Insti-tute in 1993, shortly after the Supreme Court's *Minoo Memorial* ruling, he decided that, upon graduation, he would apply to become an assistant judge. Assistant judges serve on district and family courts, or on three-judge panels, and have no significant power to render individual judg-ments. But in April 1994, the Supreme Court announced without further explanation that he would not be given an assignment as an assistant judge. Naoki Kamisaka was the only one of the 105 graduates in his class to be denied an appointment. He was the first to be rejected in seven years. Only 50 graduates of the institute have ever been denied appoint-ments upon graduation, though many others have almost certainly been discouraged by teachers at the institute from applying for judgeships.

Naoki Kamisaka had been warned by some of his instructors not to bother applying for a position as an assistant judge. He was told that because he was a party to the Minoo war memorial litigation he could not become a judge. Judges are supposed to be neutral, an instructor explained to him. A "judge should not approach such a dangerous or unpopular thing" as participating in a lawsuit.[66] Not surprisingly, the 30-year-old Kamisaka speculates that the Supreme Court's decision was due to his involvement in and protests over the *Minoo Memorial* litigation. "If my involvement in the [litigation] was the reason behind the Court's deci-sion," Naoki Kamisaka says, "it would mean that the Court itself is trying to rob the people of their right to seek a trial."[67]

The Kamisakas and supporters at a press conference after the Osaka High Court's 1994 ruling, with a diagram of the "glorified spirit cycle" in the background. (Author photo)

The Kamisakas, their attorneys, and supporters demanded some explanation for the denial. They were not alone in criticizing the Court's action. The head of the Japan Federation of Bar Associations, Kōken Tsuchiya, held a press conference in Tokyo at which he stated, "There is strong suspicion that the candidate was refused on the basis of his thoughts and beliefs. The Supreme Court should make its reasons clear."[68] Otherwise, he warned, "If the Court cannot remove the suspicion that the rejection was based on Kamisaka's background and political views, not only the public's faith in fair trials but also future legal students' motivation would be adversely affected."[69] Subsequently, 21 of the 52 prefectural bar associations issued resolutions demanding an explanation for Naoki Kamisaka's rejection.[70]

Still, such protests appeared in vain against the tightly controlled judiciary bureaucracy. Realistically, they aimed at momentarily commanding public attention and building support over the long haul for the Kamisakas' cause. Subsequently, Naoki Kamisaka filed a suit against the government. At the heart of the matter, as his supporters put it in a protest statement,

> We will never forget when the Supreme Court said, "A judge must not only be fair, but be seen as fair," in another judicial appointment case. Now, the Supreme Court is being asked not only to be fair, but to be seen as fair.[71]

The lawsuit, of course, aimed to command publicity and to make mischief. How could the Court decide a case against itself and still claim impartiality?

The Kamisakas faced another setback on July 20, 1994, when the Osaka High Court handed down its decision on their appeal of the district court's ruling in their third suit, the *Minoo Subsidy* case. The three main issues in that case were the Kamisakas' arguments that (1) Minoo's affiliate of the JAWBF was involved in promoting religious activities, (2) the city's subsidies to the local association were unconstitutional, and (3) the subsidies were not in the public interest and were unlawful.

The Kamisakas' attorneys had argued that the association was actually working against the public interest by promoting one particular religion and the religious services at the *chūkonhi* and Yasukuni, as well as in other ways supporting Yasukuni's cult of war dead. Accordingly, they maintained, as in their two earlier suits, that Minoo had violated the disestablishment provisions in Articles 20 and 89 of the Constitution. They also argued that the subsidies were unlawful under the Local Autonomy Law and Article 56 of the Public Welfare Law.

Under the Local Autonomy Law, which permits residents to file petitions for inspection of a local government's expenditures, the Kamisakas claimed that Minoo's subsidies for the local association of war-bereaved families were illegal because they were not in "the public interest." In other words, they maintained that it was not in the public interest for Minoo to subsidize a group with such close ties to Yasukuni. Under Article 56 of the Public Welfare Law, municipalities giving financial assistance to a group must enact an ordinance authorizing its supervision of the group and its expenditures. This statute had not been in place when the Kamisakas first filed their suit, but their attorneys nonetheless argued that Minoo should have to comply with its provisions.

In their appeal, they argued as well that the district court had improperly defined religious organizations as groups with common beliefs and objectives of promoting religious activities. Even leaving that issue aside, they contended that the court had misapplied its own definition when holding that the local association of war-bereaved families was not a religious organization. Finally, granting the Supreme Court's analysis in its 1993 ruling on the first two *Minoo Memorial* cases, namely, that the "essential purpose" and activities of an organization must be to promote a particular religion, the Kamisakas' lawyers claimed that the association clearly met that definition, and that Minoo's subsidies therefore violated the Constitution.

Although neither optimistic nor pessimistic, the Kamisakas, their attorneys, and supporters gathered at the Osaka High Court to hear its decision, as scheduled, at 3:00 P.M., on July 20, 1994. The presiding judge, Toshio Nakagawa, was sixty-one years old, born the same year as Reiko Kamisaka. He was joined by Judges Kazuo Komatsu and Kenichi Kitadani, both younger. The crowded courtroom was bleak, filled with an air of bureaucratic efficiency. There was no symbol of justice. Except for a high bench on which the judges were perched, the courtroom was indistinguishable from any other large governmental room.

Presiding Judge Nakagawa read briefly the unanimous decision: appeal dismissed. On every score, the Kamisakas' arguments were rejected. Closely following the Supreme Court's analysis laid down the year before, the Osaka High Court ruled that the essential purpose of associations of war-bereaved families was promoting the welfare of its constituents. According to Judge Nakagawa, neither the Japan Association of War Bereaved Families nor its local affiliate in Minoo city fit the constitutional definition of a religious organization, which he characterized as a group that believes in or promotes religion as its primary objective. The association's ties to Yasukuni and its activities in honoring war dead, although religious, were held to be only secondary activities—not primary ones, as Professor Arai had testified and the Kamisakas' attorneys had repeatedly argued.

The high court did not concern itself with even attempting to rebut the evidence and arguments to the contrary. Ignored completely was the fact that the money given by Minoo to the association was in turn donated to Yasukuni. Given that the essential purpose and activity of the association was deemed not to be directly related to Yasukuni's religious cult, subsidies from Minoo were constitutionally permissible. As for the argument that Minoo had failed to have an ordinance, as required under current law, authorizing its supervision of groups it subsidized, the Osaka High Court said that this was merely a procedural formality, a small matter that did not affect the outcome.

The Dreams of Survivors

Much had changed in the almost twenty years since the Kamisakas had brought their first suit against Minoo city officials. On the one hand, Japan's economic prosperity continued to grow. In 1993, the Liberal Democratic Party was finally out of office for the first time in thirty-eight years. This may eventually result in different kinds of appointees to the judicial bench. Mayor Nakai was also now more conciliatory. Following the announcement of the Supreme Court's decision, recalls Reiko Kamisaka, Mayor Nakai said publicly that "we should not take too much pride in the victory, for the plaintiffs are still residents of the city."[72] Minoo's *chūkonhi* war memorial still stands in front of the elementary school, but the surrounding area is no longer carefully maintained. Weeds and grass now grow in the area around it that was once covered with bright white pebbles. The area appears dirty, polluted, and contaminated by controversy. The *chūkonhi* appears at once anachronistic and yet brooding.

On the other hand, after the Supreme Court's 1993 ruling, some associations of war-bereaved families in rural parts of Kyushu and Honshu again resumed sponsoring ceremonies at local *chūkonhi* war memorials and *gokoku* (country-protecting) shrines. Although the Liberal Democratic Party lost power, conservative leaders in the government continued successfully pushing the further expansion of the Self Defense Forces' role abroad, under the guise of international cooperation. They were also now encouraged to move in that direction by the United States, among other countries. Japan's spending on the Self Defense Forces has also steadily grown and now ranks, depending on how it is calculated, third or fifth highest in military spending in the world. Defense expenditures in 1992–1993 put Japan ahead of Germany and right behind France, the United Kingdom, Russia, and the United States.[73]

Mrs. Yoshiko Furukawa and Mrs. Reiko Kamisaka discussing their lawsuit in 1994. (Author photo)

Asked whether all the years of litigation have been worth it, Reiko Kamisaka says firmly that she "doesn't consider the Supreme Court's decision to be absolute or final." Still, she adds,

> We are not optimistic, as long as the *chūkonhi* stands there it has an effect or influence over the children's subconsciousness. The children don't notice, but unconsciously they are influenced. And, of course, there is a tendency of the government to want to send the SDF abroad under the guise of international cooperation. We have to fight in order to stop the revival of the function of the *chūkonhi*. If we stop fighting, it would have a greater influence.[74]

Reiko Kamisaka's friend and fellow plaintiff in the litigation, 67-year-old Yoshiko Furukawa, agreed: "We need to continue to present the issue to the public to keep it alive. As long as wars still exist, we cannot tell when the *chūkonhi* will become alive again."[75]

At a press conference after the Osaka High Court's ruling in 1994, another survivor recalled fighting in China and the deaths on the battlefield. Rather passionately, he challenged the central argument of war-bereaved families and conservative ultranationalists, who continue to say that "because of the war, we have peace and prosperity now" and that Yasukuni's war dead must therefore be honored. "But, those who died in the war did not sacrifice their lives for the country. They all wanted to live and return home to their families. They are the only ones," the man concluded, "who can say 'because of the war, we have peace and prosperity,' and they are dead."

Members of the Kamisakas' generation would remain bitterly divided for as long as they lasted. The controversy they share, though, remains largely lost on the younger generations, who know only of Japan's postwar prosperity.

CHAPTER 5

Enshrinements for Tomorrowland

THE SUDDEN DEATH of her husband, Takafumi Nakaya, left Mrs. Yasuko Nakaya a widow. After nine years of marriage, she faced finding employment and raising her 6-year-old son, Takaharu, alone. As if her husband's death in 1968 did not cause enough grief, four years later Mrs. Nakaya learned that his soul would be enshrined as a national guardian deity at the *gokoku* (country-protecting) shrine in Yamaguchi prefecture. The enshrinement and apotheosis would take place over her repeated objections.

When the Yamaguchi *gokoku* shrine notified Mrs. Nakaya of the enshrinement and that a Shinto service would be held annually to honor her husband and others enshrined there, she became deeply depressed and bitter. She had several times refused to give her permission for the enshrinement. Although her husband had not been a Christian, he had respected her religious beliefs. In her view, the unauthorized enshrining of his soul was more than just disrespectful: it was sacrilege, a blasphemy of her Christian beliefs. The enshrinement and annual memorial ceremonies that would follow, honoring her husband and others enshrined as guardian *kami,* amounted to idolatry, a grave sin against God. Mrs. Nakaya took seriously the biblical injunction in First Corinthians: "For indeed, if there be so-called gods, whether in heaven or on earth—as indeed there are many 'gods' and many 'lords'—yet for us there is one God, the Father, from whom all being comes, towards whom we move; and there is one Lord, Jesus Christ, through whom all things come to be, and we through Him."[1]

A small, middle-aged housewife, Mrs. Nakaya gradually came to the resolution that the matter simply could not rest at that. After repeatedly pleading with the Self Defense Forces' (SDF) officers to have the enshrinement rescinded, and after consulting with her pastor, Kenji Hayashi, Mrs.

Nakaya finally decided to take the matter to court. Almost five years after the death of her husband, on January 3, 1973, Mrs. Nakaya sued the head of the Federation of Volunteer Associations, which included the local chapter of the Self Defense Forces' Friendship Association that had requested the enshrinement in the first place. She also sued the Yamaguchi liaison office of the SDF, which had assisted in the enshrinement, and the government. Her lawsuit became known as the *Self Defense Forces Enshrinement* case and captured widespread attention. It also became part of a long-running controversy that would wind its way up to the highest court in the land over the course of the next fifteen years. The Supreme Court of Japan would not hand down its ruling until June 1, 1988.[2]

Like Satoshi and Reiko Kamisaka, Mrs. Nakaya put conviction to the test and became a profile in courage. Unlike them, though, she was a Christian, a religious minority. She faced a certain uphill battle, against virtually insurmountable odds. Yet Mrs. Nakaya claims not to feel put upon because she is a Christian minority in Japan, for, as she points out, all "Christians don't think alike." Instead, she feels set apart because she thinks differently from most Japanese. In Mrs. Nakaya's words, her "case should not be seen alone. It should be placed in our ordinary life. It is deeply related to the Japanese mental structure." This is why, in challenging the government and the prevailing Japanese way of thinking, Mrs. Nakaya's cause drew support not only from Christians but from others who oppose militarism and who want to advance the cause of women's independence and, more broadly, human rights in Japan. It is also why, as Mrs. Nakaya observes, her case was "difficult for younger generations to understand,"[3] since they are largely indifferent to claims of human rights and otherwise preoccupied.

Mrs. Nakaya was also drawn into the larger political struggles of the 1970s and 1980s over the expanding activities of the SDF, veterans' groups, and associations of war-bereaved families, as well as over attempts by conservative politicians in the Liberal Democratic Party to reestablish governmental support for Yasukuni. It was against that background of political struggle that the judiciary would also determine the status of religious freedom in Japan.

Mrs. Nakaya's objections to the enshrinement of her husband's soul were difficult even for some of her neighbors and relatives to understand. Someone who wants to be, or appears to be, different, and who takes an independent stand, is generally perceived to be abnormal. Moreover, to be enshrined as a country-protecting deity *(go-koku),* loyal soul *(chū-kon),* or heroic soul *(eirei)* who died for the emperor and the country is the highest honor a person can be paid by the Japanese community and government.

In addition, Yamaguchi prefecture, where Mrs. Nakaya and her family lived, lies in the far western part of Honshu. Yamaguchi is inland yet surrounded on all sides by seas of green mountains, hazy and humid in the summer. The region is rural but has one of the greatest concentrations of Shinto shrines and religious organizations. Yamaguchi prefecture lies between those of Fukuoka on Kyushu and Hiroshima on Honshu. Both of those prefectures rank just below another western prefecture, Hyōgo, in having the most regional and local Shinto shrines in all of Japan.[4] Traditional Shinto practices and rites still have a strong pull in rural areas such as Yamaguchi, unlike large cosmopolitan areas such as Tokyo and Osaka.

Rural areas are also where leaders in the Japan Association of War Bereaved Families (JAWBF), the SDF, and veterans' groups have been especially active in encouraging affiliates to hold enshrinement ceremonies at *chūkonhi* war memorials and regional *gokoku* shrines. Furthermore, since the Meiji era there has been an East-West division in Japan, comparable in some ways to the historical North-South division in the United States. Although that division is disappearing due to social mobility and urbanization after the war (as in the United States), some citizens in the older generations still cling to such a cultural divide. To some of her neighbors, Mrs. Nakaya appeared better suited for living somewhere beyond Osaka, in the industrial corridor running from there to Yokohama and Tokyo.

Many of Mrs. Nakaya's neighbors simply could not fathom why she was making such a fuss. Even some in her church disagreed with her decision to sue the SDF and the government. Not surprisingly, given her objections and Japan's deeply rooted social pressures for conformity, she faced numerous nasty letters and phone calls in the years that followed. Some excoriated her as un-Japanese. Others said insultingly that she was Korean. Still others denied her womanhood and told her to move elsewhere.[5]

Whereas the Kamisakas' litigation centered on the constitutional separation of government from religion, Mrs. Nakaya raised that issue, as well as the untested claim of constitutional protection for the freedom of religious exercise. As with the Kamisakas' litigation, it took some time, even after Mrs. Nakaya had filed her suit, for her primary constitutional claims to crystalize. During the course of her lawsuit, some consideration was given to naming the Yamaguchi prefectural *gokoku* shrine as a party in the suit as well. This might have strengthened her claiming, as the Kamisakas had, that the provisions in Articles 20 and 89 for the separation of government from religion had been violated. Here, the SDF's Yamaguchi prefectural office had cooperated with, and arguably thereby become unconstitutionally entangled with, the *gokoku* shrine's joint enshrinement ceremony.

But the legal strategy of naming Yamaguchi's *gokoku* shrine as a party and of basing her case solely on constitutional provisions for the separation of government from religion appeared to hold little promise of success in the courts. Without naming the *gokoku* shrine as a party in her suit, Mrs. Nakaya's lawyers therefore settled on arguing that, in making an application and supplying supporting documents for the joint enshrinement, the SDF Friendship Association and the prefectural SDF office had violated clause 3 of Article 20, which provides that "The State and its organs shall refrain from religious education or any other religious activities."

In addition to appearing to offer little that would enhance their chance of winning in the courts, naming Yamaguchi's *gokoku* shrine as a party in the suit might have proven counterproductive in other ways. The media would almost certainly have portrayed Mrs. Nakaya's suit as a fight pitting adherents of Christianity against those of Shinto, which would have struck a very unresponsive cord with the public. It might have also undermined the building of support groups and any chance of moving public opinion toward the cause championed by Mrs. Nakaya and other religious minorities.

Besides claiming that the government had impermissibly become involved in a religious activity in violation of clause 3 of Article 20, Mrs. Nakaya's attorneys finally concentrated on arguing that she had a substantive right of personal privacy or autonomy that includes protection for freedom of religious beliefs under Articles 13 and 20. This is what was really at stake, and it is also what made Mrs. Nakaya's suit so novel.

Article 13 provides that "All nationals shall be respected as individuals" and guarantees the people's "right to life, liberty, and the pursuit of happiness." For Mrs. Nakaya's attorneys to argue that Article 13 guaranteed a substantive right of personal religious freedom was nevertheless innovative and unprecedented. The argument, moreover, was extremely problematic, because the guarantees of Article 13 are significantly qualified—just as the old, though very different, Meiji Constitution's guarantees for religious and other freedoms were subject to and "within the limits of law."[6]

Article 13 further stipulates that the people's rights and freedoms are guaranteed only "to the extent that [they do] not interfere with the public welfare." Article 12 imposes the additional obligation on the people to exercise their rights "for the public welfare." Hence, although Article 13 appears to hold out the promise of providing a basis for claims to a substantive right of personal autonomy and religious freedom, the article's public-welfare qualification provides a basis for the courts to do precisely the opposite, namely, to limit or deny such claims as not serving the public welfare.

The difficulty for Mrs. Nakaya's attorneys in arguing that a personal right of religious freedom is grounded in Article 13 was compounded by the fact that the Japanese words for "public" (ōyake-no or kōkyō-no) translate roughly as "governmental" or "social." By implication, the "public welfare" is synonymous with the interests of the state, the government, and, during the Meiji era, the emperor who personified those interests. As such, the "public welfare" was historically understood as opposed to and overriding private interests and claims of individual rights.[7]

The Supreme Court of Japan has also repeatedly invoked the standard of "public welfare" to limit or deny, rather than reinforce, claims to constitutionally protected rights in other areas.[8] In the so-called *Faith-Healing* case of the 1960s, for instance, the Court's Grand Bench upheld the criminal conviction of a Buddhist priestess who had attempted to cure, through faith healing, a mentally disturbed woman possessed of an evil badger spirit. Although the priestess had worked at the request of the woman's family, when the woman died the priestess alone was prosecuted, and she countered that this violated her religious freedom under Article 20. In rejecting her claim, the Court noted the "public welfare" limitations in Articles 12 and 13 and concluded that her actions had "deviated from the boundaries of the freedom of religion guaranteed in Article 20."[9]

In the district court, Mrs. Nakaya's attorneys based their argument for protecting her personal religious right in part on Article 13. But thereafter they focused on provisions in Article 20. Article 20 is more explicit about guaranteeing religious freedom and about the separation of government from religion. On both scores, Article 20 provided a better basis for her challenge to the SDF and the government. The first clause of Article 20, as we have seen, states that "Freedom of religion is guaranteed to all." The second further provides that "No person shall be compelled to take part of any religious acts, celebration, rite or practice." And the third clause bars the government from engaging in "religious activities." Still, until Mrs. Nakaya's lawsuit, these provisions had not been used or accepted as a basis for claiming a substantive right to religious freedom.

Mrs. Nakaya's lawyers would argue that those provisions guarantee individuals a substantive right of personal autonomy, or "right to be let alone,"[10] that includes respect for their religious beliefs. The government had violated those provisions when the prefectural SDF office helped arrange the enshrinement of Takafumi Nakaya's soul against his wife's wishes. In short, the government had interfered with Mrs. Nakaya's constitutional right to the free exercise of religion. Mrs. Nakaya's personal right to religious freedom had been denied because the government, in her words, "disturbed my spiritual peace to quietly remember my husband."[11]

Remarkably, Mrs. Nakaya's claim under Japan's postwar constitution was considered not merely novel but bold and virtually unprecedented. Challenges to the government based on claims to substantive personal rights also tend to be considered radical. Except for a few cases involving environmental pollution, such claims have been rejected or dismissed by the courts.[12] "It's a new concept as far as spiritual matters go,"[13] conceded one of Mrs. Nakaya's principal attorneys, Kenkichi Nakadaira. Nonetheless, her lawyers were determined to try to persuade the judiciary to enforce a substantive right to religious freedom under the Constitution.

An Accidental Death and a Calculated Enshrinement

Takafumi Nakaya's death at age thirty-seven was the result of an unfortunate but otherwise unexceptional traffic accident on January 12, 1968. He had been a first lieutenant in the Ground Self Defense Force and on a recruiting mission in northern Japan for the Kamaishi branch of the Iwate SDF prefectural recruiting office. As a young man he had joined the service before the then National Police Reserve was in 1952 converted into the National Safety Force, and in 1954 reorganized into the Land, Air, and Maritime Self Defense Forces (SDF).

The National Police Reserve (NPR) and, later, the SDF always occupied a precarious and unresolved constitutional position. Although created during the Occupation, after the outbreak of the Korean War, and with the authorization of General Douglas MacArthur, the SDF appeared increasingly to stretch to the breaking point Article 9 of Japan's peace constitution. That article not only "renounce[s] war as a sovereign right of the nation" but also specifies, in no uncertain terms, that "land, sea, and air forces, as well as other war potential, will never be maintained."[14]

The tension between the constitutional theory of Article 9 and the postwar government's policies simply grew as expenditures for the SDF steadily increased, until the constitutional objections were all but worn away. The government initially took the position that "Japan retained a right of national self-defense in international law but, by virtue of the second clause [of Article 9], could not. . . . maintain an armed force—even for the purpose of self-defense."[15] Yet in 1952, when the Japan Socialist Party charged that the expansion of the NPR into the National Safety Force and inclusion of both ground and maritime forces was unconstitutional, the government claimed the forces were not capable of effectively waging modern warfare. Hence the government asserted that the National Safety Force could not be deemed in violation of the Constitution's prohibition against maintaining armed forces of "war potential."[16]

Subsequently, the U.S.–Japan Mutual Security Treaty (Anpo) provided another, even more controversial rationalization for continued expansion of the SDF.[17] And as Japan's postwar military spending progressively grew, successive LDP governments advanced still other pragmatic rationalizations for military buildup. The SDF was said not to be a "military force" because it would serve only nonmilitary interests. Increased military spending was later defended as constitutionally permissible on the ground that the right of self-defense had never been abandoned. Later still, changing international conditions were claimed to preclude any *a priori* limitation on defense spending.[18]

Opposition to the LDP government's policy of expanding the SDF came from the Japan Socialist Party (JSP), which from the outset had challenged the constitutionality of the NPR and the SDF as a violation of Japan's peace constitution. The Communist Party also advocated the SDF's dissolution, but maintained that a Japanese People's Army had the right of self-defense. The Social Democratic Party of Japan (SDPJ) advanced a more conciliatory position, but one no less opposed to the LDP's position. The SDPJ claimed that the pacifist appeal of Article 9 did not necessitate defenseless nonresistance or rule out self-defense forces under civilian control. But for four decades the SDPJ's platform maintained that the SDF was unconstitutional. The Kōmeitō (Clean Government Party) was even more equivocal in supporting self-defense forces for the purpose of maintaining "peaceful existence."[19]

The controversy over the SDF's constitutionality was raised in the courts as well. Although the judiciary generally sidestepped the issue, it did so in ways that reinforced the conservative LDP government's pragmatic rationalizations for continuing incremental expansion of the SDF. The first case that reached the Supreme Court arose over the government's prosecution of radical demonstrators protesting the U.S.–Japan Mutual Security Treaty. They destroyed fences surrounding the Tachikawa air base, which at the time was used by U.S. forces. As a defense at their trial, the protesters claimed that the treaty and the SDF were unconstitutional. Their arguments were dismissed by the Court. In its 1959 ruling in the *Sunakawa* case,[20] the justices nonetheless declined to rule directly on the SDF's constitutionality. Yet the Court's Grand Bench asserted for the first time that Japan had an inherent and sovereign right to self-defense.

In the second case, the *Naganuma* case,[21] two hundred farmers sued the Minister of Agriculture, Forestry, and Fisheries over plans to build a missile base on Hokkaido, Japan's northernmost and most sparsely populated island. They argued that construction of the base would cause personal injury by denying them use of a forestry preserve on which the base was to be located, and also challenged the constitutionality of the SDF itself. Remarkably, the Sapporo District Court agreed and directed the ministry to retract its permit for the Defense Agency to build the base. At the same time, the district court's 1973 ruling reaffirmed Japan's sovereign right of self-defense, though suggesting that it should be exercised through nonmilitary means.

Subsequently, the Sapporo High Court reversed. It did so rather cleverly, on the grounds that the case had been rendered moot. According to the high court, the plaintiffs no longer had legal interests to assert because the government had complied with the district court's order and restored the forestry preserve. Moreover, the Sapporo High Court added *dicta* emphasizing that Article 9 bars only wars of aggression and, though declining to reach any conclusions about the SDF's constitutionality, said that the law creating the SDF evidenced no sign of aggression or militarism. On appeal, in 1982 the First Petty Bench of the Supreme Court both upheld the high court's ruling and eluded the key constitutional question.

In a third case, the Supreme Court in 1989 also evaded the central issue of the SDF's constitutionality. The *Hyakuri Base* case,[22] as it became known, originated when a farmer sold his property to a private buyer out of opposition to the government's plans to build an air base on it. Ironically, when the buyer reneged on payment, the farmer switched sides and joined the government in suing him. The would-be buyer countered that the SDF was unconstitutional and that building the base would violate Japan's peace constitution. Taking its cue from the Sapporo High Court's decision in the *Naganuma* case, the Mito District Court reaffirmed that the national self-defense was not clearly constitutionally prohibited.

The district court further held that the SDF and expenditures for it were political matters for the Diet to decide. In 1981 the Tokyo High Court—and in 1989 the Third Petty Bench of the Supreme Court—affirmed, holding that Article 9 does not apply to private acts, or give cause for suing over matters such as the sale of private property. Again the Supreme Court skirted the larger issue of the SDF's constitutionality.

Given the controversy both in and out of the courts over the SDF and LDP's stance and well-entrenched system of patronage, conservative LDP politicians, along with some right-wing constitutional-law scholars, pushed the idea of constitutional reform. Their basic aim was the elimination of Article 9 and to expressly reassert the right of self-defense under the Constitution. Yet they met repeated and overwhelming opposition from socialists, liberals, and others. In the more than forty years of postwar controversy, public opinion gradually shifted from entertaining strong doubts about the legality of armed forces in the 1950s and 1960s, to growing support for the SDF in the 1970s and 1980s.[23] Despite this shift, however, public opinion remained resistent to constitutional revision.

With no definitive ruling from the Supreme Court, and in the face of continuing expansion of the SDF, Article 9 remained a parchment guarantee but not an insurmountable constitutional barrier. Expenditures for the SDF grew to the point that, by the 1990s, Japan ranked among the top five countries of the world in military spending.[24] The SDF, to be sure, remains under civilian control, its operations severely limited by law, and, unlike the pre-1945 period, there is no conscription into the SDF. Still, the tensions and contradictions in constitutional politics have persisted in debates between the LDP and opposition parties until, as it were, the weight of time and Japan's economic prosperity, as well as interests in protecting investments abroad, virtually overshadowed serious constitutional debate or turning back.

The long-running controversy over the SDF and increased military spending was only part of the larger struggle in constitutional politics with which Takafumi Nakaya's death and Mrs. Nakaya's lawsuit became inexorably linked. Recall attorney Katsuyuki Kumano's characterization of the four stages of the prewar "glorified spirit cycle" of State Shinto: (1) education and indoctrination; (2) recruitment for the military; (3) soldiers' deaths; and, finally, (4) the disposal of war-bereaved families' grief and the comforting of the spirits of dead soldiers through enshrinements at local *chūkonhi* war memorials, regional *gokoku* shrines, and Yasukuni. It was no coincidence that, in the 1970s and 1980s, as conservative LDP politicians pressed successfully for greater spending for the SDF, leaders in the LDP also worked for renewed governmental support for Yasukuni. At the same time, branches of the SDF and the JAWBF, and other veterans' groups, stepped up their activities aimed at reviving ceremonies at *chūkonhi* war memorials and at the holding of enshrinements—enshrinements no longer just of those who had died in wars, but of those who died while in the service of the SDF during peacetime as well. During all of her husband's military service, Mrs. Nakaya never thought about such connections with the SDF. Only after his death did she come to understand the linkages in the glorified spirit cycle between Yasukuni's spiritual base and militarism.

The enshrinement of Takafumi Nakaya's soul was in fact the first time in Yamaguchi prefecture that such a ceremony had taken place at its *gokoku* shrine when the country was *not* at war.[25] His enshrinement, together with that of twenty-six other former members of the SDF, took place at the request of the local SDF Friendship Association. That association was composed of SDF members and veterans. It had the backing and assistance, as well as served the interests, of the SDF. Basically, the SDF and its supporting associations aimed to establish a new tradition. The tradition since the Meiji era of enshrining war dead would, as it were, be expanded to include the enshrinement of all departed SDF servicemen, even those who died in peacetime.

Other SDF enshrinements had been held on the rural island of Kyushu. There, the SDF, veterans' groups, and SDF friendship associations were more active and better organized. From the end of the Occupation to the Supreme Court's 1988 ruling in the *Self Defense Forces Enshrinement* case, 465 enshrinments were sponsored by the SDF and veterans' associations.[26] Still, until the one held in Yamaguchi in 1972, none had been performed on the main island of Honshu during Japan's postwar peacetime. Christian groups and opponents of militarism, therefore, immediately came out in support of Mrs. Nakaya. They were dedicated to combating what they perceived as another step backward, toward reinvigorating the prewar militarism of the emperor system. For them and for Mrs. Nakaya, this issue was no less important than her claim to a constitutionally protected right of religious freedom.

Yamaguchi's *gokoku* shrine is located a short distance down the road from the prefecture's SDF headquarters. The shrine sits hidden by pine trees and across the road from an SDF training ground, which is next to the SDF base and headquarters. A more concrete illustration of the linkages in attorney Kumano's glorified spirit cycle would be hard to come by. The physical proximity of the two underscores the close ties between Yasukuni and its regional *gokoku* shrines, on the one hand, and the SDF and militarism, on the other. Yamaguchi's *gokoku* shrine was built in 1941, in compliance with the government's 1939 directive requiring each prefecture to have one as the regional representative of Yasukuni Shrine. It now enshrines 52,099 loyal deities.[27]

Yet what function in peacetime, and under Japan's peace Constitution, could Yasukuni and Yamaguchi's or other prefectural *gokoku* shrines have? Their sole purpose as state shrines had always been the glorification of the souls of war dead and the comforting of their living survivors. This remained their function, which is precisely why it was perceived to be in the SDF's interests to hold enshrinements at regional *gokoku* shrines. Enshrinements might reinforce popular support for the expanding role of the SDF, especially during peacetime.

Beginning in the 1950s, expeditions were made to Southeast Asia to recover the bones and other remains of war dead. Those expeditions pro-

Yamaguchi's *gokoku* (country-protecting) shrine. (Author photo)

vided occasions for holding special local and regional memorial services for war dead. In 1959, at Japan's Monument to the Unknown Soldier, or National Tomb of the War Dead, in Chidorigafuchi Park, not far from Yasukuni, eighty thousand unknown war dead were memorialized in services attended by the emperor and the empress. Yet such expeditions could go on for only so long: hence the need to enshrine the souls of SDF soldiers who died during peacetime or on peacekeeping missions. That was also why opponents of militarism and the emperor system saw Yamaguchi's and other prefectural enshrinements as nothing less than a step backward, toward a return of the prewar glorified spirit cycle.

The ties between Yamaguchi's *gokoku* shrine and its prefectural SDF office ran still deeper than is suggested by the space they share. Although conveniently disregarded later by the Supreme Court, the local Federation of Volunteer Associations and the SDF Friendship Association, which had requested and sponsored the enshrinement of the twenty-seven departed SDF members, had only one employee. He worked full time for the SDF and conducted the SDF Friendship Association's business out of the SDF's headquarters in Yamaguchi. That employee of both the SDF and the SDF Friendship Association provided the vital, everyday connections serving the common goals of the SDF, the association, and the *gokoku* shrine.

By twists and turns of fate, Takafumi Nakaya's death resulted in a rather bizarre situation that eventually pushed his wife into suing the government. He had been killed instantly in Kamiaishi city, when the jeep in which he was riding hit a dump truck coming in the opposite direction.

His body was immediately taken to a hospital. Not long afterward, Mrs. Nakaya was informed by an SDF officer that there had been an accident. He also told her to get ready to submit a death report. When she asked why, the officer could not or would not tell her. In retrospect, Mrs. Nakaya suspects that the SDF wanted the report as an indication of her "implicit consent to the enshrinement." She refused to comply, and the SDF continued a number of times to call her about the report.[28]

Along with her son, Mrs. Nakaya was driven to the hospital from her home in Morioka. There, her son remained at the SDF recruiting office while she and her husband's superior, Shinichi Mizuuchi, proceeded to the hospital. Arriving around midnight, Mrs. Nakaya was promptly and without warning taken to see her husband's body. He was stretched out on a table in the hospital's mortuary. The accident, she now finally comprehended, had been fatal. (Death, particularly an untimely or abnormal death, is especially distressing given Shinto's concerns with purity and the avoidance of pollutions. The Japanese thus pay far more attention to matters of death than they do to conception or birth. This is why death is so little discussed, even by doctors, who often continue to advise their patients without telling them that they are dying.[29])

In the morning Mrs. Nakaya faced telling her son his father's fate. The next day Takafumi Nakaya's body was taken to the SDF regimental compound. The following day a regimental funeral and Buddhist ceremony were held to comfort his soul and to raise the spirits of other servicemen. Through all of it Mrs. Nakaya remained dutiful. But she would later complain that she had not been allowed to take her husband's body home. One of her attorneys, Tsuguo Imamura, described the SDF's handling of the matter as not merely insensitive but "inhumane."[30] Officer Shinichi Mizuuchi and others in the SDF dismissed such criticism as misplaced. Mizuuchi defended the SDF's holding a regimental funeral as a fitting, proper tribute, paying high respects to one who had died in the line of duty.[31]

Takafumi Nakaya's body was subsequently cremated in a second Buddhist ceremony held in Yamaguchi. His father, Yukitsugu Nakaya, paid for that ceremony. Takafumi Nakaya's remains were placed in an urn and given to his father. After that ceremony, Mrs. Nakaya and her son moved back to Yamaguchi and lived with her in-laws. She soon decided to move out with her son, however. She would find employment and begin life on her own. Her stern father-in-law expected everyone to honor the routines of his household. That meant subservience from Mrs. Nakaya, something she could no longer abide. Ten years before she had been liberated from her father's household, and her husband's death propelled her farther down the road of independence. Her decision to move out hurt Yukitsugu Nakaya, since she was the wife of his first son. But looking back, Mrs. Nakaya says that "moving out of the household was the first step to the *SDF Enshrinement* case."[32]

When Mrs. Nakaya moved out of her in-laws' house, she took some of her husband's ashes. Out of respect for her father-in-law's feelings, she initially set up a Buddhist altar in her new home and had Buddhist rites performed. Within months, though, she reconsidered that course of action. Takafumi Nakaya had not considered himself religious, whereas Mrs. Nakaya had been a Christian for over ten years. She had converted in 1958, a year before their marriage. Her childhood had been difficult, with her mother dying when she was quite young and other troubles in the household. Her grandfather had always donated at a temple, and she had thought of Buddhism as the family religion. Still, she remained unsatisfied and in some ways defiant. When she was twenty-four, a friend introduced her to Christianity, and she began attending meetings of a small missionary group. The clergyman's words about Christian love, Mrs. Nakaya says, moved her deeply, and within a year she was baptized.

Mrs. Nakaya regularly attended a church with a small congregation. Yamaguchi, like Nagasaki on Kyushu, is known for its small enclave of Catholics. In 1951, a large and impressive Xavier Memorial Chapel was built to commemorate the four-hundredth anniversary of the visit of St. Francis Xavier, a disciple of the Roman Catholic Society of Jesus (Jesuits). When it was mysteriously destroyed in a fire in 1993, arson was suspected. In any event, and in contrast, Mrs. Nakaya's church had been founded in 1881. When it was rebuilt in 1991, only sixteen old wooden pews were installed. Membership has further declined since the university in the vicinity moved. The number of parishioners has dwindled to about forty, with an average age of over sixty.

Mrs. Nakaya's husband had respected her religious beliefs, and she considered herself a devoted Christian. Upon further reflection, she decided to remove the Buddhist altar. Her husband's remains would be placed in a crypt at her church. Mrs. Nakaya wanted to remember her husband in a Christian way, according to her own religious beliefs.

Testifying in the district court—and in an extraordinary statement before the Supreme Court of Japan—Mrs. Nakaya explained that she had been moved by the desire to know "the meaning of my husband's death." The answer, her pastor had told her, would come from God and through belief. "God," she recalled Pastor Hayashi saying, "will answer it to you by your belief." Mrs. Nakaya believed, and kept "asking the meaning of my husband's death in deepening Christian belief and worshipping everyday."[33] Every week she prayed at her church, and every year on the first Sunday in November she and her son attended memorial services for her husband.

Almost four years passed. Mrs. Nakaya's life had begun to settle into a new routine of work and caring for her son, but that soon changed. On two occasions she had already rather curiously been visited by SDF staff sergeant Yutaka Anno, who was in charge of the Yamiguchi liaison office of the SDF. On those visits, without telling her for what purpose, Sergeant Anno had asked for information about her dead husband. He had obtained from her a copy of the family register *(koseki tōhon)* deleting Takafumi Nakaya's name and thereby establishing his death. Anno also made a copy of Takafumi's death certificate, which proved that he had died while in the service of the SDF. Sergeant Anno agreed to find out from his supervisors why the information was needed and promised to tell her the next time he visited. He would return, Mrs. Nakaya knew. She had mentioned that her husband had received some medals during his service, and Sergeant Anno wanted to see them.

April 5, 1972 proved to be another difficult turning point in Mrs. Nakaya's life. Arriving home from work that day, she found Sergeant Anno awaiting her. As promised, she showed him her husband's medals. He immediately began taking notes on them. In the process, and almost offhandedly, Sergeant Anno told her of the decision to enshrine her husband and other former SDF members at Yamaguchi's *gokoku* shrine. Mrs. Nakaya became irate and angry. She told him that she did not want her husband's soul enshrined: it was contrary to her Christian beliefs. Rather than argue, Anno said he would inform his superiors of her opposition and abruptly left.

As it happened, shortly after Sergeant Anno left her house, Mrs. Nakaya discovered an invitation in the day's mail. It had been sent jointly by the *gokoku* shrine's chief priest, Nagao, and the vice president of the SDF Friendship Association. Almost unbelievably, the invitation was for her to attend a joint enshrinement ceremony for twenty-seven SDF officers, including her husband. The joint enshrinement was scheduled to be conducted at Yamaguchi's *gokoku* shrine less than two weeks later, at 7:30 P.M. on April 19, 1972. Mrs. Nakaya was also requested to attend a Grand Spring Memorial Service on April 20. Angry and resentful, she immediately called her pastor. Later, she phoned the regional SDF office to protest.

In the days and weeks ahead, Mrs. Nakaya repeatedly told SDF officers and members of the SDF Friendship Association of her opposition. She pleaded with them to respect her Christian beliefs. The joint enshrinement ceremony, she was told, could not be canceled, nor could Takafumi

Nakaya be removed from the list of those to be enshrined. Too much time had already been spent arranging for the enshrinement. There was no possibility of turning back now.

Although the SDF did not tell Mrs. Nakaya at the time, it was revealed during the course of her trial that plans for the joint enshrinement had been set in motion as far back as November 1964. At a reception after a 1964 memorial service at the *gokoku* shrine, the families of twelve servicemen who had died prior to that date expressed interest in having them enshrined there as deities. That, however, was merely the beginning of a saga that would unfold into the controversy that ensnared Mrs. Nakaya and hung like a dark cloud over Yamaguchi's enshrinement of the souls of twenty-seven servicemen.

In the late 1960s, President Kazukiyo Fukuda and Vice President Hotta Takeshi of the SDF Friendship Association repeatedly approached the chief priest of Yamaguchi's *gokoku* shrine about the possibility of holding a special joint enshrinement *(gōshi)*. Servicemen who die in the line of duty may be added as "pillars"—literally enshrined on stick tablets—and venerated as *kami* at a *gokoku* shrine through various ceremonies known as *gōshi, haishi, heishi,* and *aidonohōsai.*

The ceremonies differ mainly in the prayers offered and the level of honor accorded the newly enshrined deities. These enshrinement ceremonies are conducted at shrines that have already enshrined a main guardian deity, and they accord newly enshrined deities lesser honors than those of the main *kami.* In other words, in *haishi, heishi,* and *aidonohōsai* rites, newly enshrined *kami* do not actually merge with the *kami* already enshrined there. Instead, they are loaned or rented shelter, as it were, under the main *kami's* protective roof or umbrella. *Heishi* means "to be ranked with or classed with," and *haishi* translates as "to enshrine as an associate deity." These ceremonies differ from joint enshrinements, which are known as *gōshi,* meaning "to enshrine together" or the innermost enshrinement, which has an older history rooted in the mass enshrinements of war dead.

The distinctions drawn among the various kinds of enshrinement ceremonies are subtle. Most Japanese would probably not understand them. But in the 1960s, priests at the Yamaguchi prefectural *gokoku* shrine were reluctant to undertake joint enshrinement rites. Historically, such enshrinements had been conducted only for those who died in battle or war. In short, the priests were rigid and uncertain about enshrining the souls of soldiers who had died during times of peace, albeit in the service of the SDF.

Years of uncertainty, meditation, and calculation passed. Not until the fall of 1970 did the SDF Friendship Association get an indication from the chief Shinto priest at Yamaguchi's *gokoku* shrine that a joint enshrinement might indeed be possible. The association was told that it still needed to make a formal application to the shrine for the enshrinement. In theory, a *gokoku* shrine could independently enshrine anyone who had died in the military, but in practice an application and supporting documents had to be filed first, and fees paid for the ceremonies.

Hence the SDF Friendship Association's executive committee did not actually begin work on the application for the joint enshrinement until the fall of 1970. In the process of preparing its application, the SDF Friendship Association was assisted in a number of ways by the prefectural SDF office. The head of the General Affairs Division of that office, Ikurō Nagamine, had officer Masaki Yasuda write to other SDF prefectural offices in Kyushu. Nagamine and Yasuda wanted information about other joint enshrinements of those who had died while in service during peacetime. Specifically, they sought information on whether and how many such joint enshrinements had been held. They wanted to know the pros and cons for holding them and what kinds of processes and rites—*haishi, heishi, aidonohōsai,* or *gōshi*—had been followed. SDF branches in prefectures on Kyushu responded that the enshrinement ceremonies known as *heishi* and *haishi,* which are on a slightly lower level than *gōshi* rites, had been used in the enshrinements of SDF servicemen.

The information collected by the prefectural SDF office was important. It could be used to establish a kind of precedent, an emerging practice of enshrinements in postwar peacetime Japan. Yamaguchi's joint enshrinement could, presumably, proceed safely without causing controversy. The Yamaguchi SDF liaison office gave this information to the SDF Friendship Association, which in turn gave it to the *gokoku* shrine along with its application for the enshrinement. The shrine's chief priest, Nagao, subsequently agreed to enshrine the twenty-seven servicemen in an *aidonohōsai* rite, which ranks below a *gōshi* but would accord the same level of honors as the *haishi* and *heishi* rites that had been performed for other SDF servicemen on Kyushu.

In the meantime, the SDF Friendship Association had been recruiting other groups to support the joint enshrinement. For that purpose, new groups were formed, such as the Association to Honor SDF Members Deceased While on Duty. For the costs of the joint enshrinement and related memorial ceremonies, the association raised approximately 800,000 yen (approximately $4,000). That money, as subsequently revealed at Mrs. Nakaya's trial, was kept for the association by an administrative officer of the SDF prefectural office.

When the SDF Friendship Association finally made its formal application to the *gokoku* shrine, it was approved. But the association and the SDF prefectural office continued working together. Before proceeding with the joint enshrinement, the association needed—and SDF liaison officer Nagamine obtained—necessary documents for the *gokoku* shrine. Those documents pertained to the deaths of Takafumi Nakaya and the other twenty-six to be enshrined. The information was solicited from Mrs. Nakaya and other relatives. The SDF liaison office gave it to the association's president, Fukuda, who passed it on to Priest Nagao.

Arranging for Yamaguchi's joint enshrinement was time-consuming and carefully orchestrated. The SDF prefectural office, an agency of the government, had become intimately involved in sponsoring the enshrinement ceremony. High officials in the SDF had offered their encouragement. The SDF prefectural office had obtained the necessary information on enshrinements in other prefectures that had helped persuade the priests of Yamaguchi's *gokoku* shrine to perform a joint enshrinement. SDF officers Yasuda and Nagamine then gathered the documentation on the deaths of the servicemen that was necessary for their enshrinement.[34]

Technically speaking, the local SDF Friendship Association had applied and paid for the enshrinement at the shrine, with the Federation of Volunteer Associations and the local SDF Friendship Association acting as little more than intermediaries. Coincidentally, the Federation of Volunteer Associations had been created in 1960, when left-wing students were protesting the signing of the U.S.–Japan Mutual Security Treaty. The federation's sole purpose was to support the SDF's expanded role and to help raise the morale of servicemen in the SDF.

The SDF Friendship Association also served as a kind of bridge or link in the chain between the SDF, the government, and the *gokoku* shrine, which had been a religious organization since the war but which was also a vestige of the prewar days of State Shinto. The SDF and the SDF Friendship Association had overlapping memberships, employed some of the same employees, and shared office space and other resources.

For those in Yamaguchi, it was obvious that the SDF was behind the enshrinement, just as the SDF had been behind those that had taken place earlier on Kyushu. Thus it is no wonder that it took someone like Mrs. Nakaya, someone who thought differently and who was firmly committed to her own religious beliefs, to have the courage to challenge the government over the SDF's enshrinement ceremony.

The enshrinement actually required nothing more of Mrs. Nakaya or her husband's family. Takafumi Nakaya's parents were not asked for their permission. Rather surprisingly, in light of Yukitsugu Nakaya's having been a deputy chief officer in the SDF Friendship Association and vice president of the Association of Parents of SDF Officers, he did not learn of the matter until Mrs. Nakaya raised her objections.[35] Yukitsugu Nakaya then opposed her. He supported the SDF's enshrinement of his son. His opposition to her may have made it still more difficult for some of Mrs. Nakaya's neighbors to understand her objections.

The fact that Mrs. Nakaya did not have to do anything concerning her husband's enshrinement and that his parents supported it could and would be turned against her. It could prove an Achilles' heel in her constitutional argument. Attorneys for the government and supporters of the SDF's enshrinement could be expected to argue that Mrs. Nakaya had not technically been "compelled to take part in any religious acts, celebration, rite or practice," as proscribed under Article 20 of the Constitution. What was she complaining about? Mrs. Nakaya, they were certain to counter, had no constitutional ground on which to complain or to sue. She had not been compelled to participate in any religious activity.

The joint enshrinement ceremony proceeded as planned on April 19, 1972. White-robed Shinto priests repeated solemn prayers and made sacred offerings in rites that placed Takafumi Nakaya's soul and those of the others in wooden tablets, or "pillars." Each pillar bore a name followed by the word *"kami."* In the process, the deceased were purified of the anguish and vengefulness caused by their deaths. They thereby rose above self-interest, becoming noble and worthy of veneration. Because of their merit in dying while serving their country, they were transformed from mere men *(hito)* into deities *(kami)* and country-protecting gods *(go-koku).* Their humanness and divinity became fused. Enshrined, they became *chū-kon* and *hotoke,* praiseworthy loyal souls and benevolent guardian deities. The tablets were to be kept at the shrine, where memorial services would be held annually.

The enshrinement at Yamaguchi's *gokoku* shrine exalted the souls of the servicemen for having died and for continuing to contribute to the country's prosperity. The ceremonies were precisely the same as those conducted at Yasukuni. The ceremonies also played on traditional Shinto values and practices that most Japanese take for granted. They focused attention on the importance of purity, respect for ancestors, and the interweaving of the secular and the sacred in everyday life. That is why Christians and liberals so strongly oppose the government's sponsorship of, and participation in, ceremonies at Yasukuni, *gokoku* shrines, and *chūkonhi* war memorials. It is also why their opposition often fails to generate a great deal of sympathy or public support. As Kitakyushū University professor Nobuhiko Takizawa puts it, their warnings about "the rebirth of State Shinto and militarism" and the government's running afoul of the Constitution simply "do not awake a responsive chord in the hearts of the public."[36]

About three months after the enshrinement, Mrs. Nakaya received notification that memorial services for those enshrined at Yamaguchi's *gokoku* shrine would be held on "January 12, forever." She was informed that the fees for the annual services were to be paid by the SDF Friendship Association. The notification was dated June 1, 1972 and sent from Chief Priest Nagao, but again, as later disclosed at the trial, the letter had actually been delivered by SDF officer Yasuda. Thus the government's involvement with Yamaguchi's *gokoku* shrine, a legacy of State Shinto, was further underscored.

Mrs. Nakaya renewed her protests and asked that her husband's enshrinement be rescinded. "It is quite proper for us to enshrine Takafumi Nakaya," she was told, "for he already belongs to the public after his death. Be thankful for what we did. The enshrining is also necessary in order to elevate the sense of pride among soldiers."[37] Three months after the enshrinement, Mrs. Nakaya's pastor tried in vain to intervene. He, too, was unable to persuade the local SDF office to seek a rescission of Takafuni Nakaya's enshrinement. Pastor Hayashi was told that "the Yasukuni Shrine is a 'public religion.'" No matter how uniform or how often repeated, the SDF's responses only disturbed Mrs. Nakaya even more, and drew the wrath of her pastor.

Pastor Hayashi was a crusader. He had battled with the government in the courts before; not inconsequently, he had also prevailed, just three years prior to Mrs. Nakaya's filing her suit against the SDF. For more than a decade, Pastor Hayashi had championed the cause of an alleged mass murderer, Tamotsu Okabe. Okabe, a former policeman, had resigned from the force in 1954 after being charged with trespass and theft. A year later, he was arrested for the slaying of a family of six in Niho, which is close to Yamaguchi in western Honshu. In October 1954, police discovered the bloody bodies of a farmer and his family. They initially arrested a neighbor on the suspicion that he had a grudge against them. However, after releasing him, the police arrested and charged Okabe with the crime.

Detained in jail for over three months, Okabe finally confessed, but at his subsequent trial in the Yamaguchi District Court, he recanted. Judge Masato Nagami admitted the confession, nevertheless. Following a seven-year-long trial, Okabe was sentenced to death. On appeal in 1968, the Hiroshima High Court affirmed the conviction, rejecting Okabe's contention that the police had coerced his confession. Okabe's supporters and attorneys, including Katsuyuki Kumano, appealed that decision. They maintained that the confession had been coerced, and presented evidence that three different sets of footprints were left at the scene of the crime. They also argued that Okabe's human rights had been violated when the trial judge refused to grant his request for representation by counsel.

Okabe's case thus became an important test of human rights in Japan. Pastor Hayashi and others organized a "Society to Protect Okabe" in twenty-seven prefectures to draw attention to his cause. Finally, on July 31, 1970, the Supreme Court reversed Okabe's death sentence and remanded his case for retrial. Writing for the Court, Justice Asanosuke Kusaka held that Okabe's confession was too untrustworthy to be used as evidence against him. Although the Court did not question the tactics of the police or the prosecutor, the government was forced to come up with independent evidence directly linking Okabe to the crime, which it failed to do.[38]

The final stage of Okabe's case overlapped with the emerging controversy over the SDF's enshrinement of Takafumi Nakaya. The experience had prepared Pastor Hayashi, as he would later say, for pursuing Mrs. Nakaya's cause in the courts. Moreover, he had learned how to organize supporters and how to handle reporters and the media. As a result, Pastor Hayashi "skillfully dealt with the mass media. When we went to the SDF to ask it to rescind the enshrinement," recalls Mrs. Nakaya, "the mass media followed us" and her case received nationwide coverage.[39]

"I did not want my husband's death to be used for glorifying war," Mrs. Nakaya explained much later.[40] She fiercely opposed the idolatry and militarism represented by Yamaguchi's enshrinement of her husband's soul. She could not bear his being worshipped at once in two religious traditions. The prefectural SDF office and the SDF Friendship Association had clearly conspired to enshrine her husband's soul against her wishes. Admittedly, they had not singled out Takafumi Nakaya; they merely wanted to enshrine as many servicemen as possible. Yet in doing so they had blatantly disregarded her Christian beliefs. They arguably violated constitutional guarantees for religious freedom and for the separation of government from religion. One of her attorneys, Tsuguo Imamura, quoting the late constitutional scholar Toshiyoshi Miyazawa, put the central contention of Mrs. Nakaya's case against the government bluntly: "It is a kind of violence for the state to have pressed ahead with the enshrinement coercively while being aware that she protested it."[41]

Yasukuni's Cult of War Dead

Coincidentally, at the time Mrs. Nakaya learned about the impending enshrinement of her husband's soul, she was involved in an anti-Yasukuni-bill study group. One year after her husband's death, on June 30, 1969, 244 members of the Liberal Democratic Party introduced into the lower house of the Diet a bill to reestablish governmental support for Yasukuni. The bill would provide financial support for Yasukuni, allow governmental sponsorship of ceremonies there, and provide additional subsidies for war-bereaved families. Even before it was introduced, the bill elevated to the national political stage a major underlying controversy that had run since the end of the Occupation and that would continue throughout the 1970s, 1980s, and into the 1990s.

Mrs. Nakaya immediately saw a connection between the SDF's enshrining her husband's soul in Yamaguchi and the broader political context within which the Yasukuni bill was presented. As she later testified in court, "I could not forgive them for trying to use my husband's death to provide moral support for the revival of militarism." Mrs. Nakaya had become involved in the anti-Yasukuni-bill study group because her church, the United Church of Christ of Japan, is a denomination belonging to the Japan Christian Council, which publicly opposed the bill.

The Japan Christian Council, along with other Christian groups, some Buddhist sects, and the Union of New Religions, as well as socialists and liberals, denounced the bill as unconstitutional. The Yasukuni bill was a mockery of the Constitution and a clear violation of the provisions in Articles 20 and 89 for the separation of the state from religion. Prior to the bill's introduction, these groups circulated a petition demanding that the bill not be introduced. The petition eventually collected 3,277,405 signatures. This was not all that opponents of the Yasukuni bill did in the years ahead. They held hunger strikes, sit-in demonstrations, and protest marches. The LDP's major opposition parties—the Clean Government Party, the Socialist Party, the Democratic Socialist Party, and the Communist Party—all issued protests against the bill.

Even before learning of the SDF Friendship Association's plans to enshrine her husband's soul, Mrs. Nakaya was attuned to the growing controversy over Yasukuni and the LDP's proposal to reinstitute governmental support for the shrine. Pastor Hayashi frequently arranged for guest speakers at the church study group on Yasukuni. Among them was Masahiro Tomura, a chaplain who had mounted his own crusade against Yasukuni. Another was Kenkichi Nakadaira, a Christian lawyer and former judge in one of the early suits brought by Saburō Ienaga over the government's censorship of his treatment of prewar Japan and aggression in World War II. At one of the anti-Yasukuni group meetings, Mrs. Nakaya remembers, Nakadaira had said that "someday Yasukuni must be sued."

Nakadaira also happened to have relatives who had attended Mrs. Nakaya's wedding, and he became her first attorney. Another of her attorneys, Tsuguo Imamura, was also a Christian and attended a congregation of the United Church of Christ of Japan. He had also represented the plaintiffs in the *Tsu City Ground-Purification Ceremony* case. Nakadaira, Imamura, and Kenji Koike comprised her legal team. They were joined at the appellate stage by two others, Akira Nakagawa and Takashi Kōno. All were devoted to her cause and shared her opposition to governmental support for Yasukuni.

The Yasukuni bill had the support of key LDP leaders, the National Association of Shinto Shrines, and one of the LDP's major constituents, the Japan Association of War Bereaved Families (JAWBF). Pressure to introduce such a bill had been building for a long time. Following the government's sponsorship of a May 2, 1952 memorial service for those who had died in World War II, the JAWBF called for renewed governmental funding for memorial rites at Yasukuni and launched a campaign to revive state support for the shrine. In February 1964, the JAWBF published a pamphlet, *Proposed Outline of the State Support of the Yasukuni Shrine*, and organized a Commission of the Friends of the Bereaved Families, composed of 285 LDP members in the Diet.[42] By 1966, the JAWBF had collected the signatures of 22 million supporters of reestablishing government assistance for Yasukuni. An LDP subcommittee studied the matter and by late 1967 had prepared a draft of the bill that would be introduced in the Diet. Yasukuni officials announced that the shrine would abandon its status as a religious corporation upon the bill's passage.

The Yasukuni bill sparked a major political controversy. The bill was yet another example of Japan's tactical pragmatism and almost bewildering capacity for seemingly self-contradictory engagements. The stated purpose of the bill was:

> In accordance with the spirit of the Japanese Constitution and in consideration of national feeling which desires that dead soldiers and those who died for the nation be publicly enshrined and their souls adored, the Yasukuni Shrine will enshrine them, for the comfort of their souls and in gratitude to them. We shall remember their virtues, comfort their souls, and praise their meritorious achievements. The purpose of the shrine is to preserve their great works known forever through these programs.[43]

However, while the name "Yasukuni Jinja" was to be retained and the rites and ceremonies for war dead would continue, Article II of the bill declared that the shrine "should not be interpreted as having a religious connotation." Article V further stipulated that Yasukuni "should not spread its doctrines, nor educate its believers, nor celebrate religious rites."

If the Yasukuni bill passed, at its best, the shrine's status in public law would change from that of a religious to that of a nonreligious organization, as in the prewar days. This was the *tatemae* (the principle or pretense) of the matter, the public and legal aspect of the bill. At the same time, Yasukuni's essential functions and practices would be maintained. This was more important, the *honne* of the matter (the truth or actual feelings of Yasukuni's supporters), which, as everyone understood, meant that its religious rituals and functions would continue, except now with direct governmental assistance. At its worst, then, the bill was doubletalk, mired in contradiction and a direct challenge to the constitutional disestablishment of state religion.

Supporters rallied against criticisms that the bill was a blatant assault on the Constitution. An initial study commissioned by the Diet reluctantly conceded that extensive changes would have to be made at Yasukuni in order for the bill's provisions to pass constitutional muster. The proposed changes were in fact so great as to deprive Yasukuni of much of its symbolism and religiosity. Shinto prayers would have to be omitted from ceremonies, swords and mirrors removed as objects of worship. Purification and *kami*-invoking rites, along with other rituals, would have to be eliminated.

Defenders of the bill continued to insist on Yasukuni's nonreligious function and symbolism. Forget about its prewar history as a nonreligious super-religion and its postwar legal status as a religious institution. In a rare interview, Yasukuni's deputy high priest, Terumichi Kiyama, put the matter candidly:

> War-bereaved families come here, pay reverence at the Outer Shrine, then proceed to the Inner Shrine, where the spirits reside. There they call out, "My son, I am here." They believe they are able to communicate directly with their dead ones. To express their feelings of gratitude, they come from far away and present the harvest of their land to them. It's as if living people are here. Don't you see? It's not a matter of religion anymore. . . . The sentiments of those who come to Yasukuni Shrine and of those who serve here are not religious. . . . These feelings are connected to the deepest emotions of the Japanese. This way of living, this way of thinking, is deeply rooted in this nation. As long as we continue to live according to a Japanese way, this will not change.[44]

Amid the growing storm of opposition, then transportation minister (and, in the 1980s, prime minister) Yasuhiro Nakasone took a strong public stand endorsing the bill. In a 1969 speech entitled "The Yasukuni Shrine as the Japanese Spiritual Home," delivered at Takushoku University, Nakasone articulated the basis for his advocacy of governmental support for Yasukuni, which he would repeat again and again in the coming decades. "Of course, the Yasukuni Shrine must be separate from the Shinto religion," said Nakasone, before explaining that

> In order that the Yasukuni Shrine be separate from the Shinto religion, it should be nationalized. We should resurrect the symbol of Yasukuni Shrine as the Japanese spiritual ground where we can pay our respect to those who died for the sake of the country. This should be done through the commemoration and enshrinement of their spirits. By placing the Shrine under a special legal body, it would thus come under the umbrella of the state. As long as the state exists in Japan, we should have a place where foreign dignitaries can formally attend a worship service with the Emperor of Japan. Otherwise, Japan cannot be called a state.[45]

Symbolism is important, and the symbolism of introducing the Yasukuni bill in 1969 was inescapable: it was the year of Yasukuni's centennial anniversary. The emperor paid a commemorative visit. The way for the bill's passage had ostensibly been laid three years earlier. In 1966, the Diet had passed the Bill of Amendment to the National Holidays Act, reestablishing National Foundation Day on February 11 as a national holiday. According to legendary stories and the *Chronicles of Japan,* compiled in the eighth century A.D., February 11 corresponds with the accession to the throne of the first emperor, Jimmu (Spirit of War).

The LDP and the JAWBF faced defeat of the Yasukuni bill, nonetheless. In the Diet, the bill became stalled in quarreling among members and was eventually declared void on August 5, 1969. That defeat was due largely to the strong opposition and concerted efforts of Christian and Buddhist coalitions, as well as to the opposition parties to the LDP. It also registered the difficulties of consensus-building and political change in postwar Japan.

The LDP and its supporters, particularly in the JAWBF and other veterans' groups, steadfastly refused to yield. Versions of the bill were introduced in the Diet every year from 1970 through 1973. In 1973 the bill did pass the lower house, only to die in the House of Councilors at the end of the Diet's session in 1974. Still, the controversy over Yasukuni continued.

Mrs. Nakaya's lawsuit and the Kamisakas' litigation thus ran their courses amid a robust national debate over the Yasukuni bill and resurgent nationalism. Instead of generating consensus, the Yasukini bill proved highly inflammatory, stirring the passions of factions on all sides of the controversy. Eventually, it even fragmented its own supporters. New associations and interest groups were formed to counter one another. On the one side, an Association of War Bereaved Christian Families was formed, composed of surviving families of Christians enshrined at Yasukuni. In 1975, this group issued a resolution rejecting the claims of the JAWBF and denouncing visits by the emperor and other government officials to Yasukuni.

On the other side, along with the rising tide of nationalism in the 1970s, hundreds of right-wing, ultranationalist groups emerged, including the Young Storm Association, formed within the LDP by members of factions led by Takeo Fukuda and Yasuhiro Nakasone.[46] Conservative LDP members in the Diet created another organization, the Association for Honoring the Glorious War Dead *(Eirei ni Kotaeru kai),* specifically to work with the JAWBF on exerting pressure for reinstituting the prewar practice of the emperor's and other government officials' visits to Yasukuni. The association's first president was Kazuto Ishida, former chief justice of the Supreme Court of Japan, known for his attempts during the 1970s to purge lower court judges who belonged to the Young Jurists Association. Still, as the Yasukuni bill took on various incarnations in order to evade repeated constitutional objections, its supporters began to fragment. The LDP itself became split over the bill. The Yasukuni Shrine and the Central Office of Shinto Shrines even came to oppose final versions of the bill.[47]

Besides intensifying the underlying conflict, the Yasukuni bill invited further study commissions. Much to the disappointment of the far right wing of the LDP, a 1980 study by the legal bureau of the Diet's lower house concluded that formal visits by government officials to Yasukuni would run into direct conflict with Article 20 of the Constitution. This report represented what became known as the "unified view" of the LDP and the government, but it by no means reflected a consensus. It took the position that the "suspicion of the unconstitutionality" of official visits to Yasukuni "is undeniable."

The government nonetheless pressed ahead with its efforts to resurrect the symbolism of State Shinto. In 1977, it recognized as the national anthem the *Kimigayo,* which exalts the emperor in its verses, and on October 17, 1979, the government quietly assisted in the enshrinement of fourteen convicted war criminals at Yasukuni. The next year the Diet passed a bill on "Using the Japanese Era" *(Gengō Hōan),* officially returning to the prewar practice of counting years according to each emperor's reign. In 1982, the Cabinet formally established August 15—a day recognized for honoring war dead and Japan's surrender, as well as one that coincides with *O-bon* (the Festival of the Dead)—as the Day for Mourning and Honoring the War Dead and Offering a Prayer for Peace. But this fell short of satisfying the demands of groups such as the Association for Honoring Glorious War Dead, which wanted August 15 to be declared a national holiday as well.

The battles over the Yasukuni bill continued into the 1980s. By then, legislation restoring governmental financial support for Yasukuni appeared all but precluded due to opposition from so many quarters. However, the other primary objective of the Yasukuni bill remained, namely, legitimating the symbolism of state support for Yasukuni through government officials' visits to the shrine. This became the new flashpoint of contention. On April 21, 1983, at the time of spring rites, Prime Minister Nakasone reignited the controversy by visiting Yasukuni and, while refusing to say whether his visit was official or private, signing the shrine's registry "Yasuhiro Nakasone who is Prime Minister."

Nakasone's visit to Yasukuni both signaled right-wing groups and war-bereaved families that his government supported their cause and invited a renewed uproar from opponents in Japan, as well as in China and Korea, about what they considered to be a revival of the symbolism and militarism of State Shinto. Subsequently, Nakasone told reporters that the LDP's "unified view" that official visits to Yasukuni were unconstitutional was open to different interpretations, and that he would seek a further study of the matter by an advisory committee. This was a tactic used by Nakasone to get around the Diet and focus media attention on his reforms. Nakasone had also used internal and private advisory committees to achieve administrative and welfare reforms without going through the Diet. In short, since the Diet had refused to enact the Yasukuni bill and remained unlikely to do so, Nakasone sought to bypass the Diet through use of a study committee on the issue of "official visits" to Yasukuni.

In November 1984, the study committee concluded—contrary both to critics and to the LDP's "unified view" of the matter—that official visits might be constitutional. The report reached its controversial conclusion by drawing on the Supreme Court's 1977 ruling in the *Tsu City Ground-Purification Ceremony* case. On the basis of the Court's narrow rendering of what constitutes "religious activities" under the Constitution, and reference to the "purpose and effect" of government activities, the report determined that official visits would not be unconstitutional if they were viewed as traditional social customs or social protocol. This begged the critical issue but served as a convenient, albeit controversial, cover for

Nakasone's and other Cabinet officials' visits to Yasukuni.[48] Outcries of protest continued from Christian and Buddhist groups, socialists, and liberals, as well as from officials in China and Korea. The National Council of Churches denounced the continuing movement to restore state support for Yasukuni.[49]

The controversy came to a kind of climactic head in 1984–1985, at least for the moment. Without clarifying whether his visits were official or private, Nakasone continued to go to Yasukuni in the spring and on August 15. By 1984, the campaign waged by the Association for Honoring the Glorious War Dead demanding official government worship at Yasukuni was in full swing. The association had gathered over 10 million signatures and supporting resolutions from 37 prefectural assemblies and 1,548 local governments. In mid-August of 1984, young members of the JAWBF staged a sit-in protesting the fact that there had not yet been an "official" visit to Yasukuni. The issue had become extremely volatile and again began to fragment the LDP. That same month another committee, this time a private advisory committee, was convened by the Cabinet secretary to further study the matter.

Unlike the earlier Yasukuni study committee, this private advisory committee was composed of a bipartisan group of people from outside the government. And unlike the previous report, its report, when finally delivered on August 9, 1985, did not purport to reach a consensus on the issue. The committee actually split three ways: some members supported official visits, others opposed them, and a few advocated the government's building a new national memorial independent of Yasukuni.

Yet the report contained enough to further advance the position of Nakasone's faction within the LDP. For instance, it stated that "It is natural that as representatives of the people, the government remembers the war dead. A large part of the people and the bereaved families recognize Yasukuni Shrine as the central establishment for commemorating the war dead and desire official worship by the Prime Minister and the cabinet." And a pregnant sentence full of mischief added, "Official visits by the Prime Minister and the cabinet do not require a resolution of the cabinet in order to be official and no definite form of worship, e.g., Shinto, is required."[50] The basis was thus laid for bypassing the Diet and the need for legislation authorizing "official vists" to Yasukuni.

The 1985 report on Yasukuni further complicated an already complex controversy. The issue of government officials' visits to Yasukuni had been convoluted all along, in part because the Japanese word for "visit" (sanpai) also means "to go to worship" and commonly refers to visiting a shrine or temple. Further clouding the matter was the forced distinction between "public" or "official" versus "private" governmental visits to Yasukuni. For many years prime ministers had visited Yasukuni without controversy. In 1951, prior to the end of the Occupation, Prime Minister Shigeru Yoshida paid a visit during the annual autumn festival. So did his successors Nobusuke Kishi, Hayato Ikeda, Eisaku Satō, and Kakuei Tanaka.[51] Prime Minister Takeo Miki was the first to claim that his visit to Yasukuni, on August 15, 1975, was a "private" one. He cited in support the fact that he had used neither a government car nor his official title when signing Yasukuni's registry. (Subsequently, the LDP rationalized the use of government cars by prime ministers visiting Yasukuni on the ground that it would be impractical to deny their use.)

The controversy over official visits to Yasukuni slowly escalated after the last Yasukuni bill was defeated in 1974, a full decade prior to the confrontation over Nakasone's 1985 visit. Miki's successor, Takeo Fukuda, raised the ante when he paid visits in 1977 and 1978 accompanied by his chief Cabinet secretary, though claiming that they were private visits. In 1979, Prime Minister Masayoshi Ōira, a Christian, first visited Yasukuni only days after the souls of fourteen class-A war criminals had been enshrined there. He likewise claimed that his was a private visit. Ōira's successor, Zenkō Suzuki (prime minister from 1980 to 1982), visited Yasukuni accompanied by several Cabinet members but refused to clarify whether the visit was official or private. The issue, once noncontroversial, had become highly contentious every August 15. By incremental steps, prime ministers and Cabinet members had laid the groundwork for a bolder move by Nakasone.

Prime Minister Nakasone, a former naval officer, defense chief, fervent nationalist, and champion of Japaneseness, initially followed the course of his predecessor, Suzuki. On visits to Yasukuni in 1982 and 1983, he refused to clarify whether they were official or private. When asked by reporters, he would reply, "Yasuhiro Nakasone, who is Prime Minister, paid the visit."[52] The controversy grew as more Cabinet and Diet members paid visits, often using their ministerial titles. Those visits, and the August 1985 advisory committee's report, prepared the way for Nakasone and his entire Cabinet (minus two ministers who were out of the country) to make the first "official" visit to Yasukuni on August 15, 1985, the fortieth anniversary of the end of World War II.

Nakasone's 1985 visit to Yasukuni engendered bitter opposition from within Japan and a hail of international criticism, particularly from China and other Southeast Asian countries. Nakasone initially responded that "an overwhelming majority of the Japanese people support my decision."[53] He went on to explain that

The Yasukuni Shrine has been the subject of a long-standing issue. The question is how our people will decide through consensus. It is an issue to be decided on the basis of what is supported by a majority of the people. I concluded that the visit was not contrary to the Constitution if Shintoist form was not observed in the visit [that is, if, instead of clapping and bowing twice, Nakasone only bowed once] and if the visit was made in a purely ceremonial style offering respect to the war dead.[54]

In playing to right-wing constituents and war-bereaved families, Nakasone overplayed his hand and failed to achieve his "transformation of national consciousness" based on the emperor. Protests mounted steadily from within and without Japan. Public opinion polls in the *Asahi* and *Yomiuri* newspapers found that, while most Japanese supported the symbolism of the imperial institution, only a bare majority (51 percent) supported Nakasone's "official" visit, and over one-third were "indifferent." The *Asahi* survey also revealed generational differences: more than 60 percent of those aged fifty and over supported his visit, while less than 35 percent of those under age thirty did so.[55] The Japanese public was split along generational lines, often passionately, yet on balance it was ambivalent. Such was not the case abroad, especially in China, where large anti-Japanese demonstrations took place in Beijing and other major cities.

Within months, Nakasone's government was backpedaling. It denied that the visit represented a resurgence of militarism. It even asserted doubts about the propriety of enshrining fourteen class-A war criminals in 1979. By October 1985, Nakasone had backed down from making a return visit to Yasukuni for the autumn rites, and for those the following spring. On August 15, 1986 and 1987, he again stayed away, explaining that he did so "out of respect for the feelings of neighbouring countries."[56] This became the standard line for the rest of the decade, as subsequent prime ministers also refrained from visiting Yasukuni on August 15 out of respect for neighboring countries. The issue receded into the background, for a time. Periodic visits to Yasukuni by a few Cabinet and LDP Diet members, some claiming to be doing so in their "official" capacities, keep the issue alive, as do small annual anti-Yasukuni marches in Tokyo.

Nakasone's 1985 visit to Yasukuni provoked a number of lawsuits as well. Their outcomes were far from conclusive. Conflicting and crosscutting, they became merely part of the ongoing dialogue and debate. Most of the suits were dismissed by district courts. Some wore on for years and became semi-sagas in their own right. In Fukuoka prefecture, a group of forty-three residents, led by head Buddhist priest Kosho Gunjima and including five Christians and several war-bereaved families, filed two suits. One suit alleged that Nakasone had violated constitutional provisions against state involvement with religious activities when he used 30,000 yen ($200) of public money to purchase floral offerings for his Yasukuni visit. The other sought 4.3 million yen ($28,666) in damages for the plaintiffs' "mental anguish" and "psychological damage inflicted by the unconstitutional homage" of the former prime minister. In both cases attorneys for the government countered that the visits were traditional customs, not religious acts.

The first suit was dismissed by the district and high courts in Fukuoka in 1988. A year later the district court rejected the second suit as well. In the latter case, Presiding Judge Ikuo Tomita avoided ruling on whether Nakasone had violated Article 20's provision for the disestablishment of religion. Instead, he held that Article 20 gives citizens the right to adhere to any religion and concluded that Nakasone's visit could not have infringed on that right.[57]

Another case, brought in Osaka by six families of soldiers killed in World War II, resulted in a series of far more curiously contorted decisions. The plaintiffs, including 82-year-old retired Kyoto Dōshisha University professor Yōichi Wada, demanded personal damages of one million yen each from Nakasone and the government. They alleged mental suffering caused by his unconstitutional visit to Yasukuni. As their brief put it, "We, having lost family members because of the war begun by a thoughtless state, strongly wish for peace and want to think of the deceased without interference from the state." For them, in the words of another plaintiff, Takashi Azuma, "A religious institution [was] being exploited for political reasons, a rehabiliation of militarism."[58]

Nakasone's defenders claimed to remain mystified as to why these suits were brought in the first place. "Why are people making such a big fuss?" wondered 71-year-old Kenichirō Matsuoka, the son of Yōsuke Matsuoka, the wartime foreign minister who had been hung as a class-A war criminal and later enshrined at Yasukuni. "Forty years have passed since then," he pleaded, "Please allow them to rest in peace." Likewise, Sumiko Nakai, whose husband had died during the war, voiced a common refrain: "Isn't it obligatory for the nation to pay official homage to war dead, who sacrificed their lives for the sake of the state? Our sorrows can't be healed otherwise."[59]

The Osaka District Court agreed with Yasukuni's defenders' line of reasoning. In 1989, it rejected both the claim that Nakasone had run afoul of the Constitution and the plea for damage awards. Presiding Judge Masayuki Matsuo concluded that Nakasone's visit had simply paid tribute to those who died in World War II. It did not violate the constitutional separation of government from religion. The plaintiffs' claim to a substantive right to remember the war dead without interference from the state was dismissed as groundless. In Judge Matsuo's words, their "suffering derives from a kind of outrage and unpleasant feelings over the fact that official worship took place, rather than from religious reasons."[60]

A year after the Osaka District Court's ruling, a similar suit brought by 115 members of Buddhist and Christian citizens' groups was likewise dismissed by the Kobe District Court. Their lawsuit challenged Nakasone's payment of 30,000 yen ($200) from public funds as a dedication fee to Yasukuni. Each plaintiff unsuccessfully sought 30,000 yen in personal damages for the "spiritual damage in using our taxes" for the purpose of visiting Yasukuni.[61] Following the Kobe District Court's rejection of their claims in 1990, 56 of the 115 original plaintiffs in the suit appealed the lower court's decision to the Osaka High Court.

The Osaka High Court's rulings on the appeals of the decisions of the Osaka and Kobe district courts would not come down until 1992 and 1993. In the meantime, on September 24, 1991, the Supreme Court dismissed an appeal in a related case that might otherwise have settled the controversy over official visits to Yasukuni. In the *Iwate Yasukuni Shrine Service* case,[62] the Court's Second Petty Bench, with Justice Akira Fujishima presiding, rejected an appeal by the Iwate prefectural government of a ruling handed down by the Sendai High Court on January 10, 1991.

The *Iwate Yasukuni Shrine Service* case had originated a decade earlier, in 1981, when three Iwate residents filed a suit in the Morioka District Court. They sought nullification of the prefecture's adoption of a resolution calling for the emperor, the prime minister, and Cabinet members to make official visits to Yasukuni. The resolution had been passed by the assembly, dominated by LDP members, in response to the national campaign for renewed governmental support for Yasukuni that had been waged by the Association for Honoring the Glorious War Dead. The residents argued that the resolution was unconstitutional because visits by government officials to Yasukuni would violate Article 20 of the Constitution. They also sought a refund to the prefectural treasury of the money spent on the salaries of the assembly members for the time they had spent debating and adopting the resolution.

A separate suit, filed in June 1982, became a companion case to the *Iwate Yasukuni Shrine Service* case. In it, ten other residents sought repayment of 21,000 yen ($140) that the Iwate prefectural government had donated in 1981 to Yasukuni and *gokoku* shrines. In March 1987, the Morioka District Court rejected their arguments. The district court held that official visits and public donations to Yasukuni were not religious activities. Instead, as lawyers for the government had argued, the court ruled that they were merely social courtesies paid out of respect for the war dead.

On appeal for four years, the Sendai High Court reversed the Morioka District Court. When handing down the high court's ruling on the *Iwate Yasukuni Shrine Service* case, Presiding Judge Tadao Kasuya held that official visits were "religious acts" and were therefore a violation of the constitutional principle of separation of the government from religion. As the senior judge of the high court and one who would soon be subject to mandatory retirement at age sixty-five, Judge Kasuya went out of his way to declare unconstitutional not only official visits to Yasukuni by the prime minister and other government officials but also visits by the emperor. As such, Judge Kasuya's opinion for the Sendai High Court was a kind of parting shot at the government, a farewell statement from the bench.

Judge Kasuya shrewdly stopped short of ordering repayment of the money donated by the Iwate prefectural assembly to Yasukuni. That calculated decision meant that the substantive outcome favored the Iwate prefectural government. Subsequently, however, the Sendai High Court turned this small victory for the government against the Iwate prefectural assembly. When members of the assembly sought an appeal of the high court's decision to the Supreme Court, the Sendai High Court ruled that the assembly had no standing or basis for appealing since it had basically won the case in not being ordered to repay the money donated to Yasukuni.[63] Just six months later, after the Iwate prefectural assembly persisted in appealing to the Supreme Court, the Court's Second Petty Bench agreed with the high court, dismissing the appeal for presenting no reasons that it ought to be heard.[64]

The Supreme Court's 1991 dismissal of the appeal of the Sendai High Court's ruling in the *Iwate Yasukuni Shrine Service* case was treated in the press and by some scholars as holding that government officials' visits to Yasukuni are unconstitutional.[65] This was an exaggeration: the judiciary in Japan does not work that way, that fast, or that directly and firmly. The Supreme Court generally leaves major decisions for the Grand Bench, not a petty bench, to decide. Technically, a petty bench may not declare a law or ordinance unconstitutional. Instead, the Supreme Court's dismissal of the appeal sent a mixed signal, allowing more time for the Court and other pending cases challenging the constitutionality of Nakasone's Yasukuni visit.

Chief Cabinet Secretary Misoji Sakamoto immediately disputed that the Supreme Court had ruled that official visits to Yasukuni were unconstitutional.[66] A year later, in July 1992, a panel of the Osaka High Court finally handed down its ruling on the district court's 1987 dismissal of the *Osaka Yasukuni Visitation* case. The religious nature of government officials' visits could not be denied. There was thus "reason to suspect" and a "high probability," held Judge Isamu Gotō, that government officials' visits to Yasukuni "can constitute a violation" of the Constitution. However, Judge Gotō declined to hold that the plaintiffs were entitled to compensation. He also rejected their claim of a "personal religious right" to console the souls of war dead without interference from the state. In Judge Gotō's words, "the personal religious right cannot be considered a right or benefit protected by law."[67]

When announcing the Osaka High Court's 1992 decision, Judge Gotō stressed that official visits to Yaukuni were still not publicly acknowledged to be constitutional, implying that in time they might become so. He also belabored the obvious, namely, that visits by the prime minister and Cabinet ministers create a "grave influence" in Japan and invited "objections from overseas" in "Asian countries, including China, the Koreas, the Philippines and Singapore." Even such an understated reminder of how the controversy over Yasukuni had played out during the preceding decade did little to quell passions or curtail debate. Indeed, Judge Gotō's reference to "objections from overseas" was attacked in the *Yomiuri Shimbun,* among other newspapers, as improper and irrelevant to the decision. Two weeks later, on August 15, 1992, in defiance of the high court's ruling, almost the entire Cabinet worshipped at Yasukuni. All but one member, to be sure, insisted that their visits were "private," and Prime Minister Kiichi Miyazawa stayed away so as to not provoke protests from Japan's neighbors.

Contrary to the Osaka High Court's 1992 ruling, the next year a different panel of the Osaka High Court indicated, though without expressly holding, that Nakasone's Yasukuni visit had been constitutionally permissible. This time around in the appeal of the *Kobe Yasukuni Visitation* case,[68] the presiding judge was Fumihiko Gotō (not Isamu Gotō, as in the earlier high-court decision). Judge Fumihiko Gotō dismissed the appeal of the Kobe District Court's decision. The appellants, fifty-six residents who were mostly Christian ministers and Buddhist priests, had no legal grounds for suing. Their claim of "religious personal rights" was deemed too insubstantial. Their "unpleasant feelings" over the former prime minister's visit to Yasukuni, the Osaka High Court held for a second time, were too "subjective and inadequate" to justify awards for damages.

The Osaka High Court's 1993 ruling was not the only one to go in the opposite direction from that indicated by the Sendai High Court and the Supreme Court's Second Petty Bench in the *Iwate Yasukuni Shrine Ser-*

vice case. In 1992, the Takamatsu High Court ruled that a lower court had wrongly held in 1989 that the Ehime prefectural government's donations to *gokoku* and Yasukuni shrines were unconstitutional. In the words of Presiding Judge Kazuo Takagi, "Spending such as donations to shrines remains in the realm of social protocol, and [the donations] were not considered activities that supported and promoted religion."[69] The government's donations, concluded Judge Takagi, simply showed respect for the war dead and their families.

Changes amid Continuity

By the early 1990s, the political tides appeared to be turning once again, and constitutional objections to the SDF were all but washed away. Japan sought a seat on the United Nations Security Council and a greater role in international peacekeeping. In July 1994, following a ruling by the German High Court that its Constitution did not forbid German troops from participating in U.N. peacekeeping missions, and a resolution by the U.S. Senate supporting Japan's adoption of a similar policy, the Japanese Foreign Ministry announced that, under its current interpretation of Japan's Constitution, the SDF was not prohibited from assuming the responsibilities of the country's membership on the U.N. Security Council.[70]

Later that same month, Prime Minister Tomiichi Murayama proclaimed the SDF constitutional. Murayama—the Social Democratic Party of Japan (SDPJ) leader who had come to power in a coalition government, or "marriage of convenience," with his party's longtime rival, the LDP, and the New Frontier Party—vowed to have his party reconsider its 40-year-old position to the contrary. He also now claimed that Japan's 236,000-strong SDF force was "the smallest possible force." Deputy Prime Minister Yōhei Kōno, an LDP member, said that, although the LDP had stood for constitutional revision, his party would respect Murayama's decision "in light of the changing international situation and the people's growing understanding of the Constitution."[71]

Amusement and anger, rather than renewed constitutional debate over the SDF, followed Murayama's and the SDPJ's about-face. The Communist Party blasted the SDPJ and the LDP for their opportunistic maneuvers, but otherwise the SDF's status and greater role in international missions were largely taken for granted, though legal restraints on the SDF's role remain, for the time being, in place.

On the eve of the fiftieth anniversary of Japan's Constitution, after decades of calling for constitutional revision and for amending Article 9, conservative ultranationalists had largely achieved their goal. They had done so not through the courts or by means of constitutional amendment, but through the government's successive reinterpretations of the Constitution. The government had once taken the position that the Constitution had to be amended in order to accommodate the SDF. Later, it claimed that the SDF was constitutionally permissible with respect to defending the country alone, but not for mutual defense or "collective self-defense" with other nations. Now, the government took the position that it was constitutionally permissible for the SDF to play an expanded role in international missions in the name of "collective security," since it would be operating under the guidance and authority of the United Nations.

The government had also worn down the opposition over time. Moreover, the LDP had managed to establish its counterintuitive and otherwise indefensible constitutional interpretation of Article 9 with its archrival, the Social Democratic Party of Japan, at the helm. And the SDPJ had thereby undermined its credibility with voters.

As for Yasukuni, Murayama said, "The Prime Minister and Cabinet ministers will cautiously and voluntarily make up their own minds whether they will make official visits to the shrine, while taking into account various circumstances, including the sentiment of other people in Asia."[72] Meanwhile, the JAWBF and the Association for Honoring the Glorious War Dead kept pressing ahead with their efforts to build public support for restoring governmental assistance for Yasukuni. On March 24, 1994, the latter organization placed a full-page ad in the *Sankei Shinbun* with a headline that read, "Japan is Not A Country That Invaded Other Countries." Later that summer, one of Murayama's coalition government's LDP ministers was forced to resign after publicly expressing similar sentiments. This followed Justice Minister Shigeto Nagano's resignation in May 1994, amid a storm of protest over his claiming that the so-called Rape of Nanking in 1937 was a "fabrication." And in August 1994, Murayama's minister of the Environmental Agency, Shin Sakurai, an LDP member, was forced from office as well, for asserting that Japan had not waged "a war of aggression." He had claimed that World War II actually "led to independence, the popularization of education and increased literacy in Asia."[73]

History was still being distorted, obliterated in praise of Yasukuni's cult of war dead. In October 1994, yet another minister in Murayama's coalition government came under fire for his refusal to concede Japan's aggressions in World War II. The influential head of the Ministry of International Trade and Industry (MITI), Ryūtarō Hashimoto, a right-wing LDP member and chairman of the Japan Association of War Bereaved

Families, told the Diet that it was a "delicate issue of definitions" as to whether or not Japan had committed aggression against Asian neighbors during the war. Hashimoto's remarks sparked initial demands from China and Korea that he resign. In response to questioning in the Diet, Hashimoto responded that "It was not the [Asian] countries Japan chose to fight with, but the United States, Britain, and some other countries." And he added that "taking into consideration the Soviet attacks on Japan at the end of the war and other issues, I am not willing to say we fought a war of aggression in World War II."[74]

On August 15, 1994, Hashimoto and seven of the twenty-one other Cabinet ministers paid a visit to Yasukuni Shrine. There, unlike at Nakasone's visit almost a decade earlier, they had prayed Shinto-style, bowing twice, clapping their hands twice, and bowing again once. Keeping the controversy over official visits to Yasukuni alive, Hashimoto also signed the shrine's visitors' book as "Chairman of the Japan War-Bereaved Families' Association and MITI Minister."[75] The 57-year-old MITI minister and possible future prime minister was, however, crucial to Murayama's coalition government and to trade negotiations with Asian neighbors and the United States. He was simply too powerful to dismiss from the government. And Murayama ultimately defended, rather than refuted, Hashimoto's remarks.

In anticipation of the fiftieth anniversary of the 1947 Constitution, Japan's largest daily newspaper, the *Yomiuri Shimbun,* which has a circulation of 10 million and is noted for its conservative stance, aimed to further stir national debate over revising the Constitution and recognizing the SDF's status. On November 3, 1994, the *Yomiuri* published a lengthy proposal for a new constitution. The draft document put an end to the protracted debate over the SDF's constitutionality by repealing Article 9 of the postwar peace constitution and expressly providing for "an organization for self-defense to secure [Japan's] peace and independence and to maintain its safety." It also renamed the SDF "Japan's Armed Forces" and authorized them to participate in international peacekeeping missions, as had already taken place in the early 1990s, when SDF troops were sent into Zaire, Rwanda, and Mozambique.

The proposed draft, however, also expressly banned weapons of mass destruction, stipulated that military forces were to be employed only in accord with "well-established and internationally recognized organizations" and in "observance of international law," and legally barred conscription into the military. Among other proposed provisions, the constitutional reforms also clarified the emperor's status as the symbolic head of state with respect to foreign affairs. At the same time, in recognition of the postwar judiciary's reluctance to decide constitutional issues, the draft called for the creation of a separate Constitutional Court, independent of the Supreme Court, to decide all constitutional disputes. As such, the *Yomiuri* drew criticism from both the far right and the left, along with other Asian countries, but nonetheless served to renew debate over revising Japan's postwar constitution.[76]

"Eventually, someday, we will be faced with deciding on official visits" to Yasukuni, concedes Supreme Court Justice Itsuo Sonobe.[77] In a country that places a great premium on self-professed harmony, consensus, and often unspoken agreement, great conflicts may play on and on. Consensus proves extremely elusive. Seemingly endless debate and disagreements take place. Passions run deep. Technological rather than theoretical arguments matter the most, even when disingenuous and self-contradictory. Arguments are advanced and engaged in order to gain, if only momentarily, some small tactical advantage. They may then be denied, retracted, or revised. Much later, they may be reasserted, though slightly differently. Everything depends on context. And yet the context of constitutional politics keeps changing—at times almost imperceptibly, and at other times by bold strokes. Litigation and conflict resolution in major controversies, like the one over Yasukuni's enshrinements, remain a kind of constant flirtation, ongoing and continuously changing, without consummation in the courts.

CHAPTER 6

Cool Minds, Warm Hearts

WHEN MRS. NAKAYA filed her suit against the Self Defence Forces'
Friendship Association and the government on January 3, 1973, she had
no idea the trial would drag on for five years and eight months. The
Yamaguchi District Court's decision would not come down until March
22, 1979. In the interim, there were twenty-two separate court sessions.
Each lasted a day, except for the twentieth session, which ran two days
because testimony from expert witnesses was heard in Tokyo. In 1988, fifteen years after Mrs. Nakaya initially filed her suit, the Supreme Court
finally handed down its landmark ruling in the *Self Defense Forces Enshrinement* case.

During the course of the trial, the SDF claimed three times that the
SDF Friendship Association had asked Yamaguchi's *gokoku* shrine to
rescind Takafumi Nakaya's enshrinement. The shrine's priests refused,
however, maintaining that to do so would infringe on their own religious
freedom. Mrs. Nakaya remains unpersuaded by the SDF's claims, and the
SDF Friendship Association has long since abandoned whatever efforts it
may have made to rescind her husband's enshrinement. Nevertheless, the
SDF's claims exemplify the kinds of tactics that can be used in Japan to
diffuse controversies that have become matters of litigation.[1]

Litigation against the government, as earlier noted, aims largely at
using the courts as a forum for gaining publicity and thereby, perhaps, for
shaping public opinion. When litigation raises a major public controversy,
the government typically tries to resolve it by other means—by denying
the basis for the conflict, in an attempt to evade the controversy; by mod-
erating its position; or, more often than not, by holding firm, with a view
to wearing down the opposition and riding out the controversy.

Neither the government nor the opposition generally considers the
judiciary to be an institution for resolving controversies over governmen-

tal policies. At best, courts provide "a chance for conflict resolution." At worst, they merely reinforce the position of governmental bureaucracies. "Law and the judiciary," as an attorney and former judge in Japan puts it, "is not so strong in Japan. Conflict resolution is generally not in the courts, but courts give a chance for conflict resolution."[2] Much depends on the issue, the determination of litigants and lawyers to keep the controversy alive, the bureaucracy's resolve, and how the political landscape changes during the course of the litigation.

The trial for Mrs. Nakaya's case against the government was more an educational process than an adjudication of agreed-upon facts and legal arguments at dispute. It played out in the Yamaguchi District Court, housed in an otherwise nondescript 1960s office building. The outside gives no indication that a court is within. The building could be a school or a faceless government office. The trial was held in courtroom number 21, sterile and classroom-sized. At one end of the room stands a 5-foot-high wooden bench for three judges. In the middle are two sets of tables and chairs, facing each other, for attorneys and their clients. A small gate-partition divides this section from the thirty-six seats for the press and the public. There are no emblems of justice or the authority of the law, not even the Japanese flag, which, having flown during World War II, remains too controversial. In a country that takes great pains with symbolism and that cherishes aesthetic pleasures, the courtroom reflects only the bleakness of bureaucracy. Yet Yamaguchi's district court is no different from any other lower court in Japan.

Mrs. Nakaya's quarrel with the SDF actually preceded her suit over her husband's enshrinement, and her initial confrontation reinforced what she gradually comprehended in her anti-Yasukuni study group and later experienced personally during the litigation over her husband's enshrinement. Not quite three years after Takafumi Nakaya's death, Mrs. Nakaya sued for compensation for his death while in the SDF's service. She did so after being told of another bereaved family's damages award. At the time, Japan had no system of compensating families for the accidental death of SDF servicemen.

In 1972, the year of Takafumi Nakaya's enshrinement, Mrs. Nakaya won her suit for damages over his death. But in the process of defending the government, attorneys for the SDF argued that Takafumi himself was responsible for his death. After all, the SDF insisted, he was the senior officer in charge of the driver of the jeep when it was hit by a truck coming in the opposite direction. Mrs. Nakaya could not understand either this argument or the SDF. Again she consulted Pastor Hayashi, who talked with her about political power, authoritarian thinking, and disregard for

Mrs. Yasuko Nakaya, who sued the government over the Self Defense Forces' enshrinement of her husband's soul, in front of the Yamaguchi District Court. (Author photo)

human rights. The experience, in her words, "cut her link to the SDF." Still, as a result of her suit and others, the government finally adopted a system of compensation for the accidental deaths of SDF servicemen. In this and some other areas, the judiciary triggered a governmental response: a bureaucratic scheme for informally and routinely handling such matters was created.[3] Given her success in this suit, Mrs. Nakaya was hopeful, though by no means confident, that the courts might also rule favorably in the *Self Defense Forces Enshrinement* case.

The suit brought by Mrs. Nakaya over Takafumi's enshrinement asked the court to issue an order to rescind the enshrinement, and for 10 million yen (approximately $49,000) in damages. A claim of personal damages was the only way for her, or for any litigant, to gain standing to sue. Under Article 17 of the Constitution and the State Tort Liability Act, citizens injured by civil servants may sue for reparations, although damages are usually for bodily injuries or the destruction of private property. Mrs. Nakaya's claim of personal anguish and suffering over Takafumi's enshrinement due to her Christian religious beliefs was thus hard for her attorneys to argue. At the trial's outset, she recalls, her claim was especially difficult for the judges to understand. In addition, on the first day in court, August 16, 1973, her attorneys had no evidence directly linking the SDF with the SDF Friendship Association's application for the enshrinement. Thus her attorneys were not in a position to argue that the principle of religious disestablishment had been violated. Moreover, SDF officers testified that they had not been involved in the application process and denied engaging in any impermissible activities associated with the enshrinement.

The trial proceedings were also initially consumed and clouded by conflicting testimony. Mrs. Nakaya was pitted against her husband's father. Besides testifying about her conversion to Christianity, Mrs. Nakaya claimed that her husband had neither expressed any desire to be enshrined nor considered it when joining the SDF's service. Her testimony was contradicted by Takafumi's father, Yukitsugu Nakaya. According to him, his son had said, "I want to dedicate my life to the state." Yukitsugu Nakaya also testified that he himself belonged to the SDF Friendship Association, among other veterans' groups, and introduced a letter signed by himself and Takafumi's younger brother and sister. The letter supported the SDF's enshrinement and stated that it had been his son's wish. Yukitsugu Nakaya went so far as to say that his son had joined the service in anticipation of being enshrined as a country-protecting deity *(go-koku)*. On cross-examination, however, Takafumi's father reluctantly admitted that the letter and much of his testimony had been fabricated.[4]

The trial proceeded against the background of the increasingly heated national debate over renewed governmental support for Yasukuni. Following the defeat of the fourth Yasukuni bill introduced in the Diet in 1974, the Japan Association of War Bereaved Families (JAWBF), the Association for Honoring the Glorious War Dead, the SDF Friendship Association, and many other organizations waged local and national campaigns to restore governmental support for Yasukuni. These groups sought to revive the status of Yasukuni and regional *gokoku* shrines in other ways as well. For example, both the reconstruction of Minoo city's *chūkonhi* and monuments newly built in Yamaguchi's *gokoku* shrine in the mid-1970s stand as testimonials to the dedication of SDF friendship associations, warbereaved families, and veterans' groups to restoring the symbolism of prewar State Shinto.

On the grounds of Yamaguchi's *gokoku* shrine, no less than four new war memorials were erected between 1972 and 1978, that is, between the time of Takafumi Nakaya's enshrinement and the district court's ruling on Mrs. Nakaya's suit. In 1972, a monument was constructed to officers in the Land, Air, and Maritime SDF from Yamaguchi prefecture. The next year, one was dedicated to all young soldiers from the prefecture who had died in the air force during the war. The following year, another was built to commemorate three hundred soldiers from Yamaguchi who had died in Manchuria in 1937. And in 1978, three regional veterans' groups constructed still another monument for their comrades.

These war memorials stand across the yard from Yamaguchi's *gokoku* shrine, next to two remembering stones *(kinenhi)* honoring war dead. One, which was erected in 1989, memorializes all dead imperial soldiers. The other was built in 1953 and is dedicated to those from Yamaguchi who were executed as war criminals during the Occupation. A placard on its base indicates that its construction was completed with the assistance of the SDF. Nor is this all linking Yamaguchi's *gokoku* shrine to the causes of the JAWBF, the SDF Friendship Association, and related groups, as well as to the SDF itself. In front of the shrine's donation box, in 1994, there was a petition for signatures in support of making August 15 a national holiday commemorating Yasukuni's cult of the war dead.

As if the national controversy over the Yasukuni bill and the campaigns waged in Yamaguchi and other prefectures to construct new war memorials were not enough to attract media attention to Mrs. Nakaya's case, her trial also took a surprisingly dramatic turn. Sometime between when she filed her suit in January 1973 and the date of her second court session, October 22 of that year, an insider from SDF headquarters stole one of the letters that had been sent on May 22, 1971 to SDF prefectural branches on Kyushu, asking about enshrinements there. The letter found its way into the hands of a member of the Communist Party in the Yamaguchi prefectural assembly, who passed it on to Pastor Hayashi. That letter was concrete evidence directly linking the government to the *gokoku* shrine's enshrinement of SDF servicemen.

When Mrs. Nakaya's attorneys introduced the letter as evidence in court, witnesses for the SDF and the SDF Friendship Association were forced to retract much of their earlier testimony. The SDF officers could no longer deny involvement with the enshrinement. They also had to explain their activities under cross-examination. Consequently, more details of the story of the SDF's cooperation and assistance became public. Mrs. Nakaya's lawyers—Kenkichi Nakadaira, Tsuguo Imamura, and Kenji Koike—were now able to argue that the SDF and the government had violated the constitutional separation of the state from religion.

A war memorial built in the 1970s on the grounds of Yamaguchi's *gokoku* shrine. (Author photo)

Subsequently, Nakadaira, Imamura, and Koike called expert witnesses to testify about the religious nature of Yasukuni's cult of war dead, militarism, and the constitutional guarantees in Articles 20 and 89. A prominent authority on religion in contemporary Japan, Shigeyoshi Murakami, appeared, as did a specialist on the military, Shigeo Hayashi. Both testified about Yasukuni's role in fostering prewar and wartime militarism. Three leading constitutional scholars, Tokyo University professors Nobuyoshi Ashibe and Yasuhiro Okudaira, and Shinichi Takayanagi, offered testimony in support of Mrs. Nakaya's claim to a substantive personal right of religious freedom, as well as the constitutional separation of government from religion.

Attorneys for the government apparently remained confident that the district court would come down on their side. Only one expert witness, Hitotsubashi University professor Jōji Tagami, submitted a brief on behalf of the SDF, but he did not testify for the government in court.

By March 1979, when the Yamaguchi District Court's decision was scheduled to be handed down, Mrs. Nakaya's case commanded nationwide media attention. She had a large following of private supporters and of Christian and Buddhist organizations. She rejected offers of support from socialist and communist parties, however, because she did not want her cause to become tied up with one or another of the political parties. Pastor Hayashi and others in her congregation organized a "Support Yasuko Nakaya Society" that had more than three thousand supporters.[5] Mrs. Nakaya appeared at rallies, on television, and had become a public figure. Media coverage generally ran in her favor, although nasty letters denouncing her kept coming. Even these "blackmail letters," as she refers to them, were put to a useful purpose: Mrs. Nakaya's anti-Yasukuni study group used them as "a kind of textbook" on the thinking of Yasukuni's supporters.

A Quarrel That Shaped the Constitution

On March 22, 1979, the day of the Yamaguchi District Court's decision, the crowd of supporters, opponents, and reporters was so large that police set up barricades around the court. Even Mrs. Nakaya had trouble getting into the courtroom to hear the decision. Judge Michio Yokobatake presided. Born in 1929, he was a Tokyo University graduate who, a year after deciding Mrs. Nakaya's case, was elevated to the Osaka High Court. Judge Yokobatake was joined by Associate Judge Junichi Sugimoto, born in 1943 and also a graduate of Tokyo University, along with a 28-year-old assistant judge, Yasunori Wada. Although declining to issue an order to rescind Takafumi's enshrinement, they found for Mrs. Nakaya on every other score. The government and the SDF Friendship Association were ordered to pay 1 million yen ($5,000) each in damages. More important than that outcome, however, were the court's fact-finding and legal conclusions.

The Yamaguchi District Court granted that the application for the enshrinements had originated with and been paid for by the SDF Friendship Association. However (contrary to what the Supreme Court's majority opinion would later hold), the district court proceeded to observe that, in the application process, the association had had the full cooperation of the

SDF liaison office. The court stressed that, without the SDF's assistance, the enshrinement probably would not have taken place. The court therefore deemed the application process to have been "the cooperative action of the officers of the SDF Local Liaison Office and the Friendship Association."[6] A factual basis was thus laid for finding that the government had violated constitutional provisions for the separation of the state from religion.

As for Mrs. Nakaya's claim to a substantive individual right to religious freedom, the district court took seriously her testimony about trying to understand the meaning of her husband's death on the basis of her Christian beliefs. "It cannot be denied," observed Judge Yokobatake, "that the plaintiff's legal interest in living a quiet religious life—a personal right—was interfered with when Gokoku Shrine enshrined Takafumi for his having served the state."

However, in the court's view that did not resolve the matter because, as the government's attorneys had argued, Mrs. Nakaya had not been personally compelled or coerced into doing anything in connection with her husband's enshrinement. Members of the SDF Friendship Association also had a constitutionally protected right to religious freedom. In the district court's words,

> The Friendship Association and officers of SDF Local Liaison Office as well as Gokoku Shrine did not force her to worship at the Shrine. The Friendship Association has freedom to conduct religious acts in relation to Takafumi's death. It is clear that that religious act to realize the members' religious personal right is included in the social activity of [the SDF Friendship Association].

The pivotal question, according to the Yamaguchi District Court, boiled down to a conflict between Mrs. Nakaya's and the SDF Friendship Association's equal claims to religious freedom. Giving priority to one side or the other was difficult, said Judge Yokobatake, for each had had a certain "human intimacy with the late Takafumi." There also was "no legal standard to decide the rank of legal protection" to be accorded to either side, since both were guaranteed religious human rights under the Constitution.

The Yamaguchi District Court found a way out of the bind its reasoning had created by returning to the fact that the SDF liaison office had cooperated with the association. The enshrinements were clearly a religious activity, asserted the court, thereby declining to follow or extend the Supreme Court's analysis in the *Tsu City Ground-Purification Ceremony* case. Because an application was a prerequisite for the enshrinement, the district court held that it, too, had religious meaning. This was rather tortured logic, because the shrine could have enshrined Takafumi Nakaya's soul on its own initiative—and could also claim its constitutionally protected religious freedom to do so.

This was part of the reason why the district court declined to order Takafumi's enshrinement rescinded. If the court had ruled otherwise on that issue, it would have been broadly criticized for infringing on the religious freedom of Yamaguchi's *gokoku* shrine. But by finding both that the SDF had collaborated with the SDF Friendship Association in securing the enshrinement application *and* that the application process itself possessed religious meaning, the district court was able to conclude that the government had violated clause 3 of Article 20 of the Constitution, which bars the state's participation in and support for religious activities.

Mrs. Nakaya could hardly believe she had won. She had hoped, to be sure, that the enshrinement would be rescinded. That was the only disappointing aspect of the Yamaguchi District Court's ruling; otherwise, she and her attorneys were elated. They had achieved no small victories. The district court had recognized her injuries and acknowledged her claim of "religious human rights" under the Constitution. In contrast, the SDF Friendship Association and government lawyers were sorely disappointed. The district court's embrace of constitutionally protected "religious human rights," in particular, did not sit well with the government,[7] which immediately filed an intermediate appeal to the Hiroshima High Court.

A little over three years later, just months after Nakasone came to power as prime minister, the SDF Friendship Association and the government faced another defeat in the *SDF Enshrinement* case. Presiding Judge Kaoru Ebisuda and Associate Judges Shigeo Tsuchiya and Asao Ōnishi of the high court dismissed the case, vacating the government's appeal.[8] In their brief opinion, they soundly reaffirmed the Yamaguchi District Court's decision. Notably, all three of the judges on the high court's panel had been born before and had grown up during Japan's wars. The 64-year-old presiding judge had been born in 1918; the other two, in the early 1930s.

The Hiroshima High Court agreed with the district court's finding that the SDF had been intimately involved in the process leading to Takafumi's enshrinement, and that the enshrinement process was undeniably a religious activity. The high court embraced as well the lower court's conclusion that the government had violated Article 20, clause 3 of the Constitution. The high court also upheld the claim to substantive religious human rights under the Constitution, and on that basis affirmed the district court's damages award for Mrs. Nakaya's personal suffering. Once again, Mrs. Nakaya and her attorneys had carried the day. Still, the government refused to yield and promptly appealed to the highest court in the land.

Of Rights, Rituals, and Remembrance

Almost five years passed after the Hiroshima High Court's ruling in the *SDF Enshrinement* case before Mrs. Nakaya's attorneys received telephone calls from clerks at the Supreme Court. On March 4, 1987, they learned that the government's appeal had been granted. Briefs on the merits from both sides would subsequently be filed and oral arguments heard. Mrs. Nakaya's attorneys now knew that a majority of the Supreme Court deemed the case to be very important, for they were told that the case would be heard by the entire Court, not just a petty bench. Unfortunately, Mrs. Nakaya's attorneys also knew that the Court usually grants cases review only when it plans to reverse a lower court's ruling.

All five of Mrs. Nakaya's attorneys filed individual briefs in response to the government's appeal. All but one, Kenji Koike, were affiliated with the Japan Civil Liberties Union (JCLU), and three were on its board of directors. Although affiliated with the JCLU, Kenkichi Nakadaira, Tsuguo Imamura, Akira Nakagawa, and Takashi Kōno participated in the case as individual attorneys. Unlike its counterpart in the United States, the American Civil Liberties Union (ACLU), the JCLU does not sponsor or organize litigation. Although the ACLU and the JCLU were both founded by Roger Baldwin, they differ markedly in their organization, operations, and activities. Their differences reflect, again, the widely divergent understandings in each country of the role of litigation, courts, and constitutional guarantees for civil rights and liberties.

The ACLU, founded in 1920, is older and better established than the JCLU. The founder of both organizations, Roger Baldwin, a Boston aristocrat who lived a spartan life fighting for civil liberties, organized the Civil Liberties Bureau of the American Union Against Militarism in 1917, to defend draft resisters during World War I. "Up to then," he recalled before his death in 1981, "there had been only scattered civil liberties movements [in the United States]. This was the first time the wholesale attack on civil liberties forced a nonpartisan defense of the principles of the Bill of Rights of a countrywide character."[9] In 1920, the original organization was reorganized as the ACLU, under Baldwin's direction and with the help of two conservative New York attorneys, Albert DeSilver and Walter Nelles. Other prominent civil libertarians lent their prestige to the ACLU, including trial attorney Clarence Darrow, philosopher John

Dewey, Harvard University law-school professor (and later U.S. Supreme Court justice) Felix Frankfurter, and socialist Norman Thomas.

Because of its position that political protest is an extension of free speech, the ACLU quickly became associated with labor and with liberal causes. As a result of its initiation of test cases, the ACLU greatly expanded the scope of the First Amendment's guarantees for freedom of speech, the press, and religion.[10] Among its many successes was a 1943 landmark ruling in *West Virginia State Board of Education v. Barnette.*[11] In that case, the U.S. Supreme Court held that the Jehovah's Witnesses could not be compelled to pledge allegiance to the American flag at the start of each school day. During World War II, the ACLU modified its opposition to the draft but staunchly opposed the government's internment and relocation of a hundred thousand Japanese-Americans from their homes along the Pacific coast.[12]

Although Roger Baldwin, the ACLU's founder, remained controversial for championing libertarian causes, General George MacArthur invited him to Japan during the Occupation, along with Thurgood Marshall, the head of the NAACP Legal Defense Fund (and later U.S. Supreme Court justice), among others. MacArthur asked Baldwin to advise the General Headquarters staff on civil-liberties matters. In 1947, the year Japan's new constitution went into effect, Baldwin helped found the JCLU, which counts among its members many prominent, liberal constitutional-law professors and attorneys.

Compared to the ACLU, the JCLU is extremely small; indeed, with virtually no public visibility or recognition, many Japanese have never heard of it. The JCLU has little more than 700 members, of whom 60 percent are lawyers engaged in private legal practice. It has only two paid staff members and operates out of a one-room office in downtown Tokyo that also functions as a library and conference room. In contrast, the ACLU has more than 375,000 members. Its New York headquarters alone has a staff of 125, and there are ACLU affiliates in all fifty states, as well as 200 local chapters.

The JCLU neither initiates lawsuits nor has an overarching legal strategy or campaign, explains Emiko (Amy) Furuya, the JCLU's international liaison officer and one of its two staff members.[13] Instead, the JCLU depends on volunteers and operates via nineteen committees, which range from the Freedom of Information Committee, the Supreme Court Study Committee, and the Abolition of the Death Penalty Study Committee to the International Human Rights Treaties Committee. Through its committees, the JCLU monitors civil rights violations, produces position papers and reports, and offers assistance to litigants. In short, the JCLU

works primarily to publicize its causes through publication of a Japanese-
language paper and an occasional report, *Universal Principle—Human
Rights Report from the JCLU*.[14] By these means, rather than by orchestrating
litigation, the JCLU attempts to develop consensus around its causes. Its
directors contribute their own time to assisting individuals like Mrs.
Nakaya in their appeals.

In their briefs before the Supreme Court, each of Mrs. Nakaya's attorneys concentrated on different aspects of the lower courts' rulings and reasoning. Kenji Koike's brief, for instance, concerned the nature of religious
activities and drew on some of the U.S. Supreme Court's rulings, including the landmark 1947 ruling in *Everson v. Board of Education of Ewing
Township, New Jersey*,[15] which elevated into constitutional law the metaphor of a "high wall of separation" between religion and the state. His
brief also cited more recent U.S. Supreme Court rulings and the so-called
Lemon test.[16] In particular, he noted that, under the disestablishment
clause of the First Amendment to the U.S. Constitution, the U.S. Supreme
Court had disallowed such activities as the posting of the Ten Commandments in public school classrooms,[17] and had barred public schools from
requiring students to begin each day with a "moment of silent meditation,
or prayer."[18]

Koike aimed to head off the Supreme Court of Japan's reliance on and
extension of its decade-old analysis of religious activities in the *Tsu City
Ground-Purification Ceremony* decision.[19] Japanese judges, like Japanese politicians more generally, are sensitive to international perceptions and criticisms. Through its comparisons to U.S. cases, Koike's brief demonstrated
that the Court's adoption of the *Lemon*-like purpose and effect test in the
Tsu City ruling had too narrowly construed the nature of religious activities that the Japanese government is constitutionally forbidden to support.
In other words, the lower courts in the *SDF Enshrinement* case had correctly
held that the SDF's cooperation with the SDF Friendship Association in
the enshrinement application process constituted participation in precisely the kind of religious activities that the government was prohibited
from engaging in under Article 20 of the Constitution.

Imamura, Kōno, and the other two attorneys concentrated their
briefs on supporting Mrs. Nakaya's claim of a substantive right to religious freedom or personal religious rights under Article 20, along with
advancing arguments about the constitutional separation of the state from
religion.

In their briefs and oral arguments before the Supreme Court, government attorneys in the Litigation Department of the Justice Ministry
focused on what they considered to be errors in fact-finding and legal
interpretation by the Yamaguchi District Court and the Hiroshima High

Ms. Emiko (Amy) Furuya and one of Mrs. Nakaya's attorneys, Mr. Takashi Kōno, in the office of the Japan Civil Liberties Union. (Author photo)

Court. Central to the government's argument all along was its contention that the SDF Friendship Association's application for the enshrinement had been completely independent of the activities of the SDF prefectural branch office. Attorneys for the government conceded that SDF officers had assisted in the process of preparing the enshrinement application, but argued that the SDF's assistance was far from engaging in religious activities, contrary to what the district court had held.

According to the Justice Ministry's lawyers, the SDF officers' actions had been perfunctory, merely "administrative tasks," and completely unobjectionable. As for Mrs. Nakaya's claim to a substantive personal right of religious freedom, they countered that the lower courts had wrongly granted and enforced such a right. Mrs. Nakaya, they maintained, should have been more tolerant of the religious freedom of others, such as Takafumi's father and the members of the SDF Friendship Association. Basically, the chief counsel from the Justice Ministry's Litigation Department repeated the same arguments that had been made back in the mid-1970s, during the initial trial.

On February 3, 1988, the Supreme Court heard oral arguments in its massive white-marble courtroom in downtown Tokyo. Unlike the lower courts, the Supreme Court building is impressive, though from the outside it gives no indication of housing the highest court in the land. Inside, a labyrinth of offices for law clerks and secretaries surrounds three court-rooms for the petty benches. At the center of the building, a great white-marble hall leads to the main courtroom, which sits under an iridescent dome. In front of two modern, ceiling-high, pastel-colored tapestries stands a long, dark wooden bench for the fifteen justices. As in the U.S. Supreme Court, the chief justice sits at the center. Associate justices sit on each side, in alternating order, from left to right, of their seniority on the bench. In between the high bench and seats for the press and the public are a podium and tables and chairs for attorneys and their clients.

Prior to the date set for the oral arguments, Mrs. Nakaya's attorneys had arranged with the Court for her to make a personal statement before the bench. Rarely are parties allowed to make such a personal plea to the justices. Oral arguments themselves are generally not thought to carry much weight in the Court's deliberations.[20] Infrequently do the justices ask questions of counsel. The justices and their law clerks usually base the Court's ruling on written briefs and documents. An exception was made for Mrs. Nakaya, perhaps because of the importance of the case and the media attention it commanded, or because the outcome was an all but foregone conclusion.

"I am Yasuko Nakaya. Today, I am very glad to have a chance to state my views before the Grand Bench of the Supreme Court. I thank you heartily," said Mrs. Nakaya in her opening statement, peering up at the justices. Dwarfed by the bench and the crowded courtroom, she proceeded to summarize how her case had come about, before stating her basic grievance:

> When I lived a stable and quiet life with my son, an officer of the SDF Local Liaison Office suddenly asked me for my husband's materials, in order to jointly enshrine the dead officers from Yamaguchi Prefecture in the Gokoku Shrine in Yamaguchi. I refused clearly my husband's joint enshrinement, saying to the officer, "I am a Christian and I reject your offer, as I am mourning [my husband's death] in a church." But, the SDF one-sidely ignored my objection and jointly enshrined my husband in the Gokoku Shrine. I was surprised at it and I asked the reason. The SDF only answered, "The death of the members of SDF is for the state," or "We set a bad example when we admit each one's religion." I felt disturbed and trampled down.

Mrs. Nakaya further explained that

> The relation between Yasukuni Shrine, supported by the government's Yasukuni Bill, and the responsibility of Christians [who were complacent]

during the war, which I learned in the study groups, and my husband's joint enshrining in the Gokoku Shrine overlapped with the meaning of my husband's death, which I wanted to know.

After stating her objections to the SDF's actions under Article 20 of the Constitution, Mrs. Nakaya concluded:

> I am indescribably pleased that the court of the first instance, the Yamaguchi District Court, and the court of the second instance, the Hiroshima High Court, judged my deep feeling a "religious personal right." My feeling is that I cannot give it away to anybody and I want to be let alone. Today, Japan attracts foreign countries' attention to various problems. Is it not too much to ask whether my tiny desire is respected as one of those problems? I heartily ask the Justices of the Supreme Court to give careful consideration and to make the right judgment.[21]

Only one question was posed from the bench. Chief Justice Kōichi Yaguchi wondered where Takafumi Nakaya's remains were: "In the church crypt," Mrs. Nakaya replied, simply yet unwittingly underscoring the perplexity of her claim of personal injuries over Takafumi's enshrinement.[22]

Tsuguo Imamura then proceeded to rebut the government's arguments and to make the case for what he referred to as "the sense of human rights." Central to his argument was that the religious ambivalence and pluralism in Japan, the coalescence and coexistence of Shinto and Buddhism, works to prejudice religious minorities and purists. Quoting from Ruth Benedict's *The Chrysanthemum and the Sword,* Imamura said, "The Japanese are religiously tolerant and again they are intolerant."[23]

Imamura's critical point was that religious liberty requires the majority to be tolerant of the religious beliefs of minorities. The fundamental fact remains that religious pluralism is different in countries like Japan and the United States. In Japan, different religions overlap, intersect, and blend almost without differentiation. By contrast, in the United States, a nation of immigrants and rich diversity, many different religions coexist separately and independently from one another.[24]

Religious intolerance exists in both countries but is manifested differently. In Japan, religious pluralism gives rise to an ambivalence that easily turns into intolerance toward religious minorities. When the latter stand out, as Mrs. Nakaya did or as Jehovah's Witnesses and some other Christians do, or when they ask for exceptions from generally applicable regulations due to their religious beliefs, there is simply no appreciation for their claims of religious freedom. In the United States, adherents of different religions may be intolerant of each other and try to impose their own beliefs in public schools, for example. Yet when religious liberty is threatened, different religious groups and organizations may come together, as they did in 1991–1992, after the U.S. Supreme Court's ruling cutting back on the free exercise of religion in *Employment Division, Department of Human Services of Oregon v. Smith.* [25]

Writing for the Court's majority in *Oregon v. Smith,* Justice Antonin Scalia rejected two Native American drug counselors' claims for unemployment compensation after being fired from their jobs when it was learned that they used peyote, a hallucinogen, during religious services at their Native American Church. They did not challenge their firings but claimed that the denial of unemployment compensation penalized their religious beliefs in violation of the First Amendment's guarantee of the free exercise of religion. For almost thirty years, since a watershed 1963 ruling in *Sherbert v. Verner,* [26] the Court had agreed. The Court had held that government regulations burdening individuals' religious freedom were permissible only if supported by a "compelling government interest" and when they were "the least drastic means" of advancing that interest.

As a result of *Sherbert,* federal courts carved out many exceptions from generally applicable laws for religious minorities. But Justice Scalia declined to abide by those precedents or to follow *Sherbert's* analysis. Instead, he held that there was no constitutional basis for making exceptions for religious minorities from "otherwise generally applicable laws." Justice Scalia went so far as to say that

> Leaving accommodation [of the rights of individuals and minorities] to the political process will place at relative disadvantage those religious practices that are not widely engaged in; but that unavoidable consequence of democratic government must be preferred to a system in which each conscience is a law unto itself or in which judges weigh the social importance of all laws against the centrality of all religious beliefs.

In other words, in Justice Scalia's analysis, the only recourse for religious minorities lies in the political process, not with claims of constitutional rights in the courts.

Justice Scalia's niggardly construction of religious liberty, and his rhetoric about being deferential to the government and the operation of majoritarian democracy, sparked an immediate, widespread controversy. His communitarian reasoning challenged hard-won yet settled societal expectations about religious liberty. His analysis also confused the operation of majoritarian democracy with that of a constitutional democracy, in which the rights and liberties of minorities are constitutionally safeguarded against legislative majorities and the government.[27]

A broad range of religious organizations joined together in persuading Congress to override the ruling in *Oregon v. Smith*. The Religious Freedom Restoration Act of 1993 reestablished as federal law the standards set forth in *Sherbert* as a statutory guarantee for the protection of religious minorities.[28] That coalition of religious groups included organizations as diverse—and otherwise often opposed—as the National Association of Evangelicals, the Southern Baptist Convention, the National Council of Churches, the National Conference of Catholic Bishops, the American Jewish Congress, the Mormon Church, the Traditional Values Coalition, and the American Civil Liberties Union.

Subsequently, even the Court declined to further follow Justice Scalia's analysis.[29] In spite of the Rehnquist Court's changing composition and move in more conservative directions, a majority of the justices stood firm in reaffirming the constitutional impermissibility of public schools sponsoring prayers, even at graduation ceremonies,[30] and state legislatures creating special school districts for religious communities and minorities.[31]

Religious liberty depends both on disestablishment and on the recognition of legal guarantees for the rights of religious minorities. That was Imamura's and Mrs. Nakaya's other attorneys' fundamental point. It was also why her case was so crucial. In order to prevail, the attorneys had to persuade a majority of the Supreme Court of Japan to accept their four main points of contention:

First, they maintained, as the lower courts had held, that the SDF had assisted the SDF Friendship Association in its enshrinement application and had thereby engaged in a religious activity forbidden under the third clause of Article 20.

Second, though closely related to the first and contrary to the government's arguments, they had to convince the Court that the SDF's action was itself an unconstitutional religious activity.

Third, they hoped to persuade the Supreme Court, as they had the lower courts, to recognize Mrs. Nakaya's claim to personal religious freedom under Article 20.

Fourth, there was the novel and untested claim, which the Hiroshima High Court had nevertheless granted, that Mrs. Nakaya had a "religious human right" *(shūkyōjō no jinkakuken)* under the Constitution. The government's enshrinement of her husband's soul violated that right.

On June 1, 1988, exactly six years to the day after the Hiroshima High Court's decision, the Supreme Court's Grand Bench handed down its ruling. Mrs. Nakaya took time off from her work as a day cook at a nursery center to travel the six hours by train to Tokyo the night before, so she could hear the announcement of the Court's ruling at 10:00 A.M. that morning. By a vote of 14 to 1, the justices rejected her claims on all four scores. The lower courts' decisions were overturned.

The *SDF Enshrinement* case was, as U.S. Supreme Court justices are fond of saying, a "hard case." Sometimes, as Justice Oliver Wendell Holmes also observed, "hard cases make bad law."[32] One measure of how hard the case was for the Grand Bench is the extraordinary number of concurring opinions. Separate opinions are rarely filed by justices of the Supreme Court of Japan, unlike justices of the U.S. Supreme Court.[33] Indeed, the *SDF Enshrinement* case was the only case decided by the Grand Bench in 1988 in which separate concurring and dissenting opinions were filed. Including decisions rendered by petty benches, the justices filed separate opinions in just 17 out the 5,188 cases terminated in 1988, with totals of only 22 concurring and 6 dissenting opinions.[34]

Besides the opinion delivered by Chief Justice Kōichi Yaguchi announcing the ruling in the *SDF Enshrinement* case, four separate concurring opinions were signed or joined by seven justices, along with a solo dissent. The single dissenting opinion was filed by Justice Masami Itō. A former Tokyo University constitutional-law professor, Itō was the only scholar sitting on the high bench. In addition, he was the only member also on the bench when the Justice Ministry had filed its appeal of the Hiroshima High Court's decision. Justice Itō had been appointed in 1980 on the recommendation of his longtime friend (and then chief justice) Takaaki Hattori.[35] They had become friends while spending 1954–1955 as Fulbright scholars at Harvard and Stanford law schools.

As a justice, Itō had witnessed the composition of the high bench change dramatically. In 1982, Prime Minister Zenkō Suzuki appointed two justices, Keiji Maki and Mitsuhiko Yasuoka, who would also participate in deciding the *SDF Enshrinement* case. The other twelve seats were subsequently filled by Prime Minister Nakasone, a champion of the JAWBF, the SDF, and Yasukuni. But, as noted in Chapter 3, it is the chief justice who selects and recommends to the Cabinet and to the prime minister judicial appointees to the Court, including his own successor. In 1984, Kōichi Yaguchi, perhaps the consummate judicial insider and bureaucrat, became chief justice. He influenced (if not dictated) the selection of Nakasone's eleven subsequent appointees to the Court.

Chief Justice Yaguchi was "Mr. Judicial Administration." Within

Tokyo legal circles, he was said even to know "the number of mice that live within the Supreme Court building."[36] He had been in the first graduating class of the Legal Research Institute, in 1948, and had spent most of his career rising through the ranks of the judicial bureaucracy. Prior to his appointment to the Court, he had risen to the highest position within that bureaucracy—chief of the General Secretariat. Indeed, Yaguchi had served only twelve years (or one-third) of his career on the bench deciding cases. He also had been in charge of the General Secretariat's personnel bureau in the late 1960s and early 1970s, when Chief Justice Ishida purged the judiciary of those associated with the Young Jurists Association.[37]

To be sure, not all of Chief Justice Yaguchi's nominees and Nakasone's appointees to the Court thought alike. Yet they provided the vital core for the Court's ruling. Moreover, those composing the core majority in the *SDF Enshrinement* ruling were all either career judges or, like Chief Justice Yaguchi, had spent most of their pre-judicial careers working in the Justice Ministry. With one exception, Justice Iwao Yotsuya, those justices who concurred or dissented separately had not risen through the ranks of the judicial bureaucracy and brought to the bench a diversity of experience outside the government (see Table 6).

In his opinion for the Court in the *SDF Enshrinement* case, Chief Jus-

Table 6   Japanese Supreme Court Justices and Their Positions in the *Self Defense Forces Enshrinement* Case

JUSTICE	PRIOR POSITION	YEAR APPOINTED	APPOINTED BY
Composed principal majority			
Keiji Maki	judge	1982	Suzuki
Mitsuhiro Yasuoka	judge	1982	Suzuki
Reijirō Tsunoda	administrator	1983	Nakasone
Kōichi Yaguchi	judge	1984	Nakasone
Akira Fujishima	prosecutor	1985	Nakasone
Tsuneo Ōuchi	judge	1985	Nakasone
Yasukazu Kagawa	judge	1986	Nakasone
Concurring, but critical of the Self Defense Forces			
Rokurō Shimatani	lawyer	1984	Nakasone
Masurō Takashima	diplomat	1984	Nakasone
Atsushi Nagashima	prosecutor	1984	Nakasone
Tetsurō Satō	lawyer	1986	Nakasone
Hisayuki Okuno	lawyer	1986	Nakasone
Toshio Sakaue	lawyer	1986	Nakasone
Iwao Yotsuya	judge	1987	Nakasone
Dissenting			
Masami Itō	professor	1980	Ōhira

tice Yaguchi bent over backward to support the positions taken by the Justice Ministry. Contrary to the two lower courts' finding that the SDF had supported a particular religion when assisting the SDF Friendship Association in its application for a joint enshrinement, the chief justice held that the application had been made solely in the name of the association and mainly due to its efforts. Hence the critical factual link between the SDF and the association was severed. Aware of his distortion of the record, Chief Justice Yaguchi stressed that no SDF officer had directly contacted Yamaguchi's *gokoku* shrine. Whatever assistance the officers had given to the association was dismissed as merely administrative.

As to whether the SDF's cooperation with the SDF Friendship Association constituted a religious activity constitutionally prohibited under Article 20, Chief Justice Yaguchi said that the Court had to weigh a number of factors. It had to "judge objectively the place where the said activity is done, public religious appreciation, the intent and aim of those who act, the existence or nonexistence and the extent of their religious consciousness, and the effect and influence which the activity has on the public."[38]

The decision to perform the enshrinement, he emphasized, had been solely that of the priests at the shrine. In this light, the application for enshrinement was of secondary importance, not a necessary prerequisite. The enshrinement application was thus said by Chief Justice Yaguchi to have little legal significance. Moreover, he asserted that the SDF's collaboration with the SDF Friendship Association did not constitute engaging in a religious activity. Falling back on the purpose and effect test laid down in the *Tsu City Ground-Purification Ceremony* decision, he ruled that the SDF had not transcended the "proper limits" of entanglement of the state and religion. The SDF's actions were accordingly deemed to have been "indirectly related to religion. Its intent and aim were supposed to raise the social status and morale of the SDF members," as government attorneys had argued. "Its religious consciousness was rather diluted. The activity" of the SDF, added Yaguchi, "was not considered by the public to have such effect as raising the concern for a particular religion, sponsoring, encouraging, and promoting, or oppressing and interfering with it." The SDF's activities, he concluded, were not primarily related to religion and therefore not unconstitutional.

The Hiroshima High Court's acknowledgement of Mrs. Nakaya's claims to a personal religious right under Article 20 and to religious human rights in general was rejected out of hand. Furthermore, the Yamaguchi *gokoku* shrine's enshrinement of Takafumi Nakaya's soul was held to be protected by the very guarantee for religious freedom in

Article 20 that Mrs. Nakaya had claimed. Besides turning that issue around, Chief Justice Yaguchi emphasized the importance of "a mutually generous attitude" on the part of all religious believers. He also stressed that Mrs. Nakaya had not been personally compelled or coerced into doing anything. She remained free to mourn her late husband according to her Christian beliefs, but needed to be tolerant of others' religious beliefs. Her claims were thus dismissed and the lower courts' decisions reversed.

The separate concurring opinions were more critical of the SDF, even though joining the Court's ruling. In his concurrence, Justice Atsushi Nagashima pointed out that Article 20's guarantee of religious freedom applies equally to all religions, not just "specially to so-called religious minorit[ies]." He emphasized as well that religious adherents need to be tolerant of each other, but then proceeded to criticize the SDF for its actions. In Justice Nagashima's words, "the action of the officers of SDF Local Liaison Office should have been more deliberate and their speech and action after the enshrining ran to excess." Simply put, "they should have exercised self-control as public officers."

Still sharper criticism came in an opinion filed by Justices Masuo Takashima, Iwao Yotsuya, and Hisayuki Okuno. The SDF's failure to "exercise self-control" was again criticized. In particular, they took issue with the SDF officers' telling Pastor Hayashi that Yasukuni and *gokoku* shrines were an "official religion." Yet these justices did not go as far as two other concurring justices, Rokurō Shimatani and Tetsurō Satō. Although joining in the majority's decision, they profoundly disagreed with Chief Justice Yaguchi's treatment of the first issue, that of the SDF's cooperation with the SDF Friendship Association. In their view, and that of dissenting Justice Itō, the SDF had unconstitutionally engaged in a religious activity. However, unlike Justice Itō, they rejected Mrs. Nakaya's claims to a substantive right of religious liberty. Justices Shimatani and Satō concluded that, despite the SDF's having engaged in activities that violated the Constitution, the SDF had not interfered with any legally recognizable interest on Mrs. Nakaya's part.

The final concurrence was issued by Justice Toshio Sakaue. In contrast with Justices Shimatani and Satō, he disagreed, on the one hand, that the SDF's actions had constituted an impermissible religious activity under Article 20. On the other hand, he agreed that Mrs. Nakaya had a right to religious liberty under the Constitution. He, too, thought that the SDF should have exercised more self-control and that the enshrinement had violated Mrs. Nakaya's religious interest. However, Justice Sakaue saw no reason why her feelings and claim to religious liberty should have priority over those of Takafumi's father or others, including members of the SDF Friendship Association. Hence he concurred in the judgment, though not the reasoning, of the Court.

Justice Sakaue's concurring opinion laid bare what the majority's opinion tacitly acknowledged: In the traditions of Shinto and the history of ancestor worship in Japan, the extended family of the household, not the nuclear family, worships only its own ancestors, just as the village or occupational group traditionally worships its own ancestors and no others. According to the customary understanding, Takafumi Nakaya's parents, not his widow, had first claim on his soul. Although no justice mentioned it, for the Court to have ruled in Mrs. Nakaya's favor on that issue would have cut deeply against tradition and been difficult to understand.

Although, again, no justice noted the fact, the primary exception to this exclusivity of ancestor worship based on the household or village is Yasukuni's cult of the war dead.[39] Enshrinement at Yasukuni and *gokoku* shrines severs ties with family survivors in a certain way. The departed are transformed into country-protecting deities and become part of the national polity. As a result, unless his enshrinement was rescinded, neither Takafumi Nakaya's parents nor his wife could claim a right to exclusively memorialize him.

Dissenting Justice Itō was the sole member of the Court to agree with all of Mrs. Nakaya's claims. Quoting Chief Justice Fujibayashi's dissent in the *Tsu City Ground-Purification Ceremony* case, he underscored that "even if the minority's opinion comes from their fastidiousness, their freedom of religion or conscience cannot be violated even by the rule of the majority." As the lower courts had concluded, Justice Itō found that the actions of Yamaguchi's SDF branch had gone beyond "simple practical cooperation." In supporting and assisting in the enshrinement of SDF servicemen, the SDF prefectural liaison office had run afoul of the Constitution's separation of religion and the state.

Justice Itō also criticized the majority's application, or misapplication, of *Tsu City's* purpose and effect test. Unlike former Chief Justice Fujibayashi, Justice Itō had no quarrel with the test announced in the *Tsu City Ground-Purification Ceremony* decision, but countered that the majority had minimized the cooperation of the SDF. Chief Justice Yaguchi's opinion for the majority drew too sharp a distinction between the SDF and the SDF Friendship Association, simply in order to conclude that the SDF had not aimed at, or had the effect of, advancing a religious activity. And Itō strongly disagreed with that application of the test laid down in the *Tsu City* ruling. "To judge," in his words, "that its purpose does not have religious meaning is to make unjustly light of its objective meaning." In short, in Justice Itō's view, the SDF had unquestionably become too entan-gled with the enshrinement application process, thereby unconstitution-ally supporting a particular religion and denying Mrs. Nakaya's "basic human right" to religious liberty.

The majority's ruling in the *SDF Enshrinement* case provoked an immediate outcry from Christian groups. They warned that the decision would serve to further legitimate the Nakasone administration's claim that official visits to Yasukuni were permissible. "Japan lacks a legal sys-tem to protect human rights," lamented Kazuki Nobe, a minister with the United Church of Christ and one of Mrs. Nakaya's supporters. "It is like the days of [the Japanese Empire]," he added, "when religious freedom was only allowed so long as it did not threaten the Emperor system."[40]

For her part, Mrs. Nakaya told reporters, "Through my court battle I have learned that there exists a spiritual climate in this country that has it that the state takes preference over the individual." She also criticized the Court and the judicial system for lack of independence: "I have been har-boring a notion that the Supreme Court tends to be obsequious to the [government's] power, and it is most regrettable that what I suspected was not proved otherwise."[41]

Mrs. Nakaya's lawyers and some liberal constitutional-law professors were highly critical of the majority's constitutional analysis. Moreover, leaving aside their disagreement with the Court's interpretation of the Constitution, they insisted that the majority's treatment of the SDF's actions—and its discounting of the SDF's cooperation with the SDF Friendship Association—actually violated Article 403 of the Code of Civil Procedure.

Article 403 stipulates that "Facts legally established in the original judgement shall be binding upon the court of last resort." In other words, the Yamaguchi District Court's and the Hiroshima High Court's factual finding that SDF officers had impermissibly cooperated with the SDF Friendship Association and engaged in an inherently religious activity should have bound the Supreme Court. The Court's majority should have confined itself to constitutional interpretation and the legal claims at dis-pute. Such criticism was stinging, yet it underscored how manipulative of facts and legal tests the Supreme Court of Japan can be, albeit no more so than the U.S. Supreme Court upon occasion.

The criticism that the Court had violated Article 403 of the Civil Procedure Code led to an exchange of articles in leading law journals. One of the professional law clerks at the Court even published an article attempting to counter the criticism. The justices had not manipulated or disregarded the lower courts' factual findings in violation of Article 403, the clerk argued. Instead, or so went the logic of his explanation, the majority had simply adopted a different "estimation" of those facts than had the courts below.[42]

Largely missed in press reports and scholarly criticisms of the Supreme Court's ruling was the fact that a majority of the justices had rather sharply and uncharacteristically criticized the SDF for its lack of self-control and involvement with the enshrinement of SDF servicemen. Besides dissenting Justice Itō, concurring Justices Shimatani and Satō had found the SDF's cooperation with the SDF Friendship Association unconstitutional. When those three justices are added to the five others who signed concurring opinions also critical of the SDF, a total of eight justices, or a bare majority of the Court, had censored the SDF.

In sum, the SDF's enshrinements had become too controversial. A majority of the highest court in the land disapproved. That was the crucial message of the Court's ruling in the *SDF Enshrinement* case, and it hit home in the headquarters of the SDF. Following the Court's decision, branches of the SDF did not again engage in the enshrinement of deceased SDF servicemen.[43] In ways not immediately apparent, yet critically important, a majority of the Supreme Court had spoken. A majority of the justices had stood up, more or less, against the SDF and its supporters of Yasukuni's cult of the war dead. A majority had spoken and asserted judicial independence.

The authority of a majority of the Court, which had been overwhelmingly appointed by Nakasone, coming out against the SDF's involvement with enshrinements carried enough influence to lay to rest the controversy over the SDF's peacetime enshrinements. Although generally deferential toward the government and its bureaucratic ministries, the Court may enforce constitutional norms and influence public policy, albeit infrequently and in subtle ways. As Gakushūin University law-school professor Hidenori Tomatsu puts it, "that tells you a lot about law in Japan."[44]

The ruling handed down in the *Self Defense Force Enshrinement* case was timely, and calculated to be so. Based on rumors from law clerks at the Supreme Court, speculation circulated within Tokyo legal circles that the decision had been sped up. There had been growing concerns about the SDF's possible involvement in the funeral rites for Emperor Hirohito. Agreement on that within the Court's bureaucracy had gradually emerged. A majority of the Court thought that the SDF ought to be dissuaded from fanning the flames of controversy that would undoubtedly arise over Hirohito's funeral, and over the subsequent enthronement ceremonies for his successor, his eldest son Akihito.[45]

Anticipation and planning within the government for what the press and the media referred to as "X-day," the day of the emperor's death, actually began in 1981. By 1986–1987, Hirohito appeared increasingly frail. The inevitable appeared to be not far off. At that time as well, Prime Minister Nakasone had, on the one hand, backed down from further official visits to Yasukuni due to international criticism. His government, on the other hand, was preparing for X-day and how to use the occasion both to honor the emperor and to build support for the imperial institution and the LDP's defense policies.[46]

The State, Religion, and Constitutional Politics in Everyday Life

As expected, the death of the 87-year-old Hirohito on January 7, 1989, after a reign of sixty-two years, sparked another round of controversy over the separation of the state and religion. The paradoxes of the imperial state and Shinto in Japan's postwar constitutional democracy surfaced once again, and had to be dealt with, or at least massaged, by the government. The funeral and, to an even greater extent, the accession rites for Akihito underscored how incompletely separated the government is from religion. The state and Shinto remain tightly woven together despite all the legal distinctions drawn, the denials of state support for religiosity, and the like. Article 20's guarantee of religious freedom and ban on governmental patronage for any particular religion, along with Article 89's ban on public expenditures for "the use, benefit, or maintenance of any religious institution or association," were once again up for reinterpretation, and were the basis for conflicting interpretations of constitutional politics.

The controversy over Hirohito's funeral and Akihito's enthronement rites once again divided those in older generations. Christians, socialists, and liberals again opposed right-wing traditionalists and ultranationalists in the Liberal Democratic Party, along with their constituents in groups like the Japan Association of War Bereaved Families. "Shinto gave a religious basis for Japanese ultra-nationalism, ultra-militarism," cautioned Tokai University professor Isao Satō, who had participated in the drafting of Japan's postwar constitution. He also warned that right-wingers, the JAWBF, and some in the LDP were "trying to turn back the clock by pushing for a revival of state-supported Shintoism. Their motivations," claimed Satō, "are the same in their attempts to once again institutionalize religious discrimination in favor of Shintoism."[47]

Yet even Professor Satō conceded that "the Shinto rites are an essential part of the ritual." Indeed, the funeral rites would enshrine Hirohito, posthumously known as Shōwa, in perpetuity. After more than eighteen months of mourning, the Shinto enthronement rituals for Akihito entailed his communing with his ancestor, the great Sun Goddess Amaterasu. Another Shinto ceremony would transmit to him the *kami* of the late emperor and celebrate his imperial divinity. The issue was not so much whether the government should sponsor the rituals as how best to manage them. Not-so-subtle distinctions would have to be drawn, and turning a blind eye to much of the constitutional controversy would be required in order to evade constitutional objections to the government's funding of these rites.

The controversy over the constitutional separation of the state and religion would nevertheless play out in a country so closely identified with Shinto that few liberal law professors, Christians, and other strict separationists seriously question the imperial institution. Makoto Morii, the president of Meiji Gakuin University, a Christian university in Tokyo, and other faculty did take a courageous stand. They decided that their university would not join others in calling off classes or doing anything else special when Hirohito died. Morii also publicly protested the way the media had paid homage to the ailing emperor during the last year of his life. While Morii and Meiji Gakuin University received some support, they also inspired many reactionary letters and callers. When he answered one phone call, for instance, Morii remembers the caller shouting, "Don't be stupid, you Korean! I'll kill you, you damned fool!"[48]

The Imperial Palace, the home of the emperor, who continues to preside as the highest Shinto priest and who, under the Constitution, remains "the symbol of the State and of the unity of the people," is owned and funded by the government. Moreover, distinctions between the state and Shinto are conveniently blurred. They are obscured by the Imperial Household Agency, which administers the emperor's affairs, by distinguishing among three funds: the Imperial Court budget, the Imperial Household Agency budget, and the Imperial Inner Court budget. Only the latter is used for Shinto affairs, which are deemed to be "private" and not "public," despite the fact that all three funds come from the government.

A government committee studied the constitutional concerns, and later Prime Minister Noboru Takeshita announced that the funeral would be divided into two parts. The first part would be religious, consisting of traditional Shinto rituals in a large funeral hall. The second, longer part would consist of secular mourning services. Both were nonetheless paid for by the government, at a cost estimated at 80 million dollars.[49] Neither traditionalists nor separationists were entirely satisfied with the government's solution. Members of the Social Democratic Party of Japan, the largest opposition party, attended only the secular state funeral, while members of the Communist Party attended neither ceremony. There were also some small demonstrations, and left-wing radicals set off a small bomb, without hurting anyone, on the route of the funeral procession.

The February 24, 1989 funeral for Shōwa was the largest state funeral ever staged. His death momentarily forced into focus what had for decades passed largely unspoken: Emperor Hirohito's representation of Japan's prewar and wartime aggression. His funeral, however, registered Japan's economic prosperity and stature as a postwar global power. Attended by representatives of 163 countries, the thirteen-hour funeral of rites and rituals began before dawn with private rites at the Imperial Palace. A procession then followed to Shinjuku Gyoen, a former imperial garden, where a traditional Shinto funeral hall had been constructed of cypress trees. More than half a million people lined the 4-mile-long route.

At daybreak, Akihito made an imperial address and led family members in offering food and silk clothing as final tokens of respect for his father. Following 47 minutes of Shinto rituals accompanied by ethereal flute and panpipe music, the "religious" part of the funeral concluded. A *torii* gate standing in front of the altar, along with other Shinto artifacts, was removed, signifying that the secular services would follow. Those ceremonies culminated at the end of the day on the outskirts of Tokyo, with the Shōwa's coffin being placed in a stone tomb. The granite lid was sealed and later covered with an earth mound. A year later, on January 7, 1990, the first anniversary of Hirohito's death, another ceremony marked the completion of the entire mausoleum complex built for the Shōwa.

The enthronement rites for the 56-year-old Akihito, in November 1990, proved still more costly and controversial. The nearly month-long series of rituals, ceremonies, banquets, and other festivities cost over 12 billion yen (approximately $97 million). On November 12, a set of Shinto rituals *(sokui no rei)* announcing his succession took place at three sanctuaries—the Kashikodokoro, the Koreiden, and the Shinden—inside the grounds of the Imperial Palace. Then, following a televised ceremony formally proclaiming Akihito's accession and a motorcade through Tokyo's skyscraper-dwarfed streets, the first of seven state banquets over the next five days was staged for officials and foreign dignitaries. For these ceremonies, two thrones were flown in from the ancient capitol of Kyoto. One, the Takamikura throne, symbolizes Mt. Takachihonomine on Kyushu, where the legendary grandson of the Sun Goddess Amaterasu first descended to rule over 2,600 mythological years ago. During the ceremonies, Akihito received the imperial and state seals, as well as replicas of the sacred regalia of the Imperial House.

Most controversial was the *daijōsai* ritual (Great Food Offering Festival) that Akihito performed ten days later, at an additional expense of 2.2 billion yen ($17 million). Last performed in 1926, when Hirohito assumed the Chrysanthemum Throne, the prewar *daijōsai* was believed to represent the rebirth of the emperor as a heavenly king, a living god *(arahito-gami)*. In 1990, Deputy Chief Cabinet Secretary Nobuo Ishihara rather understatedly claimed, "The government is not in a position to state whether or not the emperor assumes a divine nature."[50] Yet the Imperial Household Agency left no doubt that Akihito would duplicate prior *daijōsai* ceremonies. In other words, the LDP government sought to avoid coming to terms with the constitutional controversy.

The government was, indeed, in no position to advocate the emperor's divinity, bestowed through a Shinto ritual it had funded at public expense. Neither was there reason for doubting that Akihito would perform the ritual any differently than his predecessors, nor for denying the *daijōsai*'s significance for defenders of the imperial institution. Vaguely understood, with few written accounts of its most arcane rites, and those open to rival interpretations, the performance of the *daijōsai* is veiled even from those few officials and dignitaries invited to attend. They sit in nearby pavilions on the palace grounds. Unlike the ceremonies announcing the emperor's accession to the throne, all foreigners are excluded from the *daijōsai*.

By all accounts, the *daijōsai* is the single most important Shinto ritual in the enthronement ceremonies. After a purification ceremony in the evening, Akihito, dressed in white silk robes and accompanied by Shinto priests and chamberlains dressed in ninth-century court attire, traversed a lantern-lit corridor to enter a complex of traditional wooden buildings in the gardens of the Imperial Palace that had been constructed specifically for the ritual. In the innermost sanctum in two sacred halls, next to two straw mattresses, Akihito performed twice the rice offering ceremonies. Rice from one prefecture east and one west of the Imperial Palace was offered. The rice had been selected by Shinto priests who had examined the ashes of a burnt tortoise shell to pick the precise rice paddies from which it was to come. After the harvest, the priests had chosen each grain individually. During both the ceremonies, each lasting three hours, Akihito shared the rice, *sake*, and other foods in communion with the spirit of the Sun Goddess Amaterasu.

In performing these rites of communion, Akihito was reborn, according to alternative interpretations, either through symbolically entering Amaterasu's womb or through intercourse with his divine ancestress. Concluding at 3:30 in the morning, the *daijōsai* thereby signified the unbroken continuity of the world's oldest dynasty and established the rule of Japan's one-hundred-twenty-fifth emperor. Akihito would later pay special visits to the three shrines on the imperial grounds and travel to the Grand Ise Shrine, while messengers were dispatched to the mausoleums of preceding emperors to announce completion of the *daijōsai* and his enthronement.

Christians, some Buddhist sects, and liberals strenuously objected to the government's funding the ostensibly "private" *daijōsai* ritual. They raised obvious constitutional objections to its doing so under the prohibition in Article 20 on state sponsorship of "religious activities."[51] Japan's largest Christian organization, the National Christian Council, collected more than 180,000 signatures of Christians opposed to the *daijōsai.* The presidents of four Christian universities in Tokyo and Yokohama rather courageously issued a public declaration of protest.[52] "Only half a century ago, Japanese fought wars after being taught through Shintoism to revere the emperor as a god," explained Tōru Yuge, rector of Ferris Women's University. "Why," he asked rhetorically, "does the government then sponsor the ceremony with the identical rites if not to leave the impression that the emperor is reborn with divine qualities?"[53]

The constitutional objections raised by Christians and others carried little force against the LDP-controlled government's determination to sponsor the *daijōsai* and related ceremonies. Their objections, moreover, were easily circumvented by government lawyers accustomed to, and skilled in, the constitutional politics of lying to the government about itself. Prime Minister Toshiki Kaifu's Cabinet created a study committee that inevitably sought to legitimate its preordained conclusion. Through evasive distinctions, the religious significance of the *daijōsai* was downplayed. Public funding for its performance was justified on the ground that, though conducted as a private rite, the *daijōsai* was a public function of the Imperial Household, and hence constitutionally permissible.

Accordingly, the Cabinet's report characterized the *daijōsai* in primarily secular terms:

> The Daijōsai has its roots in harvest festivals transmitted from ancient times when rice farming was central to society. It is a ceremony in which, following enthronement, the emperor goes to a palace shrine to offer newly harvested rice to the founder of the imperial line and to the gods of heaven and earth. He then partakes of the new rice himself. Akihito gave thanks for public tranquility and for an abundant harvest of the five grains, while praying that the nation and the people will enjoy future public peace and abundant harvests. The ceremony is part of a long imperial tradition and is always per-

formed when there is an imperial succession. It is a ceremony that occurs but once in a lifetime.[54]

No more successful than the initial protests against the government's sponsorship of the *daijōsai* were lawsuits raising constitutional objections. Several suits were filed, and subsequently dismissed, against prefectural governments that paid the expenses of local officials to attend the *daijōsai* and related enthronement ceremonies.[55] Whereas plaintiffs argued that the government's funding for the *daijōsai* violated Article 20 and that, as taxpayers, they were "compelled to share part of the expenses," which amounted to "an infringement of their liberty," government attorneys effectively countered that Article 20 "merely guarantees the separation of state and religion, and that even if the state takes part in religious activities, this act itself does not constitute a violation of the Constitution if it does not force the people to take part in religious acts."[56]

As a result, all the litigation accomplished was yet another airing of the constitutional controversy over religious freedom and further recriminations from right-wing ultranationalists. The Christian ministers who led protests against the government were threatened, and the outspoken rector of Ferris Women's Univeristy, Tōru Yuge, was shot at in his study at home by a right-winger claiming that it was "heaven's punishment."[57]

In March 1995, however, the Osaka High Court at least and at last gave a modest, partial victory to the plaintiffs who had challenged the constitutionality of the government's financing of Akihito's performance of the *daijōsai* rite during his enthronement ceremonies in 1990. "There is reason to suspect that the enthronement rituals violated the separation of religion and the state," observed Judge Noriyuki Yamanaka, in announcing the high court's opinion. But he declined to award any damages to the 1,011 plaintiffs for the personal anguish they had suffered over the government's paying for the ceremony and violating the constitutional disestablishment of state support for religion. Instead, Judge Yamanaka dismissed the suit on technical grounds. The dispute was said to be moot, since the government had closed the accounts for paying for the ritual in 1990. Still optimistic and contentious, one of the plaintiffs, Hiroshi Kashima, swore to appeal that ruling to the Supreme Court. And Kashima tried to see the bright side of the high court's ruling, observing, "We lost the judgment, but the wording came very close to making our point."[58]

The continuing struggles over war's remembrance and religious freedom leave most Japanese unstirred. They are almost indifferent to both sides of the constitutional controversy over which Christian minorities and their liberal defenders clash with right-wing ultranationalists. An active minority strongly opposes the emperor and State Shinto. On the other side, the Liberal Democratic Party continues to appeal to its aging constituencies in the Japan Association of War Bereaved Families and other veterans' groups, while the far right maintains its campaigns to resurrect the prewar emperor system with frequent reminders from blaring soundtrucks cruising Tokyo's downtown streets.

Still, most Japanese appear to support the emperor only in a symbolic sense. Public opinion polls in the late 1980s found that 47 percent were "indifferent," 22 percent "favorable," and only 28 percent reported "affection" toward the emperor.[59] Interestingly, less than 20 percent of all Christians in Japan were willing to sign the petition opposing the *daijōsai.* As Reverend Nobumichi Tsuji, one of the leaders of the petition drive, conceded, most Christians have "rather warm feelings toward the Emperor, they respect him—like most Japanese."[60] A January 1990 poll by the *Mainichi* newspaper reported that barely 29 percent supported the government's funding of the *daijōsai,* while 16 percent said it should be privately sponsored and another 23 percent simply did not care.[61] Most Japanese remain ambivalent about the underlying controversy in the country's postwar constitutional politics. Basically conservative, they remain largely content to concentrate on their own economic prosperity.

As for Mrs. Nakaya, following the Supreme Court's ruling she went to Yasukuni on August 15, 1988, to address the Tokyo Conference to Prevent the Nationalization of Yasukuni Shrine. She remains an outspoken critic of renewed militarism. The nasty letters and threats stopped after the Court's decision, and life returned to normal. Mrs. Nakaya remains active in her church and in a minority-rights group against enshrinements. Every June 1, on the anniversary of the *Self Defense Forces Enshrinement* ruling, she and her supporters rally in protest at Yamaguchi's *gokoku* shrine. In 1994, Mrs. Nakaya and some local Christian attorneys were working on another letter requesting the shrine to rescind her husband's enshrinement. Another of her lawyers, Tsuguo Imamura, was contemplating a new suit based on the SDF's denial of Mrs. Nakaya's human rights under the International Covenant on Civil and Political Rights and Human Rights.[62]

Appendix A

Caseloads of Courts in Japan

YEAR	ADMINISTRATIVE AND CIVIL CASES			CRIMINAL CASES			TOTAL		
	FILED	PENDING	DECIDED	FILED	PENDING	DECIDED	FILED	PENDING	DECIDED
Supreme Court									
1952	1,801	1,666	1,275	9,994	7,668	11,178	11,795	9,334	12,453
1962	2,014	2,029	2,273	4,891	2,502	4,671	6,905	4,531	6,944
1975	2,063	1,049	2,380	3,391	1,065	3,537	5,454	2,114	5,837
1985	2,790	1,787	2,874	2,254	849	2,327	5,044	2,636	5,201
1991	3,312	1,881	3,020	1,728	631	1,783	5,040	2,512	4,803
High Courts									
1952	9,510	7,979	9,226	31,566	7,935	38,932	41,076	15,914	48,158
1962	18,131	16,212	17,494	19,508	5,983	19,139	37,639	22,195	36,633
1975	18,395	15,692	18,171	11,971	1,065	3,537	30,366	19,340	30,753
1985	21,136	13,690	21,212	8,630	2,045	8,921	29,766	15,735	30,133
1991	23,999	14,074	23,957	6,691	1,750	6,749	30,690	15,824	30,706
District Courts									
1952	196,077	75,382	183,355	516,343	41,446	518,372	712,420	116,828	701,727
1962	328,526	223,929	317,880	352,840	37,736	354,629	681,366	266,665	672,509
1975	430,911	270,611	438,304	252,995	38,571	252,879	683,906	309,182	691,183
1985	759,728	504,885	717,780	269,895	25,584	270,068	936,706	508,607	969,802
1991	628,143	387,811	619,235	194,447	17,637	194,399	822,590	405,458	813,634

Summary Courts

1952	342,322	26,984	340,723	996,573	29,504	994,986	1,338,895	56,488	1,335,709
1962	672,247	78,325	662,247	4,865,137	154,474	4,846,057	5,537,384	232,799	5,508,576
1975	625,296	57,392	438,304	2,562,046	41,998	2,560,556	3,187,342	99,390	3,190,229
1985	1,764,930	121,830	1,789,958	2,761,460	31,992	2,760,225	4,526,390	153,822	4,550,183
1991	1,196,630	80,207	1,184,606	1,453,655	10,738	1,453,332	2,650,285	90,945	2,637,938

All Courts

1952	549,710	112,011	534,579	1,554,476	86,553	1,563,468	2,104,186	193,564	2,098,047
1962	1,020,918	325,495	1,000,166	5,242,376	200,695	5,224,496	6,263,294	526,190	6,224,662
1975	1,076,665	344,744	1,088,448	2,830,403	85,282	2,829,554	3,907,068	430,026	3,918,002
1985	2,548,584	642,192	2,531,824	3,042,239	60,470	3,041,541	5,590,823	702,662	5,573,365
1991	1,852,084	483,973	1,830,973	1,656,521	30,756	1,656,263	3,508,605	514,729	3,487,081

*Excludes family courts.

Source: Supreme Court of Japan

Appendix B

Individual Opinion Writing on the Supreme Court of Japan, 1981–1993

Justice/Years of Service	Prior Position	(X) Civil (Y) Criminal	Concurrences	Dissents	Other Separate Opinions	Total
Dandō (1974–1983)	professor	X	2	6	1	9
		Y	7	5	3	15
Hattori (1975–1982)	judge	X			1	1
Kurimoto (1976–1982)	judge	X		1		1
		Y	1			1
Tamaki (1976–1982)	attorney	X		2		2
Fujisaki (1977–1984)	diplomat	X		12	3	15
		Y		2		2
Nakamura (1978–1984)	judge	X	3	4		7
		Y	6	1		7
Yokoi (1978–1984)	prosecutor	X	2	8	5	15
		Y		3	1	4
Kinoshita (1979–1986)	judge	X	2	3		5
Miyazaki (1980–1984)	attorney	X	5	4		9
		Y	1	1		2
Taniguchi (1980–1987)	judge	X	4	5	5	14
		Y	12	8	10	30
Terada (1980–1985)	judge	X	2		1	3

Itō (1980–1989)	professor	X	15	9	2	26
		Y	19		3	22
Ōhashi (1981–1986)	attorney	X	5			5
		Y	1			1
Kidoguchi (1982–1986)	attorney	X	4	3	2	9
		Y	1	2		3
Wada (1982–1986)	attorney	Y		1		1
Yasuoka (1982–1990)	judge	X	1	4	2	7
Maki (1982–1989)	judge	X	1			1
		Y	1			1
Tsunoda (1983–1990)	administrator	X	4	1		5
Yaguchi (1984–1990)	judge	X	3			3
Nagashima (1984–1988)	prosecutor	X	4			4
		Y	4	1		5
Takashima (1984–1988)	diplomat	X			1	1
Shimatani (1984–1990)	attorney	X	4	7	2	13
		Y		6		6
Ōuchi (1985–1992)	judge	X	1		1	2
Fujishima (1985–1994)	prosecutor	Y	2			2
Hayashi (1986–1987)	attorney	X	4	2		6
		Y	1			1

continued on next page

Individual Opinion Writing on the Supreme Court of Japan, 1981–1993   (cont'd)

Justice/Years of Service	Prior Position	(X) Civil (Y) Criminal	Concurrences	Dissents	Other Separate Opinions	Total
Sakaue (1986–1993)	attorney	X	1	4	1	6
Satō (1986–1990)	attorney	Y	5	1		6
		X		3	4	7
Kagawa (1986–1991)	judge	Y	2			2
		X	1	12	1	14
Yotsuya (1987–1992)	judge	X	1		1	2
Okuno (1987–1990)	prosecutor	Y	1	5		6
		X		3		3
Ōhori (1988–)	prosecutor	X	1	1		2
Sonobe (1989–)	professor	X	4	2	2	8
		Y	1	1	1	3
Kabe (1990–)	judge	X	1		1	2
Hashimoto (1990–1993)	attorney	X		1		1
Mimura (1990–1994)	administrator	X	1	1	1	3
Total:			140	138	53	331

Notes

Chapter 1: The Nail That Sticks Up

1. Although it is customary in Japan to place the family name before the given name, I have chosen to employ the English-language convention of placing the given name before the family name.

2. For further discussion of the basis for enshrinement, see Kyushiro Sugiyama, "Facts and Fallacies about Yasukuni Shrine," 8 *Japan Echo* 69 (1986).

3. I am grateful to Katsuyuki Kumano for pointing out this connection in the founding of the Japan Association of War Bereaved Families. Prime Minister Yoshida's speech is quoted and further discussed in Katsuyuki Kumano, "Minoo Chūkonhi Iken Soshō 298 nin wa naze shinda ka" (Litigation challenging the constitutionality of Minoo's monument to war dead: Why did 298 people die?), 109 *Osaka Bengoshikai* 5 (Nov. 20, 1993).

4. See Japan Association of War Bereaved Families, *Nihon Izoku kai no yonjū-nen* (Fortieth anniversary of the Japan Association of War Bereaved Families) (Tokyo: Japan Association of War Bereaved Families, 1987).

5. Reported in "War Monument Not Religious, Osaka High Court Rulings," *Kyodo News Service* (July 16, 1987).

6. Ibid; also *Kamisaka, et al. v. Nakai, et al.,* 47 Minshū 1687 (1993); at 1129.

7. For further discussion, see Mark DeWolfe Howe, *The Garden and the Wilderness: Religion and Government in American Constitutional History* (Chicago: University of Chicago Press, 1965).

8. See, e.g., *Everson v. Board of Education of Ewing Township, New Jersey,* 330 U.S. 1 (1947), and the discussion in Chapter 3, at notes 11 to 32.

9. First Amendment, U.S. Constitution.

10. See, e.g., Howe, supra note 7; Walter Berns, *The First Amendment and the Future of American Democracy* (New York: Basic Books, 1976); Stephen L. Carter, *The Culture of Disbelief: How American Law and Politics Trivialize Religious Devotion* (New York: Basic Books, 1993); and Dallin Oaks, ed. *The Wall between Church and State* (Chicago: University of Chicago Press, 1963).

11. Quoted in Leonard Levy, *The Establishment Clause: Religion and the First Amendment* (New York: Macmillan, 1986), p. 184.

12. Thomas Jefferson, Letter to Danbury Baptist Association, January 1, 1802, reprinted in Philip Kurland and Ralph Lerner, eds., *The Founders' Constitution* (Chicago: University of Chicago Press, 1986), Vol. 5, p. 96.

13. James Madison, *The Papers of James Madison,* ed. Robert Rutland (Chicago: University of Chicago Press, 1983), Vol. 14, pp. 266–267.

14. See *Everson v. Board of Education of Ewing Township, New Jersey,* 330 U.S. 1 (1947), and the discussion of the U.S. Supreme Court's rulings on the First Amendment disestablishment clause, and the sources cited, in Chapter 3, at notes 11 to 32; and in David M. O'Brien, *Constitutional Law and Politics: Civil Rights and Civil Liberties* (New York: Norton, 2nd ed., 1995), Vol. 2, Ch. 6.

15. Interview with Reiko Kamisaka, interpreted by Katsuyuki Kumano (Minoo City, May 17, 1994), based on a tape recording of Shinto priest's prayer *(Norito)* at ceremonies on April 14, 1978 and April 12, 1980.

16. Interview with Katsuyuki Kumano (Osaka, Aug. 28, 1993).

17. Ibid.

18. Interview with Mrs. Yoshiko Furukawa, interpreted by Katsuyuki Kumano (Minoo City, May 17, 1994), and letter from Katsuyuki Kumano (May 24, 1994).

19. Interview with Mrs. Hiroko Hamuro, interpreted by Katsuyuki Kumano (Minoo City, May 17, 1994).

20. Ibid.

21. Reiko Kamisaka, supra note 15, and interview with Shigeuki Uehara, translated by Professor Yasuo Ohkoshi (Osaka, July 16, 1994).

22. Furukawa, supra note 18.

23. See *Repeta v. Japan,* 43 Minshu 89 (Supreme Ct., Grand Bench, March 8, 1989); and Lawrence Repeta, "Why We Sued the Judges," 22 *Law in Japan* 49 (1989).

24. Lawrence Repeta, "International Covenant on Civil and Political Rights and Human Rights Law in Japan," 20 *Law in Japan* 1 (1987), p. 4. See also John O. Haley, "Introduction: Legal vs. Social Controls," 17 *Law in Japan* 1 (1984), p. 6.

25. See, e.g., Frank Upham, *Law and Social Change in Postwar Japan* (Cambridge: Harvard University Press, 1987), Chs. 4–5; and John Owen Haley, *Authority without Power: Law and the Japanese Paradox* (New York: Oxford University Press, 1991), Chs. 7–8.

26. For a review of the literature on interest-group litigation in the United States, see Lee Epstein, "Courts and Interest Groups," in John Gates and Charles Johnson, eds., *The American Courts: A Critical Assessment* (Washington, D.C.: CQ Press, 1991), pp. 335–372.

27. See, e.g., Richard Kluger, *Simple Justice* (New York: Random House, 1975); and Lee Epstein, *Conservatives in Court* (Knoxville: University of Tennessee Press, 1985).

28. See, e.g., Susan Olsen, "Interest-Group Litigation in Federal District

Courts: Beyond the Political Disadvantage Theory," 52 *Journal of Politics* 854 (1990); and Lee Epstein, "Debunking the Myth of Interest Group Invincibility in the Courts," 85 *American Political Science Review* 205 (1991).

29. The Japan Civil Liberties Union is discussed further in Chapter 6.

30. This case is discussed further in Chapters 5 and 6.

31. Kamisaka, supra note 15.

32. For further discussion, see Kunio Yanagita, *About Our Ancestors: The Japanese Family System* (Tokyo: Ministry of Education, 1970); Naokazu Miyaji, "What Is Shinto?" 7 *Contemporary Religions in Japan* 40 (March 1960); Naofusa Hirai, "The Principles of Shrine Shinto," 1 *Contemporary Religions in Japan* 39 (1960); and Tetsuzo Tanigawa, "National Character and Religion," 1 *Contemporary Religions in Japan* 1 (1960).

33. See Lawrence Beer, *Freedom of Expression in Japan* (Tokyo: Kodansha International, 1984), p. 249.

34. For a discussion and criticism of claims to "Japanese uniqueness," see: Sōichirō Honda, *Nippon Shinto nyūmon* (Introduction to Japanese Shinto) (Tokyo: Nihon Bungeisha, 1985); Takeyoshi Kawashima, "The Legal Consciousness of Contract in Japan," 7 *Law in Japan* 1 (1974); Michael Banton, *Racial and Ethnic Competition* (Cambridge: Cambridge University Press, 1983); Shoichi Watanabe, *The Peasant Soul of Japan* (New York: St. Martin's, 1989); Masumi Ishikawa, *Nihon Seiji no Toshi-zu* (A perspective view of politics in Japan) (Tokyo: Gendainorisō-sha, 1985); Steven Reed, *Making Common Sense of Japan* (Pittsburgh: University of Pittsburgh Press, 1993); Karel van Wolferen, *The Enigma of Japanese Power* (New York: Knopf, 1989), pp. 265–272; Roy A. Miller, *Japan's Modern Myth* (New York and Tokyo: Weatherhill, 1982); Gregory Clark, *The Japanese Tribe: Orgins of a Nation's Uniqueness* (Tokyo: Saimaru Press, 1977); Peter Dale, *The Myth of Japanese Uniqueness* (London: Nissan Institute for International Studies, 1986); Ross Mouer and Yoshio Sugimoto, *Images of Japanese Society: A Study in the Structure of Social Reality* (New York: KPI Limited, 1986); and John C. Campbell, *Politics and Culture in Japan* (Ann Arbor: University of Michigan Center for Political Studies, 1988).

35. Ben-Ami Shillony [Shichihei Yamamoto], *The Jews and the Japanese: The Successful Outsiders* (Rutland, VT: Tuttle, 1991), pp. 20, 23–25.

36. For a discussion of this episode and for works advancing theories of Japanese uniqueness, as well as anti-Semitic views in Japan, see David G. Goodman and Masanori Miyazawa, *Jews in the Japanese Mind: The History and Uses of a Cultural Stereotype* (New York: Free Press, 1995).

37. See Sachiya Hiro and Shichihei Yamamoto, "Yasukuni Shrine and the Japanese Spirit World," 8 *Japan Echo* 73 (1986). See also Robert J. Smith, *Ancestor Worship in Contemporary Japan* (Stanford: Stanford University Press, 1974).

38. For further discussion of Buddhism in Japan, see Joseph M. Kitagawa, *Religion in Japanese History* (New York: Columbia University Press, 2nd ed., 1990), pp. 86–131.

39. For further discussion, see Smith, supra note 37.

40. Jan Swyngedouw, "Religion in Contemporary Japanese Society," 13 *Japan*

Foundation Newsletter 1 (1986), p. 5. (The data were based on surveys in 1981 by NHK public broadcasting system and in 1981 by Shinpo Shrine.) See also Byron H. Earhart, *Gedatsu-kai and Religion in Contemporary Japan* (Bloomington: Indiana University Press, 1989), pp. 2–12.

41. See, e.g., Agency for Cultural Affairs, *Japanese Religion* (Tokyo: Kodansha International, 1972), pp. 89–104.

42. Agency for Cultural Affairs, *Shūkyō Nenkan* (Almanac of religion) (Tokyo: Gyōsei, 1988), p. 13. See also Hisao Takagi, "Christianity's Tenuous Foothold in Japan," *Nikkei Weekly* 2 (April 22, 1992).

43. The polls are reported in the *Daily Yomiuri* 2 (July 3, 1994), and *Yomiuri Shinbun* 8 (July 3, 1994). See also Statistics Bureau, Management and Coordination Agency, *Japan Statistical Yearbook—1992* (Tokyo: Statistics Bureau, 1992), p. 695.

44. *Kobe Technical College Case,* 813 Hanrei Taimuzu 134 (Kobe Dist. Ct., Feb. 22, 1993). I am grateful to Gakushūin University law-school professor Hidenori Tomatsu for pointing out this litigation and its significance. Interview with Hidenori Tomatsu (Tokyo, Sept. 9, 1993). In 1994, however, the Osaka High Court reversed the district court. See, "Court Backs Religion in Schools," *Japan Times* 5 (Dec. 23, 1994).

45. See, e.g., *Cantwell v. Connecticut,* 310 U.S. 296 (1940), which struck down a permit requirement for soliciting funds on public streets challenged by Jehovah's Witnesses as an infringement on their First Amendment guarantee for freedom of religious exercise; *Murdock v. Commonwealth,* 319 U.S. 105 (1943). which struck down a license tax on canvassing and soliciting as applied to Jehovah's Witnesses; *Martin v. Struthers,* 319 U.S. 141 (1943), which overturned an ordinance forbidding door-to-door solicitations as applied to Jeohovah's Witnesses; *Douglas v. City of Jeanette,* 319 U.S. 157 (1943), which held that police may not bar Jehovah's Witnesses from proselytizing on Sundays, despite objections from the community; and *West Virginia State Board of Education v. Barnette,* 319 U.S. 624 (1943), which struck down, on First Amendment free-speech grounds, a compulsory flag-salute statute challenged by Jehovah's Witnesses as a violation of their First Amendment right to religious freedom.

46. *The Tokyo School Attendance Case,* 37 Gyōsei reishū 347 (Tokyo Dist. Ct., March, 20, 1986).

47. See "Divorce on Incompatible Religious Beliefs Granted," *Kyodo News Service* (March 10, 1989); and Taime Bryant, " 'Responsible' Husbands, 'Recalcitrant' Wives, Retributive Judges: Judicial Management of Contested Divorce in Japan," 18 *Journal of Japanese Studies* 407 (1992). Notably, however, Japanese courts have held that Jehovah's Witnesses who refuse to allow blood transfusions for their children and whose children die as a result may not be prosecuted afterward. See *Kōno v. Kōno,* 1180 Hanrei Jihō 113 (Osaka Dist. Ct., Feb. 12, 1985); "Boy's Death Spotlights Jehovah's Witness Issue," *Japan Times* 3 (May 7, 1994); and "Religious Beliefs Respected: Council Recognizes Patients' Rights," *Japan Times* 3 (May 7, 1994).

48. Satoru Kaneko, "Gendaijin no shūkyō ishiki" (A modern person's religious senses) in Eisho Ōmura and Shigeru Nishiyama, eds., *Gendaijin no shūkyō* (A modern person's religion) (Tokyo: Yūhikaku, 1988), pp. 77–117.

49. Edwin O. Reischauer, *The Japanese Today* (Cambridge: Belknap Press, 1988), p. 215.

50. Keiichi Yanagawa and Yoshiya Abe, *Shūkyō-riron to shūkyō-shi* (Theories and history of religion) (Tokyo: Nippon Hōsō Shuppankyōkai, 1985), p. 20, translated and quoted by Swyngedouw, supra note 40, pp. 13–14.

51. Ian Reader, *Religion in Contemporary Japan* (Honolulu: University of Hawai'i Press, 1991), p. 14.

52. Sokyo Ono, *Shinto: The Kami Way* (Rutland, VT: Tuttle, 1969), pp. 3–4.

53. Interview with Justice Itsuo Sonobe, Supreme Court of Japan, Tokyo (July 19, 1993). See also Agency for Cultural Affairs, supra note 41.

54. *Mainichi Shinbun* (Jan. 4, 1986), reporting on a sample survey of 2,321 from Nov. 20 to Dec. 1, 1985.

55. I am grateful to Professor Takeshi Igarashi for emphasizing this dichotomy (interview, Tokyo, July 29, 1993). See sources cited in supra note 34 and cf. the essays in Byron Shafer, ed., *Is America Different? A New Look at American Exceptionalism* (Oxford: Oxford University Press, 1991).

56. See J. Mark Ramseyer, "Reluctant Litigant Revisited: Rationality and Disputes in Japan," 14 *Journal of Japanese Studies* 111 (1988); and cf. John O. Haley, "The Myth of the Reluctant Litigant," 4 *Journal of Japanese Studies* 359 (1978).

57. See Douglas D. Mitchell, *Amae: The Expression of Reciprocal Dependency Needs in Japanese Politics and Law* (Boulder: Westview Press, 1976).

58. But see Kiyomi Morioka, *Religion in Changing Japanese Society* (Tokyo: University of Tokyo, 1975). See also R. Minear, *Japanese Tradition and Western Law* (Cambridge: Harvard University Press, 1970).

59. Nihon Bunka Kaigi, ed., *Gendai Nihonjin no Hōishiki* (Japanese legal consciousness) (Tokyo: Daiichi Hōki, 1982).

60. See Kahei Rokumoto, "Problems and Methodology of Study of Civil Disputes," trans. Toru Mori, Part 1, 5 *Law in Japan* 97 (1972), and Part 2, 6 *Law in Japan* 111 (1973); Marc Galanter, "Reading the Landscape of Disputes," 31 *UCLA Law Review* 4 (1983); Haley, supra note 25, pp. 83–121; Ramseyer, supra note 56; Haley, supra note 56; and, generally, V. Lee Hamilton and Joseph Sanders, *Everyday Justice: Responsibility and the Individual in Japan and the United States* (New Haven: Yale University Press, 1992).

61. See Hideo Tanaka, *The Japanese Legal System* (Tokyo: University of Tokyo Press, 1976), pp. 260–266; R. Rabinowitz, "The Historical Development of the Japanese Bar," 70 *Harvard Law Review* 61 (1956); Percy R. Luney, "The Judiciary: Its Organization and Status in the Parliamentary System," in Percy R. Luney and Kazuyuki Takahashi, eds., *Japanese Constitutional Law* (Tokyo: Tokyo University Press, 1993), p. 123, 137; and Christopher Ocasal, "How to Count Japan's Lawyers," *Legal Times* 22 (April 6, 1992).

62. See Tanaka, supra note 61, p. 260.

63. Yasuhiro Okudaira, "The Constitution and Its Various Influences," in Luney and Takahashi, supra note 61, p. 12.

64. See Setsuro Tsurushima, "Human Rights Issues and the Status of the Burakumin and Koreans in Japan," in George DeVos, ed., *Institutions for Change in*

Japanese Society (Berkeley: Institute of East Asian Studies, 1984); and Upham, supra note 25, Ch. 3.

65. J. Mark Ramseyer, "The Costs of the Consensual Myth: Antitrust Enforcement and Institutional Barriers to Litigation in Japan," 94 *Yale Law Journal* 604, 609 (1985); J. Mark Ramseyer and Minoru Nakazato, "The Rational Litigant," 18 *Journal of Legal Studies* 267 (1990); Ramseyer, supra note 56; and Haley, supra note 56. See also the discussion of the Supreme Court and the judiciary in Japan in Chapter 3.

66. See, generally, John H. Merryman, *The Civil Law Tradition* (Stanford: Stanford University Press, 1969); and cf. Lawrence Beer, ed., *Constitutionalism in Asia: Asian Views of the American Influence* (Berkeley: University of California Press, 1979).

67. For analysis and criticism of "rights talk" and the legal culture in the United States, see: P. S. Atiyah and R. S. Summers, *Form and Substance in Anglo-American Law* (Oxford: Clarendon Press, 1987); Alan Ryan, "The British, the Americans, and Rights," in Michael Lacey and Knud Haakonssen, eds., *A Culture of Rights* (Cambridge: Cambridge University Press, 1991) p. 366; and Mary Ann Glendon, *Rights Talk* (New York: Free Press, 1991). For comparisons with Japan, see Koichiro Fujikura, "Legal Cultures of the United States and Japan: An Impressionist View," 1990 *United States/Japan Commercial Law and Trade* 642; and Koichiro Fujikura, "A Comparative View of Legal Culture in Japan and the United States," 16 *Law in Japan* 115 (1983). See also John O. Haley, *Authority without Power: Law and the Japanese Paradox* (New York: Oxford University Press, 1991), as well as the review of Haley's book by Koichiro Fujikura, "Administering Justice in a Consensus-Based Society," 91 *Michigan Law Review* 1529 (1993).

68. For further discussion, see Richard Parker, "Law, Language, and the Individual in Japan and the United States," 7 *Wisconsin International Law Journal* 179 (1988).

69. Yoshiyuki Noda, "The Character of the Japanese People and their Conception of Law," reprinted in Tanaka, supra note 61, pp. 295, 301. See also John O. Haley, "Introduction: Legal vs. Social Controls," in J. O. Haley, ed., *Law and Society in Japan: American Perspectives* (Dubuque: Kendall/Hunt, 1988), p. 16.

70. For further discussion, see Takeo Doi, *The Anatomy of Self: The Individual versus Society* (Tokyo: Kodansha International, 1985). See also Chie Nakane, *Japanese Society* (Berkeley: University of California Press, 1970); and Chalmers Johnson, "*Omote* (Explicit) and *Ura* (Implicit): Translating Japanese Political Terms," 6 *Journal of Japanese Studies* 89 (1980).

71. Ruth Benedict, *The Chrysanthemum and the Sword* (Boston: Houghton Mifflin, 1946). See also Takeo Doi, *Anatomy of Dependence* (Tokyo: Kodansha International, 1973).

72. Noda, supra note 69, p. 303. See also Haley, supra note 25, pp. 186–189.

73. For further discussion, see Aasulv Lande, "The Japanese Language," in Ian Reader, Esben Andreasen, and Finn Stefansson, eds., *Japanese Religions: Past & Present* (Honolulu: University of Hawai'i Press, 1993), p. 21.

74. Takeyoshi Kawashima, "Japanese Way of Legal Thinking," 7 *International Journal of Law Libraries* 127 (1979), p. 128.

75. Ibid., pp. 130–131.

76. For further discussion of this aspect of liberalism and privacy, see Jacob W. Landynski, *Search and Seizure and the Supreme Court* (Baltimore: Johns Hopkins University Press, 1966); Nelson B. Lasson, *The History and Development of the Fourth Amendment to the United States Constitution* (Baltimore: Johns Hopkins Press, 1937); and David H. Flaherty, *Privacy in Colonial New England* (Charlottesville: University Press of Virginia, 1972).

77. Quoted in *Frank v. Maryland,* 359 U.S. 360, 378 (Douglas, J., dissenting opinion).

Chapter 2: Paradoxes of (Dis)Establishment

1. This categorization follows that of Helen Hardacre, *Shinto and the State, 1868–1988* (Princeton: Princeton University Press, 1989).

2. For further discussions, see ibid.; and Robert Bellah, *Tokugawa Religion* (New York: Free Press, 1957).

3. For further discussion, see Shigeyoshi Murakami, *Japanese Religion in the Modern Century* (Tokyo: Tokyo University Press, 1980). See also Yoshiya Abe, *Religious Freedom under the Meiji Constitution* (Ph.D. diss., Claremont Graduate School, 1970).

4. James E. Ketelaar, *Of Heretics and Martyrs in Meiji Japan: Buddhism and Its Persecution* (Princeton: Princeton University Press, 1990).

5. See Joseph Kitagawa, *Religion in Japanese History,* 2nd ed. (New York: Columbia University Press, 1990), p. 200. For a detailed outline of legislation affecting State Shinto, see Wilhelmus H. M. Creemers, *Shrine Shinto after World War II* (Leiden: E. J. Brill, 1968), Appendix H, pp. 228–232.

6. See Hardacre, supra note 1; and Sheldon Garon, "State and Religion in Imperial Japan, 1912–1945," 12 *Journal of Japanese Studies* 273 (1986).

7. Hardacre, supra note 1, pp. 22–23.

8. For further discussion, see Hardacre, supra note 1; Daniel Clarence Holtom, *The Political Philosophy of Modern Shinto: A Study of the State Religion of Japan* (New York: AMS Press, 1984; reprint of 1922 University of Chicago Libraries ed.); idem, *The National Faith of Japan* (London: Kegan, Paul, 1938); and idem, *Modern Japan and Shinto Nationalism* (New York: Paragon, rev. ed., 1963).

9. Interview with Katsuyuki Kumano (Osaka, Aug. 28, 1993). See also Agency for Cultural Affairs, *Japanese Religion* (Tokyo: Kodansha International, 1972); Winston Davis, "Parish Guilds and Political Culture in Japan," 36 *Journal of Asian Studies* 25 (1976); and Kiyomi Morioka, *Religion in Changing Japanese Society* (Tokyo: Tokyo University Press, 1975).

10. For further discussion, see Masami Itō, "The Development of Law and Constitution in Japan," Lawrence Beer, ed., *Constitutional Systems in Late Twentieth Century Asia* (Seattle: University of Washington Press, 1992), pp. 135–140.

11. See Takeshi Muramatsu, "The Emperor as Priest-King," 16 *Japan Echo* 53 (1989); and Stephen Large, *Emperor Hirohito and Showa Japan: A Political Biography* (London: Routledge, 1992), pp. 9–14.

12. For further discussion, see Muramatsu, supra note 11; Large, supra note 11; David Titus, *Palace Politics in Prewar Japan* (New York: Columbia University Press, 1974); and Joseph Kitagawa, "Some Reflections on Japanese Religion and Its Relationship to the Imperial System," 17 *Japanese Journal of Religious Studies* 129 (1990).

13. "Okubo Toshimichi's Opinion on Constitutional Government 1873," translated and printed as Appendix II in George Beckman, *The Making of the Meiji Constitution* (Lawrence: University of Kansas Press, 1957), pp. 111–119.

14. For further discussion, see Kanzo Uchimura, *How I Became a Christian,* originally published in 1913, reprinted as Vol. 1 of *The Collected Works of Kanzo Uchimura* (Tokyo: Kyōbunkan, 1971); Abe, supra note 3, pp. 136–139; and Emil Brunner, "A Unique Christian Mission: The Mukyokai ('Non-Church') Movement in Japan," in Walter Leibrecht, ed., *Religion and Culture: Essays in Honor of Paul Tillich* (New York: Harper & Row Reprint, 1972), p. 287.

15. Reprinted in Robert Ballow, ed., *Shinto: The Unconquered Enemy* (New York: Viking, 1945), p. 68.

16. See, e.g., Saburo Ienaga, *The Pacific War: World War II and the Japanese, 1931–1945* (New York: Pantheon, 1978), Ch. 3.

17. See ibid., Ch. 2; and Gordon Daniels, "Japanese Domestic Radio and Cinema Propaganda, 1937–1945: An Overview," 2 *Historical Journal of Film, Radio, and Television* 115 (1982).

18. See Titus, supra note 12; and Byung C. Koh, *Japan's Administrative Elite* (Berkeley: University of California Press, 1989). See, more generally, Frank Upham, *Law and Social Change in Postwar Japan* (Cambridge: Harvard University Press, 1987).

19. Interview with and materials supplied by Katsuyuki Kumano (Osaka, May 13, 1994).

20. Basil Hall Chamberlain, "The Invention of a New Religion," in Appendix A of idem, *Things Japanese* (London: Kegan, Paul, 5th rev. ed., 1927).

21. Quoted in Murakami, supra note 3, at p. 109. See also Abe, supra note 3.

22. Garon, supra note 6, p. 276.

23. See Nobushige Hozumi, *Ancestor Worship and Japanese Law* (Plainview: Books for Libraries Press, 1912). See also Garon, supra note 6.

24. Quoted in Ballow, supra note 15, p. 192. See also "The Constitution and Religion," 6 *Contemporary Religions in Japan* 79 (1963), p. 82.

25. Ienaga, supra note 16, p. 107.

26. Quoted by Kwan Weng Kin, "In Devoted Pursuit of the Truth," *Straits of Times Press* 7 (April 11, 1993). See also Saburo Ienaga, "Teaching War," in Haruko Taya Cook and Theodore F. Cook, eds., *Japan at War: An Oral History* (New York: New Press, 1992), p. 441.

27. Kitagawa, supra note 12, p. 172.

28. See "Textbook Screening Upheld; Historian's 28-Year Suit Fails," *Japan Times* 2 (March 17, 1993). For further discussion of the background of Ienaga's litigation and the controversy over the Ministry of Education's screening policy, see Lawrence Beer, "Education, Politics, and Freedom in Japan: The Ienaga Textbook Review Cases," 8 *Law in Japan* 67 (1975).

29. For further discussions, see Ienaga, supra note 16; Haruko Taya Cook and Theodore F. Cook, eds., *Japan at War: An Oral History* (New York: New Press, 1992); and John Dower, *War without Mercy: Race and Power in the Pacific War* (New York: Pantheon, 1986).

30. Yoshiyuki Noda, "The Character of the Japanese People and Their Conception of Law," excerpted in Hideo Tanaka, ed., *The Japanese Legal System* (Tokyo: University of Tokyo Press, 1976), p. 301.

31. Pointed out by Professor Shōichi Kobayashi and reported in Pierre Taillefer, "Gun Attack on Hosokawa Latest in Series of Far-Right Militants," *Agence France Presse* (May 31, 1994), available on Nexis.

32. Quoted in "Hosokawa's War Remarks Condemned," *Asahi Evening News* 4 (Sept. 14, 1993).

33. See, e.g., ibid.; "Justice Chief Resigns," *Japan Times* 1 (May 8, 1994); and Kevin Rafferty, "Japanese 'Far Right' Strikes at Former PM," *Guardian* 10 (May 31, 1993), available on Nexis.

34. Radio rescript read by Emperor Hirohito (Aug. 15, 1945), reprinted in Ballow, supra note 15, pp. 193–195. See also Ienaga, supra note 16, p. 107.

35. The Imperial Rescript of January 1, 1946, reprinted in William Woodard, *The Allied Occupation of Japan, 1945–1952, and Japanese Religions* (Leiden: E. J. Brill, 1972) at Appendix E:3. See also Appendix E:4, "The Secret History of the Japanese Emperor's Renunciation of 'Divinity' in 1946."

36. See Woodard, supra note 35; and William P. Woodard, "Religion-State Relations in Japan," 24 *Contemporary Japan* 81 (1957).

37. See, e.g., Jun Eto, "The American Occupation and Post-War Japanese Literature," 38 *Studies of Comparative Literature* 1 (1980); Kyoko Hirano, *Mr. Smith Goes to Tokyo: Japanese Cinema under the American Occupation, 1945–1952* (Washington, D.C.: The Smithsonian Institution Press, 1993); idem, "The Banning of Japanese Period Films by the American Occupation," 1 *Iconics* 193 (1987); idem, "The Japanese Tragedy: Film Censorship and the American Occupation," 41 *Radical History Review* 67 (1988); and MacArthur Memorial Library and Archives, *The Occupation of Japan: The Proceedings of a Seminar on the Occupation of Japan and Its Legacy to the Postwar World* (Norfolk: The MacArthur Memorial, 1975).

38. See Justin Williams, *Japan's Political Revolution under MacArthur* (Athens: University of Georgia Press, 1979); Alfred Oppler, *Legal Reform in Occupied Japan* (Princeton: Princeton University Press, 1976); and Woodard, supra note 35.

39. See Tanaka, supra note 30, p. 653.

40. See, e.g., Edward Behr, *Hirohito: Behind the Myth* (New York: Villard, 1989); and David Bergamini, *Japan's Imperial Conspiracy* (New York: Morrow, 1971). For criticisms of those works, see Stephen Large, Book Review of Toshiaki

Kawahara, *Hirohito and His Times: A Japanese Perspective* (Tokyo: Kodansha International, 1990) and of Edward Behr, op. cit., in 17 *Journal of Japanese Studies* 508 (1991).

41. See, e.g., Charles Sheldon, "Japanese Aggression and the Emperor, 1931–1941, From Contemporary Diaries," 10 *Modern Asian Studies* 1 (1976); idem, "Scapegoat or Instigator of Japanese Aggression? Inoue Kiyoshi's Case against the Emperor," 12 *Modern Asian Studies* 1 (1978); and Shunpei Ueyama, Takeshi Umehara, and Toru Yano, "The Imperial Institution," 16 *Japan Echo* 46 (1989).

42. David Titus, "The Making of the 'Symbol Emperor System' in Postwar Japan," 14 *Modern Asian Studies* 529 (1980).

43. See Large, supra note 11; and Robert Butow, *Japan's Decision to Surrender* (Stanford: Stanford University Press, 1954).

44. Reprinted in Japanese Government, *Documents Concerning the Allied Occupation and Control of Japan, Vol. 2, Political, Military and Cultural* (Tokyo: Division of Special Records, Foreign Office, 1949), p. 175; and in Woodard, supra note 35, Appendix A:3F.

45. Reprinted in Japanese Government, supra note 44, p. 177, and discussed extensively in Woodard, supra note 35, in Ch. 6; and Creemers, supra note 5, in Chs. 3 and 5.

46. Quoted in MacArthur Memorial Library, supra note 37, p. 129. See Shigeyoshi Murakami, *Japanese Religion in the Modern Century* (Tokyo: University of Tokyo Press, 1980), p. 118.

47. See, e,g,, the discussion and debate over religious freedom of the Constitution Investigation Council, which studied the adoption of the Constitution and whether and how it should be revised in 1959–1960, in "The Constitution and Religion," in Constitution Investigation Council, *Contemporary Religions of Japan*, Vol. 3, pp. 103–115, 134–144, 220–233, 314–333 (1962); Vol. 6, pp. 79–92 (1963); and Vol. 8, pp. 145–176 (1967). See also John Maki, *Japan's Commission on the Constitution—Final Report* (Seattle: University of Washington Press, 1980).

48. WR (28 Jan. 46) WKB (Toh), quoted in Woodard, supra note 35.

49. See Woodard, supra note 35, Ch. 15; and Creemers, supra note 5.

50. See Hideo Tanaka, "A History of the Constitution of Japan of 1946," reprinted in Tanaka, supra note 30, p. 653; and Woodard, supra note 35, Ch. 7.

51. Japanese Government, *Nihonkoku Kenpō Seitei No Katei* (The making of the Constitution of Japan), *Documents Concerning the Allied Occupation and Control of Japan, Vol. 1, Political, Military and Cultural* (Tokyo: Division of Special Records, Foreign Office, 1949), p. 6. See also Tanaka Hideo, "The Conflict between Two Legal Traditions in Making the Constitution of Japan," in Robert Ward and Yoshikazu Sakamoto, eds., *Democratizing Japan: The Allied Occupation* (Honolulu: University of Hawai'i Press, 1987), p. 107.

52. Quoted in Tanaka, supra note 30, p. 659.

53. The Hussey Papers 24-G-2-4 (Asian Library at the University of Michigan).

54. Japanese Government, supra note 44, p. 221.

55. Ibid., p. 168.

56. Frank Rizzo, quoted in Woodard, supra note 35, p. 79.

57. But see Robert Ward, "Origins of the Present Japanese Constitution," 50 *American Political Science Review* 980 (1957).

58. Quoted in ibid.

59. Quoted in Tanaka, supra note 30, p. 61. See also Tanaka, supra note 50.

60. For an interesting examination of the drafting of the Constitution, see Kyoko Inoue, *MacArthur's Japanese Constitution: A Linguistic and Cultural Study of Its Making* (Chicago: University of Chicago Press, 1991). But for a good critical review of Inoue's conclusion that the Japanese and American negotiators duped each other, see J. Mark Ramseyer, "Together Duped: How Japanese and Americans Negotiated a Constitution without Communicating," 23 *Law in Japan* 123 (1990).

61. William Woodard, "The Constitution and Religion," 1 *Contemporary Religions in Japan* 32–34 (June 1960).

62. For further discussion, see Chapters 4 and 5. See also Haruhiro Fukui, "The Liberal Democratic Party and Constitutional Revision," in David Sissons, ed., *Papers on Modern Japan* (Canberra: Australian University Press, 1968).

63. See Yoichi Higuchi, "The Constitution and the Emperor System: Is Revisionism Alive?" in Percy R. Luney and Kazuyuki Takahashi, eds., *Japanese Constitutional Law* (Tokyo: Tokyo University Press, 1993), p. 57.

64. See James E. Auer, "Article Nine: Renunciation of War," in Luney and Takahashi, supra note 63, p. 69; and John Maki, "The Constitution of Japan: Pacifism, Popular Sovereignty, and Fundamental Rights," in ibid., p. 39.

65. See the sources cited in supra note 47.

66. The Yasukuni bill is further discussed in Chapter 5.

67. "Kakuryō no Yasukuni Jinja Sampai Mondai nikansuru Kondankai Hōkokusho" (The report by the research council for the question of official worship at the Yasukuni Shrine by cabinet members), *Jurisuto* 848 (Nov. 1985), p. 112.

68. See, e.g., Peter Herzog, *Japan's Pseudo-Democracy* (New York: New York University Press, 1993), pp. 99–100 and 108–118; and articles in *Hirohito and His Legacy,* a special issue of 37 *Japan Militarism Monitor* (Feb. 1989).

69. For a sophisticated analysis of the survival of the *tennō* system, see Yasuhiro Okudaira, "Forty Years of the Constitution and Its Various Influences: Japanese, American, and European," 53 *Law and Contemporary Problems* 17 (1990).

70. Shin'ichi Fujii, *Tennō Seiji* (Direct imperial rule) (Tokyo: Yūhikaku, 1944), pp. 358–359.

71. Takeo Doi, *The Anatomy of Self: The Individual versus Society* (Tokyo: Kodansha International, 1985), p. 52.

72. Nobuhiko Takizawa, "Constitutionalism in Japan," 20 *Kitakyūshū-Daigaku Hō-sei Ronshū* (Kitakyūshū University journal of law and political science) 1 (March 1993), p. 11.

73. Interview with Setsu Kobayashi (Tokyo, Sept. 9, 1993). For further discussion, see Chapter 4.

74. The Constitution of Japan, *Nihonkoku Kempō,* reprinted in Hiroshi Itoh and Lawrence W. Beer, eds., *The Constitutional Case Law of Japan: Selected Supreme*

Court Decisions, 1961–1970 (Seattle: University of Washington Press, 1978), Appendix 3, pp. 256–269.

75. *Everson v. Board of Education of Ewing Township, New Jersey,* 330 U.S. 1 (1947).

76. For further discussion, see David O'Brien, *Constitutional Law and Politics: Vol. 2, Civil Rights and Civil Liberties* (New York: Norton, 2nd ed., 1995), Ch. 6; and Henry J. Abraham, *Freedom and the Court* (New York: Oxford University Press, 6th ed., 1995), Ch. 6.

77. See, e.g., Herzog, supra note 68, pp. 108–118; Hardacre, supra note 1, pp. 144–148.

78. See, e.g., John Kie-chiang Oh, "The Fusion of Politics and Religion in Japan: The Sōka Gakkai-Kōmeito," 14 *Journal of Church and State* 59 (1972); and Daniel A. Metraux, *The Sōka Gakkai Revolution* (Lanham: University Press of America, 1994).

79. See, e.g., Tsutomu Shoji, "The Ideology of the Tennō System and Christian Responsibility," 3 *CTC Bulletin* 25 (1982); Mitsuo Miyata, "The Politico-Religion of Japan—The Revival of Militarist Mentality," 13 *Bulletin of Peace Proposals* (1982); and articles in *Hirohito and His Legacy,* supra note 68; as well as Nobuhiko Takizawa, "Religion and the State in Japan," 30 *Journal of Church and State* 89 (1988); and Koichi Yokota, "The Separation of Religion and State," in Luney and Takahashi, supra note 63, p. 205.

80. See, e.g., O'Brien, supra note 76, at Ch. 6; Stephen Carter, *The Culture of Disbelief: How American Law and Politics Trivialize Religious Devotion* (New York: Basic Books, 1993); Leonard Levy, *The Establishment Clause: Religion and the First Amendment* (New York: Macmillan, 1986); Walter Berns, *The First Amendment and the Future of American Democracy* (New York: Basic Books, 1976); Dallin Oaks, ed., *The Wall between Church and State* (Chicago: University of Chicago Press, 1963); Michael McConnell, "Religious Freedom at the Crossroads," in Geoffrey Stone, Richard Epstein, and Cass Sunstein, eds., *The Bill of Rights in the Modern State* (Chicago: University of Chicago Press, 1992), p. 115; and Kathleen Sullivan, "Religion and Liberal Democracy," in Stone, Epstein, and Sunstein, op. cit., p. 195.

81. Herzog, supra note 68, pp. 99–100.

82. See, e.g., K. Peter Takayama, "Revitalization Movement of Modern Japanese Civil Religion," 48 *Sociological Analysis* 328 (1988).

83. See Robert Bellah, *Tokugawa Religion* (New York: Free Press, 1957).

84. See Robert Bellah, "The Japanese and American Cases," in Robert Bellah and Phillip Hammond, eds., *Varieties of Civil Religion* (San Francisco: Harper & Row, 1980); and Robert Bellah, "Civil Religion in America," 96 *Daedalus* 1 (1967).

85. For further discussion, see Russell Richey and Donald Jones, eds., *American Civil Religion* (New York: Harper & Row, 1974), pp. 3–18.

86. See, e.g., Henry W. Bowden, "A Historian's Response to the Concept of American Civil Religion," in James E. Wood, Jr., ed., *Readings on Church and State* (Waco: J. M. Dawson Institute of Church-State Studies, 1989), pp. 191–192.

87. For further discussion, see Edward Humphrey, *Nationalism and Religion in America, 1774–1789* (Boston: Chipman Law Publishing, 1924); Norman Cousins, ed., *In God We Trust* (New York: Harper & Row, 1958); Sydney Mead, *The Nation with the Soul of a Church* (New York: Harper & Row, 1975); and Richard Vetterli and Gary Bryner, *In Search of the Republic* (Totowa: Rowman & Littlefield, 1987).

88. See Bowden, supra note 86; and generally Barry Kosmin and Seymour Lachman, *One Nation under God* (New York: Harmony Books, 1993).

89. See, e.g., John Swomley, *Religious Liberty and the Secular State: The Constitutional Context* (Buffalo: Prometheus, 1987); Leo Pfeffer, *Church, State, and Freedom* (Boston: Beacon Press, 1976); and Leonard Levy, *The Establishment Clause: Religion and the First Amendment* (New York: Macmillan, 1986).

90. Interview with Yoshiya Abe (Tokyo, July 15, 1994).

Chapter 3: Manipulating Law's Social Reality

1. See, e.g., Edward Lincoln, "The Showa Economic Experience," in Carol Gluck and Stephen Graubard, eds., *Showa: The Japan of Hirohito* (New York: Norton, 1992), p. 191; and Edward Lincoln, *Japan: Facing Economic Maturity* (Washington, D.C.: The Brookings Institution, 1988).

2. See Rokuro Hidaka, "Personal Retrospective," in Gavan McCormack and Yoshio Sugimoto, eds., *Democracy in Japan* (Armonk: M. E. Sharpe, 1986), p. 228; and Chalmers Johnson, "The People Who Invented the Mechanical Nightingale," in Gluck and Graubard, supra note 1, p. 71.

3. See Shigeyoshi Murakami, *Japanese Religion in the Modern Century* (Tokyo: Tokyo University Press, 1980), p. 158.

4. Law Number 43, Finance Ministry Printing Office, *Hōreizensho* (June 1979).

5. *Kakunaga v. Sekiguchi,* 31 Minshū 533 (Supreme Ct., Grand Bench, July 13, 1977), also reported in 855 Hanrei Jihō 27 (1977).

6. See, John O. Haley, "The Myth of the Reluctant Litigant," 4 *Journal of Japanese Studies* 359 (1978), pp. 381–383.

7. For further discussion of judicial federalism in the United States, see Henry J. Abraham, *The Judicial Process* (New York: Oxford University Press, 6th ed., 1993).

8. For a discussion of the U.S. Supreme Court's caseload, see David M. O'Brien, *Storm Center: The Supreme Court in American Politics* (New York: W. W. Norton, 4th ed., 1996), Ch. 3.

9. See, generally, Hiroshi Itoh, *The Japanese Supreme Court* (New York: Markus Wiener, 1989); Percy R. Luney, Jr., "The Judiciary: Its Organization and Status in the Parliamentary System," in Percy R. Luney, Jr., and Kazuyuki Takahashi, eds., *Japanese Constitutional Law* (Tokyo: Tokyo University Press, 1993), pp. 123–149; A. Didrick Castberg, *Japanese Criminal Justice* (New York: Praeger, 1990), pp. 86–89; and Lawrence W. Beer, *Freedom of Expression in Japan* (Tokyo: Kodansha International, 1984), pp. 133–160.

10. On the role of law clerks in the U.S. Supreme Court, see O'Brien, supra note 8, Ch. 3.

11. For further dicussion of the work of the *chōsakan* and the Japanese Supreme Court's decisionmaking process, see Itoh, supra note 9.

12. Interview with Justice Itsuo Sonobe (Tokyo, July 19, 1993).

13. Quoted in David Danelski, "The Supreme Court of Japan: An Exploratory Study," in Glendon Schubert and David Danelski, eds., *Comparative Judicial Behavior* (New York: Oxford University Press, 1969), pp. 121, 134.

14. Itoh, supra note 9, pp. 210–211.

15. See Administrative Office of the United States Courts, *Federal Judicial Caseload: A Five Year Review, 1989–1993* (Washington, D.C.: Administrative Office of United States Courts, 1994), p. 12.

16. General Secretariat, *Justice in Japan* (Tokyo: General Secretariat, Supreme Court of Japan, 1990).

17. The Meiji Constitution, Articles 57 and 61. On the history of courts during the Meiji era, see Hideo Tanaka, *The Japanese Legal System* (Tokyo: University of Tokyo Press, 1977).

18. For further discussion, see Chapters 4 and 6. See also Herbert Bolz, "Judicial Review in Japan," 4 *Hastings International and Comparative Law Review* 88 (1980).

19. On judicial independence in the United States, see Irving Kaufman, "The Essence of Judicial Independence," 80 *Columbia Law Review* 671 (1980). For a further discussion of judicial independence in Japan, see Setsuo Miyazawa, "Administrative Control of Japanese Judges," 25 *Kobe University Law Review* 45 (1991).

20. Constitution of Japan, 1947, Article 78.

21. For further discussion of the Occupation's "purges" and attempted cooptation of government officials, see Edwin O. Reischauer, *Japan: The Story of a Nation* (New York: Knopf, 1970), p. 225.

22. For further discussion, see Chalmers Johnson, *Conspiracy at Matsukawa* (Berkeley: University of California Press, 1972), pp. 29 and 152.

23. Some U.S. judges and courtwatchers have argued that the federal judiciary is becoming too bureaucratized in terms of acquiring larger staffs, delegating more responsibility for opinion writing, and adopting modern office technologies. See, for example, Alvin B. Rubin, "Bureaucratization of the Federal Courts: The Tension Between Justice and Efficiency," in Mark Cannon and David M. O'Brien, eds., *Views from the Bench: The Judiciary and Constitutional Politics* (Chatham: Chatham House, 1985), pp. 64–70; David M. O'Brien, "Managing the Business of the Supreme Court," 45 *Public Administration Review* 667 (1985); and Judith Resnik, "Managerial Judges: The Potential Costs," 45 *Public Administration Review* 686 (1985). But the debate over the bureaucratization of federal courts is separate from the issue of bureaucratic centralization and control over the operation of federal courts. Moreover, although Japanese courts have not incorporated modern office technologies as extensively as courts in the United States, they remain far more bureaucatically controlled than U.S. federal courts in terms of the training, appointment, and promotion of lower court judges.

24. General Secretariat, supra note 16, p. 37.

25. The appointment of Supreme Court justices is discussed later in this chapter, at infra note 43. Summary courts are generally staffed by retired inferior court judges, public prosecutors, or temporarily assigned assistant or full judges.

26. For further discussion, see Chapter 4.

27. See Takeo Hayakawa, "Age and the Judiciary in Japan," 9 *Kobe University Law Review* 1 (1973); and Takaaki Hattori, "The Role of the Supreme Court of Japan in the Field of Judicial Administration," 60 *Washington Law Review* 69 (1984).

28. Letter to the author from Katsuyuki Kumano (Aug. 6, 1994) and an interview with former Judge Teruo Ikuta published in 59 *Shūkan Kin'yōbi* (Weekly Friday) 50–53 (January 27, 1995). For other examples of lower court judges being put on fast-track careers, see Miyazawa, supra note 19, pp. 49–50.

29. Interview with Justice Sonobe, supra note 12. For other examples and further discussion, see J. Mark Ramseyer and Frances McCall Rosenbluth, *Japan's Political Marketplace* (Cambridge: Harvard University Press, 1993), pp. 156–157.

30. Interview with Justice Sonobe, supra note 12.

31. See Lawrence Beer, "Japan's Constitutional System and Its Judicial Interpretation," in John O. Haley, ed., *Law and Society in Contemporary Japan* (Dubuque: Kendall/Hunt, 1988), p. 15; and Luney, supra note 9, p. 144. But compare the assessment of the relative liberalism of lower courts and the Supreme Court in Itoh, supra note 9, pp. 269–276, finding that lower courts are not significantly more liberal than the Supreme Court.

32. Hattori, supra note 27, p. 82.

33. Based on conversations with members of the bar associations of Nagoya and Fukuoka (May 12 and June 2, 1994); and Kumano, supra note 28. See also Yoshiyuki Noda, *Introduction to Japanese Law* (Tokyo: Tokyo University Press, 1976), p. 154.

34. Interview with Shigeyuki Uehara (Osaka, July 24, 1994).

35. For another reported instance of a judge leaving the bench because his reassignment amounted to a demotion, see Peter J. Herzog, *Japan's Pseudo-Democracy* (New York: New York University Press, 1993), p. 255.

36. Kumano, supra note 28, and Judge Teruo Ikuta, supra note. 28.

37. *Itō et al. v. Sakurauchi, Minister of Agriculture, Forestry, and Fishery,* 712 Hanrei Jihō 24 (Sapporo Dist. Ct., Sept. 7, 1993). For further discussion, see Takeo Hayakawa, "The Japanese Judiciary in the Whirlwind of Politics," 7 *Kobe University Law Review* 15 (1971).

38. See Chapter 5, at note 21.

39. Quoted and discussed in Itoh, supra note 9, pp. 266–267.

40. Quoted in Frank O. Miller, "The Naganuma Case: Judge Fukushima and the *Seihokyo*," paper presented at the 1974 Association for Asia Studies meeting (New York), p. 24, as quoted by Itoh, supra note 9, pp. 266–267. See also Hayakawa, supra note 37.

41. See Luney, supra note 9, p. 141, and, more generally on environmental

pollution litigation, Frank K. Upham, *Law and Social Change in Postwar Japan* (Cambridge: Harvard University Press, 1987), pp. 28–78.

42. For other instances, see Luney, supra note 9, pp. 140–142; Itoh, supra note 9, at pp. 256–266; Herzog, supra note 35, pp. 254–255; and Hideo Tanaka, *The Japanese Legal System* (Tokyo: Tokyo University Press, 1977), pp. 558–559. For a further argument that the government punishes some but not all deviant judges, and evidence of the disciplining of those belonging to the Young Jurists' Association, see Ramseyer and Rosenbluth, supra note 29, pp. 161–181.

43. See and compare the Constitution *(Kenpō)* of Japan, Articles 6(2), 79(1), 80(1), and Court Organization Law *(Saibansho-hō)* No. 59 of 1947, Article 39(1), (2) (for the appointment of Supreme Court justices), with Article 80(1) of the Constitution and Article 40(1) of the Court Organization Law (for the appointment of inferior court judges).

44. On the drafting of the Court Organization Law, see Alfred Oppler, *Legal Reform in Occupied Japan* (Princeton: Princeton University Press, 1976), pp. 75–76.

45. See Abraham, supra note 7, pp. 35–40; and Richard A. Watson and Rondal G. Downing, *The Politics of the Bench and the Bar: Judicial Selection under the Missouri Nonpartisan Court Plan* (New York: Wiley, 1969).

46. Hattori, supra note 27, p. 72. See also Danelski, supra note 13.

47. See "Woman to Accept Supreme Court Post," *Japan Times* 2 (Jan. 15, 1994).

48. See Hideo Tanaka, "The Appointment of Supreme Court Justices and the Popular Review of Appointments," 11 *Law in Japan* 25 (1978).

49. Interview with Sonobe, supra note 12. See also Ramseyer and Rosenbluth, supra note 29, p. 153.

50. Based on the author's calculations of actual and potential service based on justices' ages at time of appointment.

51. See Tanaka, supra note 42, p. 694.

52. Court Organization Law, Law No. 59 of 1947, Article 11. See also Article 12, which further specifies that the "Expression of the opinion of each judge on written decisions shall be made giving reasons therefor explicitly."

53. For practices of dissent and concurrence in the U.S. Supreme Court, see O'Brien, supra note 8, Ch. 5.

54. For examples and further discussion, see Dan F. Henderson, ed., *The Constitution of Japan: Its First Twenty Years, 1947–1967* (Seattle: University of Washington Press, 1969), p. 127.

55. Besides the problem of selective publication of opinions, other difficulties arise from the high turnover of justices and the time lag between the actual decisionmaking and the announcement of decisions. See Itoh, supra note 9, pp. 224–232; Hiroshi Itoh, "Judicial Decision-Making in the Japanese Supreme Court," 3 *Law in Japan* 128 (1969), pp. 144–146; and Danelski, supra note 13, pp. 137–138.

56. The Supreme Court granted permission to examine all records and opinions, for which we are grateful. The Court, however, does not maintain the records for criminal cases and thus analysis of those cases was impossible.

57. Takeyoshi Kawashima, "Individualism in Decision-Making in the Supreme Court of Japan," in Schubert and Danelski, supra note 13, p. 104.

58. Professor Yasuo Ohkoshi gathered and tabulated the data here and in Appendix B from the *Saikō Saibansho Saibanshū.*

59. Kawashima, supra note 57, p. 105.

60. Interview with Justice Sonobe, supra note 12.

61. *Sekiguchi v. Kakunaga, Mayor of the City of Tsu,* 31 Minshū 606, also reported in 483 Hanrei Jihō 28 (Tsu Dist. Ct., March 16, 1967).

62. *Sekiguchi v. Kakunaga,* 31 Minshū 616, also reported in 22 Gyōsai reishū 680 (Nagoya High Ct., May 14, 1971).

63. See *Lynch v. Donnelly,* 465 U.S. 688 (1984) and the discussion of that ruling in this chapter at infra note 86.

64. Unless otherwise noted, all translations are those of Professor Yasuo Ohkoshi.

65. *Kakunaga v. Sekiguchi,* 31 Minshū 533 (Supreme Ct., Grand Bench, July 13, 1977).

66. *Lemon v. Kurtzman,* 403 U.S. 602 (1971).

67. *Walz v. Tax Commission of the City of New York,* 397 U.S. 664 (1970).

68. *Abington School District v. Schempp,* 374 U.S. 203 (1963).

69. *Engel v. Vitale,* 370 U.S. 421 (1962).

70. *Abington School District v. Schempp,* 374 U.S. 203 (1963).

71. *Epperson v. Arkansas,* 393 U.S. 97 (1968).

72. See, e.g., *Braunfeld v. Brown,* 366 U.S. 599 (1961); *McGowan v. State of Maryland,* 366 U.S. 420 (1961); and *Two-Guys from Harrison Allentown v. McGinley,* 366 U.S. 582 (1961).

73. See *Tilton v. Richardson,* 403 U.S. 672 (1971).

74. *Meek v. Pittenger,* 413 U.S. 349 (1973).

75. *Roemer v. Maryland Public Works Board,* 426 U.S. 736 (1976).

76. *Committee for Public Education and Religious Liberty v. Regan,* 444 U.S. 646 (1980).

77. *Mueller v. Allen,* 463 U.S. 388 (1983).

78. *Marsh v. Chambers,* 463 U.S. 783 (1983).

79. *Essex v. Woman,* 409 U.S. 808 (1972).

80. *Lee v. Weisman,* 112 S. Ct. 2649 (1992).

81. *Wallace v. Jaffree,* 472 U.S. 38 (1985).

82. *Stone v. Graham,* 449 U.S. 39 (1980).

83. See, e.g., *Wolman v. Walter,* 433 U.S. 229 (1977); and *New York v. Cathedral Academy,* 434 U.S. 125 (1977).

84. See, e.g., *Wolman v. Walter,* 433 U.S. 229 (1977); and Justice Stevens's dissenting opinion in *Committee for Public Education and Religious Liberty v. Regan,* 444 U.S. 646 (1980).

85. See, in particular, the dissenting opinion filed by Justice Antonin Scalia, and joined by Chief Justice Rehnquist and Justices Clarence Thomas and Byron White, in *Lee v. Weisman,* 112 S. Ct. 2649 (1992).

86. *Lynch v. Donnelly,* 465 U.S. 688 (1984). See also Wayne Swanson, *The Christ Child Goes to Court* (Philadelphia: Temple University Press, 1990).

87. Ibid., pp. 679, 681, and 685.

88. Ibid., pp. 711–712 (Brennan, Jr., dissenting opinion).

89. Interview with Professor Yoshiya Abe (Tokyo, July 15, 1994).

90. Ibid., but see the discussion in Chapter 4 at note 42.

91. See 42 *Shumujihō* 11 (March 1978), and Keiichi Yanagawa and David Reid, "Between Unity and Separation: Religion and Politics in Japan, 1965–1977," 6 *Japanese Journal of Religious Studies* 500 (1979).

92. See *Katorikku Shinbun* (Oct. 16, 1977).

93. See *Kirisuto Shinbun* (July 23, 1977).

94. Yanagawa and Reid, supra note 91, at p. 514.

95. See Table 1 in Yanagawa and Reid, supra note 91, p. 506; and David Reid, "Separation of Religion and the State: How Japanese Religions Line Up," 56 *Japan Christian Quarterly* 212 (1990).

Chapter 4: Past Remembering

1. Interview with Reiko Kamisaka, translated by Katsuyuki Kumano (Minoo City, May 16, 1994).

2. Interview with Professor Setsu Kobayashi (Tokyo, Sept. 9, 1993).

3. This discussion draws on the interviews with Reiko Kamisaka and Katsuyuki Kumano (Osaka and Minoo City, May 16 and July 21, 1994).

4. *Tomabechi v. Japan,* 7 Minshū 350 (Supreme Ct., April 15, 1953), quoted and further discussed by Nobuyoshi Ashibe in "Human Rights and Judicial Power," in Lawrence W. Beer, ed., *Constitutional Systems in Late Twentieth Century Asia* (Seattle: University of Washington Press, 1992), p. 243. See also Yasuo Tokikuni, "Procedures for Constitutional Litigation and Judgments of Constitutionality," 13 *Law in Japan* 1 (1980).

5. See Taisuke Kamata, "Adjudication and the Governing Process: Political Questions and Legislative Discretion," in Percy R. Luney and Kazuyuki Takahashi, eds., *Japanese Constitutional Law* (Tokyo: Tokyo University Press, 1993), p. 151. For a discussion of the U.S. Supreme Court's application of the "political question" doctrine, see David M. O'Brien, *Constitutional Law and Politics, Vol. 2: Civil Rights and Civil Liberties* (New York: Norton, 2nd ed., 1995), Ch. 2.

6. See *Kunihiro v. Japan,* 16 Keishū (Supreme Ct., Grand Bench, Nov. 28, 1962), voiding a law permitting the seizure of third-party evidence; *Aizawa v. Japan,* 27 Keishū 265 (Supreme Ct., Grand Bench, April 4, 1973), striking down severe punishment for the crime of patricide; *Umehara v. Japan,* 29 Minshū 572 (Supreme Ct., Grand Bench, April 30, 1975), overturning restrictions on the opening of a pharmacy near an existing pharmacy; *Kano v. Hiroshima Election Management Commission,* 39 Minshū 1100 (Supreme Ct., Grand Bench, July 17, 1985), and *Kurokawa v. Chiba Prefecture Election Commission,* 30 Minshū 223 (Supreme Ct., Grand Bench, April 14, 1976), both striking down apportionment laws; and *Hira-*

guchi v. Hiraguchi, 41 Minshū 572 (Supreme Ct., Grand Bench, April 30, 1975), invalidating a law barring the division of jointly owned forest land. See also Percy R. Luney, Jr., "The Judiciary: Its Organization and Status in the Parliamentary System," 53 *Law and Contemporary Problems* 135 (1990), p. 160; and, generally, Beer, supra note 4; and Hiroshi Itoh, *The Japanese Supreme Court* (New York: Markus Wiener, 1989).

7. See Hiroyuki Hata, "Malapportionment of Representation in the National Diet," 1990 *Law and Contemporary Problems* 35 (Spring 1990).

8. Noriho Urabe, "Rule of Law and Due Process: A Comparative View of the United States and Japan," in Luney and Takahashi, supra note 5, pp. 173 and 182.

9. *Asahi v. Minister of Health and Welfare,* 21 Minshū 1043 (Supreme Ct., Grand Bench, May 24, 1967), translated in Hideo Tanaka, *The Japanese Legal System* (Tokyo: University of Tokyo Press, 1972), pp. 793–803.

10. See especially Frank Upham, *Law and Social Change in Postwar Japan* (Cambridge: Harvard University Press, 1987). For criticisms of Upham's thesis, see Yoshiharu Matsuura, "Review Essay: Law and Bureaucracy in Modern Japan," 41 *Stanford Law Review* 1627 (1989), p. 1636.

11. Matsuura, ibid., p. 1636.

12. Ibid., p. 1637.

13. Kamisaka, supra note 1.

14. Quoted by Peter Herzog, *Japan's Pseudo-Democracy* (New York: New York University Press, 1993), p. 127.

15. *Kamisaka, et al. v. Nakai, et al.,* 1036 Hanrei Jihō 20 (Osaka Dist. Ct., March 24, 1982).

16. Interview with Shigeyuki Uehara, translated by Professor Yasuo Ohkoshi (Osaka, July 26, 1994).

17. Quoted in Herzog, supra note 14, p. 128.

18. *Nakai, et al. v. Kamisaka, et al.,* 1237 Hanrei Jihō 3 (Osaka High Ct., July 16, 1987).

19. Interview with Katsuyuki Kumano and Reiko Kamisaka (Minoo City, July 21, 1994).

20. Interview with Katsuyuki Kumano (Osaka, Aug. 28, 1993), and with Reiko Kamisaka, Yoshiko Furukawa, and Hiroko Hamuro (Minoo City, May 17, 1994).

21. Kumano, supra note 20.

22. For further discussions of the student movement, see George Packard, *Protest in Tokyo: The Security Treaty Crisis of 1960* (Princeton: Princeton University Press, 1966); Ellis Krauss, *Japanese Radicals Revisited: Student Protest in Postwar Japan* (Berkeley: University of California Press, 1974); and Patricia Steinhoff, "Protest and Democracy," in Takeshi Ishida and Ellis Krauss, eds., *Democracy in Japan* (Pittsburgh: University of Pittsburgh Press, 1989), p. 171.

23. Kumano, supra note 19.

24. *Kamisaka, et al. v. Nakai, et al.,* 34 Gyōsei reishū 358, also reprinted in 487 Hanrei Taimuzu 174 (Osaka Dist. Ct., March 1, 1983).

25. This discussion draws on Tadashi Takizawa, "Issues Raised by the Deci-

sion of the Trial Court in the 'Minoo Memorial Service Case,' " 18 *Law in Japan* 152 (1986).

26. Translated and quoted in ibid., p. 163.

27. *Nakai, et al. v. Kamisaka, et al.,* 1237 Hanrei Jihō 3 (Osaka High Ct., July 16, 1987).

28. Katsuyuki Kumano and several constitutional scholars take the position that the Osaka High Court did not use the "purpose and effect" test advanced in the *Tsu City Ground-Purification Ceremony Case,* but articles by a Supreme Court law clerk, Toshifumi Takahasi, advance the opposite view. See Vol. 45 *Hōsōjihō* 221 (Fall 1993).

29. *School District of Abington Township, Pennsylvania v. Schempp,* 374 U.S. 203 (1963).

30. *McGowan v. State of Maryland,* 366 U.S. 420 (1961).

31. *Stone v. Graham,* 449 U.S. 39 (1980).

32. *Widmar v. Vincent,* 454 U.S. 263 (1981).

33. *Minoo Subsidy* case, 39 Gyōsei reishū 997, 1291 Hanrei Jihō 3 (Osaka Dist. Ct., Oct. 14, 1988). See also "City's Aid to War-Dead Group Ruled Legal," *Japan Times* 2 (Oct. 15, 1988).

34. Minoo City Social Welfare Council Budgets for 1975 and 1979, supplied by Mrs. Reiko Kamisaka.

35. Finding of the Osaka District Court, *Minoo Subsidy* case, 39 Gyōsei reishū 997, 1291 Hanrei Jihō 3 (Osaka Dist. Ct., Oct. 14, 1988).

36. See Japan Association of War Bereaved Families, *Fortieth Anniversary of the Japan Association of War Bereaved Families* (Tokyo: Japan Association of War Bereaved Families, 1987), p. 186.

37. Interview with Katsuyuki Kumano (Osaka, May 13, 1994), and quoted in Katsuyuki Kumano, "Minoo Chūkonhi Iken Soshō 298 nin wa naze shinda ka" (Litigation challenging the constitutionality of Minoo's monument to war dead: Why did 298 people die?"), 29 *Osaka Bengoshikai* 5 (Nov. 20, 1993). Translated by Lucinda Lohman Ōta, for which I am grateful.

38. Appellant's Brief, *Kamisaka, et al. v. Nakai et al.,* 47, No. 3 Hanrei Shū (1993), p. 784.

39. Based on "Additional Rule of Pension Law for Public Servant," Article 13, Table 1; and Article 27, Table 3, *Roppō Zensho* (Tokyo: Yūhikaku, 1993).

40. Reiko Kamisaka, supra note 1.

41. Summary of points of testimony taken from "Position Statement for Reporters by Plaintiffs in Kamisakas' Suit against Minoo" (July 7, 1994), translated by Professor Hiroyuki Ōta, for which I am grateful.

42. Interview with Yoshiya Abe (Tokyo, July 15, 1994).

43. Ibid.

44. See, generally, Gerald Curtis, *Election Campaigning Japanese Style* (New York: Columbia University Press, 1971); and idem, *The Japanese Way of Politics* (New York: Columbia University Press, 1988).

45. Reported in "City's Aid to War Dead Ruled Legal," *Japan Times* (Oct. 15, 1988), p. 2.

46. Note that in the *Iwate Yasukuni Shrine Service* case, the high court said only that the officials' visits to Yasukuni were "probably not constitutional." The high court's decision is further discussed in Chapter 5.

47. Some scholars disagree that lower courts are more liberal in their rulings than the Supreme Court. Interview with former Justice Masami Itō (Tokyo, July 26, 1993). See also Hiroshi Itoh, "Judicial Review and Judicial Activism in Japan," 53 *Law and Contemporary Problems* 174 (1990). But for a contrary view, see Lawrence W. Beer, *Freedom of Expression in Japan* (Tokyo: Kodansha International, 1984), p. 137.

48. See Beer, supra note 47; and Percy R. Luney, "The Judiciary: Its Organization and Status in the Parilmentary System," in Luney and Takahashi, supra note 5, pp. 123, 144.

49. Council of State Order Number 103 (June 8, 1785). See also B. J. George, Jr. "The Japanese Judicial System: Thirty Years of Transition," 12 *Loyola of Los Angeles Law Review* 807 (1979).

50. Court Organization Law, Article 4 (April 16, 1947).

51. However, see the discussions of the Supreme Court's rulings in the *Minoo City War Memorial* case in this chapter and in the *Self Defense Forces Enshrinement* case in Chapter 6.

52. Quoted in "Court Instructs Governor to Repay Shrine Donations," *Japan Times* 1 (March 18, 1989).

53. Quoted in Norma Field, *In the Realm of a Dying Emperor: Japan at Century's End* (New York: Random House, 1991), p. 178.

54. Quoted in ibid., p. 179.

55. Reported in "Outlays for Nagasaki Shrine Are Declared Unconstitutional," *Japan Times* (Feb. 21, 1990). See *The Nagasaki Chūkonhi Case, Oka v. Motoshima, Mayor of Nagasaki,* 1340 Hanrei Jihō (Nagasaki Dist. Ct., Feb. 20, 1990).

56. Quoted in "Court OKs City Funds to Shinto-Style Monument for War Dead," *Asahi News Service* (Dec, 18, 1992). See *The Nagasaki Chūkonhi Case, Motoshima v. Oka,* 1444 Hanrei Jihō 53 (Fukuoka High Ct., Dec. 19, 1992).

57. Reported in "Government Gifts to Shrines Are Judged Constitutional," *Japan Times* (May 13, 1992).

58. *Kamisaka, et al. v. Nakai, et al.,* 47 Minshū 1687, also reprinted in 1454 Hanrei Jihō 41 (Supreme Ct., 3rd Petty Bench, Feb. 16, 1993).

59. Quoted in "Supreme Court Rules Cenotaph Funding Constitutional," *Kyodo News Service,* Japan Economic Newswire (Feb. 16, 1993).

60. Telegram from the U.S. State Department to the Supreme Commander of the Allied Powers (Oct. 11, 1945), reproduced in *Brief for Kamisaka, et al.* submitted to the Supreme Court of Japan in the case of *Kamisaka, et al. v. Nakai, et al.* (1993).

61. See the discussion of the Supreme Court's ruling in the *Self Defense Forces Enshrinement* case in Chapter 6.

62. Kumano, supra note 45; and interviews with Hidenori Tomatsu (Tokyo, Sept. 9, 1993) and Takashi Kōno (Tokyo, Sept. 8, 1993).

63. *Lemon v. Kurtzman,* 403 U.S. 602 (1971), discussed in Chapter 3.

64. Kumano, supra note 20; see also Kumano, supra note 37.

65. See "City-Funded Move of Cenotaph Upheld," *Japan Times* 2 (Feb. 7, 1993).

66. Interview with Naoki Kamisaka (Minoo City, May 16, 1994).

67. Quoted in "Court Denies Judgeship to Litigant's Son," *Asahi Evening News* (April 7, 1994), p. 3.

68. Quoted in "Activist Rejected As Judge," *Mainichi Daily News* (April 7, 1994).

69. Quoted in *Asahi Evening News,* supra note 67.

70. The number of prefectural bar associations protesting the Supreme Court's action was as of May 16, 1994. Interview with Naoki Kamisaka (Minoo City, May 16, 1994).

71. "Can a 'Silent Spring' Be Tolerated? Statement of Protest Against the Denial of Noaki Kamisaka's Appointment as an Assistant Judge," press release for reporters (April 12, 1994).

72. Interview with Reiko Kamisaka, supra note 1.

73. See *Nippon: A Charted Survey of Japan 1993/1994* (Tokyo: Kokusei-sha, 1993), p. 332.

74. Interview with Reiko Kamisaka, supra note 1.

75. Interview with Mrs. Yoshiko Furukawa (Minoo City, May 16, 1994).

Chapter 5: Enshrinements for Tomorrowland

1. *The Bible, New Testament,* First Corinthians, 8:5–6.

2. *The SDF Enshrinement Case, Japan v. Nakaya,* 42 Minshū 277 (Supreme Ct., Grand Bench, June 1, 1988).

3. Interview with Mrs. Yasuko Nakaya, translated by Professor Yasuo Ohkoshi (Yamaguchi, July 27–28, 1994). Unless otherwise noted, much of the following discussion of Mrs. Nakaya's case draws on this interview.

4. See Management & Coordination Agency, *Japan Statistical Yearbook: 1993/94* (Tokyo: Statistic Bureau, Management & Coordination Agency, 1993), p. 727. Hyōgo, Fukuoka, and Hiroshima prefectures have the largest number of reported Shinto religious organizations—4,353, 3,934, and 3,114, respectively. No other prefecture has over 2,000 Shinto organizations, and Okinawa has only 21.

5. I am grateful to Tsuguo Imamura for sharing a draft of his account of the case, *A Small Request That Was Denied: The Self-Defense Force Officer "Enshrinement" Refusal Case—The Supreme Court and the Human Rights of Minorities* (published in Japanese by Shinkyo-shupansha, 1993). See also Norma Field, *In the Realm of a Dying Emperor: Japan at Century's End* (New York: Random House, 1991), p. 148.

6. See the discussion in Chapter 2 following note 10.

7. This point is made by Nobuhiko Takizawa, "Constitutionalism in Japan," 20 *Kitakyūshū-Daigaku Hō-sei Ronshū* (Kitakyūshū University journal of law and political science) 1 (March 1993), p. 10.

8. See Lawrence W. Beer, "The Public Welfare Standard and Freedom of

Expression in Japan," in Dan F. Henderson, ed., *The Constitution of Japan: Its First Twenty Years, 1947–1967* (Seattle: University of Washington Press, 1969), p. 230; and Yasuhiro Okudaira, "The Japanese Supreme Court: Its Organization and Function," 3 *Law Asia* 67 (1972), p. 91.

9. *The Faith-Healing Case, Nishida v. Japan,* 17 Keishū 4 (Supreme Ct., Grand Bench, May 15, 1963), trans. in Hiroshi Itoh and Lawrence W. Beer, eds., *The Constitutional Case Law of Japan: Selected Supreme Court Decisions, 1961–1970* (Seattle: University of Washington Press, 1978), pp.223–225.

10. The "right to be let alone" was first coined by Samuel Warren and Louis D. Brandeis, who later served on the U.S. Supreme Court (1916–1939), in "The Right to Privacy," 4 *Harvard Law Review* 193 (1890). For a discussion of the development of the "right to be let alone" or "the right of privacy" in constitutional law in the United States, see, David M. O'Brien, *Privacy, Law, and Public Policy* (New York: Praeger, 1979); and David J. Garrow, *Liberty & Sexuality: The Right to Privacy and the Making of Roe v. Wade* (New York: Macmillan, 1994).

11. Quoted by Karl Schoenberger, "Japan Widow Loses Religious Rights Case," *Los Angeles Times* (June 2, 1988), p. 7.

12. See, e.g., Frank Upham, *Law and Social Change in Postwar Japan* (Cambridge: Harvard University Press, 1987), Chs. 2 and 4; Michael Reich, "Public and Private Responses to a Chemical Disaster in Japan: The Case of Kanemi Yusho," in John O. Haley, ed., *Law and Society in Contemporary Japan: American Perspectives* (Dubuque: Kendall/Hunt, 1988), p. 173; Julian Gresser, "The 1973 Japanese Law for the Compensation of Pollution-Related Health Damage: An Introductory Assessment," in Haley, op. cit., p. 139; and Catherine Brown, "Japanese Approaches to Equal Rights for Women: The Legal Framework," in Haley, op. cit., p. 197.

13. Quoted by Schoenberger, supra note 11, p. 7.

14. Article 9, Constitution of Japan.

15. Kenzo Takayanagi, "Some Reminiscences of Japan's Commission on the Constitution," in Henderson, supra note 8, pp. 79 and 86. See also John Maki, *Japan's Commission on the Constitution—Final Report* (Seattle: University of Washington Press, 1980).

16. See James E. Auer, "Article Nine: Renunciation of War," in Percy R. Luney and Kazuyuki Takahashi, eds., *Japanese Constitutional Law* (Tokyo: Tokyo University Press, 1993), p. 75.

17. Treaty of Mutual Cooperation and Security (June 19, 1960), United States–Japan 11 U.S.T. 1632, T.I.A.S. No. 4509.

18. See Auer, supra note 16, p. 57.

19. For a concise summary of the political parties' positions on the Self Defense Forces, see Osamu Nishi, *The Constitution and the National Defense Law System in Japan* (Tokyo: Seibundo Publishing, 1987), pp. 29–37. For further discussions of the constitutional politics of rearmament and Article 9, see Auer, supra note 16; John Maki, "The Constitution of Japan: Pacifism, Popular Sovereignty, and Fundamental Human Rights," in Luney and Takahashi, supra note 16, pp. 39–

55; John Maki, "Japan's Rearmament: Progress and Problems," 8 *Western Political Quarterly* 545 (1955); and Peter Herzog, *Japan's Pseudo-Democracy* (New York: New York University Press, 1993), pp. 218–240.

20. *The Sunakawa Case, Sakata v. Japan,* 13 Keishū 3225 (Supreme Ct., Grand Bench, Dec. 16, 1959), translated and discussed in John Maki, *Court and Constitution in Japan: Selected Supreme Court Decisions, 1948–1960* (Seattle: Washington University Press, 1978), p. 298.

21. *The Naganuma Case, Itō v. Sakurauchi, Minister of Agriculture, Forestry, and Fishery,* 36 Minshū 1679 (Supreme Ct., 1st Petty Bench, Sept. 9, 1982); *affirming* 27 Gyohan 1175 (Sapporo High Ct., Aug. 5, 1976) and *reversing* 712 Hanrei Jihō 24 (Sapporo Dist. Ct., Sept. 7, 1973). See also Nishi, supra note 19, pp. 20–22.

22. *The Hyakuri Base Case, Ishizuka v. Japan,* 43 Minshū 385 (Supreme Ct., 3rd Petty Bench, June 20, 1989).

23. See Auer, supra note 16, p. 80.

24. On Japan's spending for the military and its ranking worldwise, see *Nippon: A Charted Survey of Japan 1993/1994* (Tokyo: Kokusei-sha, 1993), p. 332.

25. This point was made by one of Mrs. Nakaya's attorneys, Takashi Kōno, for which I am grateful. Interview with Takashi Kōno (Tokyo, Sept. 8, 1993).

26. Reported in Helen Hardacre, *Shinto and the State, 1868–1988* (Princeton: Princeton University Press, 1989), p. 154.

27. Cited in pamphlet given out at the Yamaguchi *gokoku* shrine.

28. Mrs. Nakaya, supra note 3.

29. It partially explains, too, why the legalization of abortion after the war created no controversy, unlike the U.S. Supreme Court's rulings liberalizing abortion, and why abortions are considered little more than necessary, if inconvenient, operations in Japan. For a discussion of the controversy over the U.S. Supreme Court's rulings on abortion, see Barbara Craig and David M. O'Brien, *Abortion and American Politics* (Chatham: Chatham House, 1993). See also Samuel Coleman, *Family Planning in Japanese Society: Traditional Birth Control in a Modern Urban Culture* (Princeton: Princeton University Press, 1983).

30. Tsuguo Imamura, "Inhumane Self-Defense Forces," *Asahi Shimbun* (April 7, 1978).

31. Shinichi Mizuuchi, "One Word on the 'Inhumane Self-Defense Forces,'" *Asahi Shimbun* (March 29, 1978).

32. Mrs. Nakaya, supra note 3.

33. "Statement of the Appellee," Mrs. Nakaya before the Supreme Court of Japan (Feb. 3, 1988), in *Japan v. Nakaya,* 42 Minshū 277 (Supreme Ct., Grand Bench, June 1, 1988).

34. Imamura, supra note 5; and Kōno, supra note 25.

35. Kōno, supra note 25.

36. Nobuhiko Takizawa, "Religion and the State in Japan," 30 *Journal of Church and State* 89 (1988), p. 96.

37. Quoted in Robert A. Evans and Alice F. Evans, "Japan: Enshrinement," in idem, eds., *Human Rights* (Surrey: Orbis Books, 1984), p. 55. For other discus-

sions in English of the case, see Field, supra note 5; and K. Peter Takayama, "Enshrinement and Persistency of Japanese Religion," 32 *Journal of Church and State* 527 (1990).

38. Mrs. Nakaya, supra note 3. See also "Supreme Court Reverses Niho Case Death Penalty," *Japan Times* 3 (Aug. 1, 1970).

39. Mrs. Nakaya, supra note 3.

40. Quoted by Clyde Haberman, "Tokyo Journal: Shinto is Thrust Back Onto the Nationalist Stage," *New York Times* A4 (June 7, 1988).

41. Quoted in Mutsuo Fukushima, "Court Ruling on Shinto Enshrinement Triggers Concern," *Japan Economic Newswire* (June 3, 1988), available on Nexis.

42. See Yoshiya Abe, *Religious Freedom under the Meiji Constitution* (Ph.D. diss., Claremont Graduate School, 1970), p. 6.

43. Quoted in Toshi Arai, "The Yasukuni Shrine Act," 34 *Japan Christian Quarterly* 189 (1968), p. 190.

44. Terumichi Kiyama, "Meeting at Yasukuni Shrine," in Haruko Taya Cook and Theodore F. Cook, eds., *Japan at War: An Oral History* (New York: New Press, 1992), pp. 447, 449–450.

45. Reprinted in *Japan Christian Activity News* (Aug. 15, 1985).

46. See John Welfield, *An Empire in Eclipse: Japan in the Postwar Alliance System* (London: Athlone, 1988), p. 431.

47. See Nobuhito Takizawa, "Religion and the State in Japan," 30 *Journal of Church and State* 89 (1989), pp. 100–102; and Osamu Tsukada, "Yasukuni Shrine and the Emperor System," in Yoshinobu Kumazawa and David Swain, eds., *Christianity in Japan, 1971–1990* (Tokyo: Kyo Bun Kwan [The Christian Literature Society of Japan], 1991), p. 63.

48. "Kakuryō no Yasukuni Jinja Sanpai Mondai nikansuru Kondankai Hōkokusho" (The report of the Research Council for the question of official worship at the Yasukuni Shrine by cabinet members), 848 *Jurisuto* 112 (Nov. 1985); and Yoichi Higuchi, "The Constitution and the Emperor System: Is Revisionism Alive?" 53 *Law and Contemporary Problems* 51 (1990).

49. National Council of Churches, "Japanese Shintoism: The Implicit Resurgence of National Religion," reprinted in Ian Reader, Esben Andreasen, and Finn Stefansson, eds., *Japanese Religions: Past & Present* (Honolulu: University of Hawai'i Press, 1993), pp. 176–179.

50. Quoted in Herzog, supra note 19, p. 111.

51. See Kyushiro Sugiyama, "Facts and Fallacies about Yasukuni Shrine," 8 *Japan Echo* 69 (1986), p. 71.

52. Quoted in "LDP Declares Premier's Yasukuni Visit Constitutional," *Kyodo News Service* (April 14, 1984).

53. Quoted in "Hirohito Laments War Dead on Anniversary of Surrender," *Los Angeles Times* A2 (Aug. 15, 1985).

54. Quoted in "Television Interview with Yasuhiro Nakasone on Foreign Policy Issues," *BBC World Broadcasts* (Aug. 31, 1985), available on Nexis.

55. "Yasukuni Issue Remains Nakasone's Achilles' Heel," *Kyodo News Service*

(Jan. 6, 1986). See also Stephen Large, *Emperor Hirohito and Showa Japan: A Political Biography* (London: Routledge, 1992), pp. 197–200; and Yoshikazu Sakamoto, ed., *The Emperor System as a Japan Problem* (Tokyo: International Peace Research Institute Meigaku [PRIME], Meiji Gakuin University, 1989), pp. 47–48.

56. *BBC World Broadcast,* Part 3 (Aug. 16, 1986), available on Nexis.

57. *The Fukuoka Yasukuni Visitation Case, Kōrijima v. Japan,* 1336 Hanrei Jihō 81 (Fukuoka Dist. Ct., Dec. 14, 1989), and 1246 Hanrei Jihō 85 (Fukuoka High Ct., Feb. 28, 1992). See also "Civil Lawsuit Rejected on '85 Yasukuni Visit," *Japan Times* 2 (Dec. 15, 1989).

58. Quoted in "Nakasone Sued for Yasukuni Visit," *Japan Economic Newswire* (Dec. 7, 1985); and "Yasukuni Issue Remains Nakasone's Achilles' Heel," *Kyodo News Service* (Jan. 6, 1986), available on Nexis.

59. Quoted in *Kyodo News Service* (Jan. 6, 1986), available on Nexis.

60. *Osaka Yasukuni Visitation Case, Higashi v. Japan and Nakasone,* 1336 Hanrei Jihō (Osaka Dist. Ct., Nov. 9, 1989). See also "Court Rejects Suit on Nakasone's Yasukuni Visit," *Kyodo News Service* (Nov. 9, 1989), available on Nexis.

61. *Kobe Yasukuni Visitation Case, Uozumi v. Japan,* 36 Shomu Geppō 1141 (Himeji Branch of Kobe Dist. Ct., March 29, 1990). See also "Citizens' Group Sues Government for 3.45 Million Yen," *Japan Economic Newswire* (Nov. 28, 1985).

62. The Supreme Court's simple order dismissing the appeal in the *Iwate Yasukuni Shrine Service Case, Takahashi v. Inoue* and *Kagawa v. Nakamura,* is in *Civil Law Cases Orders* 163 (Aug./Sept. 1991) (Supreme Ct., 2nd Petty Bench, Sept. 24, 1991).

63. *Iwate Yasukuni Shrine Service Case, Inoue v. Takahashi, Chairman of the Assembly of Iwate Prefecture* and *Kagawa v. Nakamura, Governor of Iwate Prefecture,* 1223 Hanrei Jihō 30 (Morioka Dist. Ct., March 5, 1987), *reversed* 1370 Hanrei Jihō 3 (Sendai High Ct., Jan. 10, 1991). See also "Court Rules Against Resolution Allowing Official Shrine Visits," *Japan Times* (Jan. 11, 1991).

64. Supreme Court of Japan's dismissal of appeal from Sendai ruling is noted in *Civil Law Cases Orders* 163 (Aug./Sept. 1991) (Supreme Ct., 2nd Petty Bench, Sept. 24, 1991).

65. See, e.g., "Supreme Court Confirms Yasukuni Visits as Unconstitutional," *Japan Economic Newswire* (Sept. 25, 1991).

66. See, e.g., "Sakamoto Disputes Supreme Court Ruling on Yasukuni Shrine," *Kyodo News Service* (Sept. 25, 1991).

67. *Osaka Yasukuni Visitation Case, Higashi v. Japan and Nakasone,* 1426 Hanrei Jihō 85 (Osaka High Ct., July 30, 1992). See also "Visits to Yasukuni Are 'Probably' Illegal," *Japan Times* 2 (July 31, 1992).

68. *Kobe Yasukuni Visitation Case, Uozumi v. Japan,* 1457 Hanrei Jihō 98 (Osaka High Ct., March 18, 1993). See also "High Court Dismisses Lawsuit Over Nakasone's Yasukuni Visit," *Japan Times* 2 (March 19, 1993).

69. *Ehime Shrine Donation Case, Shiraishi v. Anzai,* 1419 Hanrei Jihō 38 (Takamatsu High Ct., May 12, 1992), reversing *Anzai v. Shiraishi, Governor of Ehime Pre-*

fecture, 1305 Hanrei Jihō 26 (Matsuyama Dist. Ct., March 17, 1989). See also "Government Gifts to Shrines Are Judged Constitutional," *Japan Times* (May 13, 1992).

70. "U.S. Senate Urges Japan to Permit full SDF Participation in U.N. Actions," *Japan Times* A1 (July 17, 1994).

71. Prime Minister Murayama's response to questions in the Diet, broadcast on television, on July 20, 1994. See also "Forces Are Legal: Murayama Admits in SDPJ About-Face," *Japan Times* 1 (July 21, 1994).

72. Quoted in "Murayama Upholds Constitution," *Japan Times* 1 (July 23, 1994).

73. Quoted in "War Remark Fells Another Japanese Minister," *Bangkok Post* A1 (August 15, 1994).

74. Quoted in "Murayama Defends Minister Over War Remarks," *Xinhua News Agency* (Oct. 25, 1994). See also William Dawkins and Tony Walker, "Hashimoto Under Fire for War Remarks," *Financial Times* 4 (Oct. 27, 1994).

75. See "Yasukuni Shrine Visits Reflect Schism in Coalition Cabinet," *Daily Yomiuri* 3 (Aug. 17, 1994).

76. See *Daily Yomiuri* (Nov. 3, 1994), available on Nexis.

77. Interview with Justice Itsuo Sonobe (Tokyo, July 19, 1993).

Chapter 6: Cool Minds, Warm Hearts

1. Interview with Mrs. Yasuko Nakaya, translated by Professor Yasuo Ohkoshi (Yamaguchi, July 27 and 28, 1994). Unless otherwise noted, quotations and much of the following discussion draw on this interview.

2. Interview with Shigeyuki Uehara, translated by Professor Yasuo Ohkoshi (Osaka, July 26, 1994).

3. For further discussion, see Yoshiharu Matsuura, "Review Essay: Law and Bureaucracy in Modern Japan," 41 *Stanford Law Review* 1627 (1989); and Frank Upham, *Law and Social Change in Postwar Japan* (Cambridge: Harvard University Press, 1987).

4. Mrs. Nakaya, supra note 1, and interview with Takashi Kōno (Tokyo, Sept. 8, 1993).

5. Reported by Robert A. Evans and Alice F. Evans, *Human Rights* (Surrey: Orbis Books, 1984), p. 53.

6. *Nakaya v. Japan and the SDF Friendship Association,* 921 Hanrei Jihō 44 (Yamaguchi Dist. Ct., March 22, 1979). Translated by Professor Yasuo Ohkoshi; unless otherwise noted, all subsequent quotations are those of Professor Ohkoshi.

7. Kōno, supra note 4.

8. *Japan and the SDF Friendship Association v. Nakaya,* 1046 Hanrei Jihō 3 (Hiroshima High Ct., June 1, 1982).

9. Quoted in "Roger Baldwin, 97, Is Dead; Crusader for Civil Rights Founded the A.C.L.U.," *New York Times* D18 (Aug. 27, 1981). See also Peggy Lam-

son, *Roger Baldwin: Founder of the American Civil Liberties Union* (Boston: Houghton Mifflin, 1976).

10. For further discussion of the ACLU, see Samuel Walker, *In Defense of American Liberties: A History of the ACLU* (New York: Oxford University Press, 1990); Lucille Milner, *Education of an American Liberal* (New York: Da Capo Press, 1971 reprint of 1954 ed.); Charles Markmann, *The Noblest Cry: A History of the American Civil Liberties Union* (New York: St. Martins, 1965); and the ACLU's magazine, *Civil Liberties*.

11. *West Virginia State Board of Education v. Barnette*, 319 U.S. 624 (1943).

12. On the internment and relocation of Japanese-Americans, see, generally, Peter Irons, *Justice at War: The Story of the Japanese American Internment Cases* (New York: Oxford University Press, 1983).

13. Interview with Emiko Furuya, Japan Civil Liberties Union (Tokyo, Aug. 5, 1993).

14. See, e.g., Japan Civil Liberties Union, *1993 Report Concerning the Present Status of Human Rights in Japan* (Tokyo: Japan Civil Liberties Union, 1993); and *Universal Principle*, published by the Japan Civil Liberties Union at 306 Atagoyama Bengoshi Bldg., 1–6–7 Atago, Minato-ku, Tokyo, 105 Japan.

15. *Everson v. Board of Education of Ewing Township, New Jersey*, 330 U.S. 1 (1947).

16. *Lemon v. Kurtzman*, 403 U.S. 602 (1971).

17. See *Stone v. Graham*, 449 U.S. 39 (1980).

18. See *Wallace v. Jaffree*, 472 U.S. 38 (1985).

19. *Tsu City Ground-Purification Ceremony Case, Kakunaga v. Sekiguchi*, 31 Minshū 533 (Supreme Ct., Grand Bench, July 13, 1977), discussed in Chapter 3.

20. This discussion draws on interviews with Kōno, supra note 4; Professor Hidenori Tomatsu (Tokyo, Sept. 9, 1993), and a draft of Tsuguo Imamura's book, *A Small Request That Was Denied: The Self Defense Force Officer "Enshrinement" Refusal Case*, which I am grateful to Mr. Imamura and Ms. Emiko Furuya for sharing.

21. Reprinted in *Japan v. Nakaya*, 42 Minshū 277 (Supreme Ct., Grand Bench, June 1, 1988), translated by Professor Yasuo Ohkoshi.

22. Kōno, supra note 4, and Imamura, supra note 20.

23. Ruth Benedict, *The Chrysanthemum and the Sword* (Boston: Houghton Mifflin, 1947).

24. For further discussion, see Yoshiaki Iisaka, "The State and Religion in Postwar History," 7 *Japan Interpreter: A Journal of Social and Political Ideas* 306 (1972).

25. *Employment Division, Department of Human Services of Oregon v. Smith*, 494 U.S. 872 (1990).

26. *Sherbert v. Verner*, 374 U.S. 398 (1963).

27. For criticism of Justice Scalia's analysis, see Justice David Souter's concurring opinion in *Lee v. Weisman*, 112 S.Ct. 2649 (1992); and David M. O'Brien, "The Framers' Muse on Republicanism, the Supreme Court, and Pragmatic Constitutional Interpretivism," 53 *Review of Politics* 251 (1991).

28. The Religious Freedom Restoration Act is further discussed in David M. O'Brien, *Supreme Court Watch—1994* (New York: Norton, 1994).

29. See, e.g., *Church of Lukumi Babalu Aye v. Haileah,* 113 S. Ct. 2217 (1993), striking down an ordinance banning "animal sacrifice" as a denial of the free exercise of religion.

30. *Lee v. Weisman,* 112 S. Ct. 2649 (1992), holding school-sponsored prayers at graduation ceremonies unconstitutional.

31. *Board of Education of Kiryas Joel v. Grumet,* 114 S. Ct. 2481 (1994). But see also *Zobrest v. Catalina Foothills School District,* 113 S. Ct. 2462 (1993), a bare majority upholding public funding for a sign-language interpreter for a deaf student attending a religious high school.

32. *Northern Securities Co. v. United States,* 193 U.S. 197 (1904), pp. 400–401.

33. For further discussion, see David M. O'Brien, *Storm Center: The Supreme Court in American Politics* (New York: W. W. Norton, 4th ed., 1996), Ch. 6.

34. Tabulated by Yasuo Ohkoshi from opinions reported in *Saibanshū.*

35. Interview with Masami Itō (Tokyo, July 26, 1993).

36. I am grateful to Lawrence Repeta for pointing this out. Letter to author, Jan. 16, 1995.

37. For further discussion, see Chapter 3.

38. *Japan v. Nakaya,* 42 Minshū 277 (Supreme Ct., Grand Bench, June 1, 1988), translated by Professor Yasuo Ohkoshi. Unless otherwise noted, all subsequent quotations are from this translation.

39. For a further discussion of this point, see Helen Hardacre, *Shinto and the State, 1868–1988* (Princeton: Princeton University Press, 1989), pp. 185–187.

40. Quoted in Daniel Sneider, "Religious Freedom Debated in Japan," *Christian Science Monitor* 10 (June 3, 1988).

41. Quoted in "Christian Loses Suit Against Husband's Shinto Enshrining," *Japan Times* 4 (June 2, 1988).

42. See Takeshi Hirano, 99 Minshū 851 (1989); and Masayoshi Mito, 42 Hōsō Jihō 674 (no. 2, 376) (1990).

43. Based on interviews with, among others, Yasuhiro Okudaira (Tokyo, Sept. 12, 1993); Kōno, supra note 4; Tomatsu, supra note 20; and Imamura, supra note 20.

44. Tomatsu, supra note 20.

45. I am grateful to Kōno, supra note 4, for initially pointing this fact out, and subsequently for the confirmations by Tomatsu, supra note 20; Okudaira, supra note 43; and Nakaya, supra note 1; among other lawyers in the Fukuoka Bar Association (Fukuoka, June 30, 1994).

46. For further discussion, see Steven Large, *Emperor Hirohito and Showa Japan: A Political Biography* (London: Routledge, 1992).

47. Quoted in "Funeral To Push Constitutional Elasticity, Scholar Says," *Kyodo Newswire, Japan Economic Newswire* (Jan. 24, 1989); and Abi Sekimitsu, "Japan Emperor's Funeral Stirs Church-and-State Controversy," *Reuter Library Report* (Feb. 21, 1989).

48. Makoto Morii, "A Crisis of Democracy," in Yoshikazu Sakamoto, ed., *The Emperor System as a Japan Problem* (Tokyo: International Peace Research Institute Meigaku [PRIME], Meiji Gakuin University, 1989), p. 30.

49. Karl Shoenberger, "World Leaders Pay Respects At Hirohito Rites," *Los Angeles Times* A1 (Feb. 24, 1989).

50. Reported by Colin Nickerson, "Japan's New Emperor Performs Sacred Rite, and Debate Ensues," *Boston Globe* 46 (Nov. 23, 1990).

51. For good summaries of the constitutional objections and further discussions of the *daijōsai,* see Koichi Oshima, "Problems of the Daijōsai: Grounds for Christian Opposition," 56 *Japan Christian Quarterly* 221 (Fall 1990); and Shigenori Nishikawa, "The Daijōsai, the Constitution, and Christian Faith," 56 *Japan Christian Quarterly* 132 (Summer 1990).

52. "Statement of Presidents of Four Christian Universities," 56 *Japan Christian Quarterly* 220 (Fall 1990).

53. Quoted in Nickerson, supra note 50.

54. Quoted in Nishikawa, supra note 51, p. 135.

55. See, e.g., *The Kagoshima Imperial Rite Case, Higo v. Tsuchiya, Governor of Kagoshima Prefecture,* 1435 Hanrei Jihō 24 (Kagoshima Dist. Ct., Oct. 2, 1992), dismissing a suit filed over the Kagoshima prefecture's appropriating funds for its governor and other officials to attend the enthronement ceremonies.

56. Quoted from briefs in "Court Begins Hearing Suit Against Enthronement Rites," *Kyodo News Service* (Oct. 30, 1990), available on Nexis.

57. Oshima, supra note 51, p. 223. For another account of threats against Christians opposing the government's sponsorship of the *daijōsai,* see *Christian Century* 1161 (Dec. 12, 1990).

58. Quoted in "The Emperor's Costly Rite," *International Herald Tribune* 4 (March 10, 1995).

59. The NHK public broadcasting system was conducted in June 1988 and is discussed by Takeshi Ishida, in Takeshi Ishida and Ellis Krauss, eds., *Democracy in Japan* (Pittsburgh: University of Pittsburgh Press, 1989), p. 47. See also Large, supra note 46, pp. 197–199; Koichi Mori, "The Emperor of Japan: A Historical Study in Religious Symbolism," 6 *Japanese Journal of Religious Studies* 522 (1979); and Osamu Watanabe, "The Emperor as a 'Symbol' in Postwar Japan," 59 *Acta Asiatica* 101 (1990).

60. Quoted in Nickerson, supra note 50.

61. Reported by Clayton Jones, "Japanese Wary of Debate Over Imperial Rite," *Christian Science Monitor* 5 (June 28, 1990).

62. Mrs. Nakaya, supra note 1. But for a critical assessment of the judiciary's unwillingness to accept human rights claims based on international treaties and law, see Lawrence Repeta, "International Covenant on Civil and Political Rights and Human Rights in Japan" 20 *Law in Japan* 1 (1987).

Select Bibliography

Abe, Yoshiya. *Religious Freedom under the Meiji Constitution.* Ph.D. dissertation, Claremont Graduate School, 1970. Ann Arbor: University Microfilms International, 1977.

Agency for Cultural Affairs. *Japanese Religion.* Tokyo: Kodansha International, 1972.

Anesaki, Masaharu. *History of Japanese Religion.* Rutland: Tuttle, reprint ed., 1963.

Arai, Toshi. "The Yasukuni Shrine Act." 34 *Japan Christian Quarterly* 189 (1968).

Ashibe, Nobuyoshi. "Consciousness of Human Rights and Problems of Equality." In Hiroshi Itoh, ed. *Japanese Politics: An Inside View.* Ithaca: Cornell University Press, 1973.

Ashizu, Yoshihiko. "The Shinto Directive and the Constitution from the Standpoint of a Shintoist." 1 *Contemporary Religions in Japan* 16 (1960).

Aston, W. G., trans. *Nihongi: Chronicles of Japan from the Earliest Times to A.D. 697.* Rutland: Tuttle, 1972.

Bachnik, Jane, and Charles Quinn, eds. *Situated Meaning.* Princeton: Princeton University Press, 1994.

Baldwin, Frank. "State and Religion in Japan: A Crack in the Wall?" 46 *Christianity and Crisis* 154 (May 5, 1986).

Ballow, Robert, ed. *Shinto: The Unconquered Enemy.* New York: Viking, 1945.

Barrett, Gregory. *Archetypes in Japanese Films: The Sociopolitical and Religious Significance of the Principal Heroes and Heroines.* London: Associated University Presses, 1989.

Beauchamp, Edward. "Education." In Takeshi Ishida and Ellis Krauss, eds. *Democracy in Japan.* Pittsburgh: University of Pittsburgh Press, 1989.

Beckman, George. *The Making of the Meiji Constitution.* Lawrence: University of Kansas Press, 1957.

Beer, Lawrence, W. "The Public Welfare Standard and Freedom of Expression in Japan." In Dan F. Henderson, ed. *The Constitution of Japan: Its First Twenty Years, 1947–1967,* p. 230. Seattle: University of Washington Press, 1969.

———. "Education, Politics, and Freedom in Japan: The Ienaga Textbook Review Cases." 8 *Law in Japan* 67 (1975).

————. "Constitutional Revolution in Japan: Law, Society and Culture." 16 *Modern Asian Studies* 33 (1982).

————. *Freedom of Expression in Japan.* Tokyo: Kodansha International, 1984.

————. "Japan's Constitutional System and Its Judicial Interpretation." In John O. Haley, ed. *Law and Society in Contemporary Japan,* p. 7. Dubuque: Kendall/Hunt, 1988.

————. "Law and Liberty." In Takeshi Ishida and Ellis Krauss, eds. *Democracy in Japan.* Pittsburgh: University of Pittsburgh Press, 1989.

————. "Freedom of Expression: The Continuing Revolution." 53 *Law and Contemporary Problems* 39 (1990).

————, ed. *Constitutionalism in Asia: Asian Views of the American Influence.* Berkeley: University of California Press, 1979.

————, ed. *Constitutional Systems in Late Twentieth Century Asia.* Seattle: University of Washington Press, 1992.

Bellah, Robert. *Tokugawa Religion.* New York: Free Press, 1957.

————. "Civil Religion in America." 96 *Daedalus* 1 (1967).

————. "The Japanese and American Cases." In Robert Bellah and Phillip Hammond, eds. *Varieties of Civil Religion.* San Francisco: Harper & Row, 1980.

Bellah, Robert, and Phillip Hammond, eds. *Varieties of Civil Religion.* San Francisco: Harper & Row, 1980.

Benedict, Ruth. *The Chrysanthemum and the Sword.* Boston: Houghton Mifflin, 1947.

Berns, Walter. *The First Amendment and the Future of American Democracy.* New York: Basic Books, 1976.

Bernstein, Gail Lee, and Haruhiro Fukui, eds. *Japan and the World: Essays on Japanese History and Politics in Honour of Ishida Takeshi.* New York: St. Martin's Press, 1988.

Bolz, Herbert. "Judicial Review in Japan." 4 *Hastings International and Comparative Law Review* 88 (1980).

Brunner, Emil. "The Unique Christian Mission: The Mukyokai ('Non-Church') Movement in Japan." In Walter Leibrecht, ed. *Religion and Culture: Essays in Honor of Paul Tillich,* p. 287. New York: Harper & Row, 1959.

Bukkyo Dendo Kyokai. *The World of Shinto.* Tokyo: Bukkyo Dendo Kyokai, 1985.

Butow, Robert. *Japan's Decision to Surrender.* Stanford: Stanford University Press, 1954.

Campbell, John C. *Politics and Culture in Japan.* Ann Arbor: University of Michigan Center for Political Studies, 1988.

————. "Democracy and Bureaucracy in Japan." In Takeshi Ishida and Ellis Krauss, eds. *Democracy in Japan.* Pittsburgh: University of Pittsburgh Press, 1989.

Carter, Stephen. *The Culture of Disbelief: How American Law and Politics Trivialize Religious Devotion.* New York: Basic Books, 1993.

Castberg, A. Didrick. *Japanese Criminal Justice.* New York: Praeger, 1990.

Center for Christian Response to Asian Issues. Symposium "Hirohito and His Legacy." 37 *Japan Militarism Monitor* 35 (1989).

Chamberlain, Basil Hall. *Things Japanese.* London: Kegan, Paul, 5th rev. ed., 1927.

Ch'en, Paul Heng-chao. *The Formation of the Early Meiji Legal Order: The Japanese Code of 1871 and Its Chinese Foundation.* Oxford: Oxford University Press, 1981.

Chouchi, Nazli, Robert North, and Susumu Yamakage, eds. *The Challenge of Japan: Before World War II & After.* New York: Routledge, 1992.

Clark, Gregory. *The Japanese Tribe: Origins of a Nation's Uniqueness.* Tokyo: Saimaru Press, 1977.

Commission on Theological Concerns, Christian Conference of Asia. 3 *CTC Bulletin* 3 (Dec. 1982).

Constitution Investigation Council. "The Constitution and Religion." 3 *Contemporary Religions in Japan* 220 and 314 (1962).

————. "The Constitution Investigation Council." 6 *Contemporary Religions in Japan* 79 and 134 (1963).

————. "The Constitution Investigation Council." 8 *Contemporary Religions in Japan* 145 (1967).

Cook, Haruko Taya, and Theodore F. Cook. *Japan at War: An Oral History.* New York: New Press, 1992.

Creemers, Wilhelmus H. M. *Shrine Shinto after World War II.* Leiden: E. J. Brill, 1968.

Crump, Thomas. *The Death of an Emperor.* London: Constable, 1989.

Cummings, William. "The Conservatives Reform Higher Education." 8 *Japan Interpreter* (Winter 1974).

————. *Education and Equality in Japan.* Princeton: Princeton University Press, 1980.

Curtis, Gerald. *The Japanese Way of Politics.* New York: Columbia University Press, 1988.

Dale, Peter. *The Myth of Japanese Uniqueness.* London: Nissan Institute for Japanese Studies, 1986.

Danelski, David. "The Supreme Court of Japan: An Exploratory Study." In Glendon Schubert and David Danelski, eds. *Comparative Judicial Behavior.* New York: Oxford University Press, 1969.

————. "The Political Impact of the Japanese Supreme Court." 49 *Notre Dame Lawyer* 955 (1974).

Dator, James Allen. "The Life History and Attitudes of Japanese High Court Judges." 17 *Western Political Quarterly* 408 (1967).

Doi, Takeo. *The Anatomy of Self: The Individual versus Society.* Tokyo: Kodansha International, 1985.

Dower, John. *War without Mercy: Race and Power in the Pacific War.* New York: Pantheon, 1986.

————. *Japan in War & Peace.* New York: New Press, 1993.

Earhart, H. Byron. *The New Religions of Japan: A Bibliography of Western-Language Materials.* Ann Arbor: Center for Japanese Studies, University of Michigan, 1983.

————. *Gedatsu-kai and Religion in Contemporary Japan.* Bloomington: Indiana University Press, 1989.

Eliot, Sir Charles. *Japanese Buddhism.* London: Edward Arnold, 1935.

Ellwood, Robert. *The Feast of Kinship: Accession Ceremonies in Ancient Japan.* Tokyo: Sophia University Press, 1973.

Eto, Jun. "The American Occupation and Post-War Japanese Literature." 38 *Studies of Comparative Literature* 1 (1980).

Evans, Robert A., and Alice F. Evans, eds. *Human Rights.* New York: Orbis Books, 1984.

Field, Norma. *In the Realm of a Dying Emperor: Japan at Century's End.* New York: Random House, 1991.

Fridell, Wilbur. *Japanese Shrine Mergers, 1906–1912.* Tokyo: Sophia University, 1970.

Fujii, Shin'ichi. *Tennō Seiji* (Direct imperial rule). Tokyo: Yūhikaku, 1944.

———. *The Essentials of Japanese Constitutional Law.* Tokyo: Yūhikaku, 1942; reprint ed., Washington, D.C.: University Publications of America, 1979.

Fujikura, Koichiro. "A Comparative View of Legal Culture in Japan and the United States." 16 *Law in Japan* 129 (1983).

———. "Legal Cultures of the United States and Japan," 1990 *United States/Japan Commercial Law and Trade* 642 (1990).

———. "Administering Justice in a Consensus-Based Society." 91 *Michigan Law Review* 1529 (1993).

Fukatsu, Masumi. "A State Visit to Yasukuni Shrine." 33 *Japan Quarterly* 19 (1986).

———. "The SDPJ's Astronomical Shift in Policy." 42 *Japan Quarterly* 76 (1995).

Garon, Sheldon. "State and Religion in Imperial Japan, 1912–1945." 12 *Journal of Japanese Studies* 273 (1986).

General Secretariat, Supreme Court of Japan. *Justice in Japan.* Tokyo: General Sectretariat, Supreme Court of Japan, 1990.

Gluck, Carol. *Japan's Modern Myths: Ideology in the Late Meiji Period.* Princeton: Princeton University Press, 1985.

Gluck, Carol, and Stephen Graubard, eds. *Showa: The Japan of Hirohito.* New York: Norton, 1992.

Goodman, David G., and Masanori Miyazawa. *Jews in the Japanese Mind: The History and Uses of a Cultural Stereotype.* New York: Free Press, 1995.

Grapard, Allan. "Japan's Ignored Cultural Revolution: The Separation of Shinto and Buddhist Divinities in Meiji *(shimbutsu bunri)* and A Case Study: Tonomine." 23 *History of Religions* 240 (1984).

Haley, John Owen. "The Myth of the Reluctant Litigant." 4 *Journal of Japanese Studies* 359 (1978).

———. *Authority without Power: Law and the Japanese Paradox.* New York: Oxford University Press, 1991.

———, ed. *Law and Society in Contemporary Japan: American Perspectives.* Dubuque: Kendall/Hunt, 1988.

Hall, John Carey. *Japanese Feudal Law.* Yokohama, 1906; reprinted ed., Washington, D.C.: University Publications of America, 1979.

Hamilton, V. Lee, and Joseph Sanders. *Everyday Justice: Responsibility and the Individual in Japan and the United States.* New Haven: Yale University Press, 1992.

Hardacre, Helen. *Shinto and the State, 1868–1988.* Princeton: Princeton University Press, 1989.

Haring, Douglas G., ed. *Japan's Prospect.* Cambridge: Harvard University Press, 1946.

———. "Religion, Magic, and Morale." In Douglas G. Haring, ed. *Japan's Prospect.* Cambridge: Harvard University Press, 1946.

Harootunian, Harry. *Things Seen and Unseen: Discourse and Ideology in Tokugawa Nativism.* Chicago: University of Chicago Press, 1988.

Hata, Hiroyuki. "Malapportionment of Representatives in the National Diet." 1990 *Law and Contemporary Problems* 35 (Spring 1990).

Hattori, Takaaki. "The Role of the Supreme Court of Japan in the Field of Judicial Administration." 60 *Washington Law Review* 69 (1984).

Hayakawa, Takeo. "Legal Science and Judicial Behavior, with Particular Reference to Civil Liberties in the Japanese Supreme Court." 2 *Kobe University Law Review* 1 (1962); reprinted in Glendon Schubert, ed., *Judicial Behavior* (Chicago: Rand McNally, 1964), pp. 325–334.

———. "The Japanese Judiciary in the Whirlwind of Politics." 7 *Kobe University Law Review* 15 (1971).

———. "Age and the Judiciary in Japan." 9 *Kobe University Law Review* 1 (1973).

Henderson, Dan F. "Abstract of Japanese Lawyers: Types and Roles in the Legal Profession." 3 *Law and Society Review* 411 (1969).

———, ed. *The Constitution of Japan: Its First Twenty Years, 1947–1967.* Seattle: University of Washington Press, 1969.

———, and John Haley, eds. *Law and Legal Process in Japan.* Seattle: University of Washington Law School, 1978.

Herzog, Peter. *Japan's Pseudo-Democracy.* New York: New York University Press, 1993.

Higuchi, Yoichi. "The Constitution and the Emperor System: Is Revisionism Alive?" 53 *Law and Contemporary Problems* 51 (1990).

Hirai, Naofusa. "The Principles of Shrine Shinto." 1 *Contemporary Religions in Japan* 39 (1960).

Holtom, Daniel Clarence. *The National Faith of Japan.* London: Kegan, Paul, 1938.

———. "Shintoism." In Edward Jurji, ed. *The Great Religions of the Modern World,* p. 141. Princeton: Princeton University Press, 1946.

———. *Modern Japan and Shinto Nationalism.* New York: Paragon, rev. ed., 1963.

———. *Japanese Enthronement Ceremonies.* Tokyo: Sophia University Press, 1972.

———. *The Political Philosophy of Modern Shinto: A Study of the State Religion of Japan.* New York: AMS Press, 1984; reprint of 1922 University of Chicago Libraries ed.

Hori, Ichiro. "Japanese Folk-Beliefs." 61 *American Anthropologist* 405 (1959).

———. "Shamanism in Japan." 2 *Japanese Journal of Religious Studies* 231 (1975).

Horio, Teruhisa. *Educational Thought and Ideology in Modern Japan.* Tokyo: Tokyo University Press, 1988.

Howe, Mark DeWolfe. *The Garden and the Wilderness: Religion and Government in American Constitutional History.* Chicago: University of Chicago Press, 1965.

Hozumi, Nobushige. *Ancestor Worship and Japanese Law.* Plainview: Books for Libraries Press, 1912.

Ienaga, Saburo. *The Pacific War: World War II and the Japanese, 1931–1945.* New York: Pantheon, 1978.

Inoue, Kyoko. *MacArthur's Japanese Constitution: A Linguistic and Cultural Study of Its Making.* Chicago: University of Chicago Press, 1991.

International Institute for the Study of Religions. "Sōka Gakkai and the Nichiren Shu Sect (I)." 2 *Contemporary Religions in Japan* 55 (1960).

Iriye, Akira. *Power and Culture: The Japanese-American War, 1941–1945.* Cambridge: Harvard University Press, 1981.

Ishida, Takeshi. "Popular Attitudes toward the Japanese Emperor." 2 *Asian Survey* 29 (1962).

Ishida, Takeshi, and Ellis Krauss, eds. *Democracy in Japan.* Pittsburgh: University of Pittsburgh Press, 1989.

Ishii, Ryosuke, ed., and William Chambliss, trans. *Japanese Legislation in the Meiji Era.* Tokyo: Kasai Publishing, 1968.

Ito, Marquis Hirobumi, translated by Baron Miyoji Ito. *Commentaries on the Constitution of the Empire.* Tokyo: Chūō Daigaku, 1906; reprinted ed., Washington, D.C.: University Publications of America, 1979.

Itoh, Hiroshi. "Judicial Decision-Making in the Japanese Supreme Court." 3 *Law in Japan* 128 (1969).

———. *The Japanese Supreme Court.* New York: Markus Wiener, 1989.

———. "Judicial Activism in Japan." In Kenneth Holland, ed. *Judicial Activism in Comparative Perspective* 188. London: Macmillan, 1991.

Itoh, Hiroshi, and Lawrence W. Beer, eds. *The Constitutional Case Law of Japan: Selected Supreme Court Decisions, 1961–1970.* Seattle: University of Washington Press, 1978.

Japanese Government. *Documents Concerning the Allied Occupation and Control of Japan, Vols. 1 and 2, Political, Military and Cultural.* Tokyo: Division of Special Records, Foreign Office, 1949.

Johnson, Chalmers. "Japan: Who Governs? An Essay on Official Bureaucracy." 2 *Journal of Japanese Studies* 1 (1975).

———. "Omote (Explicit) and Ura (Implicit): Translating Japanese Political Terms." 6 *Journal of Japanese Studies* 89 (Winter 1980).

Kataoka, Tetsuya. *The Price of a Constitution: The Origin of Japan's Postwar Politics.* New York: Crane Russak, 1991.

Kato, Genchi. *A Study of Shinto.* London: Curzon, 1926.

———. "The Three Stages of the Shrine Shinto Religion." 3 *Japan Christian Quarterly* 116 (1928).

Kawahara, Toshiaki. *Hirohito and His Times: A Japanese Perspective.* Tokyo: Kodansha International, 1990.

Kawashima, Takeyoshi. "Individualism in Decision-Making in the Supreme Court of Japan." In Glendon Schubert and David Danelski, eds. *Comparative Judicial Behavior* 103. New York: Oxford University Press, 1969.

———. "Japanese Way of Legal Thinking." 7 *International Journal of Law Libraries* 127 (1979).

Kawazoe, Noboru. "The Ise Shrine." 9 *Japan Quarterly* 285 (1962).

Ketelaar, James Edward. *Of Heretics and Martyrs in Meiji Japan: Buddhism and Its Persecution.* Princeton: Princeton University Press, 1990.

Kida, Ken-ichi. "The Imperial System and Multiple Discriminations." 3 *CTC Bulletin* 8 (1982).

Kishimoto, Hideo. "The Constitution and Religion." 3 *Contemporary Religions in Japan* 103 (1962).

———, ed., and John Howes, trans. *Japanese Religion in the Meiji Era.* Tokyo: Ōbunsha, 1956.

Kitagawa, Joseph M. "The Japanese *Kokutai* (National Community): History and Myth." 13 *History of Religions* 209 (1974).

———. *On Understanding Japanese Religion.* Princeton: Princeton University Press, 1987.

———. *Religion in Japanese History.* New York: Columbia University Press, 2nd ed., 1990.

———. "Some Reflections on Japanese Religion and Its Relationship to the Imperial System." 17 *Japanese Journal of Religious Studies* 129 (1990).

Kiyama, Terumichi. "Meeting at Yasukuni Shrine." In Haruko Taya Cook and Theodore F. Cook, eds. *Japan at War: An Oral History.* New York: New Press, 1992.

Krauss, Ellis. *Japanese Radicals Revisited: Student Protest in Postwar Japan.* Berkeley: University of California, 1974.

Kudo, Takuya. "The Faith of Sōka Gakkai." 2 *Contemporary Religions in Japan* 1 (1961).

Kumazawa, Yoshinobu, and David Swain, eds. *Christianity in Japan, 1971–1990.* Tokyo: Kyo Bun Kwan (The Christian Literature Society of Japan), 1991.

Large, Steven. *Emperor Hirohito and Showa Japan: A Political Biography.* London: Routledge, 1992.

Lay, Arthur. "Japanese Funeral Rites." 19 *Transactions of Asiatic Society of Japan* 507 (1891).

Lebra, William. *Okinawan Religion: Belief, Ritual, and Social Structure.* Honolulu: University of Hawai'i Press, 1966.

Leibrecht, Walter, ed. *Religion and Culture: Essays in Honor of Paul Tillich.* New York: Harper & Row Reprint, 1972.

Levy, Leonard. *The Establishment Clause: Religion and the First Amendment.* New York: Macmillan, 1986.

————. *Original Intent and the Framers' Constitution*. New York: Macmillan, 1988.

Luney, Percey R. "The Judiciary: Its Organization and Status in the Parliamentary System." 53 *Law and Contemporary Problems* 135 (1990); reprinted in Percy Luney and Kazuyuki Takahashi, eds., *Japanese Constitutional Law*. Tokyo: Tokyo University Press, 1993.

Luney, Percy R., and Kazuyuki Takahashi, eds. *Japanese Constitutional Law*. Tokyo: Tokyo University Press, 1993.

MacArthur, Douglas. *Reminiscences*. New York: McGraw-Hill, 1964.

MacArthur Memorial Library and Archives. *The Occupation of Japan: The Proceedings of a Seminar on the Occupation of Japan and Its Legacy to the Postwar World*. Norfolk: The MacArthur Memorial, 1975.

Maki, John M. *Court and Constitution in Japan: Selected Supreme Court Decisions, 1948–1960*. Seattle: University of Washington Press, 1978.

————. *Japan's Commission on the Constitution—Final Report*. Seattle: University of Washington Press, 1980.

Marshall, J. *Japan's Successor Generation: Their Values and Attitudes* (1985).

Matsuura, Yoshiharu. "Review Essay: Law and Bureaucracy in Modern Japan." 41 *Stanford Law Review* 1627 (1989).

Matsunami, N. *The Japanese Constitution and Politics*. Tokyo: Maruzen & Co., 1940.

McMullin, Neil. *Buddhism and the State in Sixteenth-Century Japan*. Princeton: Princeton University Press, 1985.

————. "On Placating the Gods and Pacifying the Populace: The Case of the *Gion Goryo* Cult." 27 *History of Religions* 270 (1988).

————. "Historical and Historiographic Issues in the Study of Pre-Modern Japanese Religions." 16 *Japanese Journal of Religious Studies* 3 (1989).

Metraux, Daniel. *The Sōka Gakkai Revolution*. Lanham: University Press of America, 1994.

Mitchell, Richard. *Janus-Faced Justice: Political Criminals in Imperial Japan*. Honolulu: University of Hawai'i Press, 1992.

Miyaji, Naokazu. "Shinto Symbols." 7 *Contemporary Religions in Japan* 3 (1966).

Miyanaga, Kuniko. *The Creative Edge: Emerging Individualism in Japan*. New Brunswick: Transaction Books, 1991.

Miyata, Mitsuo. "The Politico-Religion of Japan—The Revival of Militarist Mentality." 3 *CTC Bulletin* 12 (1982).

Miyazawa, Setsuo. "Administrative Control of Japanese Judges." 25 *Kobe University Law Review* 45 (1991).

Moos, Felix. "Religion and Politics in Japan: The Case of the Sōka Gakkai." 3 *Asian Survey* 136 (1963).

Mori, Koichi. "The Emperor of Japan: A Historical Study in Religious Symbolism." 6 *Japanese Journal of Religious Studies* 522 (1979).

Morioka, Kiyomi. *Religion in Changing Japanese Society*. Tokyo: University of Tokyo Press, 1975.

Morley, John, ed. *The Fateful Choice: Japan's Advance into Southeast Asia, 1939–1941*. New York: Columbia University Press, 1980.

Mouer, Ross, and Yoshio Sugimoto. *Images of Japanese Society: A Study in the Structure of Social Reality.* New York: KPI Limited, 1986.

Murakami, Hyoe. *Japan: The Years of Trial, 1919–1952.* Tokyo: Kodansha International, 1983.

Murakami, Shigeyoshi. *Japanese Religion in the Modern Century.* Tokyo: University of Tokyo Press, 1980.

Muraoka, Tsunetsugu. *Studies in Shinto Thought.* Tokyo: Yushodo, 1964; Westport: Greenwood, reprint ed., 1988.

Nakamura, Hajime, and Philip Wiener, trans. *Ways of Thinking of Eastern Peoples: India—China—Tibet—Japan.* Honolulu: East-West Center Press, 1964.

Nakane, Chie. *Japanese Society.* Berkeley: University of California Press, 1970.

Nishi, Osamu. *The Constitution and the National Defense Law System in Japan.* Tokyo: Seibundo Publishing, 1987.

Nishi, Toshio. *Unconditional Democracy: Education and Politics in Occupied Japan, 1945–1952.* Stanford: Hoover Institute Press, 1982.

Nishikawa, Shigenori. "The Daijōsai, the Constitution, and Christian Faith." 56 *Japan Christian Quarterly* 140 (Summer 1990).

Noda, Yoshiyuki. *Introduction to Japanese Law.* Tokyo: University of Tokyo Press, 1976.

Nosco, Peter, ed. *Confucianism and Tokugawa Culture.* Princeton: Princeton University Press, 1984.

Oaks, Dallin, ed. *The Wall between Church and State.* Chicago: University of Chicago Press, 1963.

O'Brien, David M. *Storm Center: The Supreme Court in American Politics.* New York: W. W. Norton, 4th ed., 1996.

———. *Constitutional Law and Politics, Vol. 2: Civil Rights and Civil Liberties.* New York: W. W. Norton, 2nd ed., 1995.

Oh, John Kie-chiang. "The Fusion of Politics and Religion in Japan: The Soka Gakkai-Komeito." 14 *Journal of Church and State* 59 (1972).

Okudaira, Yasuhiro. "The Japanese Supreme Court: Its Organization and Function." 3 *Law Asia* 67 (1972).

———. "Forty Years of the Constitution and Its Various Influences: Japanese, American, and European." 53 *Law and Contemporary Problems* 17 (1990); reprinted in Percy R. Luney and Kazuyuki Takahashi, eds., *Japanese Constitutional Law.* Tokyo: Tokyo University Press, 1993.

Ono, Sokyo. *Shinto: The Kami Way.* Rutland, Vt.: Tuttle, 1969.

Ooms, Herman. *Tokugawa Ideology: Early Constructs, 1570–1680.* Princeton: Princeton University Press, 1985.

Oppler, Alfred. *Legal Reform in Occupied Japan.* Princeton: Princeton University Press, 1976.

Oshima, Koichi. "Problems of the Daijōsai: Grounds for Christian Opposition." 56 *Japan Christian Quarterly* 221 (1990).

Parker, Richard B. "The Bureaucratization of Policymaking in Postwar Japan." 18 *American Journal of Political Science* (Nov. 1974).

————. *Patterns of Japanese Policymaking: Experiences from Higher Eduation.* Boulder: Westview Press, 1982.

————. "Law, Language, and the Individual in Japan and the United States." 7 *Wisconsin International Law Journal* 179 (1988).

Perry, John C. *Beneath the Eagle's Wings: Americans in Occupied Japan.* New York: Dodd, Mead, 1980.

Pfeffer, Leo. *God, Caesar, and the Constitution.* Boston: Beacon Press, 1975.

————. *Church, State and Freedom.* Boston: Beacon Press, 1976.

————. *Religion, State, and the Burger Court.* Buffalo: Prometheus Books, 1985.

Powles, C. "Yasukuni Jinja Hoan: Religion and Politics in Contemporary Japan." 49 *Public Affairs* 491 (1976).

Pyle, Kenneth. *The New Generation in Meiji Japan: Problems of Cultural Identity, 1885–1895.* Stanford: Stanford University Press, 1969.

Ramseyer, J. Mark. "Reluctant Litigant Revisited: Rationality and Disputes in Japan." 14 *Journal of Japanese Studies* 111 (1988).

Ramseyer, J. Mark, and Frances McCall Rosenbluth. *Japan's Political Marketplace.* Cambridge: Harvard University Press, 1993.

Reader, Ian. *Religion in Contemporary Japan.* Honolulu: University of Hawai'i Press, 1991.

Reader, Ian, Esben Andreasen, and Finn Stefansson, eds. *Japanese Religions: Past & Present.* Honolulu: University of Hawai'i Press, 1993.

Reed, Steven R. *Making Common Sense of Japan.* Pittsburgh: University of Pittsburgh Press, 1993.

Reid, David. "Japanese Christians and the Ancestors." 56 *Japan Christian Quarterly* 24 (1990).

————. "Separation of Religion and the State: How Japanese Religions Line Up." 56 *Japan Christian Quarterly* 212 (1990).

Reingold, Edwin. *Chrysanthemums and Thorns.* New York: St. Martin's Press, 1991.

Reischauer, Edwin O. *The Japanese Today.* Cambridge: Belknap Press, 1988.

Repeta, Lawrence. "International Covenant on Civil and Political Rights and Human Rights in Japan." 20 *Law in Japan* 1 (1987).

————. "Why We Sued the Judges." 22 *Law in Japan* 49 (1989).

Richey, Russell, and Donald Jones, eds. *American Civil Religion.* New York: Harper & Row, 1974.

Richie, Donald. *A Lateral View: Essays on Culture and Style in Contemporary Japan.* Berkeley: Stone Bridge Press, 1992.

Saeki, Shoichi. "Is a Shinto Renewal Possible?" 17 *Nanzan Bulletin* 32 (1993).

Sakamoto, Yoshikazu, ed. *The Emperor System as a Japan Problem.* Tokyo: International Peace Research Institute Meigaku (PRIME), Meiji Gakuin University, 1989.

Sakata, Yoshio. "Changes in the Concept of the Emperor." 2 *Zinbun* 1 (1958).

Sansom, George. *A History of Japan to 1334.* London: Cresset Press, 1939.

Satow, E. M. "The Shinto Shrines of Ise." 1 *Transactions of Asiatic Society of Japan* 99 (1874).

———. "Ancient Japanese Rituals—Part I." 7 *Transactions of Asiatic Society of Japan* 97 (1879).

———. "Ancient Japanese Rituals—Part II." 9 *Transactions of Asiatic Society of Japan* 182 (1881).

Schaller, Michael. *The American Occupation of Japan: The Origin of the Cold War in Asia.* New York: Oxford University Press, 1985.

Shikita, M. "Law Under the Rising Sun." 20 *Judges Journal* 42 (1981).

Shillony, Ben-Ami [Shichihei Yamamoto]. *Politics and Culture in Wartime Japan.* Oxford: Clarendon Press, 1981.

———. *The Jews and the Japanese: The Successful Outsiders.* Rutland, VT: Tuttle, 1991.

Shiroyama, Saburo. *War Criminal: The Life and Death of Hirota Koki.* Tokyo: Kodansha International, 1977.

Shoji, Tsutomu. "The Ideology of the Tennō System and Christian Responsibility." 3 *CTC Bulletin* 25 (1982).

Shupe, Anson. "Conventional Religion and Political Participation in Postwar Rural Japan." 55 *Social Forces* 613 (1977).

Siemes, Johannes. *Herman Roesler and the Making of the Meiji State.* Tokyo: Sophia University Press, 1968.

Smith, Robert J. *Ancestor Worship in Contemporary Japan.* Stanford: Stanford University Press, 1974.

Sorauf, Frank. *The Wall of Separation: The Constitutional Politics of Church and State.* Princeton: Princeton University Press, 1976.

Special Issue. "The Emperor System and Religion in Japan," 17 *Japanese Journal of Religious Studies* (June–Sept. 1990).

Stokes, Anson Phelps. *Church and State in the United States: Historical Development and Contemporary Problems of Religious Freedom under the Constitution.* New York: Harper & Brothers, 1950.

Sugiyama, Kyushiro. "Facts and Fallacies about Yasukuni Shrine." 8 *Japan Echo* 69 (1986).

Supreme Commander for the Allied Powers. Government Section. *Political Reorientation of Japan.* 2 Vols. Grosse Pointe: Scholarly Press, 1968; originally published by the U.S. Government Printing Office, 1949.

Swomley, John. *Religious Liberty and the Secular State: The Constitutional Context.* Buffalo: Prometheus, 1987.

Swyngedouw, Jan. "Secularization in a Japanese Context." 3 *Japanese Journal of Religious Studies* 283 (1976).

———. "Japanese Religiosity in an Age of Internationalization." 5 *Japanese Journal of Religious Studies* 87 (1978).

———. "Religion in Contemporary Japanese Society." 13 *Japan Foundation Newsletter* 1 (1986).

Takayama, K. Peter. "Revitalization Movement of Modern Japanese Civil Religion." 48 *Sociological Analysis* 328 (1988).

————. "Enshrinement and Persistence of Japanese Religion." 32 *Journal of Church and State* 527 (1990).

Takeda, Kiyoko. *The Dual Image of the Japanese Emperor.* London: Macmillan, 1988.

Takizawa, Nobuhiko. "Religion and the State in Japan." 30 *Journal of Church and State* 89 (1988).

————. "Constitutionalism in Japan." 20 *Kitakyūshū-Daigaku Hō-sei Ronshū* (Kitakyūshū University journal of law and political science) 1 (March 1993).

Takizawa, Tadashi. "Issues Raised by the Decision of the Trial Court in the 'Minoo Memorial Service Case.'" 18 *Law in Japan* 152 (1986).

Tanaka, Hideo. *The Japanese Legal System.* Tokyo: University of Tokyo Press, 1976.

————. "The Appointment of Supreme Court Justices and the Popular Review of Appointments." 11 *Law in Japan* 25 (1978).

Tanigawa, Tetsuzo. "National Character and Religion." 1 *Contemporary Religions in Japan* 1 (1960).

Taniguchi, Yasuhei. "The Post-War Court System as an Instrument for Social Change." In George DeVos, ed. *Institutions for Change in Japanese Society.* Berkeley: Institute for East Asian Studies, 1984.

Tipton, Elise. *Japanese Police State: Tokkō in Interwar Japan.* Sydney: Allen and Unwin, 1990.

Titus, David. *Palace Politics in Prewar Japan.* New York: Columbia University Press, 1974.

————. "The Making of the 'Symbol Emperor System' in Postwar Japan." 14 *Modern Asian Studies* 529 (1980).

Tokikuni, Yasuo. "Procedures for Constitutional Litigation and Judgments of Constitutionality." 13 *Law in Japan* 1 (1980).

Tomura, Masahiro. "The Dual Structure of the Emperor System in Japan," 3 *CTC Bulletin* 1 (1982).

Tsuji, Kiyoaki. "The Bureaucracy Preserved and Strengthened." 11 *Journal of Social and Political Ideas in Japan* 88 (1964).

————, ed. *Public Administration in Japan.* Tokyo: University of Tokyo Press, 1984.

Tsukada, Osamu. "The Church, Theology and the Emperor System." 3 *CTC Bulletin* 18 (1982).

————. "Yasukuni Shrine and the Emperor System." In Yoshinobu Kumazawa and David Swain, eds. *Christianity in Japan, 1971–1990.* Tokyo: Kyo Bun Kwan (The Christian Literature Society of Japan), 1991.

Tsuneishi, Warren. *Japanese Political Style.* New York: Harper & Row, 1966.

Uchimura, Kanzo. *How I Became a Christian.* Originally published in 1913, reprinted as Vol. 1 of *The Collected Works of Kanzo Uchimura.* Tokyo: Kyobunkan, 1971.

Umegaki, Michio. *After the Restoration: The Beginning of Japan's Modern State.* New York: New York University Press, 1988.

Umehara, Suyeji. "Ancient Mirrors and Their Relationship to Early Japanese Culture." 4 *Acta Asiatica* 70 (Tokyo: Bulletin of the Institute of Eastern Culture, 1963).

Upham, Frank. *Law and Social Change in Postwar Japan.* Cambridge: Harvard University Press, 1987.

van Wolferen, Karel. *The Enigma of Japanese Power.* New York: Knopf, 1989.

———. "Japan's Non-Revolution." *Foreign Affairs* 54 (Feb. 1993).

von Mehren, Arthur, ed. *Law in Japan: The Legal Order in a Changing Society.* Cambridge: Harvard University Press, 1963.

Wada, Manabu. "Sacred Kinship in Early Japan." 15 *History of Religions* 319 (1976).

Ward, Robert, ed. *Political Development in Modern Japan.* Princeton: Princeton University Press, 1968.

Ward, Robert, and Yoshikazu Sakamoto, eds. *Democratizing Japan: The Allied Occupation.* Honolulu: University of Hawai'i Press, 1987.

Watanabe, Osamu. "The Emperor as a 'Symbol' in Postwar Japan." 59 *Acta Asiatica* 101 (1990).

Welfield, John. *An Empire in Eclipse: Japan in the Postwar Alliance System.* London: Athlone, 1988.

Whitney, Courtney. *MacArthur: His Rendezvous with History.* New York: Knopf, 1955; reprint ed., Westport: Greenwood, 1977.

Wigmore, John, ed. *Law and Justice in Tokugawa Japan,* 3 Vols. Tokyo: Kokusai Bunka Shinkokai, 1969.

Williams, Justin. *Japan's Political Revolution under MacArthur.* Athens: University of Georgia Press, 1979.

Woodard, William. "Religion–State Relations in Japan." 25 *Contemporary Japan* 81 (1957).

———. *The Allied Occupation of Japan 1945–1952, and Japanese Religions.* Leiden: E. J. Brill, 1972.

Yamasaki, M. "Signs of New Individualism." 11 *Japan Echo* 8 (1984).

Yanagawa, Keiichi, and David Reid. "Between Unity and Separation: Religion and Politics in Japan, 1965–1977." 6 *Japanese Journal of Religious Studies* 500 (1979).

Yanagita, Kunio. *About Our Ancestors: The Japanese Family System.* Tokyo: Ministry of Education, 1970.

Yasaki, M. "The Word of Law and Matters Legal." 20 *Osaka University Law Review* 25 (1973).

Yokota, Koichi. "The Separation of Religion and State." In Percy Luney and Kazuyuki Takahashi, eds. *Japanese Constitutional Law.* Tokyo: Tokyo University Press, 1993.

Name and Subject Index

References to illustrations appear in **boldface**

Abe, Yoshiya: 62, 96, 102, 115–116
abortion: 238 n. 29
Akihito, Emperor: 63; enthronement
    controversy about, xi, 58, 202–203,
    205–208
Allied Occupation: ix, 3, 25, 47, 51–57, 71,
    114, 131, 147, 151, 162, 169, 189
American Bar Association: 76
American Civil Liberties Union: 14–15, 188–
    189, 195
American Jewish Congress: 195
American Judicature Society: 76
ancestor worship: 6, 18, 30, 33, 38, 46, 200
Anglican Church: 105
Anno, Yutaka: 155
Antichristian: 8
Anzai, Kenji: 122
Aoyama, Kōichi: 84
Arai, Ken: 115, 139
Asahi, Shigeru: 99–100
Asahi Evening News: 131, 170
Ashibe, Nobuyoshi: 95, 102
Association for Honoring the Glorious War
    Dead: 75, 166–168, 172, 176, 182
Association of Parents of SDF Officers: 159
Association of Shinto Shrines: 61, 96
Association of War Bereaved Christian Fami-
    lies: 166
Association to Honor SDF Members Deceased
    While on Duty: 157
associations of war bereaved families: 3–4, 9,
    14, 54, 61, 98, 103–104, 106–107,
    109, 113, 115–116, 123–125, 140
Azuma, Takashi: 171

Baldwin, Roger: 188–189
Battle of Okinawa: 52, 124
Bellah, Robert: 62
Ben-Dasan, Isaiah: 17
Benedict, Ruth: 29, 193
benevolent neutrality toward religion: 61, 89
Bible: 22, 89
Black, Hugo: 60
Blackmun, Harry: 93
Board of Shrine Rites: 45–46, 53
Brennan, William: 93
Britain: 177
buddhas: 9, 20–21, 25, 35, 67, 127
Buddhism: 28, 95, 154, 193; Hinayana, 19–
    20; Mahayana, 19–20; and political par-
    ticipation, 38; separation from Shinto
    of, 32–38
Buddhist: affiliation, 21; anti-Buddhist
    storm, 36; *butsudan* (altar), 20, 35, 154;
    ceremonies, 9–10, 18–19, 86, 107, 127,
    133, 154, 172; organizations, 15, 121,
    165, 168, 185, 207; priesthood, 16, 35;
    temples, 19, 35; traditions, 20
Bunce, William: 54
Burakumin: 27
Bureau of Religion: 39
Bureau of Shinto: 36
Bureau of Shrines: 39, 44–45
Bureau of Shrines and Temples: 39
bureaucracy: 99–100, 180. *See also* judicial;
    State Shinto
Burger, Warren: 88–90, 92–93, 96
Burger Court: 88–91
Burton, Harold: 61

259